D0484061

PRAISE FOR *NO GREATER VALOR*

"Who are we as a nation? What defines us? What has made us a great nation? All these questions are answered in *No More Valor*. Dr. Corsi shows how we are losing our identity and our honor because we are losing our faith—the faith upon which America was built. It was the Judeo-Christian values of the founders that gave rise to the courage that birthed a nation founded on unalienable rights and the consent of the governed. It was this same faith that sustained the defenders of freedom in December 1944, where outnumbered US forces won a decisive battle because of their reliance on the same Creator as their forbears."

—Lt. Gen. William Boykin (Ret),
executive vice president of the
Family Research Council

"At a time when Americans' deepest spiritual values are under withering attack from both without and within, Jerome Corsi arrives with reinforcements. Focusing his brilliant analytical and journalistic skills on one of the most inspiring battles of WWII, Corsi skillfully recreates the Siege of Bastogne where US forces, led by the fabled Screaming Eagles of the 101st Airborne, rely on a combination of raw American courage and Divine intervention to seal the Allied victory."

—David Kupelian, best-selling author
of *The Marketing of Evil* and
managing editor of WND.com

"The Siege at Bastogne and its outcome is one my favorite events of WWII. I had the opportunity at West Point to study in great detail this battle of valor, survival, and victory of our 101st Airborne Division and other assigned units against overwhelming Nazi infantry and panzer units. We said 'Nuts' to a German demand for surrender and God blessed the troops with a break in the weather for our soldiers to get Allied air support and push back the German forces. Thank you, Jerry, for writing this book and bringing back the memories of brave Americans who were dedicated to survive and defeat the enemy."

—Paul E. Vallely MG, US Army
(Ret), chairman of Stand Up
America

"Using firsthand accounts, diaries, and the recollections of those who were there, Jerome Corsi's *No Greater Valor* tells the powerful story of the role of faith during the Siege of Bastogne. From chaplains, to enlisted men, to General Patton, we come to realize just how deeply these heroes of World War II struggled to reconcile their Christian beliefs with the horrors of war. *No Greater Valor* is a must read."

—Grover Norquist, president of Americans for Tax Reform (ATR); contributing editor to the *American Spectator* magazine; and author of *Rock the House* and *Leave Us Alone: America's New Governing Majority*

"*No Greater Valor* puts the reader at the Siege of Bastogne with vivid imagery and stories of courage and circumstance. Corsi also reminds us that God was with our Allied troops in this battle, whose outcome changed the course of history. This is a compelling, informative, and inspiring book."

—Herman Cain, CEO of THE New Voice, Inc.

"The Allied defense of Bastogne against Hitler's final frenzied blitzkrieg is well known to students of World War II—but most do not know about the focus of Jerry Corsi's moving book *No Greater Valor*: General George Patton's deep faith in a God who would respond to the fervent prayers of His people. No understanding of the Siege of Bastogne or the Battle of the Bulge is complete without appreciating Patton's invocation of God's intervention and the chaplains who composed the prayers calling for it. Dr. Corsi has made a major contribution to the scholarship of that important turning point in our history."

—Colin A. Hanna, president of Let Freedom Ring

"My friend Jerry Corsi has written yet another superb book on one of the most important battles of the most important war of the 20th century, which once again clearly demonstrates that God's hand rests on America."

—Richard Viguerie, chairman of ConservativeHQ.com

"*No Greater Valor* is much more than the typical WWII military history anthology, but rather it is a living account of the heroism and faith of the brave Americans who stopped a Nazi counterattack on Bastogne in 1944—which if successful, could have given Hitler sufficient time to develop an atomic bomb and thus have changed the outcome of the war. The depth and detail of *No Greater Valor* is presented in a manner that allows the reader to 'be in the battle' and witness both the faith of the men and the intervention of God that led to victory. *No Greater Valor* is a must read for every Christian high school and homeschool parent as it depicts the America of the Greatest Generation and the bravery and faith that undergirded it."

—William J. Murray, chairman of the
Religious Freedom Coalition

"Dr. Corsi brings a personal, refreshing, fast-paced angle to the Battle of Bastogne, one of the great American victories of WWII. Outnumbered and outgunned, Americans fought and prayed and died and won for God and country. Whether you believe or not, it is certain that the force of faith made a difference on that Christmas Day so long ago. A singular achievement recommended to anyone who loves great writing."

—Stephen Freifeld, MD

"I couldn't put *No Greater Valor* down. The courage of these brave men fighting in a noble cause with faith in God, and then seeing the hand of God at work, was wonderful to read and tremendously inspiring. This book is a gift to future generations. Thank you, Jerome Corsi!"

—Rich Bott, president and CEO of
the Bott Radio Network

NO GREATER
VALOR

NO GREATER
VALOR

The Siege of Bastogne and the Miracle
That Sealed Allied Victory

Jerome R. Corsi, Ph.D.

NELSON
BOOKS
An Imprint of Thomas Nelson

Published in Nashville, Tennessee, by Nelson Books, an imprint of Thomas Nelson. Nelson Books and Thomas Nelson are registered trademarks of HarperCollins Christian Publishing, Inc.

Thomas Nelson titles may be purchased in bulk for educational, business, fund-raising, or sales promotional use. For information, please e-mail SpecialMarkets@ThomasNelson.com.

All Scripture quotations are taken from the KING JAMES VERSION of the Bible. Public domain.

All maps used in the book were found in the various Bastogne collections at the National Archives and Records Administration (NARA) at College Park, Maryland, with minor alterations to remove technical military notes in the originals.

All photos used in this book were found in the archives of the 101st Airborne Division at the Don F. Pratt Museum on the military base at Ft. Campbell, Kentucky.

Library of Congress Control Number: 2014950943

ISBN: 978-1-59555-521-2

Printed in the United States of America

14 15 16 17 18 RRD 6 5 4 3 2 1

For my father, Louis E. Corsi,
whose memory inspired me to write this book

—⁂—

That they shall drive thee from men, and thy dwelling
shall be with the beasts of the field, and they shall make
thee to eat grass as oxen, and they shall wet thee with
the dew of heaven, and seven times shall pass over
thee, till thou know that the most High ruleth in the
kingdom of men, and giveth it to whomsoever he will.

—DANIEL 4:25

If my people, which are called by my name, shall humble
themselves, and pray, and seek my face, and turn from
their wicked ways; then will I hear from heaven, and
will forgive their sin, and will heal their land.

—2 CHRONICLES 7:14

CONTENTS

INTRODUCTION

I have been fascinated by the Siege of Bastogne since I was a child. My father served in World War II with the Army Air Corps. Although he was fortunate enough never to have been called upon to be in battle, many of his friends were combat veterans who fought in Europe or the Pacific.

As a child, the question, "What did you do in the war?" was never far from my mind when I was with my father's wartime buddies. Though many were reluctant to discuss their experiences, the subject of Bastogne came up frequently. I remember that those veterans, even those who had not fought at Bastogne, still regarded the battle as a final turning point of the war. The courage and the rugged determination of a small group of paratroopers, joined by just the right number of armored and artillery units, held these veterans in awe. I recall distinctly the stories they told as I read books written by the men who fought at Bastogne.

The Siege of Bastogne continues a legacy of military history that connects with the Battle of Thermopylae in 480 BC. On a narrow coastal pass, some three hundred Spartans and approximately six thousand soldiers from other Greek cities under the leadership of King Leonidas of Sparta held for days against the vastly overwhelming invading forces of the Persian Empire numbering perhaps as many as one hundred thousand soldiers led by the Persian king Xerxes I.

In December 1944, as World War II in Europe showed promise of ending with the defeat of Nazi Germany by Christmas, all such hopes were thwarted on December 16, 1944, when Hitler launched a daring, last-ditch-effort counterattack in the Ardennes Forest in Belgium with a classic blitzkrieg ("lightning-war") maneuver. Hitler planned that the spearhead of his attacking force would drive to Antwerp with the goal of dividing Allied forces and denying the Allies their main port of resupply.

What has fascinated me was how the Siege of Bastogne, fought at Christmas, was won by a small group of American soldiers who largely believed in God in accordance with the Judeo-Christian traditions that have steeled American soldiers against foreign enemies since 1776. In the opening sentence of the Declaration of Independence, our Founding Fathers made reference to the "Laws of Nature and of Nature's God" as the entitlement for our pursuit of liberty from Great Britain and establishing a new nation. Our Founding Fathers' goal in establishing the United States was to secure for themselves and their progeny "the unalienable Rights" endowed to us as human beings by the Creator. The Siege of Bastogne in World War II served as a testament to the courage and determination with which a God-fearing military could enter combat even though overwhelmed by an opposing enemy force. Called from bivouac, the troops of the 101st Airborne drove through the darkness of night in the midst of a fierce European winter to a nondescript little Belgian village simply because the generals felt the town had to be held.

In the tradition of combat chaplains that stretches in American history back to the Revolutionary War, the 101st was accompanied by Chaplain Lt. Col. Francis L. Sampson, a Catholic priest known as "Parachute Padre," as they were rushed from bivouac in France largely in open trucks to defend Bastogne. Father Sampson first jumped into combat with the 101st Airborne Division on D-Day, followed by jumping into combat once again with the 101st in Operation Market Garden. As I researched the Siege of Bastogne for this book, I became determined to tell as a centerpiece of the narrative the story of Father Sampson's faith in God as well as his courage under fire.

In World War II, there were more than twelve thousand Protestant ministers, Catholic priests, and Jewish rabbis who joined the Chaplain Corps, who, armed only with Bibles and Torahs, ministered to provide spiritual strength and guidance to America's armed forces. Almost no man or woman in uniform in the United States was without benefit of clergy if he or she wanted it, observed minister and historian Lyle Dorsett, PhD, in his

2012 book, *Serving God and Country: US Military Chaplains in World War II*. "Not every Jewish person in the armed forces could always find a rabbi," Dorsett noted, "but Protestant and Catholic chaplains did their utmost to scour the base and find one or, if necessary, contact the nearest town or city for a civilian rabbi to help."[1] Characterizing World War II chaplains as men of faith who took exceptional risks under fire to save souls, Dorsett tells the story of a young infantry officer along the Belgian-German border who crawled out of the Ardennes Forest holding a compress on his wounded leg.

> Falling off the front line to get stitched up, Lt. Henry Cobb looked up to see a chaplain rushing into the woods, where the Germans were raining down a storm of artillery shells on the battered Americans who had been caught by surprise in the Battle of the Bulge. Cobb recalled that he recognized the chaplain as the priest who had given him and some other soldiers Holy Communion several hours earlier. The Catholic priest was charging full speed toward the woods, into an inferno of fire, smoke, deafening explosions, and splintering trees. The wounded officer yelled, "Where in the devil do you think you are going, Father? All hell is breaking loose up there." The chaplain ran past Cobb, muttering, "That is why I need to be there."[2]

Dorsett stressed that the brave men who voluntarily left the relative comfort of their civilian ministry callings to care for the spiritual needs of the twelve million men and women who served in America's armed forces during World War II were important because, as William Arnold, US Army chief of chaplains during the war, phrased it, "Battles are won by military power, but wars are won by spiritual power."[3]

At Bastogne, US forces led by the Screaming Eagles of the 101st Airborne Division, outnumbered and surrounded, held the Belgian crossroads town through Christmas despite repeated day and night attacks by Nazi panzer divisions, punctuated by the Luftwaffe's bombardment from the air. As Hitler launched his Wacht am Rhein offensive, US troops who seemed within weeks of going home victorious took up arms once more and rushed into battle, prepared to die if necessary in the eleventh hour of the most deadly war up to that moment in human history.

Those brave US soldiers who fought and died at Bastogne had not been induced to enlist by the promise of the GI Bill (not signed into law by FDR until June 22, 1944), which would offer college after the war with a federal government–sponsored tuition, or the opportunity to buy a first home with a government-subsidized zero-down mortgage, nor were they motivated by a signing bonus (those did not exist), or by a paycheck (which was meager and typically saved to send back home to a waiting and worrying mother, father, or wife). Those who rushed into the breach to defend Bastogne were motivated by their faith in God, their devotion to family at home, their brotherhood with their comrades-in-arms, and their conviction that their cause was right. Moral resolve then left those who rushed to defend Bastogne no other choice but to put their lives and limbs at risk. How else can we explain why those who fought at Bastogne suffered frostbite, hunger, and sleep deprivation that even today we find remarkable to contemplate?

It is my hope that writing this book will serve as witness that the generation of Americans born to and raised by those who fought in World War II still acknowledge no greater valor has ever been shown by Americans in war than was shown by the Americans who fought the Bastogne siege. Equally with the Minutemen of Lexington and Concord who went forth on their town squares to confront the British, we owe special thanks for our freedom today to those Americans who gave, as Abraham Lincoln so well phrased it for the heroes of the American Civil War, the last true measure of their devotion for a more noble cause. In writing this book, I hoped to inspire readers to join with me in resolving in this seventieth anniversary year commemorating the battle that those who bled and died on the soil of that obscure Belgium town did not do so in vain.

Truly, the story of the Siege of Bastogne is larger than life. The 101st was ordered out of Camp Mourmelon without proper winter clothes or fighting gear. During the next few desperate hours that stretched into days, all that stood in the way of the Wehrmacht advancing in a final desperate battle to salvage the Führer's tragically flawed vision of a thousand-year Reich were the quickly mustered 101st Airborne and other brave units that rushed to join them on the battlefield. Had the US military not risen to the defense of Bastogne, Hitler's Wehrmacht might just have turned the tide of the war in Europe.

At Bastogne, in addition to the courage of the troops, the generals rose to exhibit a rare form of leadership capable of finding victory in adversity. True to form, the artillery general thrust into leadership of the 101st Airborne Division turned back the Nazi offer of surrender with a one-word reply that electrified American forces around the globe. "Nuts!" Gen. Anthony McAuliffe told the Germans, sending them on their way back across German lines along with their white flag. On the surface, the fact that this brigadier general happened to lead the 101st Airborne into action at Bastogne was as much an accident of war as any other happenstance of the battle. At 0800 hours on Sunday, December 17, 1944, McAuliffe, the highest ranking officer of the 101st present at that time, was ordered to prepare to move out of Camp Mourmelon to join Maj. Gen. Troy H. Middleton, the VIII Corps commander in the Ardennes. Who could have realized at that moment that McAuliffe, a previously unknown and relatively insignificant subordinate artillery officer, would end up leading the 101st Airborne in one of the most courageous defensive actions in US military history? This was only one of the many aspects of the Siege of Bastogne that appeared to those who fought the battle even at the time to be providential, almost as if the hand of God was guiding decisions so as to bring the battle to a successful conclusion.

McAuliffe's one-word defiant rejection of the German surrender ultimatum rang so true that it inspired to heroic action no less than Gen. George Patton, the military genius without whom the United States may never have defeated Nazi Germany. The story that fittingly completes the saga of the Bastogne siege is the historic forced march Patton engineered in pivoting the Third Army north to relieve Bastogne. That Patton ordered the chaplain of the Third Army to write a prayer asking God for favorable weather fits into what the troops saw as more evidence that the battle they were fighting was providentially determined. When the weather broke unexpectedly after the chaplain delivered Patton his prayer, God seemed to deliver on schedule the Christmas miracle the US military needed to win the day.

Ever since I was a child, I have wondered if an army of atheists could have won at Bastogne. In graduate school at Harvard, pursuing a PhD in political science, I first read the history of the Peloponnesian War written in ancient Greece by the historian Thucydides.[4] From my first reading, I was captivated by Thucydides' narrative of the Athenian invasion of Sicily. He made abundantly clear the daring battle strategy of Alcibiades likely would have been successful, if only the Athenian democracy had not recalled him from Sicily for impiety. The Athenian people held Alcibiades responsible for a shocking sacrilege committed just before the armada sailed. With Alcibiades recalled to Athens, the Athenian armed forces invading Sicily fell under the leadership of Nicias, a general Thucydides says was one of the most pious military leaders Athens had in the Peloponnesian War. Yet the Athenian army fell to inglorious defeat under the command of Nicias, with Nicias ultimately suffering a brutal execution by the Sicilians in a remote stony quarry outside Syracuse. Thucydides' lesson is clear: belief in God alone is not sufficient to trump brilliance devising a superior military strategy in warfare.[5]

Yet, the idea that an army of atheists can have victory over a God-fearing foe is one of the military truths that has always made the Siege of Bastogne so intriguing to me. Yes, among the Germans fighting at Bastogne there were soldiers and commanders who believed in God. But Hitler and his minions—the producers of the Holocaust, one of the most horrific tragedies in human history—remain judged appropriately as evil even in our secular era. Hitler's Wehrmacht fighting at Bastogne could have won the battle despite the fact that Hitler and his cause were evil. Today, we have allowed ourselves to become so politically correct that merely characterizing radical Islamic terrorism can be interpreted as hate speech. Consider the case of a military hero like Gen. William G. "Jerry" Boykin, who ended a distinguished thirty-six-year army career that included having played a founding role in creating the US Army's Delta Force simply because he expressed his faith in God in a manner considered inappropriate. General Boykin commented on the "war on terrorism" declared by President George W. Bush by daring to claim the United States holds the righteous ground because we are a Christian nation with our roots in the Judeo-Christian tradition. To make the offense even more severe, he went on to claim the true enemy in the war on terror was Satan, the evil genius Boykin asserted motivated the heinous acts committed by radical Islamic terrorists.[6]

I decided to write this book as a follow-up to my 2013 book, *Bad Samaritans: The ACLU's Relentless Campaign to Erase Faith from the Public*

Square. There I explored how the ACLU has twisted the First Amendment and Thomas Jefferson's articulation of a "wall of separation" between church and state to transform what previous generations of Americans understood as "freedom *of* religion" into what current generations of Americans believe can only be "freedom *from* religion." In *Bad Samaritans*, I argued that since the end of World War II, the United States has witnessed the ACLU wage a "war on God," determined to systematically remove any and all references to Judeo-Christian faith from our public schools and our public squares.

I was distressed when the US military in 2013 threatened to court-martial soldiers and chaplains for proselytizing religion to troops not initially receptive to a biblical message, despite the importance evangelical work has always played in the historical mission of Christianity. I am especially troubled for our future when the Obama administration's decision to abandon the "Don't Ask, Don't Tell" standard for military conduct means the LGBT community is now pressing to have joining the ranks of the US military declared a Constitutional right. How long will it be before a Christian chaplain faces discipline and possibly court-martial for refusing to perform a same-sex marriage of two military personnel the chaplain feels violates his or her Judeo-Christian religious beliefs? Will the United States lose our moral compass should the Bible ever be prohibited from our military bases?

Granted, Mussolini's fascist government in Italy joined with the Vatican in ratifying the Lateran Accords on June 7, 1929, concluding a historic agreement that joined together the Italian state with the Catholic Church.[7] Every Italian soldier marching into battle in Ethiopia in 1932 carried a copy of a new collection of prayers, *Soldier, Pray!* The booklet included the following admonition: "Go where the Fatherland sends you and God calls you, ready for everything. . . . Trust even if God asks you to sacrifice your life. . . . Soldier of Italy, your sacrifice, united with the sacrifice of Our Lord Jesus Christ, God among men, will achieve the salvation and greatness of the Fatherland."[8] Yet even the blessing of Mussolini and Pope Pius XI could not make Italy's invasion of Ethiopia into a war that the League of Nations, or any other international body, could accept as a morally necessary war. What distinguished Bastogne was the unique combination of a war against Hitler still perceived today as a just and morally necessary war, fought at Christmas by God-fearing military forces that perceived their success in battle as an answer by God to their prayers. In the final analysis, we have to ask this: Can it be said that those US military who fought at Bastogne were distinguished because their uncommon heroism and valor touched the heart of God to intervene in the battle in their favor?

In the ancient world, that question would not have been considered foolish or naïve. The Roman emperor Constantine attributed his victory over Maxentius at the Battle of the Milvian Bridge on AD October 28, 312, to the intervention of God and a vision in which God promised, *In hoc signo vinces,*" which translated from Latin reads, "In this sign you will conquer." According to Christian tradition, God promised that if Constantine and his army fought under the Chi-Rho sign (the first two Greek letters in "Christos"), the Roman army would triumph. No less an expert than Edward Gibbon in his classic *Decline and Fall of the Roman Empire* could credit Constantine's victory as a pivotal point in history in which the ancient Romans abandoned pagan vices to embrace Christian virtue as the moral foundation needed to perpetuate their empire. To the ancient mind, the idea that God intervened to change the fate of human history was as comfortable and as normal an idea as the concept today is considered naïve at best. While the modern, secular world is determined to dismiss the importance of God in human events, the ancients even in the pagan world feared prayer aimed at winning the favor of God as all-important to their success.

As the war in Europe came to a bloody conclusion, Hitler was still as dangerous as a cornered lion fatally wounded but not yet dead. On December 25, 1944, all Hitler lacked to win the war was the one atomic bomb that he insanely believed would save the Nazis even at the bitter, brutal end. That was one Christmas Day that Hitler most certainly did not celebrate as his panzer stood stalled in the snowy fields of winter battle, stopped in its tracks by lack of petrol. As I hope to demonstrate in this book, even if the point cannot be proved, those Americans who fought and won the Siege of Bastogne believed the Christmas miracle that turned the battle in their favor may never have happened had they not had faith in God.

A last factor that led me to write this book involved a more pragmatic consideration: the Siege of Bastogne was distinguished by the presence of US military historian Lt. Col. Samuel Lyman Atwood (S. L. A.) Marshall. During World War II, Army chief of staff George Marshall had insisted, with the full support of President Franklin D. Roosevelt, that field histories collected even as a battle ended were essential to preserving the immediacy of the events experienced in combat. S. L. A. Marshall pioneered in the army's oral history effort. Drawing on his experiences as a journalist before the war, Marshall was in the field asking questions almost before the shooting stopped. Stephen E. Everett, in his valuable overview of military oral history, *Oral History: Techniques and Procedures*, noted Marshall had a remarkable ability for asking questions "that guided soldiers through the battle, step-by-step, and elicited personal experiences and detailed information about what occurred during the fighting."[9]

It took me two years searching in US archives to find S. L. A. Marshall's records. Misfiled and not properly catalogued, I came upon his collection of oral histories by surprise one day while researching unit military histories stored away in boxes for some seven decades and now preserved on the shelves of the National Archives and Records Administration in College Park, Maryland. These oral histories are fascinating not only because they reflect the thoughts of the participants before history determined the proper way the battles had to be recalled but also because they were taken and given by men many of whom went on subsequently to be wounded or killed in battle. The vibrancy of the pages is felt despite the distance of years and the complexity of later events.

Marshall first developed his oral history techniques after a fierce night engagement on Makin Atoll in the Gilbert Islands, in the Pacific theater battle fought November 20–23, 1943. There, Marshall interviewed members of the 3rd Battalion, 165th Infantry, and experimented with how best to take their oral histories immediately after they emerged from battle. Subsequently, shortly after D-Day he traveled to Normandy to interview combatants from the 82nd and 101st Airborne Divisions. "These interviews constitute the basic record of the airborne assault, because the widely scattered and hard-pressed airborne troops kept few written records," Everett notes.[10] Six months later, during the Battle of the Bulge, Marshall and his assistants Capt. John G. Westover and Lt. A. Joseph Webber interviewed members of the 101st Airborne Division and its attached units in Bastogne. The historians conducted their first interviews just four days after the German siege ended. Their efforts resulted in the collection of official records as well as oral histories later published as *Bastogne: The First Eight Days*, a book that has become an indispensable source for all students of Bastogne.[11]

As a journalist, I was fascinated that thanks to the efforts of S. L. A. Marshall and his team of historians, I could read what commanders like General McAuliffe thought immediately after the battle, expressed in the general's direct language and simple eloquence. To someone like myself with no real military experience, it was eye opening to read McAuliffe explain how his prior military experience prepared him to understand that being surrounded did not necessarily constitute what most thought were desperate straits, but could actually be construed as a tactical advantage. While almost everyone except McAuliffe, including the Nazis themselves, saw the US military predicament at Bastogne as a lost cause, McAuliffe explained to S. L. A. Marshall and his historians how and why he could see being surrounded by German forces as an opportunity. The after-action field interviews Marshall and his team of researchers collected permitted me, reading them fifty years later, to see the battle through the eyes of the officers who fought there. Reading these histories, I began to understand and I hope to express to the reader how the response "Nuts!" came immediately to McAuliffe's mind. Finally, I began to appreciate why this simple one-word response reverberated through American forces worldwide like electricity, moving even a battle-hardened veteran of Gen. George Patton's status to drive himself and the men of the Third Army to the extraordinary limits that they achieved, relieving the besieged troops at Bastogne.

Twenty years ago, in 1994, the fiftieth anniversary of the battle, I read for the first time George Koskimaki's book *The Battered Bastards of Bastogne*, originally published in 1989.[12] My childhood interest in the battle was rekindled instantly. During the next two decades I resolved that if at all possible I would write a history of the battle, but not a volume that competed with the many excellent professional military histories that have already been written. Instead, I resolved to pursue what has always fascinated me about the battle: Is it possible to make the case even today that the faith of those who fought at Bastogne invited God to play a direct hand in how the battle turned out? Or, have we become so jaded by our modern secular world that we can no longer appreciate how the men who fought at Bastogne explained to themselves the "miracle" of their victory at Christmas 1944? I know how my father's wartime buddies would have felt.

I wrote this book to reexamine the importance of God in our Judeo-Christian historical tradition in a world certain again to be, as Thomas Hobbes warned, "nasty, cruel, brutish, and short" once again in the future. "Under God" and "In God We Trust" are parts of America's commitment. If America ever turns its back on God, we should not be surprised if God ends up being equally willing to forget us. That the few brave defenders of Bastogne held on and won is a remarkable story by itself. That the power of faith in a being supreme to ourselves played a pivotal role in the outcome, that the "moral fiber" of our combatants won over a powerful but godless enemy is a lesson for future warriors of our country. We should all be proud of the committed and dedicated Americans who fought and won the Battle of Bastogne, thankful to God for the Christmas miracle that sealed Allied victory.

SECTION I

"HOLD BASTOGNE!"

The one standing order that General Middleton gave
General McAuliffe before leaving Bastogne on the
morning of 19 December was: "Hold Bastogne."

—Hugh M. Cole, US Military Historian, *The Ardennes: Battle of the Bulge*, 1988[1]

T he Battle of the Bulge began on Saturday, December 16, 1944, just nine days before Christmas, with an artillery barrage. At 0530 hours, the German Wehrmacht under the overall command of seasoned General Karl Rudolf Gerd von Rundstedt opened up along the entire eighty-five-mile frontier of the dense Ardennes Forest in Belgium, pounding American positions for a full thirty minutes.

The Ardennes frontier demarking Allied offensive advances and German defensive positions ran roughly parallel to the Belgian-German border, in an area from Losheim, Germany, in the north down to a point where the Our River crosses the French-German border.[2] Maj. Gen. Troy H. Middleton, commander of the US VIII Corps assigned to the First Army, was charged with defending the Ardennes frontier as the Allied rush across France and Belgium stalled in November and December 1944. The Ardennes Forest is commonly described as a region of rugged hills, high plateaus, deep-cut valleys, flowing rivers, and a restricted road network.[3] The Germans in both world wars had already launched historic offensive campaigns against France from the Ardennes.

They repeated this tactic in the dawn hours of December 16, 1944, launching a major counteroffensive the Germans labeled the *Wacht am Rhein* or "Watch on the Rhine." Hitler chose his code name carefully and cleverly, as if all he had planned was a defensive action designed to protect the German homeland rather than a surprise panzer charge through the dense Ardennes Forest. That way no alarm would be sounded, even if the Allies managed to intercept one of the few messages Hitler allowed his commanders to send openly as German forces moved quietly into place. This massive and terrifying breakout would have to come off as a total surprise, a daring offensive move no United States general would ever have imagined possible.

What Hitler dreamed he would set in motion that cold December morning was nothing less than a plan to slaughter those American troops who dared stand and fight, while sending to flight in terror the few improperly positioned American troops defending the Ardennes. Those troops, Hitler knew, were either raw recruits that had never seen battle or seasoned veterans already mauled from having desperately fought their way across the continent of Europe. Only six months before, on June 6, 1944, the Allies had gained a foothold on Europe with the daring and costly D-Day invasion. Now, as the depth of winter 1944 settled into Europe, the Allies were stalled on the doorstep of Germany, after an end-run attempt planned by British field marshal Bernard Montgomery had failed to break into Germany from the north through the Netherlands in a daring paratrooper-led sweep codenamed Operation Market Garden.

Now it was Hitler's turn to try a daring sweeping motion with a massive tank-charged offensive that aimed to retake Antwerp. Hitler envisioned entrapping and killing a large number of the Allied forces opposing him in Belgium. In Hitler's way stood Lt. Gen. Troy Houston Middleton, a soldier-educator who came up in the US Army not through West Point, but as a military cadet in the four-year college program at Mississippi A&M. Born October 12, 1889, on a plantation near Georgetown in Copiah County, Mississippi, Middleton was truly a son of the Confederacy. Both of his grandfathers had fought with distinction for the Confederate States of America in the Civil War. Middleton enlisted in the army on March 3, 1910, after taking the train to Buffalo, New York, where he started off as company clerk in the 29th Infantry Regiment at Fort Porter.

He fought with distinction as commander of the 39th Infantry Regiment during the Argonne Offensive in September and October 1918, in the vicinity of the Meuse River. There on October 11, the Germans gassed Middleton and his entire regiment. Describing that action, Middleton recalled he was faced with a German enemy well dug-in throughout the Bois de Foret. "I gave orders that everybody should shoot," Middleton explained, "in what is commonly known today as marching fire—under the theory that if we were shooting, the defending Germans would naturally conclude that we could see them, or at least this would force them to keep their heads down."[4] For more than a mile, the 39th advanced in a skirmish line through the dense forest. "You never heard such a racket in your life. We walked right on through the wood to its northern edge. This was the farthest advance of Fourth Division troops into enemy territory, putting us right on the edge of the Meuse River beyond Brieulles."[5] Middleton was promoted to colonel two days after his twenty-ninth birthday, making him the youngest officer in the American Expeditionary Force to achieve that rank. For his bravery in the Bois de Foret action, Middleton later received the Distinguished Service Medal.[6]

After World War I, Middleton served at a succession of military schools, including the United States Army Infantry School at Ft. Benning, Georgia, the US Army Command and General Staff College at Ft. Leavenworth, Kansas, and the Army War College in Washington, DC. In 1937, Middleton retired from the army after he was offered the opportunity to be the dean of admissions for a higher salary at Louisiana State University in Baton Rouge. On the Monday after the Japanese attacked Pearl Harbor, Middleton wired the War Department saying he was in good physical condition and available for military service should the department choose to have him. The War Department responded to Middleton's telegram, telling him he should report to active duty as a lieutenant colonel on January 20, 1942.[7]

With his square face, gentle smile, and ever-present eyeglasses, Middleton looked more like a country doctor than a military commander. Still, none other than the Supreme Allied Commander himself, Dwight D. Eisenhower, personally had selected him to be appointed a Corps commander. Before dawn on December 16, 1944, Middleton was asleep in his comfortable campaign caravan next to his headquarters in Bastogne. The German shelling woke him up. Middleton soon learned several German divisions had attacked his defenses all across the Ardennes sector.[8] "I could hear the big guns there in Bastogne," Middleton remembered. "By 10 a.m. I had word that elements of sixteen different German divisions had been identified in the attacking force."[9] It would take all Middleton could muster to rally US defenders sufficiently to slow Hitler's winter offensive. In the early hours of the attack what Middleton feared most—that his lines of defense would collapse and be routed as the Germans advanced—looked like it was happening.

At approximately 0600 hours, the artillery barrage along Germany's entire Western Front began coming to a halt as squads of Nazi infantry led by panzer tanks advanced out of the Ardennes in the fog and mists familiar to December winter mornings in those dense woods. Hitler's desperate eleventh-hour counterattack designed to turn the fortune of the war in Europe back in Germany's favor had begun.

Hitler hoped to win a military victory that might force the Allies—the United States, England, France, and the Soviet Union—to agree to peace terms more favorable to Nazi Germany than the unconditional surrender the Allies had been pressing since the Morocco Conference in 1943. The concept of "unconditional surrender" in US history dates back to the Battle of Fort Donelson, Tennessee, during the American Civil War, when Brig. Gen. Ulysses S. Grant forced Confederate brigadier general Simon Bolivar Buckner, the fort's commander, to agree to unconditional surrender before Grant would halt hostilities. Ever thereafter, the general's initials, "U. S. Grant," morphed into "Unconditional Surrender Grant." President Franklin D. Roosevelt revived the concept of unconditional surrender during the January 1943 summit meeting with British prime minister Winston Churchill, held in the Anfa Hotel in Casablanca, French Morocco, when the two heads of state agreed on the terms Allies would require the Axis powers of Nazi Germany, Fascist Italy, and Imperial Japan to accept as a condition of bringing World War II to an end.

Perhaps success in the Wacht am Rhein winter offensive would not be sufficient to win the war for Germany, but Hitler had reason to anticipate that striking a decisive blow with his surprise attack out of the Ardennes might win him a ceasefire and ultimately a peace on terms that would allow the Nazi regime to remain in power after the war. If all went well for Hitler, the Nazis in their drive through Bastogne to the port city of Antwerp, Belgium, would divide the British forces in the north from the American forces in the south, isolating large pockets of Allied troops such that they could be behind enemy lines and cut off from resupply. In the first few hours of what the Allies soon called the "Battle of the Bulge," military strategists on both sides realized the success or failure of Hitler's bold gamble would depend on whether or not the Allies could slow Hitler's advance in time to reorganize defenses and bring up reinforcements. By dawn December 17, the morning of the second day of Hitler's offensive, the focal point of the Allied effort to stop Hitler had begun to focus on a small Belgian town called Bastogne.

On December 18, 1944, the New York Times alerted readers to the German offensive with a headline that read, "Nazi Offensive Pierces First Army Lines." Drew Middleton reported, "A German offensive against the southern flank of the American First Army bit several miles into Belgium today and crashed across the Luxembourg frontier in two areas. Several German armored infantry divisions are being employed in Field Marshal Karl von Rundstedt's counterblow, which is described here as a major effort."[10] Middleton's report was accompanied by another story written by Times reporter Harold Denny. "The German counteroffensive that started yesterday moved into our lines today and with increased power. It looks like the real thing," Denny wrote. "It is too early yet to gauge its possible extent and scope and whether this is to be Germany's final all-out effort to stave off defeat. But the rate at which the Germans are throwing in divisions, including some crack ones, shows that this is a serious, major counter-offensive and serious exertions will be needed to meet it."[11]

Yet the news of Hitler's counteroffensive reported in New York on December 18, 1944, was not definitive enough to shatter the expectations of a war-weary US public that peace in Europe was on the horizon. While the war movies were still playing on the silver screen in New York City, first-run feature films were already prefiguring happier times. Judy Garland and Margaret O'Brien were starring in *Meet Me in St. Louis* playing at the Astor at Broadway and 45th Street; John Wayne and Ward Bond were featured in the Western *Tall in the Saddle* at the RKO Palace on Broadway and 47th Street; and Mickey Rooney and Elizabeth Taylor were featured in *National Velvet* at Radio City Music Hall in Rockefeller Center.

During the next few days, hopes for peace by Christmas were shattered as the nation began praying Bastogne would be the place the German advance would stall.

CHAPTER 1

THE 101ST AIRBORNE
CALLED FORWARD

Less than thirty-six hours after the start of the German counteroffensive, General Hodges, seeing the VIII Corps center give way under massive blows and having thrown his own First Army reserves into the fray plus whatever Simpson's Ninth could spare, turned to Bradley with a request for the SHAEF Reserve. Eisenhower listened to Bradley and acceded, albeit reluctantly; the two airborne divisions would be sent immediately to VIII Corps area. Orders for the move reached the chief of staff of the VIII Airborne Corps during the early evening of 17 December and the latter promptly relayed the alert to the 82nd and the 101st.

—Hugh M. Cole, US Military Historian, *The Ardennes: Battle of the Bulge*, 1988[1]

G en. Omar N. Bradley, as Eisenhower's second-in-command and the operational commander of all Allied forces in the European theater, was responsible for translating Eisenhower's strategic command decisions into operational orders given to various Allied units in the field during the Battle of the Bulge. As he evolved a battle plan for countering Hitler in the Ardennes, Bradley reached a decision that holding

Bastogne was strategically important. "My decision to hold Bastogne, at all costs, had been anticipated by Middleton even as his front was crumbling to pieces," Bradley noted. "When I called Troy to give him the order to hold that crucial road junction, he replied that he had already instructed his troops there to dig in and hold."[2]

Still, Bradley had in mind that Middleton's holding action at Bastogne was only temporary. Discussing his plans to defend should the Germans counterattack in the Ardennes, Bradley wrote: "If the Germans hit his sector, Middleton was to make a fighting withdrawal—all the way back to the Meuse River if necessary. We chose specific defensive positions he would hold. Since there were only a few roads through the area, we thought our tactical air forces could interdict them with relative ease, further delaying the Germans. Middleton was to locate no gasoline or food dumps, or anything else of value to the enemy, within that line of withdrawal."[3] Bradley's plan was that Middleton should withdraw as slowly as possible, giving Bradley time to bring up reserve units to join the battle.[4]

The news from the front was not good on the morning of December 17 as members of the SHAEF general staff gathered around a map. The Nazis were pressing Middleton's VIII Corps defense so hard that the units assigned there were beginning to fall back in confusion. The major reserves available were the 82nd Airborne and the 101st Airborne then in bivouac in France. "I think we should put them there," said Maj. Gen. J. F. M. Whiteley, the SHAEF assistant chief of staff, and "G-3," the officer in charge of SHAEF operations and combat deployment, pointing to Bastogne. "The place has the best road net in the area." Eisenhower and Bradley conferred by telephone, joined by Gen. Walter Bedell Smith, generally known as "Beetle" Smith, Eisenhower's chief of staff at SHAEF.[5] "It appeared then that the enemy objective was no less than Liège and the Meuse River," Bradley recalled. "We three—and the staff present—agreed that our immediate defensive strategy would be first to hold the north and south 'shoulders' of the penetration, second to block the westward rush by holding the road hubs of St. Vith and Bastogne, and third to prepare strong defenses behind the Meuse River. Von Rundstedt might reach the Meuse, but he would go no farther. Ike gave orders for his reserve 82nd and 101st Airborne Divisions to race to the Bastogne–St. Vith areas to reinforce units of the 7th, 9th, and 10th Armored

Divisions. In addition, he ordered that the 11th Armored and the 17th Airborne Divisions be rushed from England to replace SHAEF reserve and help defend the Meuse River line."[6]

Bradley knew that von Rundstedt might be able to reach the Meuse River, but he was determined he would let him go no farther. Holding crossroad towns like St. Vith and Bastogne would delay Rundstedt's advance. With Hitler's tanks edging toward them in the difficult winter terrain, capturing these two crossroad towns quickly was vital to the Germans' success. Bradley's first goal was to prevent the Wacht am Rhein offensive from adhering to the tight schedule both Hitler and the Allied command knew was critical. In launching the Ardennes counteroffensive, the Germans had the advantage of surprise. But once the counteroffensive had been launched, time worked to the German's disadvantage. The units available to Rundstedt were the last Hitler had and reinforcements were virtually non-existent, while all the Americans needed was time to deploy whatever forces were immediately available to delay the Germans so reserves could be fully engaged. In the final analysis, the 82nd and the 101st Airborne Divisions were important, but expendable. From the moment Hitler's Wacht am Rhein offensive began, how the generals on both sides played for time was the critical element that would ultimately determine the outcome of the battle.

The Fifth Panzer Army under General Hasso von Manteuffel brought four divisions against the Bastogne sector of Middleton's VIII Corps defenses. Manteuffel, like Rundstedt, was the son of a distinguished Prussian military family. In 1916, while fighting for the German infantry on the Western Front during World War I, Manteuffel had been wounded in battle. In Hitler's offensive against Stalin, Manteuffel commanded the 7th Panzer Division in Russia, and in 1944 was given command of the Gross Deutschland Panzer Division. He was one of the most decorated officers in the German army, holding the Iron Cross of the Knights Degree with Swords and Diamonds.[7] With his extensive experience in battle, Manteuffel had joined Rundstedt in objecting to Hitler's plan for launching a counteroffensive in the Ardennes. Like Rundstedt, Manteuffel appreciated the difficulty of bringing large forces through the Ardennes in winter, since the tanks would have to travel on the limited network of roads available. Like Rundstedt, Manteuffel ultimately accepted his command in the Wacht am

Rhein offensive, finally conceding it was futile to oppose Hitler in this last-ditch effort to stave off defeat.

As the battle began, Manteuffel knew that if he did not reach the Meuse River quickly, the Americans would have time to bring up sufficient defenses to deny him the crossing, causing the Wacht am Rhein offensive to stall. In their 2012 book, *No Silent Night: The Christmas Battle for Bastogne*, military historians Leo Barron and Don Cygan discussed a Wehrmacht planning meeting of senior officers before the winter counteroffensive was launched. "With such limited routes of travel toward the Meuse, road hubs like the Belgian towns of Bastogne and St. Vith became decisive terrain," Col. Heinz Kokott, commander of the 26th Volksgrenadier observed. "He [Kokott] realized what many of the other officers in the room must be thinking, but were afraid to yet voice: if the Wehrmacht failed to seize those two towns early on, it would be almost impossible to reach the Meuse River in four days."[8]

At the start of the battle, General Baron Heinrich Freiherr von Lüttwitz, the commander of the 47th Panzer Corps was having trouble advancing against the dogged defense of the 28th Infantry Division to the east of Bastogne. Gen. Fritz Bayerlein, the commander of the distinguished Panzer Lehr Division, who came to prominence as Field Marshal Erwin Rommel's chief of staff during the North African campaign, was not able to dislodge the 28th in their defense of Hosingen and Holzhtum on the road to Bastogne. Bayerlein estimated the Americans had delayed his Panzer Lehr Division a crucial thirty-six hours. With this news, Manteuffel realized his precious timetable was coming apart, in the first hours of the battle, with the prospect developing that Bastogne would not fall to a quick strike, but could develop into a prolonged defense and a troublesome siege.[9] Still, the left flank of the 28th Infantry was forced to withdraw to the west bank of the Our River and the right flank was pushed even further. But it was in the center of the 28th that the Germans made their greatest penetration, with one enemy salient thrusting through some eight miles and another some six miles.[10] In the first day of battle on December 16, the Germans had advanced to within eleven miles of Bastogne.[11]

"The woods are full of Jerries! The woods are full of Jerries!" The shouts went up as K Company, 112th Infantry Regiment of the 28th Infantry Division, was attacked outside Bastogne in the early morning hours of

December 16, 1944. Lt. Ralph Larson, the platoon leader, knew the panicked, almost hopeless warnings from the forward guards meant trouble. "It was a cry I shall never forget," Larson recalled after the war. Larson ordered his men to leave their bunkers and occupy the forward ring of foxholes and slit trenches the unit had dug when they occupied this forward position. Larson knew they needed to defend themselves from any Germans that might emerge attacking from the woods. "There was no time for reflection," Larson said. "Instinctively I grabbed my helmet and carbine, as did the other two platoon members who had been sleeping in that particular dugout."[12] Suddenly, a flare shot up and illuminated the area long enough for the Americans to see the distinct shapes of German soldiers a couple of hundred yards away in the woods, moving toward them.

Up and down the line, Larson remembered, the Yanks opened fire with M1 Garands and Browning Automatic Rifles, commonly known simply as BARs. Suddenly, Larson heard the Bunsen-burner-like sound of a flamethrower. "A German flamethrower went into action, barely missing our positions," he explained. "Rifle shots blared back and forth from both sides." The flamethrower found a victim somewhere in the distance, and the unfortunate GI burned like a torch for a few minutes before he collapsed in a charred heap. Twenty minutes later, when the firefight was over, Larson surveyed the damage, realizing he had lost his two forward sentries, and his temporary platoon sergeant was missing. He was told the man who was scorched to death was from the 3rd Battalion, but Larson did not know his name. There were four dead in the woods. Several others were wounded. Larson and the other Americans could hear the wounded Germans moaning somewhere in the darkness. Larson felt he had defended his position against a German patrol, but he had no idea he had just encountered the leading forces of the 560th Volksgrenadiers Division. All night long, thousands of them had worked their way through the no-man's-land and the wooded forests that honeycombed the area, wrote Professor John C. McManus in his 2007 book *Alamo in the Ardennes*.[13]

By 1600 on December 16, German engineers attacking Bastogne had finished constructing armor-capable bridges at Gemund across the Our River and were moving Mark IV and Mark V Panzer tanks from the 2nd Panzer Division and Panzer Lehr into the battle; Manteuffel hoped his forces would have been across the Our River that morning, so they could dart into Bastogne while the American defenders were still in shock.[14] But that had not happened. To Manteuffel's surprise, the disoriented infantry-men of the 28th reorganized quickly and fought back.

At Lutzkampen, another small Belgian town outside Bastogne, the Germans still had not crossed the Our even as the sun was setting. There the infantrymen of the 28th held off the Germans all day as the German tanks accompanied by hundreds of infantry soldiers attacked the southern end of the town. From a foxhole, Private Alexander Hadden of Company B, 112th Infantry of the 28th watched the advance of "the huge, black, obscene shapes" of a column of seven advancing German tanks. "They approached up the road from the middle of Lutzkampen toward one of the farmhouses used by the company," Hadden recalled. "All of a sudden there was a horrendous detonation from the cannon of the lead tank and the house collapsed and fell inward on itself in a shower of sparks."[15] Small-arms fire erupted, tracers whizzed back and forth, and the Americans were mowing down columns of German infantry. But the tanks kept coming. One of them was a flame-thrower. Private First Class Charles Huag of Company B heard screams. "We witnessed the most horrible thing any GI dreams of," he said. A flame-thrower tank had stopped some fifty feet from an occupied foxhole. "As the two kids sat there helplessly, a gigantic stream of roaring fire shot in on them," Huag remembered, thinking it was hard to imagine a more horrible death. "They had been burned to a crisp."[16]

By evening, the German tanks turned around and headed back into Lutzkampen. A lieutenant from Company B jumped from his foxhole, obvi-ously high on adrenaline, and shouted, "We licked 'em!"[17] In their fury at being stopped, the Germans unleashed a massive artillery barrage battering Company B, Professor McManus noted. While damaged physically and psy-chologically, the infantry of the 28th Division still held the bridges crossing the Our at Lutzkampen. Doggedly, the 28th threw Manteuffel's timetable into disarray on this, the first day of the Battle of the Bulge.

CONFUSION AT CAMP MOURMELON

On December 16, as the Wacht am Rhein offensive began, the head-quarters of the 101st Airborne Division was at "Camp Mourmelon" in

Mourmelon-le-Grand in France. This was the Champagne country near Reims, about 150 kilometers (93 miles) northeast of Paris, a drive of some two hours by automobile, where the 101st was enjoying a much-deserved rest. But in the next few hours, their command assignment was going to change. The 101st Airborne consisted of three parachute infantry regiments, each with approximately 130 officers and 2,200 enlisted men: the 501st Parachute Infantry Regiment, or PIR; the 502nd PIR; and the 506th PIR. The 327th Glider Infantry Regiment rounded out the 101st Airborne's fighting power. Combined with various additional units including artillery and engineering, the 101st Airborne leaving Camp Mourmelon to head to Belgium was estimated at 805 officers and 11,035 men. The 82nd, also in bivouac in France, and the 101st were the best combat-tested reserve divisions available to SHAEF for immediate deployment to reinforce the Ardennes front. At that time, both divisions were under the command of Gen. Matthew Ridgway, commanding officer of the XVIII Airborne Corps.

At 0800 hours on the morning of December 17, Brig. Gen. Anthony "Tony" McAuliffe received a phone call from of the staff of the XVIII Airborne Corps ordering him to prepare for an immediate departure to join Middleton's VIII Corps in the Ardennes. General Ridgway at that time was preparing to leave XVIII Airborne Corps rear headquarters in Wiltshire, England, to rush to France. This order was reaffirmed when at 2030 hours Lt. Col. Ned D. Moore, chief of staff of the 101st and the officer McAuliffe had assigned to organize the pullout from Mourmelon, received a call from Col. Ralph D. Eaton, chief of staff of the XVIII Airborne Corps, confirming General Ridgway's directive. Eaton told Moore the destination of the 101st was to be Werbomont, a small Belgian town to the northwest of Bastogne. At 2100 McAuliffe assembled the division staff and explained, "All I know is that there has been a breakthrough and we have got to get up there."[18] He directed the division staff to prepare the various units of the 101st to move out of Camp Mourmelon immediately, without waiting for the men on pass in Paris or elsewhere to get back to camp.

Combat journalist MacKenzie accurately stated that McAuliffe, when he assembled division staff that evening, was operating on the very sketchy information then available to the 101st's G-2 intelligence officer, Lt. Col. Paul A. Danahy. "What exactly was the situation at the front? The information that Danahy had furnished General McAuliffe was passed on to the group. What exactly were they supposed to do?"[19] The problem was that nobody seemed to know for sure. MacKenzie observed that a circle had been drawn with black crayon around the speck on the map labeled "Werbomont" in eastern Belgium. Lt. Col. Julian J. Ewell, the commander of the 501st Parachute Infantry Regiment, noticed that across the area at the German border "ARDENNES" was printed in type larger than that designating the populated areas. "That," Ewell proclaimed, pointing, "is where the Germans always come out of Germany looking for trouble."[20]

Ewell did not mention that he had visited Bastogne in recent weeks, eager after the intense combat in Holland to take "a busman's holiday." Anxious to satisfy his curiosity about the ancient battlefield, Ewell had taken a personal tour of Bastogne and the vicinity. As a result, Ewell had the unique advantage among all the officers of the 101st that he had personally walked in recent weeks every square inch of the Bastogne battlefield, providing him with information and insight that was to prove invaluable in the days ahead.

MacKenzie noted that Ewell and Kinnard had fought together as battalion commanders in Normandy and part of the time in Holland. "Each had one of the 501st Regiment's three infantry battalions until Ewell was promoted to the regimental command and Kinnard to G-3 of the Division," MacKenzie wrote. These were young officers, with Ewell, Kinnard, and the 101st's G-2 Danahy all twenty-nine years old. Still, they were veterans of combat. "'Julian acts like he was born on a Battlefield," Kinnard told Danahy. Both Danahy and Kinnard were graduates of West Point in 1939. MacKenzie commented that Ewell, who seemed too large for his 5-foot–11-inch frame had seen his weight drop to 135 pounds from the rigor of airborne life. MacKenzie noted Ewell was born in Oklahoma, an army brat like Kinnard, who "fell into a slouching gait and a mountaineer drawl when he was in battle dress." MacKenzie commented there was "an air of stealth in Ewell's movements, as though he had been fashioned for the paratrooper's brand of behind-the-enemy-lines fighting."[21]

"Each man took into battle an overriding obligation never to let the other fellow down," MacKenzie wrote. "It was never put into words. It was acknowledged only in actions."[22] MacKenzie noted that along with this obligation to the individuals around him, each airborne volunteer carried into combat an unwritten rule of conduct implied in the admonition of Maj. Gen. William Carrey Lee, the first commanding general of the division at its activation in 1942: "Let me call your attention to the fact that our badge is the great American Eagle. This is a fitting emblem for a Division that will crush its enemies by falling upon them like a thunderbolt from the skies."[23] A heart attack just before the D Day invasion at Normandy forced General Lee to relinquish his command to Maj. Gen. Maxwell B. Taylor. With a reputation for intellectual attainments, Taylor's ferocity in battle set the example for Screaming Eagle deployment in combat. MacKenzie noted that as Taylor sprang out of airplanes "fierce and glowering," he parachuted down with a knife and gun ready "for any foe who might be waiting there in enemy territory to resist his establishment of a command post from which he could attack in all directions."[24]

When the 101st Airborne was called into action on December 17, the division's commander, Taylor, was in Washington discussing with the Pentagon operational changes in the unit. He was making the case that the 101st should be reassigned to the Pacific theater. Word among the troops was that Taylor, believing the war in Europe was winding down, "was eager to bloody a Screaming Eagle talon in Asia before it was done."[25] Upon hearing the 101st had been called to the front, Taylor immediately took an airplane to England, but he did not arrive in France in time to join the division before it moved into action. Brig. Gen. Gerald J. Higgins, Taylor's assistant division commander, was in England along with five senior commanders of divisional units and sixteen junior officers, working to provide a detailed after-action review of the unit's participation in the fiasco that developed out of Operation Market Garden in Holland. McAuliffe was upgraded from "rest-camp commander"[26] to battlefield leader simply because he was the top officer of the 101st present when the call to action came.[27]

Just being there in Camp Mourmelon on December 16 and 17, 1944, it turns out, was one of the most decisive moments in McAuliffe's military career.

MCAULIFFE TAKES COMMAND

Unlike many in the US military command in World War II, McAuliffe was too young to serve in the American Expeditionary Force in World War I. Born in Washington, DC, on July 2, 1898, McAuliffe was a student at West Virginia University from 1916 to 1917. He graduated from West Point in November 1918, the month World War I ended. Between the two world wars, McAuliffe had excellent army training, having attended the US Army Command and General Staff College at Ft. Leavenworth, as well as graduating in June 1940 from the US Army War College. Prior to the United States joining World War II, McAuliffe had a comfortable "armchair job" in weapons development at the Pentagon. An ordinance expert, McAuliffe was well qualified to command the 101st's artillery.[28] On D-Day, he parachuted into Normandy with the 101st, and during Operation Market Garden, he entered Holland by glider.

When the Siege of Bastogne started, McAuliffe was forty-six years old, three years younger than Gen. Maxwell Taylor, but still an "old man" to many of his young regimental commanders—a fact McAuliffe reinforced by his practice of referring to himself as "Old Crock" when in the presence of his younger associates.[29] McAuliffe was squarely built and he had a reputation as a man of quiet but direct speech who could express his thoughts clearly and concisely, without mincing words. "A realist, methodical and chary of haphazard adventuring," was the way MacKenzie best described McAuliffe.[30] Bastogne was McAuliffe's chance to assume divisional command, and he jumped at the opportunity.

On the following morning, December 18, Maj. Gen. James M. Gavin, commander of the 82nd Airborne and in temporary command of the XVIII Airborne Division until General Ridgway returned from England, learned in a meeting with First Army that the 82nd was going to be reassigned from Middleton's XVIII Airborne Corps to V Corps under Gen. Leonard Gerow. When the 101st and the 82nd departed bivouac in France, both divisions knew they were headed northeast into Belgium, but neither realized they would be fighting under different corps commanders in different sectors of the battle. While the 101st ended up being assigned to the defense of Bastogne, the 82nd headed into Belgium, ultimately assigned to the defense of St. Vith, another small Belgian town, about thirty-five miles to the northeast of Bastogne.

"On the morning of December 17, Eisenhower made the critical decisions of the entire battle, and did so without consulting anyone outside his own staff," wrote historian and best-selling author Stephen E. Ambrose in *Band of Brothers*, his 1999 classic account of Easy Company, 506th Parachute Infantry Regiment, 101st Airborne Division. "He declared the crossroads city of Bastogne as the place that had to be held no matter what. (Bastogne is in a relatively flat area in the otherwise rugged hills of the Ardennes, which is why the roads of the area converge there.) Because of his offensives north and south of the Ardennes, Ike had no strategic reserve available. He decided to use the paratroopers to plug the holes in his line and to hold Bastogne."[31] This was the brilliance of US command that Hitler may have failed to fully appreciate in deciding his strategy for the Wacht am Rhein offensive. The US military in World War II was successful largely because initiative was considered all-important, with units in combat relying on the calculation that field commanders best knew what needed to be done simply because they were closest to the action. In the final analysis, improvisation was key to the ability of the US military to respond successfully to Hitler's surprise counteroffensive.

On December 18, at approximately noon, an advance party headed by Danahy and consisting of representatives of each unit in the 101st along with a company of engineers was ready to depart Camp Mourmelon. The advance party was responsible for identifying and preparing an assembly area near the front lines where the 101st could assemble and reorganize, waiting for assignments into the battle.[32] Leaving Camp Mourmelon, the 101st advance party believed they were headed toward Werbomont, about 137 miles to the northeast of Camp Mourmelon. But as the morning progressed, General Middleton changed the orders, directing the 101st to proceed to Bastogne instead. The after-action reflections of Lt. Col. H. W. O. "Harry" Kinnard, the 101st's G-3 operations officer, stressed the initial confusion the 101st faced upon going into battle. Kinnard noted that when the advance party arrived at a crossroads location outside Werbomont, Danahy met Lt. Col. Ireland of the 82nd Airborne and was told, "You are not supposed to be here. You are due thirty miles from here, in Bastogne." Danahy replied, "I want maps."

Maps were scarce and Danahy was having trouble getting anyone to part with a map until Danahy threatened to report to General Gavin the names of the officers who were refusing to cooperate. Danahy got his maps and headed out for Bastogne, but the delay was costly. Kinnard commented: "The advance party was far distant from the sector and did not reach Bastogne in time to accomplish its mission."[33] Had the advance party been given Bastogne as the correct location upon leaving Camp Mourmelon, Danahy and the others would have been at Bastogne by 1630 on December 18, in plenty of time to make advance preparations for the 101st trailing behind.

At approximately 1230 hours, some fifteen minutes after the advance party departed Camp Mourmelon for Werbomont, General McAuliffe set off from Camp Mourmelon in a command car, taking with him Kinnard and his first aide, 1st Lt. Frederic D. Starrett. McAuliffe was anxious to see with his own eyes exactly what the German advance looked like.[34]

The day before, on December 17, when word came down that a German offensive had begun in the Ardennes, Fred MacKenzie, an experienced combat reporter for the *Buffalo Evening News*, was at Camp Mourmelon, embedded with the 101st. Before moving to Buffalo to work there for the *Evening News*, MacKenzie had worked several years for the Associated Press in Pittsburgh and then for the *Pittsburgh Sun-Telegraph*. He first met McAuliffe by coincidence at the Scribe Hotel in Paris around December 14, at a press conference in which McAuliffe and his G-2 intelligence officer Lt. Col. Paul Danahy were outlining the role the 101st played in the Holland campaign. At that first meeting at the Scribe Hotel, MacKenzie asked to accompany the Division, and McAuliffe agreed MacKenzie could come with them to Camp Mourmelon, thinking that having a reporter along might produce some good news for readers back home.

On December 18, when the 101st was suddenly being called to the front, MacKenzie asked a second time to be part of the action. "When the hurry call came for us to move north by truck, Fred asked to go," McAuliffe explained in the foreword to MacKenzie's 1968 book, *The Men of Bastogne*. "I told him he might be exposed to many dangers and discomforts. But he was already hooked by the remarkable *esprit de corps* and rollicking humor of the airborne soldiers and was determined to see them in action. Thus he became the only correspondent with us during the Siege of Bastogne."[35] McAuliffe knew that once MacKenzie went into combat with the 101st, there would be no turning back. MacKenzie for his part was willing to take the risk to have a front-row seat as the only correspondent going into action with the 101st to counter the German offensive. For a journalist of MacKenzie's experience and ability, he couldn't pass up the opportunity, regardless of the danger, to accompany the 101st into action as it was being rushed to the front to stem the tide of the daring Nazi surprise counterattack.

McAuliffe respected MacKenzie's courage. "During the battle, Fred was the target for some typically rough paratrooper humor," McAuliffe wrote. "He was well liked by everyone, however, and became a specially privileged personality. He went everywhere, had entrée to command posts, signal and supply installations and aid stations. He visited me several times."[36] During the Siege of Bastogne, MacKenzie was in constant danger of being killed or wounded. In chapter 6 of his book on the Bastogne siege, *The Men of Bastogne*, MacKenzie related a story of four men killed in their bunks near the command post by an exploding shell. What MacKenzie neglected to mention was that five men had bunked there and only one man survived, because he was at the command post typing when the shell hit. "Fred was that man," McAuliffe recorded. [37]

McAuliffe departed from Camp Mourmelon in a hurry to get to Werbomont where he expected to receive his combat orders from command elements of the XVIII Airborne. "Step on it!" was McAuliffe's order to the command car driver as they departed camp.[38] Ironically, even though McAuliffe left Camp Mourmelon after Danahy's advance party, McAuliffe arrived at Bastogne ahead of Danahy by a quirk of fate. As we shall soon see, on the road to Werbomont, McAuliffe decided that, since he left first, he had time to take a slight detour, choosing to enter Werbomont by way of Bastogne. McAuliffe knew Middleton's headquarters were in Bastogne, so he figured why not go to Bastogne first to get briefed in person by the corps commander?

Here in the narrative describing how McAuliffe left Camp Middleton to head for the front, army historian S. L. A. Marshall, the author of the classic 1946 book, *Bastogne: The Story of the First Eight Days*, interrupted to make an important comment: "Then occurred an odd sequence of events in which Fate might have played a stronger hand against 101st Division had it not been for several circumstances."[39] This was an unusual comment for a military general interested in recording immediate field histories from actual combatants just hours or days out of a battle. Military historians may speak of a commander's experience or intuition, but rarely in military history going back to Caesar's *Commentaries* on the Gallic War of 58–50 BC do serious military historians speak in terms that suggest the direct intervention of God into the affairs of warriors as an essential element determining the outcome of a great battle.

Yet, what Marshall perceived was what many who fought at Bastogne perceived. The initial confusion of rushing reinforcements to the front required commanders to improvise, to rely on intuition to make decisions, since in the early hours of the Siege of Bastogne none of the Allied commanders had any real idea how the German counteroffensive had been organized, what Nazi units they would face in battle, or what objectives the Nazi commanders had been assigned by German high command to achieve. In retrospect, Marshall was among those who marveled at how decisions commanders like McAuliffe made on the spot ended up being the best possible decisions that could have been made even with complete and accurate knowledge of the battlefield. One way to interpret the sequence of events that helped bring the 101st to enter the Siege of Bastogne was pure luck, good or bad luck depending on how you saw Bastogne—as an opportunity to get killed or as part of a "Rendezvous with Destiny," the phrase crafted to title the divisional history of the 101st Airborne in World War II. Yet, was it pure luck that the 101st was one of only two units Eisenhower had available in reserve close enough to Bastogne to be called into battle soon enough to have a chance of stopping the Germans? Was it simply luck that General Taylor was in the United States when the Battle of the Bulge began?

About an hour after the 101st's advance party left Camp Mourmelon, General Ridgway arrived by air. His departure from Wiltshire, England, started at 2:15 on the morning of December 17, when he received a surprise call from First Army headquarters in Spa, Belgium. He was awakened to learn the Germans were smashing through the Ardennes with a sizable force, and the previous day Eisenhower had released his XVIII Airborne Corps from theater reserve unit status to combat status, reassigned to First Army command. With one division in England, the 17th Airborne, and two divisions in France, the 82nd and the 101st Airborne, Ridgway decided to move his staff and equipment to the Continent as fast as possible. He contacted Troop Carrier Command and rounded up every available C-47 to make the trip. By dawn, 55 C-47s left England bound for France with Ridgway and his entire staff contingent. Ridgway was lucky in that his C-47 fleet contained the last airplanes to leave England for forty-eight hours, as a heavy fog rolled over the English Channel.[40] The 17th Airborne was stuck in England until December 23, when weather cleared sufficiently to fly the 17th Airborne to France via emergency night flights.

When he arrived at Camp Mourmelon, Ridgway was still uncertain about decisions made higher up by Eisenhower and Bradley at SHAEF. He decided to go directly to General Taylor's empty office and use his phone to call his SHAEF directly. In the ensuing conversation, Ridgway learned his 101st Airborne Division was headed to Bastogne, reassigned from him to Middleton and VIII Corps, while the 82nd Airborne Division was headed to St. Vith, under the command of Gerow and V Corps. As the telephone conversation ended, General Higgins, the assistant division commander for the 101st, entered General Taylor's office and learned Ridgway was headed to Bastogne.

Higgins and the various officers with him also departed England and headed for France as soon as they learned the 101st Airborne had been called to action. One of the youngest generals in the American army at the time, Higgins was a six-foot, 185-pound bundle of muscle who managed to get back to Camp Mourmelon as the 101st were boarding trucks to depart. Once Higgins hooked up with the 101st, he assumed the same position of assistant division commander under McAuliffe as he had held under Taylor. Ridgway was so anxious to get to Bastogne that he left immediately, not realizing that Higgins had also been ordered to Bastogne. This left Higgins to travel alone. McAuliffe had left instructions that Higgins was to get forward as fast as possible, and Higgins calculated the route via sedan would be less encumbered than the route he would have to take to get there in a command car.

CHAPTER 2

THE SCRAMBLE TO REACH BASTOGNE

The two divisions [the 82nd and the 101st Airborne] had little organic transportation—after all they were equipped to fly or parachute into battle—but in a matter of hours the Oise Section of the Communications Zone gathered enough ten-ton open trucks and trailers plus the work horse two-and-a-half-tonners to mount all the airborne infantry. . . . To alert and dispatch the two veteran airborne divisions was a methodical business, although both moved to the front minus some equipment and with less than the prescribed load of ammunition. This initial deployment in Belgium presents a less ordered picture, blurred by the fact that headquarters journals fail to square with one another and the memories of the commanders involved are at variance, particularly as regards the critical decision (or decisions) which brought the 101st to Bastogne and its encounter with history.

—Hugh M. Cole, US Military Historian, *The Ardennes: Battle of the Bulge*, 1988[1]

C amp Mourmelon is outside the village of Mourmelon-le-Grand, around twenty miles to the southeast of the cathedral town of Reims, in the French Champagne region. Stephen Ambrose appropriately pointed out that Mourmelon had been a military garrison town for nearly two thousand years, dating back to 54 BC when Julius Caesar used the area as a campground for his Roman legions. The French army had maintained barracks in Mourmelon for hundreds of years. Ambrose adds that Mourmelon, located between the Marne River to the south and the Aisne River to the north, is on the traditional invasion route toward Paris. "Mourmelon was in an area that had witnessed many battles through the centuries," Ambrose wrote. "Most recently the area had been torn up between 1914 and 1918. The artillery craters and trenches from the last war were everywhere. American Doughboys had fought in the vicinity in 1918, Château-Thierry and Belleau Wood."[2] Here the 101st was in bivouac for refitting, following seventy-two continuous days of combat action in the ill-fated Operation Market Garden in Holland, an unsuccessful plan to shorten the war devised by British field marshal Bernard Law Montgomery, 1st Viscount Montgomery of Alamein.

The men of the 101st had welcomed the opportunity to rest. But Ambrose noted that after a few days of rest, the troops needed an outlet for their energy. The 101st borrowed football equipment from the air force, flown in from England, and organized a Christmas Day Champagne Bowl between the 506th and 502nd Parachute Infantry Regiments, with tryouts held and practice scheduled for three hours a day. On December 1, the 82nd and the 101st enjoyed a pass to go into Reims, where there was more than enough champagne to get the troops tipsy and induce fistfights. On December 4, all passes to Reims were canceled because, as one trooper expressed it, "The boys won't behave in town."[3] Then, at the conclusion of dinner one evening, the men got paid, and predictably gambling broke out, with many men blowing three months' pay, or gaining a windfall, in the hours and days that followed. USO shows were scheduled, with New York Giants baseball star Mel Ott and movie stars Marlene Dietrich and Mickey Rooney entertaining the troops. Passes to Paris for forty-eight hours were issued in limited quantity, usually by company, and a few thirty-day furloughs back to the United States were handed out in drawings.

George Koskimaki, a 101st combat veteran, compiled in his important 1994 book *The Battered Bastards of Bastogne* the story of some 530 veterans of the 101st who at his request wrote about their combat experiences. There, Koskimaki reports the account of Sgt. Donald Woodland, who attended a Sunday church service while the men of the 101st were garrisoned in Mourmelon. "Today was an ordinary Sunday in the life of this enlisted man," Woodland wrote years after the battle. "I recall attending church service in the large auditorium of Camp Mourmelon. We were 'under orders' from Captain Stach to go to church every Sunday and to pray for our lost men. The captain himself was there in his spit and polish uniform. We sat near him but not with him." Woodland was particularly impressed during the Consecration of the Mass when eight paratroopers, immaculately attired in dress uniform, silently filed out and flanked both sides of the altar. A command was given and the troopers brought their M1 rifles to "Present Arms." At the conclusion of the service, the troopers filed quietly from the altar. "Today, on every Sunday that I attend church service, my mind goes back to Camp Mourmelon and the presentation of arms," Woodland recalled.[4]

THE SCRAMBLE TO LEAVE CAMP

The bivouac in Mourmelon came to an abrupt end on the evening of December 17, when the alert to move out the next morning began to circulate. A call went through army channels to the military police in Paris to round up and get back to Camp Mourmelon those who were in Paris on forty-eight-hour passes. PFC Amos Almeida recalled:

> We were given a very much-needed rest. We went to Paris and had a ball. While in Paris, the MPs came and called out everyone who was wearing a Screaming Eagle patch, telling us there was an emergency and we were to return to our base at once. At that time I was having dinner and I didn't even touch it. They put us on a truck and took us back to Mourmelon. Our rest did not last long.[5]

Back at camp, the men scrambled to find winter clothes and equipment. All fighting equipment had been turned in when the 101st first arrived at Camp Mourmelon. Division supply doors were swung open and the men were told, "Take what you need and be sure you have enough. No forms to sign—no red tape—help yourself!"[6] The problem was that paratroopers who went to the supply company to pick up equipment found they were out

Members of the 501st Parachute Infantry Regiment of the 101st Airborne Division load onto trucks at Camp Mourmelon for the movement to Bastogne, Belgium. December 18, 1944.

of luck. There were no winter boots or overcoats. If they could find weapons, ammunition was not available. "The men had hastily grabbed together anything useful: bazookas, machine-guns and rifles, as well as blankets and thick army overcoats," wrote Guy Franz Arend, a student of the battle who was born in Bastogne and was almost single-handedly responsible for opening the Bastogne Historical Center in the center of town in 1950. "Not everyone had these, and the soldiers who did not were to shiver in their new olive-green field jackets or in their lightweight beige windbreakers," he continued. "They were, however, able to carry with them as many K rations as they wanted from the pile that had been dumped near the trucks, and the men helped themselves."[7]

Sergeant Robert Bowen, a soldier with the 401st Glider Infantry Regiment assigned to the 101st Airborne, remembered that the soldiers departing Camp Mourmelon packed everything, as if they would never return. "I insisted that every man take an overcoat and overshoes as ordered,"

Bowen wrote. "The overcoat seemed to weigh a ton after being soaked by rain and the overshoes were like anchors, especially in deep snow. I also insisted on taking an extra blanket in bedrolls."[8] Still, with most of the men lacking winter clothing, the paratroopers of the 101st stood packed in open-air trailers, with no choice but to endure the 107-mile drive from Camp Mourmelon. "We marched to a waiting line of open-backed trucks as darkness fell," Bowen continued. "Jammed aboard like olives in a jar, we left for Belgium. It was a long cold ride with a biting wind chilling us to the bone. The headlights of the trucks were on despite being in a combat zone. We raced through small towns and we headed northeast, civilians with anxious faces cheering and waving to us. Were we to be their saviors again, I wondered? After five years of war, I was sure they'd had enough."[9] Most of the 101st Airborne's 107-mile trip from Camp Mourmelon to Bastogne was made in rain and snow flurries, with those departing last making the entire trip in darkness.[10]

Because of bad weather, there was no way the 101st Airborne could be parachuted into Bastogne. Instead, the Transportation Corps acted quickly to call in all available trucks and trailers throughout France. To arrange the truck convoy, MPs stopped every truck they could find in the region of Paris and ordered them to Mourmelon, even if it meant dumping loads of gear and supplies by the roadside. In the segregated armed forces of the World War II era, most of the truck drivers were African Americans from the famed "Red Ball Express." Even those who had been on the road for many hours were ordered to head to Mourmelon as fast as possible, without stopping for anything. The transportation of the 82nd and the 101st to the front was complicated because of the large volume of US troops retreating from the Bastogne region on the very road they needed to travel. Throughout the night, all parts of the 101st Airborne caravan heading to the front in Belgium were forced to buck the mass of vehicles streaming back from the front lines in retreat. S. L. A. Marshall noted:

> Every time the column of retreating vehicles came to a halt for a few minutes, some of the drivers fell asleep from exhaustion. When the road was again free for a few minutes and the forward vehicles got in motion, these sleeping drivers formed new traffic blocks back along the column. To keep things moving at all, it was necessary for officers and MPs to continue

patrolling up and down the column, ready to rouse any slumberer who had tied things up.[11]

William "Wild Bill" Guarnere and Edward "Babe" Heffron, 101st paratroopers, recall:

> As we advanced, infantry troops were running toward us, scared as can be. We're going forward, they're running back. A lieutenant named Rice, I don't know where he was from, he was stopping these kids, making them pile their weapons, clothes, ammo in one big pile. They threw their stuff down and ran. The pile was getting bigger and bigger, so as we walked past, we fished through it and grabbed whatever we could carry. First thing I grabbed was ammo. You tried to load up on guns, ammo, and grenades. Food and clothes were secondary. When your hands were full, you threw what ammo you found in someone else's hands.[12]

Guarnere noted the retreating soldiers were wearing shoulder patches that identified them as 28th Infantry.

> I'm telling you I never seen men with a look like that in my life, running, scared to death. No helmets, no weapons. They threw everything down, they threw their bandoleers down, they threw everything down. The kids were out of breath, yelling, "Don't go up there, there are so many Germans, they're gonna kill everybody!" We said, "That's our job!" They said, "But there's a million of them."[13]

Guarnere stopped one of the retreating soldiers and asked him what unit he was with. "He mentioned some artillery. I said, 'Jesus, I hope you at least lowered your gun and blew them.' He said, 'No, we didn't have time.'" Guarnere was shocked. He reflected that one of the leaders in the 101st would have ordered, "Stand your ground," and that order would have prevailed. "We were more ashamed than anything else," Guarnere concluded. "These were American soldiers."[14]

The process of assembling the trucks and trailers required to transport the 101st to the front began as darkness fell on Sunday, December 17, with the first trucks arriving at Mourmelon early the next morning. According to the after-action report of the 101st Airborne, total division strength including attached units came to 805 officers and 11,035 enlisted men.[15]

A transportation corps after-action report of the 101st Airborne summarized the logistics as follows:

> At 0900 hours on the eighteenth (eleven and one-half hours after the initial order) the first serials arrived at Mourmelon. Those from Paris had traveled approximately 102 miles and those from Rouen approximately 155 miles. Some of the drivers had started fresh; others, however, had been on the road when intercepted, peremptorily unloaded, and dispatched on the new assignment. The last vehicle of the 380 trucks dispatched from the two initial points arrived at Mourmelon at 1720 hours on the eighteenth of December.
>
> Loading of the approximately 14,000 men of the 101st began within ten minutes of arrival of the first serial. At 1915 hours, twenty-three and one quarter hours after the initial order for the vehicles, the divisional G-4 officer informed the chief of staff and Major Mahoney that the last man had been out-loaded.[16]

The report added that the truck convoy ran as far as Bouillon, Belgium, "with the lights blazing." The report noted: "It was a calculated risk taken by the 101st for the sake of speed. The German air force was active that night of the eighteenth but none of the planes came down to stop the lighted troop movement."[17] All the trucks got to the front without losses.

To appreciate just how risky the night convoy with headlights blazing was, realize that one Nazi Messerschmitt fighter airplane sighting the trucks could have called in a Luftwaffe airstrike that could have caused chaos simply by strafing the exposed trucks traveling without air cover or anti-aircraft gun support. Traveling that night through Belgium, the men in the column contemplated these factors, aware of the danger. "I looked back toward the rear of the column and all I could see was bright headlights," remembered PFC Charles Kocourek. "I remarked to the man next to me that this must be pretty serious—going into combat with the lights blazing."[18] The same thought occurred to 1st Lt. Alfred J. Regenburg, assigned to G Company of the 327th Glider Infantry Regiment. "The situation was so urgent that we travelled all night with head lights blazing," he noted after the war. "Had the weather broken and the German air force spotted us, the results would have been devastating."[19]

Sgt. Steve Koper was driving a jeep in the convoy to Bastogne. Koper remembered a command car impatiently trying to pass him along the very congested highway. "It was foggy," Koper recalled. "Suddenly an olive drab vehicle cut in front of me. I think it was a Packard. It was General Higgins. I almost hit him. He was trying to pass the convoy but a column of trucks was coming toward us."[20]

Capt. Jim Hatch of the 502nd also encountered Higgins on the highway.

> We had a sedan behind us that was giving us a bad time trying to pass us. I finally got out and went back to see what this fellow's problem might be. Guess what? It was General Higgins trying to get ahead of everybody since he had received word before he left that the 101st was placed under the command of VIII Corps which was located in Bastogne and that was to be the assembly area for the 101st units. Needless to say, we let him pass and now we had positive word as to our next higher headquarters and would head straight to Bastogne.[21]

Arriving at Mande-Saint-Étienne, Higgins found a captain of the 28th Infantry blocking the road. "Our division is coming up here to fight, Captain," Higgins insisted, "and we must use this road to bring them in." The captain balked, replying that he could not move because he had orders to block the road to stop deserters getting away. "Get the . . . things out of the road," Higgins barked, fingering the holster of his pistol.[22] Higgins gave the captain a direct order to get his vehicles in a single file along the road at once, and just to make his point clear, he set himself about immediately directing the drivers to move off to the side of the highway.[23] Wisely, the captain got the idea and complied.

Journalist MacKenzie also made specific mention of the scene encountering Higgins on the road to Bastogne. "The ordeal went on and on: stop, start, move a few feet ahead, stand still in the cold and dark," MacKenzie noted of the convoy. "Except for the muffled sound of the engines and the grinding gears, the column stood or moved in utter silence. Not a shout was heard. No voice was given to misery too great for expression. They crawled along by inches, sunk in a vast coma, a nightmare of misery, despondency, and dread."[24] Suddenly, the figure of a big man standing in the middle of the road and waving his arms loomed up off the left front fender of 1st Sgt. Joe Hayes's lead jeep in the headquarters company section of what had developed into a mile-long column. The figure in the road was motioning Hayes to turn off to the left. "They passed him so near that the jeep almost brushed him," MacKenzie wrote. "'That's Gerry Higgins,' muttered a voice from the backseat. Joe Hayes suddenly became lively, his voice enthusiastic as he confirmed, 'Yea-a-a-h! He's a great guy.'"[25]

THE PARACHUTE PADRE

Born on February 29, 1912, in Cherokee, Iowa, Father Francis L. Sampson was a Catholic priest who graduated from Notre Dame University in 1937. After attending St. Paul's Seminary in Saint Paul, Minnesota, he was ordained a Catholic priest on June 1, 1941. Following ordination, Father Sampson served St. Joseph Parish in Neola, Iowa, and taught at Dowling High School in Des Moines until World War II began. Although he had only been ordained one year, he asked for and received permission from his bishop, Gerald T. Bergan of Des Moines, to enlist in the army. He volunteered to be a paratrooper while attending the Chaplain School at that time held at Harvard University. After completing the Chaplain School, Father Sampson was commissioned as a first lieutenant in the army in 1942 and assigned to the 501st Parachute Infantry Regiment of the 101st Airborne Division. He recalled in his autobiography:

> At this time the army asked for volunteer chaplains for the paratroopers. Like a zealous young businessman starting out in a strange town, I was ready to join anything out of a sheer sense of civic duty. Frankly I did not know when I signed up for the airborne that chaplains would be expected to jump from an airplane in flight. Had I known this beforehand, and particularly had I known the tortures of mind and body prepared at Fort Benning for those who sought the coveted parachute wings, I am positive

that I should have turned a deaf ear to the plea for airborne chaplains. However, once having signed up, I was too proud to back out. [26]

On D-Day, June 6, 1944, Sampson became the first chaplain to take part in the Normandy invasion when he jumped into France with the 501st Parachute Infantry Regiment. "I lit in the middle of a stream over my head and grabbed my knife to cut my bags from me (my Mass kit, doctor's kit, etc.), but I could scarcely move to free myself," he recalled. "The canopy of my chute stayed open, and the strong wind blew me down stream about a hundred yards into shallow water." In those hectic first minutes of his combat experience, Father Sampson realized he managed to survive the first hurdle: landing alive. "I lay there a few minutes exhausted and as securely pinned down by equipment as if I had been in a straitjacket," he recalled. Father Sampson jumped with the same three hundred pounds of equipment the other paratroopers jumped with, but instead of carrying a weapon and ammunition, he carried a couple of extra sets of blood plasma, and as he mentioned, a doctor's field kit plus a complete Mass kit. "It took me about ten minutes to get out of my chute (it seemed an hour, for, judging from the fire, I thought that we had landed in the middle of a target range). I crawled back to the edge of the stream near the spot where I landed, and started diving for my Mass equipment. By pure luck I recovered it after the fifth or sixth dive."[27]

Father Sampson realized none of the other men of the 501st had landed anywhere near him. "The whole area was swamp with deep little streams running through it," he wrote. "As I started to get my bearings, I looked for the lights to assemble on. I later learned that we were several miles from where we were supposed to jump, and that the ack-ack of the Germans had forced the planes to disperse and dump us where they could." He soon realized not being dropped where initially planned had saved his life. "Later, I learned this too had been fortunate; for the path finders with the assembly lights had landed on the proper DZ, and many had been killed almost as soon as they landed."[28] Then he spotted his assistant not far away, still struggling to get out of his parachute. "We got together and made for the nearest hedgerow that would offer cover," he continued. "We no sooner got there than a plane on fire came straight at us. It crashed about a hundred yards in front of us and threw flaming pieces over our heads. We prayed for the men who were in the plane and then watched and prayed for the men in two other planes that were crashing about a mile away. My assistant had lost his weapon in the stream, so we welcomed two of our men who came crawling along the hedgerow."[29] So began Father Sampson's career in World War II combat.

One of Father Sampson's exploits after landing behind enemy lines on D-Day is often cited as the story upon which the hit movie *Saving Private Ryan* was loosely based.[30] The story, as told by Father Sampson, involved a soldier named Sgt. Frederick Niland. "When the regiment was bivouacked near Utah Beach waiting for the boats to take us back to England, a young soldier by the name of Fritz Niland came to see me," Father Sampson recalled in his autobiography *Look Out Below!* "He was very troubled in mind. The company commander of his brother, who was with the 508th Regiment, told Fritz that his brother had been killed and was buried in the Sainte-Mère-Église cemetery. We jumped in my jeep and drove the twenty miles back to that town."[31] Father Sampson checked the cemetery roster and could not find William Niland listed there, though he did find a Roland Niland listed. Frederick Niland choked back the realization that that was his brother too. Unfortunately, Father Sampson located William Niland buried a few blocks away from the grave they initially searched. "After saying a few prayers at the grave, we went to another cemetaery [sic] just a few blocks away where we found the grave we were looking for originally," Father Sampson continued.[32]

Then, the news came that a third brother had been killed in the Pacific. Father Sampson detailed Niland's grief:

> As we were driving back to the bivouac area, Fritz kept saying over and over again, more to himself than to me, "What will poor Butch do now? What will poor Butch do now?"
>
> "Who is Butch, son," I asked.
>
> "Butch? Oh, she's my mother." I looked at him and wondered if he were suffering from combat exhaustion and the terrible shock of this afternoon's discovery. He must have read my thoughts, for he explained, "We four boys always called mom 'Butch' these last few years. That's because, when we wanted to listen to swing orchestras and jive bands on the radio, mom would always turn on 'Gangbusters' or some other program about gangsters . . . she liked those. Now I'm the only son left."[33]

Back at Utah Beach, Father Sampson initiated the paperwork to get Sgt. Frederick Niland out of the war, determined that his mother deserved to have the one remaining of her four sons survive the war. "Mrs. Nyland [sic] had received three tragic wires within the week," Father Sampson noted. "However, we managed to get Fritz sent back to the states, so [his mother] still had one son to comfort her."[34]

Jumping with the 101st into Holland for Operation Market Garden, Father Sampson landed in water a second time. "We jumped at one o'clock," he remembered about the jump on September 16, 1944, over Holland. "Just after I left the door, I saw a large castle below with a wide moat encircling it. My chute opened well, but I had scarcely got my bearings again when I saw that I was swinging onto the top of another man's chute. I called out, '*Look out below!*' and tried to slip in the opposite direction, but it was too late. I landed almost in the middle of his chute and sank as if in quicksand I lay down and tried to roll off. In the meantime my own chute collapsed and hung down, and now his chute was in danger of collapsing. I rolled off and both of our chutes blossomed out again just in time."[35] After separating themselves, the two paratroopers managed to land safely. "I was less than a hundred feet from the water," he continued. "That was the closest I ever came to death in jumping, I think. We both lit squarely in the middle of the moat, but fortunately the water was only about four feet deep. Since we were not nearly as heavily loaded down as in Normandy, we were able to make the edge and help each other over the moat wall and the fence surrounding it."[36]

At Camp Mourmelon with the 101st Airborne after Operation Market Garden, Father Sampson found himself teased by Col. Julian Ewell, the executive officer who took over the command of the 501st Parachute Infantry Regiment after the previous commander, Col. Howard R. Johnson, was mortally wounded in combat and died en route to the 101st Airborne Division's hospital in Nijmegen. Father Sampson had great respect for Colonel Ewell. He wrote:

> Col. Julian Ewell took over the regiment, and he will always stand out in my mind as the near-perfect example of the officer and gentleman. Whenever a company was going to be given a particularly difficult and dangerous mission, he would notify Chaplain Engel [a Protestant minister assigned

as a chaplain to the 501st] and myself so that we could hold respective services. He had the keenest droll wit that I have ever known.[37]

When introducing replacement troops to his staff at Camp Mourmelon, Colonel Ewell had the opportunity to demonstrate that wit. "When he finally came to me, he said, 'Men, this is Father Sampson,'" the Parachute Padre remembered. "He will take care of you fish-eaters [slang for Catholics]. In Alabama he lit into the Chattahoochee; in England he lit in a lake; in Normandy he lit in a creek; in Holland he lit in the canal. And I guess, if he ever jumps in the Sahara Desert, he will land in a puddle left by some cockeyed camel."[38] Chaplain Engel was present and he almost fell off his seat laughing, Father Sampson noted. But then, Ewell introduced Chaplain Engel. "Now you left-footers [slang for Protestants], this is Chaplain Engel, the Protestant chaplain, and if I catch any of you saluting or wearing the uniform the way he does, I will have you court-martialed." This time it was Father Sampson's turn to laugh. But returning to their offices, Father Sampson worried that Chaplain Engel might have been hurt by the remark. Father Sampson explained he knew Colonel Ewell and he was sure Ewell "only intended to rib him." Engel evidently could handle it. "Father Sampson," he said soberly, "I've just been thinking. You know, I believe that the frequency of your immersions must be a providential sign that you should have been a Baptist."[39]

At Camp Mourmelon on December 18, 1944, Father Sampson was awakened at 0200 hours and informed the 101st Division was moving to the front to fight back a major German offensive in the Ardennes Forest. When packing to leave, the whole regimental band appeared at his barracks to ask a favor. Not having participated with the 501st in combat either on D-Day or the subsequent Operation Market Garden, the regimental band had received nothing but derision from the other paratroopers. "Father," their spokesman said, "we have been ordered to stay behind again. We joined the paratroopers because we want to fight in this war." Father Sampson knew he could not give the regimental band a green light to disobey orders. "What can I do about it?" he asked. The men asked the chaplain to intervene for them with Colonel Ewell, the commander of the 501st PIR. "Speak to the colonel?" Father Sampson replied. "He'd throw me out of his office if I bothered him now. Besides, he's up at division headquarters, I'm sure, getting his instructions." The band members suggested they might just jump on some of the trucks when they pulled out, since they worried this might be their last chance to get into combat before the war was over. "I shrugged my shoulders," Father Sampson recalled. "I was on the spot and evaded the question; but at least I didn't say 'No!' They must have guessed that I personally thought the colonel would be mighty glad to have a few extra men to bolster our thinned-out companies." In the end, it turned out all right. "Each company in the regiment found a couple of band members with them later at Bastogne, and from all I heard, they gave an excellent account of themselves," Father Sampson wrote. "Several of them were wounded, but none that I know of were killed. Thus they regained in full measure the respect of the other men of the regiment."[40]

The pullout from Camp Mourmelon was accomplished in such a hurry that there was no time to get the whole regiment together for Mass. "Nor did I have time for confessions," Father Sampson recalled. "I said Mass, and just before we pulled out, I went around to each company, called the Catholics together, gave general absolution, and distributed Holy Communion."[41]

Father Sampson threw his combat equipment and bedrolls into his jeep and headed out of Mourmelon accompanied by Chaplain Engel. Father Sampson recalled the incident involving General Higgins on the road to Bastogne. "Roads were jammed with vehicles going both ways," he observed. "A truck commander leading his forty or fifty trucks westward [retreating from the front around Bastogne] had jammed the division's ten-mile-long convoy trying to get to Bastogne in a hurry. When General Higgins, our division deputy commander, ordered the captain to take his trucks off the road, he refused. General Higgins pulled his .45 out and ordered the captain once more. This time he saw the wisdom of prompt obedience. Emergency called for emergency measures."[42]

On his way back into combat, Father Sampson mused on the fighting effectiveness of the 501st PIR, commanded by Colonel Ewell.

> The regiment was no longer just a collection of individuals; it was a single weapon of war. It had to be; it had to stop in the next few days the last and most desperate attempt of the German army to reclaim the offensive. The

Germans failed to do so only by the smallest of margins. Had they been successful, the war might have been extended by at least another year.[43]

Father Sampson fully appreciated the seriousness of his mission to accompany the troops into combat. In the introduction to his autobiography he noted:

> I should like to make the observation that a priest sees war from a different standpoint than almost anyone else. He is far more interested in what is going on inside men than in what is going on outside them. To him the souls of men are even more involved in combat than their bodies; their spiritual resources are more vital to real success than any material factors. The eternal life of a man is as much at stake there as his physical life, and the sacraments of Penance and the Holy Eucharist were healing the wounds of his soul while blood plasma, penicillin, and the sulfa drugs were healing the wounds of his body. And it is quite possible that in the providence of God many a man was the better prepared for death that came, not as a thief in the night, but as an ever-expected guide to his eternal home. As a priest, I write from this point of view.[44]

THE ORDER OF BATTLE LEAVING CAMP MOURMELON

Before departing for Werbomont, McAuliffe left orders for the motor march from Mourmelon to proceed as follows. First the 82nd Airborne would depart. McAuliffe calculated the 82nd had been out of action a bit longer than the 101st and was somewhat better prepared to return to combat. The 82nd grabbed the first trucks to arrive at Mourmelon, departing before dawn on Monday, December 18.

While the 82nd was on the road, Allied high command decided to order the 82nd Airborne to the defense of St. Vith, a city northeast of Bastogne in immediate need of reinforcement. Had the 101st left Camp Mourmelon first, conceivably the history of Bastogne would have involved the heroism of the 82nd Airborne, not the 101st.

In ordering how he wanted the 101st to leave Camp Mourmelon, McAuliffe commanded the 501st PIR, the unit headed by Colonel Ewell, to leave first, with the result that Ewell would be the first to get to Bastogne. Middleton, as we shall soon see, was very happy to realize that among the first of the 101st to arrive at Bastogne was a commander with firsthand knowledge of the battlefield terrain.

In World War II, an Airborne Division typically was divided into four regiments including three parachute infantry regiments, each of which was capable of operating as a separate fighting unit in the field.

Each regiment had its own command structure broken down first into battalions and then into companies. The famous Easy Company made popular by Stephen Ambrose's highly successful *Band of Brothers* book and television series was E Company, 2nd Battalion, of the 506th Parachute Infantry Regiment, one of the three parachute infantry regiments constituting the 101st. At the time of the Siege of Bastogne, Capt. Richard "Dick" Winters commanded the 2nd Battalion of the 506th. In writing his book *Beyond the Band of Brothers*, Winters described Easy Company as follows: "[Easy] Company included three rifle platoons and a headquarters section. Each platoon contained three twelve-man squads and a six-man mortar team squad. Easy also had one machine gun attached to each of its rifle squads, and a 60mm mortar in each mortar team."[45] Stephen Ambrose commented that at the peak of its effectiveness, Easy Company "was as good a rifle company as there was in the world."[46] At the company level, the fighting units were typically organized in three-or four-man squads, with each squad having a specialized purpose. A squad, for instance, could be a reconnaissance squad assigned for advance positioning in combat, a machine gun squad, or a rifle squad. Ambrose quotes Private Kurt Gabel as saying of the Easy Company squads: "They would literally insist on going hungry for one another, freezing for one another, dying for one another. And the squad would try to protect them or bail them out without the slightest regard to consequences, cussing them all the way for making it necessary."[47]

As it turned out, the 101st had more artillery than would normally be the case with a conventional infantry division. Historian Hugh Cole summarized as following the combat configuration of the 101st on December 18, 1944:

The division was smaller than a conventional infantry division (it numbered 805 officers and 11,035 men), but the organization into four regiments was better adapted to an all-around or four-sided defense than the triangular formation common to the regular division. The 101st had three battalions of light field pieces, the modified pack howitzer with a maximum effective range of about eight thousand yards. In the place of the medium artillery battalions normally organic or attached to the infantry division, the airborne carried one battalion of 105-mm howitzers. Also the airborne division had no armor attached, whereas in practice at least one tank battalion accompanied each regular division.[48]

Cole also observed the 101st Airborne Division's defense of Bastogne benefited greatly from the "odd bits and pieces of armored, artillery, and tank destroyer units which were en route to Bastogne or would be absorbed on the ground" by the 101st to coalesce ultimately into a "balanced" combat force.[49]

Col. Ralph M. Mitchell, in his important 1986 study, *The 101st Airborne Division's Defense of Bastogne*, makes the point that the 101st's artillery firepower was unusually strong. "In addition to its own artillery of four battalions, the division had at its disposal a field artillery group consisting of two 155-mm gun battalions and a 4.5-inch howitzer battalion," Mitchell noted. "It also had one 155-mm gun and two 105-mm howitzer battalions (which had fallen back after initial German assaults on 16 December). In all, that meant that as many as ten field artillery battalions could have supported the division at any one time."[50]

When alerted for movement to Bastogne, the 101st Airborne's artillery units were in the process of being reconstituted for action. Many of the howitzers in poor condition from Operation Market Garden were repaired or replaced before the road march to Bastogne began. "Anticipating a departure from their traditional airborne role, the artillerymen reconfigured for land movement and consequently carried with them far more ammunition than they would, or could, otherwise have taken via aircraft," Mitchell observed. "Without the additional loads, they would have run out of ammunition before aerial resupply was possible."[51]

The 105mm howitzer and the 150mm howitzer were the American workhorse field artillery pieces in the Ardennes campaign. The 105mm howitzers were easy to load and served as excellent defensive weapons against the type of tank-supported infantry charges the Nazis tended to make in trying to penetrate the Bastogne defenses. The 105mm howitzer had a range of about 10 kilometers (around 6.2 miles), while the larger and more lethal 150mm howitzer could send a shell almost twice as far. The 105mm howitzer was considered 50 percent lethal within a range of 20 meters, approximately 65.5 feet, while heavier ninety-pound shells of the 150mm howitzer were equally lethal within 30 meters, 98.5 feet, of impact. Infantry commanders in World War II also found anti-aircraft weapons could be used as artillery pieces to combat tank and infantry attacks. In Bastogne, the anti-aircraft batteries available to the 101st in the attached 81st Airborne Anti-Aircraft Battalion were quickly shifted to be used as artillery pieces along the main line of resistance, or MLR, to reinforce the defensive perimeter.[52]

MCAULIFFE REACHES BASTOGNE

Departing Camp Mourmelon from Bastogne at around 12:25 p.m. on Monday, December 18, McAuliffe and his companions—his G-3 operations officer, Lt. Col. Harry Kinnard; his first aide, 1st Lt. Frederic D. Starrett; and war correspondent Fred MacKenzie—drove as fast as they could.

Fred MacKenzie described the journey as follows: "The driver pushed the command car along expertly at high speed over the road. His passengers relaxed after a time into the somnolent state of expeditionary soldiers unable to guess at and unwilling to speculate on what lay ahead of them."[53] They passed the historic French and Belgian battlefields of Verdun and Sedan as they swept eastward over rolling hills and then north into dense forest country. MacKenzie noted the misty weather cleared once they were out of Camp Mourmelon, but the chill of approaching winter was still in the air. "From time to time they caught up and passed elements of the 82nd Airborne Division, also headed for Werbomont," MacKenzie noted.[54]

"When he had been traveling for approximately three hours and obviously was far ahead of his own troops, General McAuliffe announced a decision that would turn out to be one of several miraculously fortunate ones," MacKenzie commented, bringing to mind the similar observation of S. L. A. Marshall.[55] As they approached Bois de Herbaimont, some thirty miles southwest of Werbomont and nine miles northwest of Bastogne, McAuliffe decided to make a detour. McAuliffe determined he would go to VIII Corps headquarters and let Middleton brief him on the battle situation before he met his troops at Werbomont.[56] At the crossroads leading to Werbomont in the northeast and Bastogne in the southwest, the military police recognized General McAuliffe and let him pass, pointing out the most direct route to Bastogne.

After the car traveled nine or ten miles southeast, the forest area opened up so that the occupants saw a long slope leading down to a sweeping plain with Bastogne situated in the middle, MacKenzie noted. The town was a quaint Belgian village with a railroad track running through the middle headed north and south, and country crossroads entering and leaving the town as if it were an old telephone switchboard. A tall church steeple near the center punctuated this "ancient town in the dreariest part of the Ardennes Forest region,"[57] as MacKenzie described it, with the tallest buildings in the town appearing no higher than five stories. As they drove the command car into town, many of the town's thirty-seven hundred citizens stood in doorways or peered from windows, wondering how long it might be before the Germans were back. After the German invasion in 1940 through the Ardennes heading toward Paris, Bastogne became a headquarters for German troops. Once in town, McAuliffe observed units of the 28th Infantry and the 9th Armored that were in the process of pulling out in retreat. "The soldiers for the most part seemed to be in transit or preparing to quit town," MacKenzie observed.[58] "Most of the men looked furtive, beaten. Obviously they were in retreat and not headed for the front."[59] From the many military vehicles they observed in Bastogne heading south out of town, McAuliffe and the others judged the tide of battle was moving westward, with the Germans most likely advancing rapidly on Bastogne from the east, meeting with very little Allied resistance.

McAuliffe found Middleton's headquarters located in what was known as the Heintz Barracks on the northwestern outskirts of Bastogne. Built by the Belgian Army in 1934, the Heintz Barracks were intended to billet the Belgian regiments organized to defend the Ardennes. From the beginning of the German occupation until the liberation of Bastogne on September 10, 1944, the barracks had been used as a Wehrertüchtigungslager, a boot camp for Hitler Youth.[60] They consisted of a series of long, one-story brick structures distinguished by a row of evenly spaced windows, with chimneys for wood- or coal-burning stoves punctuating the buildings' gently sloping roofs. At approximately 1600 hours on Monday, December 18, McAuliffe found Middleton's headquarters in the basement of the largest building in the complex.

McAuliffe was in for some surprising news. When he arrived at Middleton's headquarters at Bastogne, Middleton explained a command decision had been made higher up the chain that the 101st was to fight at Bastogne, not at Werbomont. But there was still some uncertainty. General Gavin, then the acting commander of the 82nd Airborne, was still under the impression that the 82nd and the 101st were still under the command of General Ridgway's XVIII Airborne Corps. But Gavin did not arrive until after dark. By then, Middleton had explained to McAuliffe that it was his impression the 101st Airborne had been reassigned to Middleton's command as part of VIII Corps.[61]

"There has been a major penetration," General Middleton explained to McAuliffe. "Certain of my units, especially the 106th and 28th Divisions, are broken." As Middleton explained to McAuliffe the battle situation, McAuliffe was calm, journalist MacKenzie observed, although others in the command headquarters showed signs of a bad case of nerves. Middleton was reluctant to give McAuliffe orders until General Gavin arrived and the command structure could be clarified with General Bradley.

As McAuliffe studied the crayon markings on the map overlay, it became apparent that the German attack was spread along the entire eighty-five-mile Ardennes Forest frontier, with the Nazis attacking V Corps to the north as hard as they appeared to be attacking Middleton's VIII Corps. "The turn of events hardly could have been more staggering to General McAuliffe and his G-3," MacKenzie wrote. "A confrontation with the enemy was at most only hours away, their Division was headed for the wrong place, headquarters had no specific assignment for McAuliffe, and the only help he had at hand was that of his young G-3 [Lt. Col. Harry Kinnard] and youthful aide-de-camp [1st Lt. Frederic D. Starrett]."[62] McAuliffe's immediate concern was the safety of his troops. He was concerned the 101st might be in jeopardy before they had any chance to form for battle, especially since Danahy and the advance party were headed to Werbomont and no assembly area around

Bastogne had been chosen for the 101st to arrive. As MacKenzie observed, McAuliffe, as he stood around and listened to Middleton describe the battle map, was in no mood to cool his heels while higher authorities decided "the lofty matter of which among the higher commands would have the authority to tell him what to do."[63]

THE 10TH ARMORED ARRIVES

A few minutes after General McAuliffe arrived at General Middleton's VIII headquarters, Col. William L. Roberts arrived with definite orders that his Combat Command B of the 10th Armored Division had been assigned to the defense of Bastogne under the command of Middleton at the disposal of the VIII Corps commander.[64] Roberts was born on September 18, 1890, making him truly the "old man," senior in years to both Middleton and McAuliffe. Roberts was a graduate of the West Point class of 1913 and had served as instructor in armored tactics at the Command and General Staff School at Ft. Leavenworth, Kansas. By 1940, Roberts was assigned as professor of military science and tactics at the Citadel in Charleston, South Carolina.

In World War II, United States armored divisions were generally organized for combat into two brigade-size combat commands, A and B, with a third combat command, designated R for "Reserve," typically held back to fill in when A or B battalions were resting, refitting, retraining, or simply exhausted from previous actions.[65] The 10th Armored CCB under the command of Colonel Roberts was known as the "Tiger Division," whose motto was "Terrify and Destroy."[66]

Roberts, under the command of General Patton's Third Army when Hitler's Wacht am Rheim offensive began, got to Bastogne as soon as was humanly possible. Under orders from General Patton's Third Army to reinforce Middleton's VIII Corps, Roberts moved CCB out of its reserve area in Rémeling, France, southeast of Luxembourg, at 1320 hours on Sunday, December 17, and headed the approximately seventy-five miles directly northeast to the Bastogne area.

After a forced march through the night, CCB reached Arlon, Belgium, just south of Bastogne, in the late afternoon of December 18. Roberts ordered CCB to wait there until he had the opportunity to confer with General

Middleton and receive further instructions. Fortunately, Middleton and Roberts were old friends who needed little time for formalities. Middleton wasted no time in explaining that of the seven roads leading out of Bastogne, three were seriously threatened at that moment: the road running out of Bastogne north to Noville; the road heading east through Mageret and Longvilly, where the CCR of the 9th Armored Division was doing its best to hold back the German advance; and the road southeast to Marvie and Wardin.

John S. D. Eisenhower, the son of Dwight D. Eisenhower, reconstructed the conversation between Middleton and Roberts in his 1969 book about the Battle of the Bulge, *The Bitter Woods*, with Middleton asking the first question:

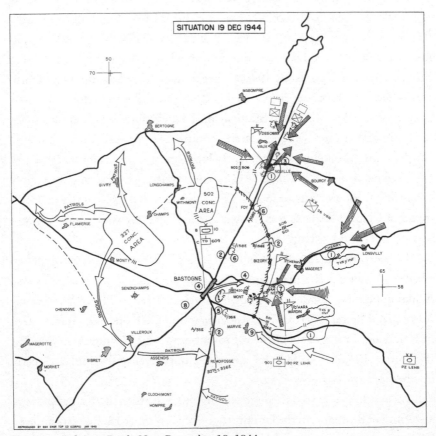

Bastogne, Belgium: Battle Map, December 19, 1944

"Robbie, how many combat units can you make out of your combat command?"

His friend looked concerned. "What do you have in mind?"

"I need a combined arms team to advance out and guard each of these three roads."

"That's no way to use armor."

"Robbie," said Middleton, "I may not know as much about the employment of armor as you, but that's the way I have to use them."

Roberts thought for a moment. Obviously Middleton had an exceptional situation on his hands. Mentally setting aside the "Dos and Don'ts of Armor" doctrine he had taught at Leavenworth, he organized CCB into three teams without further protest.[67]

S. L. A. Marshall pointed out that Roberts accepted the order without complaint, although at the moment he believed dividing his force over so great an area would make his combat command ineffective. Fortunately, Roberts accepted that Middleton knew the battle situation better than he did.[68] Marshall noted in *Bastogne: The First Eight Days* that Middleton's decision to deploy as he did three teams from Roberts' CCB was "the initial tactical step which led finally to the saving of Bastogne."[69]

What Roberts and the 10th Armored brought to Bastogne were armored vehicles, in particular Sherman tanks, without which a successful defense of Bastogne would have been almost impossible to launch. Facing top German panzer tank units, Middleton needed the 10th Armored Division CCB to have any chance of holding Bastogne.

Various units assigned to the 101st, such as the 705th Tank Destroyer Battalion, were also equipped with tank destroyer armored vehicles. The M10 tank destroyer was built on the M4 Sherman tank chassis and looked much like an M4 Sherman tank. Like its counterpart, the M18 "Hellcat" tank destroyer, both fighting vehicles were designed to reduce the armament in order to increase the speed. The M18 was capable of reaching speeds of up to sixty miles per hour, compared to the much slower and heavier M4 Sherman tank that was the workhorse of units like the 10th Armored Division CCB. M10 and M18 tank destroyers were built with open-topped turrets in which their 76mm gun was mounted, with the turret capable of a 360-degree traverse, allowing the tank destroyer to fire in all directions. Tank destroyers were designed to kill tanks, though often field commanders used tank destroyers to support infantry, or at times to supplement field artillery.[70] In battle, M10 and M18 tank destroyers served well in "hit-and-run" combat tactics, avoiding pitched battles with the much heavier and better-armored German panzer tanks. The Sherman tanks of the 10th Armored's CCB combined with the 705th's tank destroyers were a formidable combination in the rapidly approaching encirclement of Bastogne.

The German workhorse tank in the Battle of the Bulge was the Panzer Mark IV armed with an excellent 75mm high-velocity gun, considerably superior to the M4A3 Sherman tank's 75mm low-velocity gun. The M4 Sherman was light and fast but the tank's frontal armor was only two inches thick, making M4 Sherman even more vulnerable to German panzer assault. The Mark V Panzer weighed forty-five tons, making it more armored than the twenty-five-ton Mark IV tank. The Mark V Panzer was also armed with a 75mm high-velocity gun and was considered relatively immune to the M4 Sherman in a frontal attack. The Mark V was generally the German favorite in the Ardennes fighting.

The Mark VI "Tiger" came in two versions, a Tiger I, which weighed sixty tons, and an even heavier Tiger II, weighing in at seventy-one tons. An estimated twenty Tiger I tanks fought for the Germans in the Ardennes, while perhaps as many as fifty Tiger II tanks fought in the campaign. The heavier armor made the Tiger tanks superior to the M4 Sherman, but the Tiger tanks were plagued by mechanical problems that made them less reliable in combat. The Tiger tanks were also gas-guzzlers, a disadvantage that was especially troublesome for the Germans in the Ardennes campaign.[71]

A BATTLE OF ARMOR OR A PARATROOPER-COMMANDED ARTILLERY BATTLE?

Throughout Monday, December 18, Middleton and Bradley had been in contact to clarify key strategic concerns. "Bradley had now agreed on the importance of holding Bastogne and supported Middleton's employment of the 101st Airborne Division, plus CCB of the 10th Armored Division for this purpose," military historian John Eisenhower wrote. "This was a sober decision: Bradley realized full well that Bastogne might easily be cut off, but he was willing to accept the risk. Moreover, he had learned that General Eisenhower would cancel Patton's attack in the Saar and turn the Third Army north toward Bastogne regardless of the situation of the garrison there."[72] But still Bradley insisted Middleton himself must pull out VIII Corps headquarters from Bastogne to the nearby town of Neufchâteau, about seventeen miles southwest of Bastogne. Middleton accepted these orders, though he decided not to leave Bastogne until he had briefed both McAuliffe and Roberts, informing them both were to fight under his VIII Corps command.

Now with Middleton scheduled to leave Bastogne the next morning, he still needed to settle a conflict he saw developing between McAuliffe and Roberts. McAuliffe and Roberts still clashed over who was going to be boss, the 10th Armored CCB commanding the 101st Airborne or the other way around. Roberts argued he did not want to have a paratrooper commander whose specialty was artillery tell his armored divisions what best to do in battle. McAuliffe, for his part, argued that it made no sense to have a general who was acting division commander report to a colonel in charge of a combat command unit that constituted one-third of a division in strength. "With Middleton departing for Neufchâteau the next morning, unity of command for the bastion of Bastogne became a question of prime importance," John Eisenhower wrote. "Sensing this, McAuliffe proposed that Colonel Roberts' CCB, 10th Armored, be attached to his 101st Division. Roberts bristled; he was suspicious of the way armored forces might be employed by an untutored airborne division." McAuliffe was sympathetic, but he had his own point of view. John Eisenhower wrote, "Not only had he [McAuliffe] a high regard for Roberts, but he realized that on the regular army list, Roberts was nine years his senior at West Point and some pride might be involved. McAuliffe himself made no claims to be an expert on armor, but he was a matter-of-fact man and got straight to the point. 'Do you suppose that my entire division should be attached to your combat command?' he demanded."[73]

Middleton settled the argument by insisting McAuliffe and Roberts had to work together for the time being, saying he would resolve the question of combat command at a later date. The key point was that Roberts had CCB at Arlon to the immediate south of Bastogne and was ready right then to deploy his troops into battle; at 1600 on December 18, the 101st was still in trucks en route to Bastogne, with the last units not scheduled to leave Camp Mourmelon until 2000 hours, some eight hours later.

In his oral history with S. L. A. Marshall's field team after the battle, General McAuliffe said:

> I asked Middleton to attach the armor to me. Colonel Roberts spoke up then and said: "What do you know about armor?" I replied: "Maybe you want the Division attached to your combat command." Well, nothing was done about it. Middleton decided that the armor should support me and not be attached. He called me next day and reversed that decision. By that time I was cut off and surrounded. I didn't raise the question again. Middleton decided to change the order as the situation changed.[74]

McAuliffe was referencing a call Middleton finally made to Roberts on December 20, announcing formally that he had decided CCB would be attached to the 101st Airborne Division. "Your work has been satisfactory," Middleton explained to Roberts. "I'm attaching you to the 101st, because I have so many divisions that I can't take time to study two sets of reports from the same area."[75] Roberts, accepting this order immediately, moved his headquarters from the Hotel LeBrun in Bastogne to the Heintz Barracks where McAuliffe was then headquartered, in order to more effectively implement the decision that the 10th Armored CCB was now officially under McAuliffe's command. This decision sealed the command structure, placing McAuliffe in command of all units fighting at Bastogne, regardless whether the units were armored, artillery, anti-tank, or anti-aircraft in nature.

GENERAL RIDGWAY ARRIVES

At 2030 hours on December 18, General Ridgway arrived at General Middleton's headquarters. He was still acting on the presumption he would command the 101st at Bastogne under the XVIII Airborne Corps, but he also thought he would be commanding the 82nd at Werbomont, some twenty-five miles to the north. To resolve the situation, Ridgway called First Army headquarters. In the conversation that ensued, Ridgway and

Middleton "got the new instructions which changed the problem of each and which at last set the lines along which the 82nd and 101st Airborne Divisions, late of SHAEF reserve, would operate in the Ardennes."[76] Bastogne was to remain under the command of General Middleton's VIII. General McAuliffe would be the field commander of the 101st, and all other units at Bastogne would fight under the direct command of McAuliffe. General Ridgway's XVIII Airborne Corps, minus the 101st, was to operate north of Bastogne, in a variety of assignments that included Ridgway commanding the 82nd Airborne in the defense of St. Vith.

One of the first conclusions McAuliffe came to regarding the defense of Bastogne was that it was likely the Germans would encircle the village before long. In his oral history after the battle, McAuliffe admitted, "I realized as soon as I got to Bastogne that we would be cut off. The way the thing seemed to be moving and the lack of anything in front of us that might stabilize the situation pointed in that direction." This realization was a key reason that Bradley at the level of the Twelvth Army Group to insist that Middleton get out of Bastogne before he was trapped there. As commander of the VIII Corps, Middleton had responsibilities beyond Bastogne. Being surrounded by the enemy and unable to get in or out of Bastogne could easily have limited essential direct contact Middleton needed to communicate with his field commanders in other locations.

Finally understanding that Allied high command did not want him to play a role in the defense of Bastogne, Ridgway departed Bastogne right after the call with Bradley on the evening of December 18, to establish his headquarters at Werbomont. But first Middleton managed to persuade him that a few hours' sleep would be a good idea. Departing Bastogne on the morning of December 19, Ridgway did not take the most direct route to Werbomont through Houffalize, but instead chose the more westerly approach through Marche. Unbeknownst to him at the time, this saved Ridgway from "what might have been a very unpleasant encounter" with the advancing German 116th Panzer Division.[77] Ridgway, in writing his memoirs, attributed this choice of route to "God's guidance."[78]

Clearly, Ridgway wanted to command at Bastogne. The idea of a small group of encircled warriors fighting to the death to defeat an enemy with a numerical majority was a textbook opportunity any battle commander with

West Point experience would appreciate. Ridgway knew that good opportunities do not come around often or without difficulty. Even to get himself to West Point, Ridgway had to fight hard, especially after failing the entrance exam the first time he applied. So, too, Ridgway must have sensed the Siege of Bastogne was the chance of a lifetime. Ridgway had already distinguished himself in the invasion of Sicily and the subsequent campaign in Italy. But the height of glory to which he aspired awaited him in the next war, when he commanded the Eighth Army with distinction in Korea.

MCAULIFFE FINDS AN ASSEMBLY AREA

After his initial conversation with General Middleton, General McAuliffe realized that the responsibility for finding an assembly area near Bastogne for the 101st Division now fell to him. Given the truck traffic congestion of retreating men and vehicles pushing south from the Bastogne area, Danahy's advance party did not reach Bastogne until approximately 0300 hours on Tuesday morning, December 19. Ironically, as we noted earlier, the 101st advance party traveling with the 101st's G-2 intelligence officer Col. Paul Danahy was the first of the 101st to leave Camp Mourmelon and the last to actually arrive.

While there was still light left as night descended on December 18, McAuliffe, along with his G-3 colonel Kinnard and 1st lieutenant Starrett, drove out from Bastogne to select an assembly area for the arriving 101st troops. McAuliffe chose a roughly triangular area northwest of Bastogne that was defined by the village of Champs to the north, Mande-Saint-Étienne to the southeast, and Hemroulle to the southwest. Again, this was a fortuitous decision in that this particular area ended up being the best possible place on the battlefield for the 101st to assemble. S. L. A. Marshall observed: "It was a snap decision, yet it influenced the campaign importantly because it placed the division in a sheltered forward assembly area until it was ready to strike."[79] John Eisenhower in *The Bitter Woods* commented that the assembly area McAuliffe selected was ideal in that each unit of the 101st had to go only a minimum distance to its initial point of deployment in the battle, and the 101st Division artillery was perfectly placed for the defense of the area, in that even without moving, "it could go into business."[80]

G-3 operations officer Harry Kinnard explained the situation as follows: "McAuliffe personally was responsible for the designation of the area, and it later proved that by instinct and with almost no opportunity for reconnaissance he had established a center of gravity in the one area in which was most liable to keep the general defense of Bastogne in balance."[81] Kinnard further explained that in searching for a bivouac area for the 101st, he took with him the few maps Middleton could spare at VIII Corps headquarters in Bastogne, maps of the area being at a scarce premium for all commanders as the battle began. After a few minutes of looking for the advance party in vain, McAuliffe and Kinnard "took a spin" around the area west of town and within a few minutes, just before darkness closed around them, McAuliffe told Kinnard where he wanted the bivouac established.

When Danahy finally got to Bastogne, McAuliffe was relieved to see him. "I told Harry [Kinnard] you wouldn't do that to me if you could help it," McAuliffe ribbed Danahy upon seeing him. "Thank you, General," was all the relieved G-2 could bring himself to respond.[82] Danahy and Kinnard ended up being McAuliffe's constant companions and closest confidants throughout the Siege of Bastogne. Combat journalist Fred MacKenzie noted that Danahy, of Irish descent, and Kinnard, Scottish, complemented each other. MacKenzie commented that when Danahy was on his feet, "his sturdy body bounced in graceful movement,"[83] while Kinnard "looked like a Boy Scout, smooth-cheeked, delicately handsome" at five-feet-seven-inches tall, weighing 145 pounds.[84] What caught MacKenzie's eye was that McAuliffe and Danahy were of approximately the same age, same weight, and same height, "and appeared to be overtrained physically, all fat having been drained by the rigorous airborne life from bodies that looked as though they should have been heftier."[85] Though there was a seventeen-year difference in their ages, McAuliffe and Danahy "were alike in many ways," MacKenzie insisted. "Danahy's good humor and brash behavior appealed to McAuliffe, whose entire adult life had been regulated in military service, where a disposition for natural fun did not often find expression."[86] In McAuliffe's presence, Danahy curbed his rebel nature, observing "the rules of military decorum more rigidly in McAuliffe's presence than with any other soldiers, generals included."[87] Danahy was reared in Buffalo, New York, where MacKenzie had worked as a newspaper reporter before the war.

Through the night of December 18, the 101st filed into the assembly area. The rush to Bastogne was the first time the 101st Airborne had entered combat other than by jumping from a C-47 or riding in gliders, typically CG-4A and British Horsa gliders.[88] When they arrived at the front, the only "jump" required for the 101st to enter combat was the tailgate jump to dismount the trailer or truck that transported them.

Military historians Leo Barron and Don Cygan noted the men of the 101st arrived at Bastogne complaining and stamping their feet in the cold, after having traveled 107 miles in more than eight hours through freezing sleet and icy cold rain. Many had been fully exposed to the elements, having been huddled in the back of what amounted to open-topped "cattle cars." The historians quoted Bob MacDonald, the commander of Baker Company, 1st Battalion, 401st Glider Infantry, as summing up the feeling pretty well: "The whole trip was miserable. It was foggy, it was cold, and occasionally snowing en route. The men were so crowded in the trucks that only half of them could attempt to sleep on the floor, while the remainder stood and took it." Barron and Cygan observed cynically that this was not exactly how the men of the 101st Airborne Division wanted to spend their days leading up to Christmas.[89] As might be expected, the paratroopers complained mightily about the trucks. "The trucks had no benches, and . . . little in the way of springs," Ambrose wrote of the open-air trailers. "Every curve sent men crashing around, every bump bounced them up into the air. It was hard on the kidneys—relief came only when the trucks stopped to close up the convoy—and on the legs."[90]

In contrast, Father Sampson and Chaplain Engel were happy to arrive at Bastogne. "By sheer luck we found the regimental CP [Command Post]," Father Sampson noted in his autobiography. "Colonel Ewell had his staff and battalion commanders there; he was pointing out on a map what little he had been told about the situation. When he finished, he looked around and said, 'Any questions?' All the officers just looked at him with open mouths. Ewell broke into one of his rare laughs, 'Cripes, what a mess, huh?' The tension relaxed. 'Well, nuts! The situation is bound to clarify some in the morning. In the meantime the enemy are sure to be just about as confused as we are.' With his frank appraisal and cool manner, Ewell reminded these officers that they were the finest leadership our country could provide for any regiment."[91] Ewell then spotted Father Sampson and Chaplain Engel. "Hi, Chaplains," he said. "How about putting a petition in to your Boss for clear weather tomorrow? We're going to need some air support. How about a cup of tea?" Ewell poured some hot water into two cups, took out a much-used tea bag from his pocket, and dunked it a few times in each cup. "A greater sacrifice for a buddy could not be expected," Father Sampson commented.[92]

BASTOGNE CIVILIANS FLEE TO SAFETY

As the defense of Bastogne took shape, many of the citizens of Bastogne knew from past experience what was likely coming. Some hunkered down, determined they would stay with their homes and possessions, even if they knew they would have to survive in their basements, typically without toilets or other facilities, with minimal food and no ability to cook. Others packed up and left. Their experience in World War I, and now again in World War II, was that when war came to your village, war came to your living room. Army military historian Charles B. MacDonald in his 1985 book, A Time for Trumpets, commented that at first the people of Bastogne were not aware that a great battle had started. "For the civilian population of Bastogne, the first day of the German offensive, December 16, was calm," MacDonald wrote. "Since it was a Saturday, the shops along the Grand Rue were doing a bustling business. Not until the next morning, as the congregation in the Church of the Franciscan Fathers spilled out after Mass into the Place St. Pierre, was there anything other than rumor that something unusual might be happening."[93] But by the morning of the third day, Monday, December 18, the approaching sound of artillery was clear and American stragglers began to enter the town. "By midday, some of the people were leaving, pushing carts, pulling children's wagons piled high with possessions," he noted.[94] Still, some three thousand of the town's residents remained in Bastogne for the duration of the siege.

The family in the horse cart pictured on the dust jacket of this book left their home in Bastogne before the fierce fighting of the siege took place. Looking at the photograph carefully, it is clear the battle at Bastogne is in the early stages because the streets are not yet crowded with American troops. The streets also show no signs of rubble from the German air bombardment, which leveled and destroyed most of the buildings standing and in relatively good shape in the photograph. Finally, the streets are clear of snow, reflecting the battle is yet in the early stages, in the hours before the peak of the severe winter weather that was about to hit Bastogne.

The photograph was printed in the 1969 book *When the Third Cracked Europe*, where author Gen. Paul Harkins correctly identified the people.[95] In and behind the wagon are the members of the sizable Claude family, evacuating their home in Bastogne to seek refuge in safer environments. Harkins recounted that a five-man Signal Corps team had set up their communications equipment in the cellar of Marcel Claude's butcher shop. Below the photograph of the Claude family, leaving Bastogne, Harkins produced a second photograph showing three members of the surviving Claude family after the war, taken around 1969 in Bastogne. The second photograph appeared to have been taken in fall or early winter, as the family members are not as bundled up as they were in the earlier photograph from December 1944, when the family was fleeing Bastogne. In the second photograph taken after the war, the members of the Claude family are seen wearing light coats and sweaters. The caption describing the three surviving members of the Claude family reads: "Marcel, Jr., now runs the family business since his father is retired. Mme. Claude, who is in the front seat of the wagon, is shown today with her husband (who was hidden by the horse) and a son. Charles, who was seventeen then, is walking, with cap on, immediately behind the cart."

CHAPTER 3

A MASSIVE INTELLIGENCE
FAILURE

Hitler's optimism and miscalculation, then, resulted in the
belief that Germany had the material means to launch and
maintain a great counteroffensive, a belief nurtured by many
of his trusted aides. Conversely, the miscalculation of the
Western Allies as to the destruction wrought by their bombers
contributed greatly to the pervasive optimism which would
make it difficult, if not impossible, for Allied commanders
and intelligence agencies to believe or perceive that Germany
still retained the material muscle for a mighty blow.

—Hugh M. Cole, US Military Historian, *The Ardennes: Battle of the Bulge*, 1988[1]

I n what has to be one of the greatest failures in military intelligence in
World War II—perhaps second only to the failure to anticipate the
Japanese attack on Pearl Harbor—Hitler amassed the forces needed to
launch the Wacht am Rhein offensive virtually undetected. How did Allied
command allow it to happen?

The idea of a bold, swift German offensive through the Ardennes
can be traced back to the Schlieffen Plan developed by Count Alfred von

Schlieffen, formerly the chief of the German General Staff, and his strategic plans that began in 1894 and culminated with his Grand Memorandum of 1905. The original concept was that if Germany were to face fighting a war on two fronts, both the Western Front versus France and the Eastern Front versus Russia, German troops could mount a bold offensive out of the Eifel Mountains aimed at piercing through the dense Ardennes Forest to take troops defending Belgium by surprise. The Schlieffen Plan envisioned a swift offensive designed to cut through the heart of France to Paris with a grand flanking movement sweeping into France from the north through Belgium. Once France was defeated, German troops deployed on the Western Front could be redeployed to fight Russia in the east, eliminating the need to fight on two fronts simultaneously. The risk could be taken, Schlieffen calculated, because Russia would take six to eight weeks to mobilize troops after a war had been declared, largely because of deficiencies in the Russian railway system. This delay, he calculated, would give Germany time to defeat France and transfer troops from the Western Front to the Eastern Front in time to deal a crushing blow to Russia.[2]

In August 1914, at the beginning of World War I, Germany implemented the Schlieffen Plan, attacking Belgium through the Ardennes, only to be met by French forces under the command of French chief of staff Gen. Joseph Joffre. Rather than cut through to Paris as planned, the advancing German armies were stopped at the outskirts of Paris. The First Battle of the Marne, fought September 5–12, 1914, involved a French counterattack aided by the British that held the German advance to the Marne River. Repulsed in the battle, the Germans abandoned their hopes for a quick defeat of France and withdrew into what developed into four years of trench warfare along the Western Front. But rather than abandon the Schlieffen Plan, German military strategists preparing for World War II refined the plan to include a blitzkrieg attack. Hitler launched his World War II offensive against France out of the Ardennes on May 10, 1940, sweeping into France through Belgium in a swift move that allowed the Germans to occupy Paris on June 14, 1940.

"The German advance through southern Belgium and Luxembourg in 1914 had demonstrated that a huge modern force could be concentrated via rail in the abrupt, broken country of the Eifel, and from thence be moved afoot or ahorse through the worst of the Ardennes mass," wrote US military historian Hugh M. Cole. "The events of 1940 proved that mechanized forces could move speedily through the Ardennes, and more, that not only was Hitler correct in his insistence on the use of large mechanized forces in the Ardennes, but that the professionals in the OKH [German High Command, Oberkommando des Heeres] who had opposed him were wrong."[3] In launching the Wacht am Rhein offensive on December 16, 1944, Hitler had calculated to launch his counteroffensive when German meteorologists were forecasting winter storms sufficiently severe to ground Allied air attacks, making it nearly impossible for the Allies to turn back the offensive merely by relying upon the strong tactical advantage of Allied air power. He was also counting on difficult snowbound terrain to hinder Allied efforts to move fresh troops to the front to reinforce what Hitler believed would be stunned defenders routed by shock into disarray and a hazardous retreat.

What Hitler had discounted was the possibility that Allied supreme commander Dwight D. Eisenhower would act decisively to deploy to the front tough, seasoned combat units then being held in reserve, despite the hardships of winter. Hitler mistakenly assumed Eisenhower and the Allied high command would fail to take immediate, decisive action because they would be forced to operate under the type of political constraints he had imposed typically throughout the war on German military high command. Hitler hoped President Roosevelt and British prime minister Churchill would panic in response to the Nazi counterattack and hesitate in their response.

But the contrast in cultures between the American and German military was dramatic. Where Eisenhower and Bradley improvised instinctively, the German high command had been trained to follow orders without question. The German military high command launched the Wacht am Rhein offensive, even though they were doubtful of its success, simply because the offensive was Hitler's idea. They understood the winter weather would be an equal if not more crucial disadvantage for the Germans than it was for the Allies. German high military command also anticipated Eisenhower and Bradley would fight back with whatever fighting units the US commanders could find to put in the field. But no one in the German high military command dared oppose Hitler, not even when they were convinced that Hitler's eleventh-hour counteroffensive reflected not sound military planning but the wishful thinking of a dictator who had limited military training. To the professionals in the German high military command, Hitler's military decision-making frequently had proven to be disastrous, beginning with his decision to break his non-aggression pact with Stalin to attack Russia on June 22, 1941. Many in Germany's high military command ridiculed the idea that a German offensive launched through the Ardennes in December 1944, as Europe entered an exceptionally cold and stormy winter, could be compared with or modeled after the Ardennes offensive launched in May 1940, when Europe was emerging from spring weather to enter the favorable combat months of summer.

But Hitler was right in calculating that Eisenhower and the entire Allied command in Europe would be caught completely by surprise when the German artillery salvo opened on December 16, 1944. That Saturday morning, unaware that the German counteroffensive had started, Eisenhower signed the guest book at Louis XIV Chapel at Versailles, just outside Paris, where he attended the marriage of two junior members of his staff, his orderly, Sgt. Michael J. "Mickey" McKeogh, and Women's Army Corp sergeant Pearlie Hargrave. Immediately following the wedding, Eisenhower returned to his suite in the elegant Trianon Palace Hotel in Versailles, to preside over the champagne and cake wedding reception attended by his field commander General Bradley. Bradley wrote that Ike made an appearance at a wedding reception in Versailles before he and Ike returned to Ike's suite at the Trianon. "Later, we cracked a bottle of champagne to celebrate Ike's promotion [to five-star general]," Bradley recalled. "We then played five rubbers of bridge."[4]

Throughout World War II in Europe, Eisenhower and the Allied high command occupied the best hotels, enjoying the finest French champagne and wine, especially in and around Paris, but also throughout France and into Belgium, while troops in the field suffered the hardship of winter. Through two world wars, one of the constants in Europe, ironically, was the top-tier French hotels, which remained essentially the same regardless of whether their clients at the time were French generals, German generals, or US generals. What has remained basically the same from 1914 until today is the French waiters continued to judge the quality of their guests by the wine they order, their appreciation for the subtleties of French haute cuisine, and their willingness to tip generously, regardless whether the exigencies of war at any particular time limited the wine list or the availability of particular French delicacies normally on the menu.

Throughout the Battle of the Bulge, Bradley remained in a luxury hotel in Luxembourg. Despite being generally described as a "soldier's soldier," Bradley often exhibited surprising detachment from battlefield realities. Writing his histories in comfort after the war, Bradley expressed sympathy for the hardship and heavy casualties GIs suffered in the intense and costly battles waged in October and November 1944 in the Hürtgen Forest and the Roer River dam area, as the Allied advance across Europe was stopped by determined German defenses. Bradley wrote the dogged combat was complicated by "a wholly unexpected onslaught of trench foot" that Bradley blamed on "late-arriving, ill-designed cold-weather footwear," which he attributed to causing an additional twelve thousand non-battle casualties.[5] But, when it came to the Battle of the Bulge, Bradley had much more to explain than simply why US military command could not supply GIs fighting the Nazis with adequate winter footwear.

EISENHOWER AND BRADLEY REACT

On December 16, 1944, Bradley was second in command to Eisenhower, with operational command over all Allied forces in Europe. Eisenhower, as supreme allied commander in Europe, acted more like a corporate CEO who viewed his responsibility as setting grand strategy while resolving disagreements and personality conflicts among his subordinate command officers. Eisenhower was constantly challenged, negotiating differences in culture and military procedure between the French, the British, and the Americans, a task made more difficult by the especially high regard in which British field marshal Montgomery held himself despite a legacy of military setbacks, including his flawed battle plan that developed into Operation Market Garden in Holland, the fiasco from which the 101st Airborne was recovering in Camp Mourmelon.

As evening progressed into night on Saturday, December 16, 1944, Eisenhower and Bradley, safely ensconced in Eisenhower's suite in the Trianon Palace, quit their comfortable card game, as grim battle reports flooded in from the Ardennes front. Never leaving the Trianon, the two commanders remained through the night huddled together, monitoring the increasingly alarming reports of enemy attacks pouring from the front into SHAEF headquarters.

"At first Ike and I were frankly astonished that Volksgrenadier [or "People's Troops"] divisions could mount an offensive," Bradley wrote. Hitler's Volksgrenadier divisions were known to have been hastily assembled combat units consisting predominately of young boys, old men, wounded veterans from military divisions that no longer existed, and others considered typically unfit for military duty, led by a few hardened veteran Wehrmacht soldiers. "However," Bradley continued, "it gradually became apparent—Ike sensed it before I did—that this was no spoiling attack by Volksgrenadier divisions but rather an all-out offensive by three German armies: the Sixth Panzer, Fifth Panzer, and the Seventh, with perhaps as many as twenty-four divisions attached."[6] At dawn of Sunday, December 17, Eisenhower and Bradley began receiving German military radio messages decoded by the code-breakers at Bletchley Park in England, the location of the Allied team that earlier in the war had secretly cracked the German code for the "enigma machine." Reading these top secret "Ultra messages," Eisenhower and Bradley reacted with alarm to Rundstedt's order launching the German counteroffensive. Rundstedt had urged the Nazi forces about to launch the Wacht am Rhein counteroffensive, with brave words: "Mighty offensive armies face the Allies. Everything is at stake. More than mortal deeds are required as a holy duty to the homeland."[7]

Bradley, responsible for configuring the Allied defense along the German frontier, had assigned the primary responsibility of defending the Ardennes Forest to Gen. Drew Middleton's VIII Corps attached to the First Army. To Middleton's north, Gen. Courtney Hodges was preparing to lead the First Army in a renewed offensive against the dams along the Roer River. To Middleton's south, Gen. George Patton, leading the Third Army, was preparing to mount a full-scale attack in the Saar area. In arraying his troops for a renewed Allied winter offensive, Bradley had taken a calculated risk in allowing the weakest link in the Ardennes sector to be the approximately eighty-five-mile stretch Middleton defended between Hodges and Patton. "It was held by Troy Middleton's VIII Corps, now attached to Hodges's

First Army," Bradley wrote. "Even though we were well aware that Hitler had launched his 1940 attack on France through the Ardennes, we did not consider it an unusually dangerous area. Ultra told us it was only lightly manned by transient divisions or the newly created Volksgrenadier divisions composed of sailors and airmen."[8] At first, Bradley found it hard to admit he was wrong. His first reaction was to presume the Nazi counterattack on Middleton's VIII Corps was a feint, a secondary German offensive designed as a tactic to take Allied attention away from the real German offensive Bradley expected the Nazis would launch in the south to block Patton's advance with the Third Army into the Saar.

Eisenhower disagreed. "I was instantly convinced this was no local attack," he wrote in his 1948 memoirs, *Crusade in Europe*.[9] Eisenhower reasoned from history that it was not typical for the enemy to attempt a minor offensive in the Ardennes. "It was through this same region that the Germans launched their great attack of 1940 which drove the British forces from the Continent, and France out of the war," Eisenhower wrote. "That first attack was led by the same commander we were now facing, Rundstedt. It was possible that he hoped to repeat his successes of more than four years earlier."[10]

Eisenhower knew that Hitler and Rundstedt had a stormy relationship, but he also knew that Hitler had no choice but to turn to Rundstedt when the war became deadly serious. US military historians of World War II have typically held Rundstedt in high regard, in part because Rundstedt had little respect for Hitler's military acumen. "A wizened, venerable old soldier (he was almost seventy), Rundstedt was to most Germans the paragon of all that was good and right about the German officer corps," wrote Charles B. MacDonald, one of the most respected of the official US military historians in World War II. "Hitler disliked him intensely, partly because he was such an obvious exemplar of that elite corps with its plumy elegance, whose officers, Hitler knew, saw him in his role as supreme military commander as an imposter, and partly because Hitler knew also that in private conversations Rundstedt referred to him mockingly by his rank in the Great War as 'the Corporal.'"[11]

Specifically, Rundstedt used to refer privately to Hitler as "that Bohemian corporal,"[12] a double insult implying not only that Hitler had little military experience of any real value but also that he was born in Austria, not in Germany. Hitler was not granted German citizenship until 1932, a year before he was appointed chancellor.

Eisenhower believed that for Hitler to reinstate Rundstedt and put him in command of this offensive, the German attack pouring out of the Ardennes in the winter of 1944 had to be the real deal. Hitler had fired Rundstedt in 1941 on the Russian front for ordering his forces to retreat from Rostov during a major Russian counteroffensive. Worried about the anticipated Allied invasion in Europe, Hitler recalled Rundstedt to active duty in March 1942, appointing him to command Oberbefehlshaber West, or OB West, the overall German military forces on the Western Front, to defend against the Allied invasion at Normandy. After the Allied invasion on D-Day and the subsequent Allied breakout from Normandy, Hitler fired Rundstedt a second time, but only after Rundstedt advised Hitler and the German high military command facing the Allied advance into France, "Make peace you fools!"[13] When Hitler recalled Rundstedt the third and final time to prepare for the Ardennes counteroffensive, Rundstedt made it clear he held Hitler's plans in disdain. "It was a nonsensical operation," Rundstedt scoffed, "and the most stupid part of it was the setting of Antwerp as a target. If we had reached the Meuse we should have gotten down on our knees and thanked God—let alone tried to reach Antwerp."[14]

When the Nazi counteroffensive in the Ardennes began, Eisenhower and Bradley knew they had to act quickly and decisively. Among the available reserves they could bring into the battle, the generals identified two seasoned paratroop divisions assigned to the XVIII Airborne Corps under Gen. Matthew Ridgway, located near Reims, France. These divisions, the 82nd and the 101st Airborne Divisions, were battle groups Eisenhower immediately identified as "battle-tested formations of the highest caliber." The 82nd Airborne Division was given the nickname "All American" because when the unit was organized at Camp Gordon, Georgia, in 1917, members of the division came from all forty-eight states. The 82nd Airborne was known by a distinctive shoulder patch featuring an "AA" on a red field, with a blue banner above saying "Airborne," surrounded by a stylized wing and topped with a five-pointed star. The 101st Airborne, organized at Camp Shelby, Mississippi, in 1918, bore the famous "Screaming Eagle" shoulder patch, displaying a side view of a white-crested bald eagle with a clearly visible red tongue, apparently squawking angrily. The 82nd and the 101st had both distinguished themselves in combat in the D-Day invasion and during Operation Market Garden. Montgomery had not released the 82nd and 101st Airborne Divisions from his combat command until after Operation Market Garden concluded in late November 1944. In *Crusade in Europe*, Eisenhower commented that both divisions had taken heavy losses in the recently concluded and costly Operation Market Garden offensive in Holland and were not yet fully rehabilitated.[15]

"I finally got to bed around midnight. But I could not sleep," Bradley wrote, reflecting on how the day ended on Saturday, December 16. "I lay awake most of the night mulling over the impact of this massive attack. We had been caught flat-footed. We had to reorganize our strategy, not only to contain the attack but also to make Hitler pay a high cost for mounting it. If we played our cards right, we had a chance of destroying the German army west of the Rhine. It would demand a radical shift in our thinking and strategic planning. We must break off all offensive attacks, turn the full weight of Hodges south and the full weight of Patton north."[16] On December 17, Bradley returned to his headquarters in the city of Luxembourg and kept in hourly contact with Eisenhower by telephone during the next few critical days.[17]

The battle in Normandy and the pursuit of the Wehrmacht across France and Belgium had cost the Allies more than 160,000 casualties, 500 tanks, and 100 artillery pieces. Moreover the rapid pace of the advance, with Allied forces in December 1944 some seven months ahead of Eisenhower's pre-invasion schedule, left battle units in bad need of rest and reinforcement.[18] Yet, among Allied commanders, the success pushing the Nazis back into Germany had been breathtaking. When in the first week of October 1944, Gen. George Marshall, the army chief of staff, traveled from Washington, DC, to Paris to visit in person with Eisenhower and Bradley, there were high hopes the war against Germany might be concluded rapidly. The military intelligence analysis of the Allied offensive in late November 1944 found Hodges's First Army and Patton's Third Army had captured nearly sixty thousand German soldiers, the manpower equivalent of five or six divisions. SHAEF analysts reported continued Allied pressure along the front was costing the Germans some nine thousand permanent or long-term casualties each day, the equivalent in manpower of another five divisions per week.[19] "He [Marshall] was bubbling with optimism about the course of our campaign," Bradley noted. "He believed that if we kept the pressure on the Germans, we could probably wind up the war by Christmas. His optimism was based on overly rosy intelligence reports emanating from the combined chiefs of staff."[20]

The hope of ending the war before New Year's Day 1945 was dashed by the logistical difficulty of keeping US forces supplied. In September 1944, the Allied forces in Europe were using twenty thousand tons of provisions, six million gallons of gasoline, and two thousand tons of artillery ammunition every twenty-four hours. These supplies needed to be trucked over the three-hundred-mile distance from Cherbourg and the Normandy invasion beaches to the front.[21] By fall 1944, the US troops advancing over Europe were deemed to be "running on empty," in bad need of opening up the port of Antwerp closer to the front.[22]

Moreover, the Nazis persisted in a series of fierce defensive battles in the Hürtgen Forest in the Roer River dams area in Germany. As the fighting got closer to the German homeland, the Nazis fell back into defensive positions, determined to use the difficult terrain to stop the Allied push into Germany. Both sides took heavy casualties. Military historian Carlo D'Este in his 2002 book, *Eisenhower: A Soldier's Life*, described the fighting in the Hürtgen Forest in starkly brutal terms. "In a series of misguided engagements often compared to the worst battles of World War I, the First Army commander, Lt. Gen. Courtney Hodges, flung one division after another into the bloody cauldron of the Hürtgen in November 1944," D'Este wrote.[23] "Heavily defended by the Germans, the forest became a deathtrap that consumed men at a shocking rate in a series of futile and costly frontal attacks that gained nothing." D'Este noted that before the Hürtgen Forest was captured in mid-December 1944, eight different American divisions had taken casualties that amounted to 24,000 Americans killed, wounded, or captured.[24] The fighting along the Roer River during the autumn of 1944 produced losses for the First and Ninth Armies amounting to 57,000 combat casualties, plus another 70,000 due "to the ravages of the elements."[25] When the fighting along the Roer River finally ended, D'Este noted, "the Germans remained in control of the vital Roer dams, and the Allies were left with a hollow victory in what was undoubtedly the most ineptly fought series of battles of the war in the West."[26]

By mid-December 1944, the Allied offensive came to a virtual halt. Eisenhower had no choice but to pause and allow time to develop new, more proximate supply lines from the port liberated at Antwerp, giving the Pentagon much needed breathing room to rush fresh replacement troops, equipment, and supplies to Europe. It should be no surprise that Antwerp was the main Nazi objective in the Wacht am Rhein offensive. If the Wehrmacht could recapture Antwerp, "they would cut off a major artery the Allies used to supply their forces."[27]

GERMAN STEALTH PREPARATIONS FOR BATTLE

Under the overall leadership of Rundstedt, Field Marshal Walther Model commanded Hitler's Wacht am Rhein offensive in the field. Commanding the 3rd Panzer Division for the invasion of Russia, Model displayed such remarkable energy that by the fall of 1941, he was promoted to command the 51st Panzerkorps. Barely six months later, he was awarded command of the German Ninth Army. In 1943, at fifty-three years old, he was promoted as then the youngest field marshal in the Germany army.[28] Model went about his job diligently, ignoring Rundstedt's disdain for Hitler. Model planned to throw three armies into the Ardennes: the Sixth SS Panzer Army under General Sepp Dietrich; the Fifth Panzer Army under General Hasso von Manteuffel; and the Seventh Army under General Werner von Brandenberger. In total, this German force would number 850 panzer tanks and self-propelled assault guns. In his combined assault force, Model commanded twenty-two divisions in his planned first wave of the counterattack and another four in a second wave. At the start of the battle, Model commanded approximately 250,000 men, 382 tanks, 335 assault guns, and 2,623 artillery pieces in the first assault, with another 55,000 men with 561 tanks and assault guns waiting to the east to form the second wave of the attack. Facing this force were 83,000 American troops, with 242 tanks, 182 tank destroyers, and 394 pieces of artillery.[29]

The Allied high command was perplexed trying to figure out how the Germans were able to move into position a force of this size for a massive counterattack without being detected. There were many reasons for this US intelligence failure. Until the Strategic Bombing Study was conducted after the war, US military commanders had little appreciation that the massive bombing of German factories had done little to stop the German production of war equipment. Under the genius direction of Albert Speer, the Germans managed to decentralize manufacturing out of buildings destroyed by massive US strategic bombing from the air, such that by the end of the war the Nazis were producing almost as many tanks and airplanes as had been produced at the beginning of the war. The only strategic bombing that had a major impact on the Nazi war machine was the destruction of German oil refineries, synthetic oil manufacturing plants, and chemical facilities.[30] In December 1944, Hitler could still put into the field of battle a panzer army with tanks technologically superior to the tanks used by the Allies. The success of the Wacht am Rhein offensive depended in large part on the Nazi forces under Model's command being able to capture Allied fuel depots. Put simply, the Allied military intelligence in December 1944 badly underestimated Hitler's yet-remaining war machine. Even if the Germans lacked fuel, they still had the tanks and other military equipment needed to launch the counteroffensive in the Ardennes.

The Allied high command had considered the Ardennes region to be a relatively quiet zone where troops could be sent for rest, so much so that the Ardennes in December 1944 became known to the soldiers in the field as a "ghost front."[31] At the beginning of the German attack on December 16, 1944, the VIII Corps under General Middleton defended the Ardennes by relying primarily on two battle-weary divisions, the 28th Infantry Division and the 4th Infantry Division, both of which had taken heavy casualties in the Hürtgen Forest, plus two inexperienced divisions, the 106th Infantry and the 9th Armored, to cover an eighty-five-mile frontier that stretched from Aachen in the north, through the Ardennes, to Luxembourg in the south. The 106th Infantry Division, newly arrived in Europe, had spent only four days on the line, and Middleton had held the 9th Armored Division in reserve to support the other three. The 106th Infantry Division and the 9th Armored Division had never fired a shot in anger, and the 28th and 4th Infantry Divisions were badly beaten up from combat that had only just ended.[32] "The defense in the Ardennes was almost casual, with the only excitement coming from the nightly patrols into no-man's-land conducted by either side," noted military historian Danny S. Parker. "Historically the region was a European resort area, replete with hot springs and quaint castled towns. And so it became for the fortunate American soldiers stationed there. 'Lucky guys,' a veteran 2nd Division man leaving the Ardennes chided a newcomer of the US 106th Division, 'you're going to a rest camp!'"[33]

Before the battle started, the Allies had reports of increased German activity in the area of the Ardennes, but Allied military intelligence officers, not expecting Hitler could possibly be preparing to attack, had largely discounted the reports. Then, too, the Nazis took steps to hide their preparations. German military units had moved into position mostly at night, with troops reaching their final assembly areas in the last hours before the attack began. Moreover, by keeping radio traffic, telephone conversations, and coded messages to a minimum, the Germans negated efforts by the Allies to detect German plans in advance by intercepting command communications. By 1943, British Ultra teams monitoring enigma machine coded messages often knew German plans by the time Wehrmacht commanders in the field received their orders.[34] Generals Bradley and Eisenhower were particularly sensitive about the failure to detect in advance the German counteroffensive. "The fallacy that crept into our thinking was that since Ultra had not specifically forecast or suggested a major strategic counterattack, there was no possibility of one," Bradley wrote in his 1983 autobiography, *A General's Life*.[35]

From Ultra intercepts in November 1944, Bradley learned along with Eisenhower and the Allied high command that Rundstedt had resumed command of Hitler's Western Front. This misled Bradley into concluding incorrectly that Hitler had selected Rundstedt, because Rundstedt, as a professional soldier, would conduct a textbook defense against the US offensive. Bradley also mistakenly believed that Hitler had been badly injured in the attempt to assassinate him in his Wolf's Lair field headquarters near Rastenburg, East Prussia, on July 20, 1944, when Lt. Col. Claus Schenk Graf von Stauffenberg detonated a bomb in a conference room where Hitler was present. On December 5, when members of the House Military Affairs Committee visited Bradley's headquarters, one of the congressmen asked him if he thought Hitler, who had not made a public appearance since the assassination attempt, was incapacitated due to lingering injuries from that incident or from some other illness. Bradley responded that it was possible Hitler was out of action, noting that the command of the German army on the Western Front had been returned to competent command drawn from the German General Staff. Then Bradley remarked flippantly about Hitler, saying, "If he [Hitler] is ill, I wish he'd recover and take command again."[36]

As Bradley explained in his 1983 autobiography, "What I meant was that if Hitler were directing strategy on the Western Front, he might very well order another desperate and disastrous offensive like the one at Mortain." The German counterattack at Mortain was a Hitler-concocted move designed to push the Allies back into the English Channel at Normandy after the D-Day invasion. The result, however, was precisely the opposite. Seizing the opportunity presented by Hitler's counterattack at Mortain, Bradley ordered Patton to attack to the north. As a result, US forces surrounded and easily defeated the Nazis. "Such an offensive might enable us to destroy the German armies west of the Rhine, just as we had west of the Seine," Bradley continued. "This would put an end to our stalemate and grinding war of attrition and enable us to cross into eastern France, Belgium, Holland, and Luxembourg, pursuing a mangled and fleeing army in fast-moving open warfare."[37]

"Our immediate plan in the northern sector was to continue the pressure, seize control of the Roer dams, then cross the Roer River and strike for the Rhine," Bradley explained. Bradley knew from a steady flow of Ultra intelligence reports that Rundstedt had created a strong panzer reserve near Cologne in what was the Sixth Panzer Army. Also, he knew from Ultra that the Fifth Panzer Army had been withdrawn from the field for refitting and the addition of fresh troops. "We anticipated that when we crossed the Roer, Rundstedt would counterattack us with his panzer reserves (principally the Sixth Panzer Army) in the good tank country between the Roer and Rhine rivers." Bradley considered that to be the "proper professional solution to the threat we posed to Rundstedt."[38] The assumption that Rundstedt was in charge and that future operations would be more or less by the book was universally held in the Allied high command, Bradley noted.[39] "We were all wrong, of course—tragically and stupidly wrong," Bradley confessed. "After the experience of Mortain, it should have occurred to at least one of us that as we pushed Germany to the wall, Hitler might very well do something crazy and desperate again. That was his style."[40]

In his earlier autobiography published in 1951, *A Soldier's Story*, Bradley also admitted Middleton's VIII Corps only thinly defended the Ardennes sector. Still, he was willing to take a calculated risk manning the Ardennes front so sparsely with so many green troops. "But if we were inclined to play it safe by preparing for trouble in the Ardennes, we should have to call off the winter offensive, strengthen Middleton's VIII Corps front, and brace him with reinforcements to meet this danger of counterattack," Bradley wrote. "Clearly there were not enough troops for both a winter offensive and a secure defense everywhere else on the Allied line. To push on in the attack—or bed down until the spring: these were the alternatives we faced."[41] Bradley argued that nothing less than an unequivocal indication of an impending attack in the Ardennes could have convinced him to quit the planned winter offensive, and no intelligence officer had been able to show him indisputable evidence that the Germans were assembling for a counterattack in the Ardennes. In the final analysis, Bradley insisted, "Indeed no one came to me with a warning on the danger of counterattack there."[42]

It is impossible to read Bradley's long treatises written after the war regarding the lead-up to the Battle of the Bulge as anything but agonized self-justification. Had McAuliffe not held at Bastogne, the history of World War II in Europe could have had a drastically different ending. Most likely, the American forces had sufficient depth of reinforcements and resupply to defeat Germany, even had the German Wacht am Rhein reached Antwerp. But had Hitler succeeded, the logical candidate to play "fall guy" for the disaster was Bradley, and Bradley's writings on the Battle of the Bulge suggest he knew that.

Allied military intelligence failed to anticipate Hitler's Wacht am Rhein offensive because, truthfully, Rundstedt was right: the idea of a German winter offensive in the Ardennes at this stage of the war made no sense, not to professionally trained and battle-experienced military commanders on both sides of the conflict. Sepp Dietrich, formerly Hitler's chauffeur, promoted by the Führer to be the commander of the Sixth SS Panzer Army, perhaps expressed the sentiment best, famously saying, "All Hitler wants me to do is to cross a river, capture Brussels, and then go on to take Antwerp. And all this at the worst time of the year through the Ardennes when the snow is waist deep and there isn't room to deploy four tanks abreast, let alone armored divisions. When it doesn't get light until eight and it's dark again at four and with re-formed divisions made up of kids and sick old men—and at Christmas."[43] Still, if the outcome of the Battle of the Bulge could have been determined by the first hours or days of combat, Hitler's gamble might have worked. But, as journalist and World War II historian Max Hastings pointed out in his 2004 book, *Armageddon: The Battle for Germany, 1944–1945*, victory in World War II battles typically "hinged upon the ability of the attackers to sustain momentum, reinforcing constantly as fresh troops passed through tired ones, feeding forward the huge supplies of ammunition and fuel necessary to keep punching, while the defenders were rushing men, tanks, aircraft to the battlefield."[44]

Throughout his life, Bradley was defensive about his decision to leave the Ardennes lightly defended:

> Our failure to foresee that those signs pointed to an attack through the Ardennes ironically enough spared us heavier casualties when it came. For had we doubled our divisions across Middleton's thin VIII Corps front, we could not have withstood the weight of Rundstedt's powerful offensive. With the twenty-four divisions he was to throw into the Bulge, the enemy could have broken a hole anywhere in our line. He may not have been able to advance as far as he did had he dragged through heavier defenses, but he would have undoubtedly inflicted more casualties upon Middleton's troops in the effort.[45]

Basically, Bradley took a calculated risk. With limited troops available, he decided to make his first objective the resumption of the First and Third Army offensives, not the reinforcing of Middleton's VIII Corps held along the Ardennes in defense. "There was a calculated risk involved in manning the Ardennes front so thinly with so many green troops, but I thought the gamble was negligible," Bradley explained in his 1983 autobiography. "In the remote event the Germans launched a spoiling attack in this sector, with our great mobility we could quickly cut it off by diverting troops south and north from Hodges's and Patton's armies. Such an attack—another Mortain—would even be welcomed. It would certainly fail, affording us the opportunity to destroy German elements at small loss to us."[46] He continued, writing, "Lacking the resources to continue our offense *and* defend the Ardennes in depth, my defensive plan for the Ardennes was broadly based on *mobility*, at which we had proved ourselves unequaled, rather than *concentration*."[47]

Instead of engaging in rationalizations, Eisenhower was more direct in his willingness to take blame for having failed to anticipate the German attack. Eisenhower admitted that intelligence reports prior to the start of the German counteroffensive had indicated the enemy was increasing infantry formations, causing Eisenhower to experience a growing anxiety about the weakness of Allied defenses in the Ardennes. Eisenhower confessed he questioned the decision to use the area of the Ardennes defended by Middleton's VIII Corps as a place to rest tired troops. The problem, Eisenhower argued, was that he had gotten used to hearing predictions of doom and gloom from military intelligence, so much so that he tended to discount the likelihood the Germans would actually launch a counterattack. "The commander who took counsel only of the gloomy intelligence estimates would never win a battle; he would forever be sitting, fearfully waiting for the predicted catastrophes," Eisenhower argued in *Crusade in Europe*.[48] The general acknowledged the Allies remained on the battle plan he had personally prescribed, along with the decision to remain on the offensive, even if that meant some defenses had to be weakened. "This plan gave the German opportunity to launch his attack against a weak portion of our lines," Eisenhower admitted. "If giving him that chance is to be condemned by historians, their condemnation should be directed at me alone."[49]

Patton was less forgiving than Eisenhower. On December 16, while Bradley was still at Eisenhower's headquarters in Versailles, Bradley telephoned Patton at Patton's headquarters in Nancy, France, to explain that a major German counterattack was underway. Bradley wanted to redeploy the 10th Armored Division then assigned to Patton's Third Army and being held in reserve near Thionville, just south of the Luxembourg-French border. Bradley planned to use the 10th Armored to attack the German flank in case the Nazis broke through on Middleton's front. "George, get the 10th Armored on the road to Luxembourg," Bradley ordered Patton, explaining that he planned to reassign the 10th Armored away from Patton so the division could be attached to Middleton's VIII Corps. Patton objected, as Bradley expected he would, arguing he needed the 10th to break through into the Saar in the offensive he planned to launch on December 19, in three days' time.[50]

Patton disagreed with Eisenhower's assessment that the German counteroffensive in the Ardennes was the main event. Instead, Patton sided with Bradley's initial presumption that it was likely a spoiling attack aimed at throwing the Allies off balance for the real offensive planned against Patton in the south. "I hate . . . to do it, George, but I've got to have that division," Bradley insisted. "Even if it's only a spoiling attack as you say, Middleton must have help."[51] Bradley recorded that within a few minutes Patton issued orders by phone. Patton not only issued the order to move the 10th Armored, as Bradley had requested, he also ordered the Third Army to pull out of its eastward attack, change direction ninety degrees, and move toward Luxembourg, attacking north.

Ladislas Farago, in his esteemed 1964 biography of Patton, *Patton: Ordeal and Triumph*, observed Patton's immediate decision to pivot the Third Army north was key in the ultimate course of the battle. "Inspired and, as it turned out, invaluable though his order was, it was the product of sheer intuition," Farago wrote. "For Patton really did not know what the Germans were up to, and where and how their offensive would lose its venomous sting."[52] Clearly, Patton wanted to hedge his bet that Hitler's counteroffensive was a feint. If the Ardennes counteroffensive turned out to be the main event, Patton did not want to take the chance on his Third Army being a sideshow.

SECTION II

THE DEFENSE OF BASTOGNE TAKES SHAPE

Even Hitler—a strategic illiterate—came to recognize the importance of Bastogne. He had ordered that centers of resistance be bypassed but specifically stated that the swift capture of Bastogne was critical to the operation.

—Samuel W. Mitcham Jr., US Military Historian[1]

In the first hours of the German Wacht am Rhein offensive, Bastogne became a focus for both the Allied and the Nazi high command. Initially, the German commanders in the field felt their prospects for quickly capturing Bastogne were excellent.

As the Battle of the Bulge began, the future of Bastogne hinged on whether General Middleton could hold the town long enough for reinforcements to arrive. This outcome was by no means certain, given the collapse of Allied front lines under the initial assault launched from the Ardennes. Still, with only thinly dispersed troops available, including the inexperienced troops of the 106th Infantry and the 9th Armored Divisions, plus the battle-hardened but seriously decimated 28th Infantry and the 4th Infantry Divisions, Middleton stood and fought.

General Rundstedt's original battle plan had counted on the Fifth Panzer Army under General Manteuffel to take Bastogne quickly. Manteuffel in turn called for General Lüttwitz, the commander of the 47th Panzer Corps, to attack Bastogne as his primary objective, relying heavily on the Second Panzer Division, the Panzer Lehr Division, and the 26th Volksgrenadier. Realizing in the early hours of the battle on December 16 that the US 28th Infantry Division was thinly deployed along the eastern side of the Our River in enemy territory to the east of Bastogne, Middleton quickly pulled the 28th back across the Our; he also deployed the 9th Armored Combat Command Reserve to reinforce the 28th to the northeast and the southeast of Bastogne.

Manteuffel planned to be in Bastogne by noon on Sunday, December 17. If Middleton could do anything about it, that was not going to happen. Middleton hurriedly placed a perimeter around Bastogne, determined to defend towns at about a twenty-five-mile radius to the east of the city in a half-circle from Houffalize in the north around to Wiltz in the South.

CHAPTER 4

THE GERMANS SENSE
A QUICK VICTORY

The German High Command was aware that the two American
airborne divisions had orders to enter the battle; in the late
afternoon of 18 December intercepted radio messages to this
effect reached OB WEST. German intelligence knew that the
Americans were moving by truck and so estimated that none of
these new troops would appear in the line before noon on the
19th. . . . The 2nd Panzer Division's successes during the night of
18 December against the outpost positions east of Longvilly had
netted forty American tanks, and the apparent crumbling of the last
defenses east of Bastogne promised quick entry to that city on the
19th. The German staffs believed that the two divisions would be
deployed along a front extending from Bastogne to the northeast.
In any case the German attack was unfolding about as scheduled
and three German divisions were bearing down on Bastogne.

—Hugh M. Cole, US Military Historian, *The Ardennes: Battle of the Bulge*, 1988[1]

In the early hours of defending Bastogne, Middleton relied heavily on
the 28th Infantry Division. The division, known as the "Keystone
Division," one of the oldest continuously serving divisions in the US
Army, bore a red shoulder patch in the shape of a keystone, honoring the

Pennsylvania Army National Guard units from which the division was formed. The 28th traces its proud lineage back to 1747, when Benjamin Franklin organized artillery and infantry units to help defend Philadelphia against French and Spanish privateers.[2] The 28th was a distinguished World War II battle division that had marched down the Champs Elysée. Battered in the Hürtgen Forest, the 28th was now resting in the Ardennes where it had been resupplied and refitted.[3] When the Battle of the Bulge began, the 28th "was up to strength, the new replacements were being assimilated, and the morale was good." The problem was a problem the 28th had in common with other divisions in the VIII Corps in that "its frontage was excessive."[4]

DAYS OF DESPERATE DEFENSIVE FIGHTING

South of St. Vith, one of Lüttwitz's first objectives was to take the city of Clerf, Luxembourg, some twenty-five miles almost directly east of Bastogne. Maj. Gen. Norman Cota, the commander of the 28th, called Lt. Col. Hurley Fuller, the commander of the 110th Infantry Regiment defending Clerf, and instructed him in no uncertain terms that Clerf must be held at all costs. "No one comes back!" Cota ordered.[5]

Fuller was an "old soldier" who had seen combat in the Argonne Forest in World War I, and he continued to harbor bitter memories of that bloody engagement, giving him a cantankerous disposition that rankled many of his superior officers.[6] Ironically, Fuller's irascibility had caused him to be relieved of commanding a regiment of the 2nd Infantry Division during the Normandy campaign. Fuller appealed to his old friend Troy Middleton, then at VIII Corps headquarters near Cherbourg, to plead his case. Middleton, also a World War I veteran, decided to ask General Bradley to give Fuller another chance. Just before the start of the Battle of the Bulge, Fuller joined the 110th Infantry Regiment of the 28th Infantry Division, stationed to hold the thinnest section of the VIII Corps line.[7]

In the intense battle to defend Clerf, Fuller's position was overwhelmed by advancing Germans. Fuller held on until 1800 hours, December 17, when Col. Meinrad von Lauchert's 2nd Panzer Division broke through and rolled into town. A German panzer tank rolled right up to the Claravallis Hotel, where Fuller had located his headquarters. "Fuller's staff fought off the German infantry for about half an hour, but the panzers wrecked the hotel, which was soon literally coming down around ears," observed military historian Samuel W. Mitcham Jr. in his 2002 book, *Panzers in Winter*. "He and the surviving members of his staff ducked out the back door and tried to escape to the west, but most of them did not make it. Colonel Fuller, who tried to infiltrate through the woods with a blinded soldier holding on to his belt, was captured. The next day, 102 members of the Headquarters Company surrendered, and the 110th Infantry ceased to exist."[8]

The defense of Clerf typifies the fierce holding action the outgunned and outmanned US forces waged against the advancing Germans. Those who fled became stragglers not because they ran in fear, but because the Germans brought to bear overwhelming force. "It is impossible to assess in hours the violence done the 2nd Panzer Division timetable at Clerf, but it is clear that the race by this division to Bastogne was lost as a result of the gallant action by the 110th Infantry in front of and at the Clerf crossings," wrote US military historian Hugh Cole.[9] The defenders of Clerf made their last radio contact with the 28th Division as late as 0528 on the morning of December 18, Cole reported, but the final word came from the enemy. The Mark IV Battalion of the 3rd Panzer Regiment came clanking into Clerf, determined to play cat and mouse with the remaining American defenders. "Bullet fire from the old stone walls was no menace to armored vehicles," Cole wrote, "bazooka teams sent down from the château were killed or captured, and the German battalions moved on north and west toward Bastogne. But the German infantry were more vulnerable and their march was delayed for several hours before engineers and self-propelled 88's finally set the riddled château afire and forced the Americans to surrender."[10]

Having smashed Clerf, Lauchert's 2nd Panzer Division pushed on to Allerborn, Luxembourg, a village about halfway from Clerf to Bastogne, defended by the 9th Armored's Combat Command Reserve, or CCR. "Then, suddenly, the 2nd Panzer Division, led by the dashing Colonel Lauchert, emerged from the darkness and launched a surprise attack," military historian Mitcham wrote. "Spearheaded by his Tigers and panzers, his men quickly knocked out several Shermans, half-tracks, and armored cars; overran CCR's roadblocks; and inflicted severe casualties on the American infantry."[11] In retreat, the US troops fell back to Longvilly, a town only about five and a half miles to the northeast of Bastogne. There, the CCR survivors joined the US 158th Engineer Battalion that had already laid almost one thousand anti-tank mines within three miles of the town, on the Bastogne perimeter.

But instead of advancing on to Bastogne, Lauchert turned the 2nd Panzer northwest on a secondary road and passed through the hamlet of Bourcy, heading for Noville, to the north of Bastogne. Lauchert's orders were to bypass Bastogne and get to the Meuse River as fast as possible so he could capture crucial river crossings. The German high command had assigned taking Bastogne to the 26th Volksgrenadier and Panzer Lehr Divisions.[12] On the morning of December 19, General Cota still held Wiltz to the south-east of Bastogne, but just barely.

On the evening of Monday, December 18, Lüttwitz received an inter-cepted radio message informing him that two American airborne divisions, the 82nd and the 101st Airborne, were headed toward Bastogne. But the veteran panzer general was not worried. He calculated that the American reinforcements could not possibly arrive before noon on December 19, and by then Gen. Fritz Bayerlein, the commander of the elite Panzer Lehr Division, would certainly have captured Bastogne.[13] Mitcham was highly critical of Bayerlein's abilities as a commander, writing, "Certainly Bayerlein's perfor-mance during the Battle of the Bulge was quite poor, and, on one critical day, he was more interested in seducing a captured American nurse than in the activities of his division."[14]

East of Longvilly, the 2nd Panzer had knocked out some forty American Sherman tanks, and Lüttwitz had every reason to anticipate the Bastogne defenses were on the verge of crumbling. Counting on Bayerlein, Lüttwitz saw no reason he should deny Lauchert permission to move rapidly north-east, bypassing Bastogne for the Meuse River, a primary objective of the German counteroffensive.[15] From Longvilly, Bayerlein had a clear route to attack Bastogne by just traveling east on the Longvilly road, passing through Mageret and Neffe to hit Bastogne from the east with a rolling vengeance. But instead of advancing rapidly, Bayerlein satisfied himself with cutting the road between Longvilly and Mageret, missing a chance during the night of December 18 to seize Bastogne while the US forces were in disarray. This decision ended up being for the Nazis one of the most costly blunders of the entire Wacht am Rhein offensive.

Mitcham reported that Bayerlein's initial mistake in not attacking Bastogne immediately was that he stopped to ask Belgian civilians if the roads to the small towns of Oberwampach and Niederwampach were good. "They replied they were. They were lying," Mitcham wrote.[16] Bayerlein started down the road in the lead tank and got a short way before the road turned into mud. Bayerlein pressed on, reaching Niederwampach, six miles from Bastogne, before 2000 hours on December 18. "An hour later he reached Mageret and was on the main road to Bastogne," Mitcham continued. "Here, he paused and asked another Belgian civilian for information. The civilian, who was an Allied sympathizer (like most Belgian civilians), replied that an American armored force of 50 Shermans, 25 self-propelled guns, and dozens of other armored vehicles had passed through Mageret, heading east. He also said it was being commanded by an American major general." Bayerlein bought the story, convinced Mageret was defended by a divisional-size American force. As a result, he confined himself to cutting the Longvilly-Bastogne road, deploying his tanks east of Mageret and laying mines. "Actually, Mageret was defended by very weak forces," Mitcham wrote. "Bastogne was his for the taking, but Bayerlein let the opportunity pass."[17]

The Bastogne After-Action report of the 28th Infantry Division noted that starting December 16, the division met the full blow of at least six divisions in Rundstedt's offensive in the German drive to the west across the Our River. "By fighting in place, until surrounded, with everything at the Division disposal, including artillery, engineers, headquarters personnel of all units to include Division Headquarters, and then fighting a way out to delay again, the Division gave the higher command four days to bring forces to the vicinity of Bastogne and organize its defenses." The report credited the action of the 28th with having saved Bastogne from falling into German hands.[18] Had the 28th Infantry collapsed upon being attacked, Manteuffel may have succeeded in taking Bastogne by noon, December 17. But the 28th fought with distinction such that now Lüttwitz was going to be satisfied if the Nazis took Bastogne by noon, December 19. Given determined US resistance, the Wehrmacht timetable was clearly slipping. When the 28th finally collapsed on December 18, the good fortune was that Colonel Roberts had just arrived at Bastogne, ready to send his 10th Armored CCB into combat to hold the German advance that the 28th Division had managed to stem in the first three full days of the battle.

When Wiltz finally fell on December 19, recognition again was given to the valiant defense. "The fall of Wiltz ended the 28th Division's delaying action before Bastogne," noted historian Hugh Cole. "Other American troops now had to take over the actual defense of that all-important road center, but without the gallant bargain struck by the 110th Infantry and its allied units—men for time—the German plans for a *coup de main* at Bastogne would have turned to accomplished fact."[19] Cole noted the 28th paid a high cost for this delaying action, with "the 110th Infantry virtually destroyed, the men and fighting vehicles of five tank companies lost, the equivalent of three combat engineer companies dead or missing, and tank destroyer, artillery, and miscellaneous units engulfed in the battle."[20] Cole praised the action of the 28th in the defense of Bastogne, writing, "In the last analysis the losses inflicted on the enemy may have equaled those sustained by the Americans—certainly the Germans paid dearly for their hurried frontal attacks against stone-walled villages and towns—but the final measure of success and failure would be in terms of hours and minutes won by the Americans and lost to the enemy."[21] S. L. A. Marshall also paused in his narrative of the Siege of Bastogne to credit the 28th Infantry Division with absorbing much of the shock of the initial German attack, permitting Middleton to hold on long enough for reinforcements to begin arriving.[22]

A PLAN TO ORGANIZE THE STRAGGLERS

Father Sampson turned out to be an acute observer of "combat fatigue," a peculiar phenomenon he came to realize could affect soldiers in strange ways. To illustrate the point, Father Sampson often told the story of a paratrooper who distinguished himself with the Screaming Eagles in both Normandy and Holland, and was credited with knocking out a German tank with his bazooka. The paratrooper had volunteered for several very successful patrols and on one mission wiped out a machine-gun nest, for which he was decorated. "But the lad just couldn't stand artillery, and when the Germans were throwing in a few 88s at us, he lay in his foxhole shaking like a leaf and crying," Father Sampson recalled. Daily, the paratrooper got worse, though he resisted being evacuated. Finally, his hysterical fear of artillery became a morale factor, "for fear and hysteria are contagious." What was diagnosed as "combat exhaustion" eventually made the paratrooper useless to his regiment. "There were numerous other cases in which men had been subject to as much fear and horror as they were capable of enduring, then broke under the pressure of further demands too great for them to sustain," Father Sampson continued. "These men were as sick and as serious casualties of battle as those wounded by bullets or by fragments of enemy shells, and their evacuation was just as honorable. But they were sometimes to suffer even further by the false accusations of their comrades, or by their own unfair suspicions regarding their courage."[23]

US Army medical doctors Lt. Col. Roy Grinker and Maj. John Spiegel specialized in military psychiatry, applying their specialty to working with combat soldiers overseas in active theaters of operations and combat returnees suffering from war neurosis who were hospitalized for rehabilitation. In their classic 1945 work, *Men Under Stress*,[24] Grinker and Spiegel's study of air force fliers led them to conclusions that "challenged the view that combat fatigue and other war-related symptoms could be ascribed to character faults."[25] A typical military assumption was that only "cowards" ran away from combat. What Grinker and Spiegel established was that a very thin line separated the "normal" soldier from the soldier considered to be a "coward." They came to realize that every person in combat has a psychological breaking point. Grinker and Spiegel found that soldiers experiencing "battle fatigue" needed to be taken off the line, given something to eat, and a chance to get warm and sleep for a while. Some soldiers snapped back rapidly and were ready to return to the battle. In the Siege of Bastogne, those stragglers who did not snap back right away were quickly abandoned as veteran troops learned how to distinguish those soldiers so psychologically damaged by battle that they were not worth the effort trying to save.

Before Colonel Roberts left his initial conference with Middleton on the evening of December 18, he wanted to discuss what could be done about the stragglers who were continuing to drift into Bastogne. Though all three of these commanders—Middleton, Roberts, and McAuliffe—had been born in the nineteenth century, only Middleton and Roberts shared the experience of having fought with the American Expeditionary Forces in World War I. As noted earlier, World War I was over by the time McAuliffe, the youngest of the three, graduated from West Point. Middleton and Roberts both had fought at the Second Battle of the Marne and experienced firsthand the one hundred thousand stragglers—the "walking wounded"—that so disgraced the American First Army by mid-October 1918. The Château-Thierry district became a rendezvous for American soldiers "Absent Without Leave," or AWOL. These troops roved the countryside and banded together to steal provisions from French villages to survive. "In the fall of 1918, MPs arrested some fifteen to twenty stragglers each week around Château-Thierry, but this meager effort made no discernible dent in this community's vitality because a steady influx of new delinquents continually replenished it," observed World War I historian Jennifer Keene.[26]

"Sir," Roberts addressed Middleton politely, "there will be stragglers. I want authority to use these men."

Among the stragglers, both Roberts and Middleton knew from their experience in World War I that there were likely to be a few worth returning to battle. Many of the stragglers had run from the field of battle simply because they had no alternative. Surprised by overwhelming German forces, many US soldiers stood and fought until they ran out of ammunition. Many of the stragglers drifting into Bastogne could be persuaded to go back into battle, provided they were given a cup of coffee and something to eat, and maybe a chance to sleep. Middleton granted Roberts' wish. There was another reason Roberts wanted to round up the stragglers. As he noted in his oral history after the battle, Roberts was concerned the large number of stragglers moving through Bastogne could slow down his efforts to get the 10th Armored CCB into the battle. "The stragglers jammed the roads as groups moved south and east," Roberts recalled. "The confusion bordered on panic in some cases. The only way CCB could move through Bastogne was by commandeering MPs along the route, sometimes putting out MPs of our own."

Roberts knew that rounding up stragglers was not likely to be either easy or popular. To have the authority he needed to get the job done quickly and efficiently, Roberts asked Middleton to put in writing permission for Roberts to round up the stragglers. Middleton agreed, issuing the following confirmation: "190706 [December 19, 0706 hours] Major General Middleton directs that you [Colonel Roberts] have the authority to take over all or any part of the Reserve Command of the 9th Armored in case they show the slightest inclination to retire. Anything you do to prevent falling back in that area will be given fullest backing."[27]

With written permission in hand, Roberts went about assembling what he called "Team SNAFU," with SNAFU being the acronym constructed from one of the favorite sayings of World War II fighters: "Situation Normal, All Fouled Up" (with typically a more colorful phrase substituted for "Fouled Up"). Roberts appointed an officer from the 110th Infantry Regiment of the 28th Infantry Division, Capt. Charles Brown, to head SNAFU. Together, Roberts and Brown looked in particular for infantrymen without rifles, artillerymen without howitzers, and tankers without tanks. "Roberts set up a detail in the town square to assign the men—many of whom were hollow-eyed, semi-coherent—a place to sleep and to feed them a hot meal," noted US Army military historian Charles B. MacDonald in his 1985 book, *A Time for Trumpets*. "Within twenty-four hours, most were sufficiently recovered to join Team SNAFU."[28] MacDonald noted that the stragglers were mostly from CCR of the 9th Armored and from the 28th Infantry Division. Brig. Gen. George A. Davis, with Middleton's permission, took some three hundred of the men who wore the red Keystone shoulder patches to rejoin the division. MacDonald estimated that Team SNAFU ended up numbering about six hundred men, used to man close-in roadblocks on the edges of Bastogne, to form small task forces, and to serve as individual replacements in various units in the field.[29]

In his oral history after the battle, Roberts recalled his efforts to organize stragglers into Team SNAFU.

On the 19th [December 19], two hundred to two hundred and fifty stragglers were picked up. In the next week this figure was raised to seven hundred to eight hundred. A number of these men were men of the 9th Armored, but the majority were from the 28th Infantry. It wasn't difficult to stop the stragglers when they went through town, for the MPs at the crossroads in the southwest corner of town sent everyone not of the 101st Division over to the 10th Armored CCB area. Headquarters Company had plenty of food, and a hot meal was always ready.

Roberts noted the stragglers were billeted in the buildings around the center square in Bastogne. "The name SNAFU was applied to the situation and stuck," Roberts commented. "Team SNAFU was organized under casual officers in the group. All of these stragglers were short of equipment, and there was very little transportation with them."[30]

Trucks and stragglers heading west through Bastogne, Belgium. December 19, 1944. Note men without equipment. Many of these stragglers were collected, reequipped, and formed into Task Force SNAFU.

More efficient than scavenging equipment from dazed men in rout was raiding the supply depots of now dysfunctional combat units that had been assigned to VIII Corps before the battle, including the 9th Armored CCR and the 28th Infantry Division. Stephen Ambrose in *Band of Brothers* recounts the story of 2nd Lt. George C. Rice assigned to the 10th Armored Division CCB.

He [Rice] jumped in his jeep and drove to Foy, where he loaded the vehicle with cases of hand grenades and M-1 ammunition, turned around and met the column coming out of Bastogne [going into combat on the night of December 18]. He passed out the stuff as the troopers marched by, realized the need was much greater, returned to the supply dump at Foy, found a truck, overloaded it and the jeep with weapons and ammunition, drove back to the oncoming column, and had his men throw it out by the handfuls. Officers and men scrambled on hands and knees for the clips of M-1 ammo. The firefight noise coupled with the panic in the faces of the retreating American troops made it clear that they were going to need every bullet they could get. Lieutenant Rice kept it coming until every man had all he could carry.[31]

Capt. George McCormack, commander of the 907th Glider Field Artillery Battalion, reported in the narrative of the unit's December activity that "the fortunes of war had smiled upon the men of his battalion," relating the following about the selection of a château one mile east of Bastogne as a command post: "This château had been formerly used as a headquarters for the American Red Cross club-mobiles in this vicinity, and there was a considerable amount of sugar, donut flour, butter, and other edibles stored in the buildings adjacent thereto. This food supply was shared with other units in our area, and it proved to be invaluable later inasmuch as it was flour to make hotcakes for breakfast, donuts and hotcakes for supper until other rations arrived."[32] Stories from the men who fought at Bastogne often mention how grabbing a stack of hotcakes, even without syrup or butter, was a morale booster, both because of the welcome change of some hot food and because of the cherished memories of breakfast back home. Soon, pancakes appeared on everybody's breakfast menu and were welcome simply because they were warm.[33]

The US military requisitioned from local farmers, with a promise to pay later, a fairly good supply of potatoes, poultry, and cattle. In an abandoned corps warehouse was found 450 pounds of coffee, 600 pounds of sugar, and a large amount of Ovaltine. An abandoned corps bakery provided flour, lard, salt, and a small amount of coffee. Prowling around Bastogne, supply officers found a large store of margarine, jam, and flour in a civilian warehouse, assuring flapjacks for several more days. Although the remedy may merely ultimately only have made the ailment worse, some two thousand burlap bags that were found among the groceries were rushed out to the infantrymen in the foxholes to wrap around their feet to compensate for the lack of arctic overshoes.[34]

As Roberts' CCB prepared for battle, the total strength of his three combat teams was about seventy-five tanks and twenty-eight hundred officers and enlisted men. Rapidly approaching Bastogne on the night of December 18 were the advance elements of some three hundred German tanks and fifty thousand fighting men whose mission was to take Bastogne and to take it fast.[35]

HITLER'S WEATHER

Critical to Hitler's decision to launch his Wacht am Rhein offensive on December 16 was the weather. His final decision hinged on a forecast by Dr. Werner Schwerdtfeger, one of the most brilliant German meteorologists in charge of the forecasting section at the weather center in Berlin. Hitler waited until Schwerdtfeger predicted a window when the bad weather would ground Allied bombing attacks and severely restrict the use of Allied air support for several days in the west. "The hanging mists and ground fog that are so common in the Ardennes in December gave another advantage; a natural veil to cloak and deny the enemy long-distance observation of German assault forces," wrote military historian Danny S. Parker. "This was the gloomy and inclement weather, 'Hitler's Weather,' that prevailed when the offensive was launched on December 16."[36]

On the morning Hitler launched the attack, the temperature stood at 28 degrees Fahrenheit, reaching 38 degrees that day. Deep snow still remained on the ground that was frozen in patches. But the same weather that grounded US air strikes also impeded the off-road mobility of Hitler's tank forces as they worked to negotiate the marshy Ardennes plateaus.

On December 18, an Atlantic high-pressure system caused a large-scale thaw that made off-road movement even more difficult. The heavy ground fog began to lift, suddenly exposing advancing German troops to Allied firepower. "By December 20, the thaw had melted practically all the snow contributing to the mud that was evident nearly everywhere," Parker wrote. "The ground fog was extremely heavy in the mornings and visibility in some cases was less than one thousand yards. Coupled with the terrain this had the effect of considerably reducing the effectiveness of armor."[37] Parker also pointed out the potential of artillery was also reduced simply because the forward observers the US relied upon to zero in the artillery strike could not see their targets. On December 21 and 22, the high ground began to freeze, leaving many of the roads in the Ardennes slippery and treacherous.

Through December 22, Bradley despaired over the weather. "Each day our gloom had deepened as the Ninth Air Force's youthful meteorologist opened the daily briefing with his dismal repetitious report," Bradley noted. "And each morning [Gen. Hoyt] Vandenberg [commanding officer, Ninth Air Force], in a chair next to mine, pulled his head a little tighter into his leather flying jacket. On more than one hundred socked-in airfields from Scotland to Brussels, an Allied air force of more than four thousand planes waited for the end of Rundstedt's conspiracy with the weather."[38] By December 22, a winter storm had developed, bringing with it a dismal mixture of snow, rain, and fog. No break in the weather was expected until after December 26. The prospects of resupplying Bastogne by air any time soon were not good. Equally problematic with fighter planes and bombers grounded, Middleton's few available ground forces at Bastogne were left to fend for themselves.

CHAPTER 5

BASTOGNE BUYS TIME

Many people assume that the 101st Airborne Division was *solely* responsible for the defense of Bastogne and the surrounding area. Granted, the Screaming Eagles did supply the greatest number of soldiers and played the "starring role" in the drama that unfolded around this tiny critical crossroads town, but the limelight enjoyed by the American paratroopers does not detract from the attention that should be paid to the remarkable accomplishments of the tankers of the 10th Armored Division who preceded the 101st Airborne's arrival at Bastogne.

—Michael Collins and Martin King, *The Tigers of Bastogne*, 2013[1]

Colonel Roberts left his initial conference with Middleton in Bastogne to return to his troops waiting a mile south of Bastogne along the road to Arlon. Now, having agreed with Middleton regarding a strategy to deploy his forces into the battle, Roberts dispatched the teams around Bastogne as follows: Team O'Hara to Wardin, Team Cherry to Longvilly, and Team Desobry to Noville. By 1800 on December 18, Roberts set up his CCB command post in the Hotel LeBrun in the center of Bastogne.

TEAM CHERRY HEADS OUT

The first 10th Armored CCB unit to go into battle was "Team Cherry," headed by Lt. Col. Henry Thomas Cherry Jr., the commanding officer of the 3rd Tank Battalion. Cherry, a 1935 West Point graduate, was born on July 15, 1911, in Macon, Georgia, making Cherry the oldest of the CCB's three team leaders. Before fighting at Bastogne, Cherry had received a Silver Star for gallantry in action in France and in the vicinity of Merzig, Germany, during the period from November 16–27, 1944. His citation noted Cherry, with utter disregard for his own safety, had led a rescue party over open ground to a hill occupied by the enemy one thousand yards away, where he assisted in the rescue of a wounded officer who was in immediate danger of being killed by enemy fire.[2]

On the road south of Bastogne, Roberts told Cherry to move into position near Longvilly, to the east of Bastogne. Cherry managed to get his tanks and men on the road before dark on December 18. All Roberts could tell Cherry was that the enemy was advancing from the east and certain elements of the 9th Armored CCR were in the vicinity of Longvilly. Cherry put Lt. Edward Hyduke in command of an advance column with orders to move along the road from Bastogne toward Longvilly. Hyduke led his men through the villages of Neffe and Mageret, pulling up just short of Longvilly at 1920 hours. From the high ground around the town, Hyduke could see ahead that all the streets in Longvilly were completely filled with vehicles from the 9th Armored's CCR.[3]

Lt. Carl W. Moot Jr. of the 420th Armored Field Artillery Battalion recalled arriving at Longvilly as part of Team Cherry. "It was after dark when we moved up near the German position," Mott wrote. "We went through the little town of Mageret and everything was quiet. At Longvilly we stopped just short of the town and pulled off to the side of the road and waited. It is my recollection that we were planning to jump off from Longvilly the next morning. We had always been on the offensive, and I think everyone on the team expected us to take the offensive next morning and start pushing the Germans back."[4]

Seeing Team Cherry pull up outside Longvilly, the command post of the 9th Armored's Combat Command Reserve in Longvilly asked for Cherry to come forward to meet with them. A captain from the CCR headquarters offered to lead Cherry to the headquarters, but after traveling a considerable distance forward, Cherry realized they had gone too far, passing the town by about a mile. Cherry ordered the captain to turn around. After finally reaching the 9th Armored's CCR command post in Longvilly, Cherry determined the unit was preparing to retreat. Cherry returned to his column outside of town and found his tanks refueling along the road. He instructed Hyduke to take a reconnaissance patrol and establish an advance position before dawn. With the main body of Task Force Cherry about one thousand yards short of the town, Cherry ordered the unit to wait until the CCR in Longvilly began to move out. Sensing a pause in the battle, Cherry decided he would take the opportunity to return to CCB headquarters in Bastogne to meet with Colonel Roberts. As he headed back to Bastogne, Cherry was fired on in Mageret, but he figured some "trigger-happy" US soldiers had fired on him by mistake. At 2300 hours, Cherry met with Roberts in Bastogne. What Cherry did not know was that he had encountered the lead elements of Gen. Fritz Bayerlein's Panzer Lehr Division.

Cherry reported to Roberts the situation of CCR in Longvilly was confused. "Throughout the night, there were stragglers on the road [between Bastogne and Longvilly]. Most of them were trucks and half-tracks, mainly from the 9th Armored Division and the 28th Infantry Division. A number of them were halted to gain information of the enemy, but they could give nothing except the enemy was six miles east on the main road. When asked what the Germans had, they said, 'Tanks, tanks, tanks,' and kept on moving to the rear."[5] Roberts ordered Cherry to provide cover so the 9th Armored CCR could withdraw back to Bastogne. Roberts also ordered Cherry to hold Longvilly. Cherry was delayed getting back to his troops because the fire he received coming through Mageret was from Germans who had cut the road between Longvilly and Mageret as General Bayerlein advanced with the Panzer Lehr Division. At 2340 hours, the 9th Armored CCR began to move out from Longvilly, with Cherry trying to get back to his troops and Team Cherry providing cover for the 9th Armored CCR in Cherry's absence.

Positioned outside Longvilly, Lt. Carl W. Moot Jr. was frustrated that he did not have a map of the area around Longvilly. He spent several hours poring over the maps he had by flashlight inside his closed tank. Around 0200 or 0300 hours, in the middle of the night, he called the 420th Battalion Headquarters to complain he had not received any maps. He recalled:

> I was informed that they could not or would not bring them to me and that I would have to get by with what maps I had. This upset and angered me because I needed maps coordinates to initiate an artillery mission. A little later I was monitoring the 3rd Tank Battalion radio channel and learned that the town of Mageret, behind us, had been invaded by the Germans after we went through, and there was a fight going on to reopen the road through it. I then understood why Battalion Headquarters could not send any maps to me. I drew in some coordinate lines past the edge of the one map and located the approximate location for Longvilly on them, so that I would have some sort of approximate coordinates to call in if and when I wanted to adjust some artillery fire.[6]

When Cherry finally got to Neffe, a town on the way to Mageret from Bastogne, he encountered a wounded enlisted man who reported that his vehicle had been shot up at Mageret. A sergeant confirmed to Cherry that a German patrol had entered Mageret just after midnight. Cherry radioed Capt. William Ryerson in his team outside Longvilly and ordered him to send out a patrol to determine the enemy strength at Mageret. Ryerson sent out two squads of infantry in a half-track. Within a few minutes, this patrol located three enemy tanks and an infantry force they guessed to be about a company in strength, occupying positions around the crossroads at Mageret. "When confirmation of the reports that the Germans were in Mageret was radioed to Colonel Cherry, he prepared his headquarters group to make a stand at Neffe and in the château CP [Command Post] south of the town," journalist Fred MacKenzie commented in his book *The Men of Bastogne*. "Colonel Roberts now had to deal with this unexpected development: the enemy had not appeared frontally at Longvilly, but instead had come in behind the main force of Team Cherry and was less than three miles east of Bastogne. Still Roberts expected the main blow at Longvilly."[7] MacKenzie commented that the advance element of German armor at Mageret in the last hours of darkness as December 19 dawned was "as near on the east to the Bastogne prize as was the 101st Airborne Division bivouacked at Mande-Saint-Étienne on the west."[8]

Colonel Roberts and Cherry finally concluded that Team Cherry had been cut off at Longvilly and would have to remain under Hyduke's command, with the likelihood being that Longvilly could not be held. At 0830 hours, Colonel Cherry ordered Hyduke to hold his ground at Longvilly, while the 9th Armored CCR tried to fight its way back through Mageret. Cherry picked as a command post a château-style country mansion built with strong stone walls. Here, about three hundred yards south of Neffe, he decided he would wait to monitor developments. The result was confusing. Cherry's command post force was just outside Neffe; as the battle developed along the road to Longvilly, the main body of Task Force Cherry joined the retreating 9th Armored CCR in attempting to get back to Bastogne by fighting through the German forces that had moved into Mageret under cover of night. The only part of Task Force Cherry that stayed at Longvilly was the original advance guard under the command of Lieutenant Hyduke. "By daybreak of the 19th Hyduke was set up on three sides and ready to defend the rear," S. L. A. Marshall wrote. "However the closing of the road at Mageret by the Germans had kept many of Combat Command Reserve's vehicles from withdrawing, and after taking to the road, they sat there blocking all traffic." Marshall noted the action resumed on the morning of December 19. "The morning engagement opened with the sighting of two enemy tanks about 1500 yards southeast of Longvilly but the visibility was so poor because of fog that only the vague outlines of the tanks could be seen. A shot from the Germans hit a tank in the Combat Command Reserve group along the road, locking the turret. All of the American armor returned the fire and both enemy tanks went up in flames. After this there was a prolonged shelling of Longvilly."[9]

Several days earlier, VIII Corps Signal Company had occupied the château Cherry now occupied as his command post. On pulling out, the Signal Company left written on the walls, "We'll be back. The YANKS." Seeing this, the men of Cherry's headquarters replied, "We'll be back? . . . [W]e're here to stay!" Through the night of December 18 and into the next morning, the Germans continued attacking Cherry's headquarters, finally surrounding the château on three sides and covering the fourth side on the west with 20mm cannons and machine guns. Cherry held out after ordering that the automatic weapons be dismounted from all vehicles and shifted to the château.

On the night of December 19, the 9th Armored CCR was in disarray and attempting to retreat from Longvilly. The Germans were in Mageret within three miles of Bastogne, and the only troops standing in their way were Colonel Cherry with a small group defending his château command post at Neffe. General Manteuffel was furious with Bayerlein for getting lost on side roads and, as we saw earlier, taking directions from civilians who were not sympathetic to the German counteroffensive, only to become diverted and bogged down at Mageret. Manteuffel supposedly commented angrily that if Bayerlein was incapable of reading a map, he should have asked

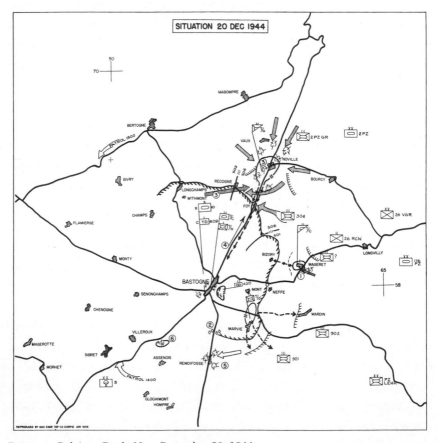

Bastogne, Belgium: Battle Map, December 20, 1944

one of his staff officers to do it for him.[10] Manteuffel's point was Bayerlein should have taken Bastogne before Team Cherry moved in to provide support for the retreating 9th Armored and resistance to the German advance.

TEAM O'HARA MOVES OUT NEXT

The easiest deployment the night of December 18 for the three task forces fell to Lt. Col. James O'Hara and his Team O'Hara. A very tall man, O'Hara, thirty-two years old, seemed to be always smiling, no matter what the situation was. This earned him the nickname "Smiling Jim."[11] O'Hara was born at West Point, New York, on August 9, 1912, the son and grandson of West Point graduates. He completed his studies at the West Point Military Academy in 1936. Thanks to his almost constant smile, the men serving under him found it difficult to tell for certain what his moods were or how serious the situation in the field of combat might be.[12] On December 23, 1944, he would win a Silver Star for his bravery in commanding an attack in the vicinity of Marvie, Belgium, just outside Bastogne, that repelled the enemy's second attack that night.[13]

After the 9th Armored CCB's main column cleared the road, O'Hara ordered his command to head southeast on the road to Wardin. At 1725, Team O'Hara occupied the high ground south of the town, just short of the woods. "The night was quiet except for stragglers coming through," O'Hara noted in his after-action oral history. "Most of these were from the 28th Infantry Division and seemed generally to be rear echelon people. They rode in vehicles, but their columns and knowledge of the enemy were wildly confused." Donald Nichols of Company C, 21st Tank Battalion, of the 10th Armored CCB, recalled moving up to the front with Team O'Hara. "We had to pull over to the side of the road during the night to let other units traveling to the rear, to escape the German drive from their front," Nichols noted. "We asked where they were going but their reply was, 'Give them [expletive], Yank,' our only communication with the retreating soldiers."[14] The stragglers were those escaping from Wiltz, farther to the southeast. Team O'Hara put out a few security outposts for the night and let the stragglers pass without attempting to stop them. "No strong defense was made," O'Hara noted, as the night of December 18 passed without incident.[15]

TEAM DESOBRY DEPLOYS THROUGH BASTOGNE

Maj. William R. Desobry, the commanding officer of the 20th Armored Infantry Battalion of the 10th Armored Division, headed the third task force. Desobry, the youngest of the three CCB team leaders, was born in Manila, Philippines, on September 11, 1918, to Col. and Mrs. E. Desobry. Unlike the other two team leaders, Desobry was not a West Point graduate. Instead, he graduated in 1941 from the Georgetown University School of Foreign Service where he received a commission into the US Army through the ROTC. "Des," as his friends knew him, always put his troops first, making an effort to communicate with them despite his many bureaucratic assignments in the army. As we will see, Desobry displayed exceptional courage at Noville, just a few miles north of Bastogne, where he was severely wounded and almost lost his life. Today there is a street in Bastogne named after him. He received a Silver Star for his bravery on December 19, 1944, leading a command of an armored task force composed of tanks, infantry, tank destroyers, assault guns, and mortars with a mission of holding Noville at all costs.[16]

While the first two teams got through Bastogne during the daylight, it was already dark before Team Desobry was ready to leave the village. Before departing, Desobry went to see Colonel Roberts, a senior commander with whom the youthful Desobry, often described as "boyish," had a close relationship. "For a number of years Desobry had known the older man well," S. L. A. Marshall observed. "He [Desobry] was talking now to a man who was not only his commander but whom he regarded as a second father."[17] As Roberts explained to Desobry his mission to hold Noville, the colonel cautioned him. "It will be a close race to get there before the enemy," he explained. "You are young, and by tomorrow morning you will probably be nervous. By midmorning the idea will probably come to you that it would be better to withdraw from Noville. When you begin thinking that, remember that I told you that it would be best not to withdraw until I order you to do so."[18] This advice was to appear providential the next day when Desobry had exactly the reactions Roberts had predicted.

Journalist Fred MacKenzie confirmed the close relationship the boyish Desobry had with Colonel Roberts, also noting that Roberts was virtually a second father to Desobry. Desobry always had confidence in what Roberts told him, knowing that the Old Man had fought the Germans as a young man in World War I. "That is the way it was," MacKenzie wrote. "Loyalty to Roberts and what he represented versus the tremendous anxiety clutching at them all; and Roberts had to win or all would go down the drain with the panicky derelicts overrunning the roads and spreading their infection."

MacKenzie commented that the night was big with the makings of defeat. "From the last minutes of daylight they carried into the darkness vivid recollections of colossal disaster: haggard stragglers on foot and in vehicles, long lines of guns, equipment dragged from airfields, hospitals, Red Cross clubs, and more guns, many more than the Tigers could muster, all fleeing headlong from the front." Roberts looked at these young lives with a mixture of hope and sadness. "Each man moved in a dark closet of varying dimensions, heard noises trying to be hushed, saw wraith forms slink by, shrinking away when straying words were spoken to them. Roberts talked at many. He regenerated a few."[19]

As Desobry's Sherman tanks, tank destroyers, and half-tracks prepared to roll through Bastogne on their way north to Noville, Desobry confidently addressed his hastily assembled force. "Put those tank destroyers on point and gather all the ammo you can lay your hands on," he told his men. "Good luck and God be with you."[20] Desobry ordered his men to allow the armored vehicles and men retreating from Noville to pass through the lines as he headed out of Bastogne. Military historians Michael Collins and Martin King commented in *The Tigers of Bastogne* that Desobry was concerned the additional vehicles would end up congesting the streets of Noville and increase his vulnerability to enemy artillery. Collins and King concluded Desobry seemed to have sensed he was headed toward something big because he had incorporated infantrymen and engineers into the task force, with the plan that the engineers would set up obstacles and barriers to function as road blocks hindering the forward movement of German armored divisions. What Desobry did not know was that he was headed to a "perfect storm" of attacking Germans determined to break through his small force as they rushed to bypass Bastogne to the north, determined to reach the Meuse River to the west.[21]

"Team Desobry consisted of fifteen medium tanks, five light tanks, a company of infantry transported in M3 half-tracks, and a platoon of five M10 tank destroyers," Collins and King wrote. "They were accompanied by a unit of mechanized cavalry in three armored cars and six Willy's jeeps. Unbeknownst to Team Desobry, heading in the direction of Noville was the entire 2nd Panzer Division, commanded by Col. Meinrad von Lauchert. The 2nd Panzer had already dispersed the 28th Division's 110th Infantry Regiment at Clervaux, about seventeen miles to the east, and hammered the task forces of the 9th Armored Division's CCR. Now Lauchert's panzers were planning to meet up with Gen. Fritz Bayerlein's feared Panzer Lehr and General Kokott's 26th Volksgrenadier divisions, which were approaching Bastogne from the east. Team Desobry had no idea of the magnitude of the task ahead of them."[22]

Heading north from Bastogne on the road to Noville, Desobry was not certain what he faced ahead. He recalled after the battle:

> They said that O'Hara had been sent out to the southeast to block a road coming to the town of Wiltz, which was a high-speed road, and Cherry was moving out to the town of Longvilly to block that road, and I was going due north to a town of Noville and I was to block that road. They really didn't know what the situation was, except the Germans had broken through the 28th Division somewhere to the east of us; that Germans were using American equipment and some of them were dressed in American uniforms and some of them civilian uniforms. So you had to watch out for that.[23]

Leaving Bastogne, Desobry had only a hastily constructed overlay he had made from the few maps available when the battle began. Desobry acknowledged that even his orders from Colonel Roberts were broadly stated, leaving him to figure out the situation when he got there.

> I was to go to this town of Noville and if there were any Germans in it, I was to knock them out and seize the town. If there weren't any, I was to hold the town, the town of Noville. And I asked, "Well, if I get into trouble, can I withdraw or the like?" And they said, "No, you are to stay there." So I said, "How in the heck do I get to Noville?" And nobody knew how to get

through Bastogne to Noville and so I sent a guy off to find an MP and he found a Corps MP. I met him outside and I said, "I [have] to go to Noville and I'd like him to lead me up there." And he said, "He wasn't about to leave Bastogne." And I said, "Well can you get me through Bastogne and get me headed on the road to Noville?" And he said, "Sure, I'd be glad to do that."[24]

The MP led Desobry's column through the winding roads of Bastogne, and then, when the column got to the outskirts of the town, the MP pointed that Noville was about two towns up the road, heading straight. From there, the MP went back to Bastogne and Desobry sent out a recon platoon to search out Noville.

After passing through the village of Foy, Team Desobry arrived at Noville at around 2300 hours on December 18, with the major part of his force arriving by 2:00 a.m., on what was then December 19. Desobry's task force consisted of a company of Sherman tanks from the 3rd Tank Battalion and a company of the 20th Armored Infantry Battalion, with engineers, medics, and scouts—in all, about four hundred men.[25] Pleasantly surprised, Desobry found there were no Germans yet there. What Desobry did not know was that the 2nd Panzer Division was now only hours away. Still, given the warning he received from Roberts, Desobry decided to place his troops in defensive positions, anticipating correctly that a fierce battle was about to start. Desobry, MacKenzie noted, set up his command post in Noville, "warm with determination to prove his mettle to the colonel."[26] Team Desobry in Noville to the north of Bastogne was separated from Team Cherry to the east in Longvilly by five miles of terrain running up and down small hills and across shallow valleys. Another five miles separated Team Cherry from Team O'Hara to the southeast of Bastogne, positioned astride the road to Wiltz.[27]

Walter Lepinski of the 20th Armored Infantry Battalion remembered passing through Foy on his way to Noville with Task Force Desobry. Just outside Noville, word was passed to Lepinski that Captain Geiger wanted him to come forward and report. He recalled:

I moved forward to report to Captain Geiger, who said to me that he and I were going into town and pick the spots to place the platoons and gun positions. Captain Geiger and I left the platoon and walked into town, it was not very far, and after we passed the first house, which was on the left hand side of the road, we went into town and walked around the area. Once he decided where to place each platoon he called the column to move up to the town. I asked Captain Geiger, "Captain, in the case of a withdrawal, what is the alternative route back?" He said to me, "Our orders are to stay here and battle to the last man." My heart dropped. At that point there was no firing, small arms or artillery, it seemed so strange. It continued to get dark. I was there with him as he placed each company into positions and I got my men into their position as well. That night my men and I slept on the floor of this schoolhouse that we found on the left side of town, I didn't know it was a schoolhouse until I saw the desks there. I was tired as all [expletive] . . . and I slept.[28]

"Task Force Desobry was preparing to make an epic stand against overwhelming numbers," Collins and King stressed. "Desobry's Company B was to defend the ridge to the northwest and Company A was allocated to the northeast. The job of Company C was to cover the southern half of the perimeter while the armored group was held in the center of the town ready to strike out in any direction."[29] Desobry's positioning of his troops was designed to take full advantage of the terrain; Noville is on relatively high ground itself, but two ridges from about eight hundred yards dominate the village, one in the southeast and the other running from north to northwest.[30] "In this natural amphitheater of the Ardennes, the defenders were screened by fog and at the same time could see little of their distant surroundings," journalist Fred MacKenzie wrote. "As the day advanced, the fog started to behave like a theater curtain, rising and falling periodically. It was as though the curtain was separating into scenes the lethal play that would go on until the next afternoon."[31]

Throughout the night, stragglers from the 28th Infantry and 9th Armored continued filtering into Noville. Desobry, following Colonel Roberts' instructions, drafted into his task force any of the stragglers he thought he could use. "The infantry came into the line usually in groups of three or four. Many of them had discarded all fighting equipment; few were able to say where they had been; none had maps, and none was able to pinpoint the area where he had last seen the Germans," noted S. L. A. Marshall.

"It became the experience of Team Desobry that these stragglers who came to Noville singly or in small groups were of almost no value to the defense; when the action started, they took to the cellars."[32]

At around 0400 in the early morning hours of December 19, Desobry noticed the flow of stragglers stopped abruptly, signaling that the battle for Noville was about to start. Walter Lepinski, sleeping in the schoolhouse, did not find refuge there for long. "It didn't seem that I slept at all when all of a sudden all [expletive] broke loose," he recalled. "Small arms, burp guns, and artillery, everything was going on outside the window of my schoolhouse. I jumped up and told the men that we needed to get out of here. My half-track was parked alongside the building facing away from the main street. I manned the .50 caliber and it was gray outside with a lot of fog out."[33] Suddenly, Lepinski found himself in the center of the action and the artillery fire was constant:

> We were in a staggered formation in that area, and the half-track to my right had two buildings or sheds in front of them and he would fire between the two buildings. The road north of my position was sloped down and on the road that ran parallel to the road we were on had a column of German tanks that were lumbering towards where we had come from, they never fired, but we kept losing them in the fog. The fog kept rising and falling, and when I could see I lined my barrel over a hedgerow that was fifteen feet in front of me, so that I could see my tracers bouncing off the tanks. Even when I could not see them I could continue to fire since I was lined up. It was one [expletive] of a hectic time, a lot of fire and smoke. I sat up there like a duck in the pond, nothing to protect me, but most of the fire came from the other side of the street.[34]

Lepinski was awarded a Bronze Star with Oak Leaf Cluster for his action in Noville firing on enemy tanks with the .50 caliber machine gun mounted on his half-track. "While he was directing fire, the enemy were attacking within three to five hundred yards, using 88mm guns, machine guns, and mortars," his Bronze Star citation read. "By his courage and complete disregard for his personal safety, Sergeant Lepinski assisted in knocking out at least four enemy tanks, thereby enabling his unit to save important vehicles and equipment."[35]

CHAPTER 6

THE "HOLE IN THE
DOUGHNUT" DEVELOPS

Early Wednesday [December 20], German panzer, infantry
and parachute divisions swelled around Bastogne like a tidal
wave, slashed the last remaining road leading into the city,
completely surrounded the 101st. That day when Corps [VIII
Corps] called by radio telephone to ask the [Screaming]
Eagle situation, Lt. Col. H. W. O. Kinnard, Division G-3,
replied: "Visualize the hole in the doughnut. That's us."

—"Bastogne: The Hole in the Doughnut," *The Story of the 101st Airborne Division,* 1947[1]

The three CCB Task Force teams of the 10th Armored were on the move into the field of combat at Bastogne that Monday evening, December 18, 1944, just as the first unit of the 101st Airborne was about to arrive at the assembly area to the east of Bastogne, having completed the drive from Camp Mourmelon.

THE 501ST ARRIVES AT BASTOGNE

"At Bastogne, the 101st Division played in luck from the beginning and the luck began weeks before the siege started," S. L. A. Marshall commented in *Bastogne: The First Eight Days*. "In the early part of November a young lieutenant colonel, Julius Ewell, commanding the 501st Parachute Infantry in the Neder Rijn in Holland, took a busman's holiday and spent two days of his leave in Bastogne." But the good fortune did not stop there. "It was the luck of war that in giving the march order before leaving Camp Mourmelon, General McAuliffe had put the 501st Parachute Infantry at the head of the column. It was the luck of war again that Ewell got away well in advance of the column on December 18 and was the first commander to arrive in the vicinity of the bivouac."[2] Those religiously inclined might not see this as luck, but as the hand of God intervening in the battle, arranging seemingly random events so as to advantage the Americans coming to the defense of Bastogne. As noted earlier, in other passages of his classic work, Marshall is less circumspect, claiming various battlefield events were not due to luck, but were "providential," a reference that more clearly attributes outcomes to the influence of God.

When he got to Bastogne from Camp Mourmelon, Ewell ran into a wire-stringing detail establishing telephone communications, and he asked what they were doing. It turned out these two men were from the 101st Airborne, such that all Ewell had to do was follow the wires to end up where General McAuliffe had established his headquarters. Even more fortunate, the 101st started arriving at the bivouac area outside Bastogne at 2230 hours just before midnight on Monday, December 18, 1944, a half hour earlier than Ewell originally expected, so that by 2400 the 101st Airborne was safely in position. This gave General McAuliffe the advantage of having at least one regiment in place ready to be dispatched to battle in the first hours of Tuesday, December 19.[3]

Following the wire lines, Ewell reached the schoolhouse in Bastogne where General McAuliffe had established his first headquarters. Pleased to see Ewell had arrived, General McAuliffe rushed him over to Middleton's VIII Corps headquarters in the Heintz Barracks on the northeastern outskirts of town. When Ewell entered the war room at the corps headquarters, red blotches on the map overlay marked the enemy's advance. "It looks like it's got the measles," Ewell announced in his characteristic drawl, causing Generals McAuliffe and Higgins to laugh.[4]

Leaving headquarters, Ewell took his staff officers and headed to various road junctions in Bastogne to see what more they could learn about the battle situation from men retreating from the front.[5] In his after-action oral history of the battle, Ewell's assessment of the situation was grim. "No one knew exactly where the Germans were," he said. "The general situation at corps was one of panic. I do not think any other word fits the case. After a while it became clear to me that any quest for information concerning the enemy, other than going out bodily after it, was useless." He recalled:

> During the evening of 18 December, I met many groups of men, Americans, coming down the roads from the north and northeast. I stopped some of them. They would say to me rather dumbly, "We have been wiped out," and then they would keep on going. They did not know where they had been. They did not know where there were proceeding. It was useless to talk to them. I tried it several times and so did others around me. Finally we realized we were wasting our time and then we paid almost no attention to them.[6]

Despite his efforts, Ewell ended up no more certain about the battle situation around Bastogne than he had been when he first arrived at General Middleton's corps headquarters and commented the map looked like measles.

Back at headquarters in Bastogne, Middleton and McAuliffe were having difficulty settling upon the best plan for deploying the 501st PIR. Finally, McAuliffe suggested they should use "a good old Leavenworth solution." McAuliffe had attended the US Army Command and General Staff College, and Middleton had taught there. Both understood what McAuliffe meant. Put simply, a "Leavenworth solution" was a practical solution that worked to solve a complex military problem, not an academic solution designed to win a good grade.[7] Here the "Leavenworth solution" involved a decision to send Ewell's regiment on the road toward Longvilly as quickly as possible, realizing Germans advancing against Team Cherry were only a few miles away.

Middleton approved the plan, and McAuliffe called for Ewell. In his oral history after the battle, Ewell remembered that Middleton was perfectly cool and calm, that he seemed to know what he was doing. McAuliffe, on the other hand, appeared to Ewell to be "a little rattled," upset that there was not more definite information at corps headquarters about the Nazi advance.[8] Pointing to the road to Longvilly heading east out of Bastogne, McAuliffe gave Ewell his orders: "Ewell, move out along this road at 0600 hours, make contact, attack, and clear up the situation." Ewell listened quietly. "Yes, sir," he said, saluting and leaving without a question.[9] In his after-action report, Ewell recalled coolly, "I was vaguely familiar with this terrain, which gave me more confidence than if I had been a complete stranger to it."[10]

After the battle, McAuliffe had nothing but praise for Ewell:

> There were many men and commanders in any operation who did outstanding things. But it is something to put yourself in Ewell's place. He made the greatest gamble. It was dark. He had no knowledge of the enemy. I could tell him what he was likely to meet. I said to him, "Ewell, move out at 6 a.m. along this road (pointing to map). Make contact, attack, and clean up the situation." He didn't bat an eye or ask a question. He said, "Yes, sir," saluted, and went on his way. We had picked up a few more maps, and he had twenty for his regiment. He is a cool commander, possessed of an eye for ground and a good tactical mind. No man has more courage. He was the right man for the spot I put him in.[11]

Summarizing his decision to send Ewell along the road to Longvilly, McAuliffe explained himself simply, "I sent Ewell out because I thought it most likely that they would roll down on us from that direction."[12] As it turned out, McAuliffe had guessed correctly.

Realizing the 101st Airborne was going to have to carry the defense of Bastogne for several days, McAuliffe decided to err on the side of caution. Even though he had defined Ewell's mission as a regimental one, McAuliffe decided initially to authorize Ewell not to lead out the entire 501st Paratroop Infantry Regiment, but a combat team instead consisting of an infantry battalion, an anti-aircraft battery, and a platoon of reconnaissance troops.[13] "McAuliffe had decided right at the beginning that a successful defense of

Bastogne depended on the utmost harboring of his reserves at every stage of operation," S. L. A. Marshall observed, "and having sent Ewell forth, he [McAuliffe] decided to sit on Bastogne with the rest of his [101st Airborne] Division until something new developed."[14] Whether the German advance into Bastogne from the east could be stopped now depended on how successfully Ewell could relieve Cherry.[15]

EWELL AND THE 501ST HEAD OUT

At exactly 0600 hours on the morning of Tuesday, December 19, Ewell left the bivouac area with the various contingents assembled from the 501st. The 1st Battalion, commanded by Maj. Raymond V. Bottomly Jr., took the lead position, followed by Battery B of the 81st Airborne Anti-aircraft Battalion and seven 57mm guns. Before departing, Ewell had instructed his commanders that if they met opposition, they were to take it "slow and easy." Ewell knew his 501st, nicknamed the "Geronimos" were good at adapting the Apache chieftain's tactics of attacking the enemy by throwing themselves directly on a target. While that approach worked in Normandy and Holland, Ewell was convinced, given what he had seen of Bastogne during his November holiday, his best chance of success lay in the more cautious tactics of "fire and maneuver." Ewell stressed, "I don't want you to beat the enemy to death."[16]

The thick fog reduced visibility to somewhere between an average of four hundred and six hundred yards, reminding Ewell of the Gettysburg battleground in the Civil War. At the first intersection past Bastogne, Ewell realized the 1st Battalion in the advance guard position had taken the wrong turn in the predawn fog and were heading southeast toward Marvie. His knowledge of the terrain helped Ewell solve the problem quickly. "Once outside the town, the 501st commander began recognizing features of the landscape he had noted in November during his Ardennes invasion-route study," journalist Fred MacKenzie noted. "The road to Longvilly bent slightly northward along a hillside at the intersection of another road leading southeast into a broad, shallow valley. The column guides had led the troop down the latter."[17] Realizing this, Ewell promptly recalled Bottomly and set the 1st Battalion along the correct road, heading east out of Bastogne, toward Neffe, Mageret, and Longvilly.

One mishap of the wrong direction was that the reconnaissance platoon, which had gone farthest down the wrong road, reentered the column on the right road behind the battalion column.[18] The recons had to race through the entire column to get back to their lead position.[19] Approaching Neffe, between 0800 and 0900 hours, the 1st Battalion met resistance from German infantry supported by two Mark IV tanks. As Middleton recalled, "The reconnaissance troops were back where they belonged when a German machine gun began firing on them half a mile west of Neffe. The paratroopers went into the ditches. When a German tank joined the serenade they left the ditches for higher ground."[20]

Ewell quickly realized he could not utilize his 57mm anti-tank guns because the German tanks were firing from the back slope of the hills around the roadblock. This involves a military position classified as "defilade," in which a tank advances upward on a hill to the point where only the tank's cannon protrudes over the hill, allowing the tank to fire while the hilltop protects the tank turret and body from direct enemy fire. Fighting their way through Neffe, a roadblock stopped the 501st advance just west of Neffe at a road junction headed north to Bizory. These were typical Belgian rural villages that Ewell described as amounting to little more than a group of large farmhouses in a quiet valley.[21] Some hundred yards back from the skirmish line west of Neffe, Ewell noticed a stone house snuggly set into a kind of pocket on the hillside that he thought would make a good command post. The house created a defilade of its own against artillery or tank fire coming from German forward positions to the east. Though Ewell did not realize it immediately, Cherry's château stonehouse command post was nearby, just south of Neffe.

Troopers from the 501st remembered Ewell remaining calm at Neffe, even though the fighting was chaotic. "Colonel Ewell's jeep had come to a stop about ten feet in front of me at the sounds of resistance," PFC John Trowbridge recalled. "I had never been that near to the Colonel, nor did I remember hearing his voice before. His calm, cool composure had a reassuring effect on those near him. I can't remember his exact words, as he spoke on the radio, but it meant the same as 'Hold on right where you are!'"[22] In sharp contrast, PFC Lawrence C. Lutz recalled another incident that morning. "Just west of Neffe, we were challenged by machine gun fire and we hit the ground," he wrote, describing his action with Ewell's 501st as the regiment moved east on the road to Longvilly. "Immediately, a fire fight developed, and after some time, we were ordered to dig in with the 3rd Platoon of 'B' Company on the left of the Bastogne-Longvilly road." That is when the incident occurred. "Sgt. George Adomitis jumped out of his fox-hole screaming like he was badly hit. A couple of the troopers knocked him down and shortly after, they took him away. Later I learned that he had died. I was told that Adomitis' mind had taken all the combat it could and that he stood up to end it all. This was just the start of the killing and destruction to take place in the next month."[23]

At approximately 1000 hours on the morning of December 19, Ewell became convinced that the 1st Battalion was stopped outside Neffe and he had no choice but to call the 2nd Battalion out of Bastogne.[24] The 2nd Battalion took more than an hour to fight through traffic in the attempt to leave Bastogne and get on the road to Longvilly. Finally, at 1203 hours on December 19, the 2nd Battalion took Neffe in heavy combat. Having secured Neffe, Ewell decided he would take Bizory, another small town to the north of Neffe. Ewell ordered Maj. Sammie Homan with one company ahead to explore a long ridge he felt could be strategically important when he next planned to order the 2nd Battalion forward to take Bizory. S. L. A. Marshall commented, "His decision, so casually made, probably contributed as much to the salvation of Bastogne as anything that happened during the first few critical days."[25] The irony was that when the Germans saw Ewell attempting to extend the 501st in a sweep forward, this was the last thing the Germans expected. "Until it happened," Marshall continued, "they [the Germans] had been meeting small or disorganized units they quickly encir-cled and overcame. The shock of the discovery threw them off stride. They recoiled, hesitated and lost precious, unreclaimable hours and opportunity because of their own confusion."[26] Ewell's aggressive attack caused Bayerlein to become even more cautious, military historian Samuel Mitcham noted in *Panzers in Winter*. "Instead of clearing the Longvilly road to the north, as he had originally planned, the Panzer Lehr leader now decided to divide his command," Mitcham wrote.[27] Leaving strong forces along the Mageret-Neffe road, Bayerlein turned southwest with the bulk of his division, determined to probe the American offenses, instead of launching a concerted attack. "Another day was lost," Mitcham concluded.[28]

Middleton also observed the impact Ewell's arrival on the field of battle had on Bayerlein: "The Germans interpreted the appearance of Ewell's force as part of a larger attack on the Panzer Lehr forces at Neffe."[29] As Ewell prepared to engage his 2nd Battalion in the push for Bizory, he asked for artillery support. The 501st artillery units came forward on the double, taking positions to fire on the enemy from protected positions chosen so the enemy could not fire back effectively. The lightweight 105mm guns made such a noise that Bayerlein was sure US tanks were firing upon him. In the ensuing artillery barrage, Bayerlein's Panzer Lehr force took eighty casualties from the shelling. "Besides the 101st's artillery, Bayerlein kept hearing rifle fire from his left, from Team Cherry's small headquarters force shut up in Château Neffe," Middleton observed. "Bayerlein's hearing must have become super acute: he was now imagining two battalions of infantry in the attack coming from Château Neffe and a squadron of tanks pushing out from Bastogne. Thus he went back to the comparative safety of Mageret."[30]

FATHER SAMPSON ENTERS THE BATTLE

"The first day was not too bad, and our casualties were not very heavy," Father Sampson wrote in his autobiography, *Look Out Below!* "Ewell had been right; the Germans had apparently been so confused by the variety of reports from their patrols that they had paused just long enough for Ewell to get his battalions in position in time to be able to blunt the point of Rundstedt's spear-thrust into Bastogne."[31]

Father Sampson noted the 501st regimental headquarters had moved into a Catholic junior seminary in Bastogne. "We always seemed to headquarter in a church building," he wrote. "The rector of the seminary came to me with a problem. 'I have about thirty boys here,' he said. 'Do you think I should try to get them out of Bastogne or not?'" Father Sampson found it impossible to answer. "I can't tell you, Father," he responded. "I really don't know what would be best. There may be some fighting in the city later on. Do you have a deep basement where you can take the boys if it comes to that? On the other hand, we know that we are just about surrounded and in a day or so may be entirely surrounded . . . we may be now, for all I know." In the end, Father Sampson commented he was not much help to the rector.[32]

As the 501st entered the battle, the fighting was fierce. George Koskimaki, in his book *The Battered Bastards of Bastogne*, relates the poignant story of a medic, Technician 5th Grade Leon Jedziniak, who went with Father Francis Sampson to the aid of a wounded soldier. Jedziniak wrote: "Just outside of Bastogne, the unit was pinned down by machine gun fire. We crawled to a ravine by a viaduct that had a railroad track. The call 'Medic up front!' came back. I learned a wounded man was lying in an exposed position beside the railroad tracks about seventy-five yards ahead. Father Sampson, a rifleman, and myself advanced to where the wounded man was lying."[33] Despite concluding the man had little chance of survival, Jedziniak and Sampson had advanced seventy-five yards under sniper and tank fire to where the wounded man was lying unconscious. The three dragged him back to US lines in the face of heavy enemy fire that forced them to crawl their way back. Jedziniak's citation for a Bronze Star Medal noted a bullet went through his jacket and another threw dust into his eyes, temporarily blinding him. Still Jedziniak and Father Sampson succeeded in bringing the soldier to a safe position from which he was evacuated.[34]

Father Sampson described as follows what appears to be the same story, the experience of rescuing a wounded soldier as the 501st moved toward its objective on December 19, 1944:

I attached myself, for the time being, to a company just a mile or so east of the city. A soldier told me that there was a man a couple hundred yards down the road in a culvert by the railroad tracks. He was wounded and he called out for a priest (a rare request under the circumstances, for a man just doesn't count on a priest being on hand everywhere). I asked the soldier to take me to him and grabbed an aid man to help me. A German tank had been knocked out on the road between us and the wounded man, but a German was still manning the machine gun on the tank. As we skirted his immediate area and started to climb through the fence, he let go at us. The soldier leading us had the upper bone of his arm shattered by a bullet. We all three took a dive in that ditch by the railroad track. The wounded soldier pointed out with his good arm where the man I was looking for was located. The medic and I went to him. We were pinned down by crossfire. I lay down beside the wounded man, heard his confession and anointed him. He uttered not a word of complaint but expressed his thanks. He felt everything was going to be all right now. The aid man indicated with a shake of the head that the man didn't have a chance, but we carried him back to our position and some other men took him to the aid station. I never heard whether he lived or not; he was not from our regiment.[35]

EWELL REGROUPS

While Colonel Ewell's 2nd Battalion took the village of Bizory without incident, he recognized the 3rd Battalion was still tied up in a traffic jam in Bastogne, such that by noon on December 19 they had scarcely moved. Ewell finally got them going, ordering Lt. Col. George M. Griswold to march the battalion to Mont, a hamlet lying to the south of Neffe. Ewell also ordered Griswold to send Company I of his 3rd Battalion down the road to Wiltz, to the southeast of Bastogne, to cover the 3rd Battalion's flank. Griswold was prevented from taking Mont by fire from the Panzer Lehr tanks on the higher ground near Neffe, making it impossible to cross the forbidding open stretch of land in the mile or so that separated Mont from Neffe. Griswold fell back to Neffe, while Company I joined up with elements from Team O'Hara of the 10th Armored Division Combat Command B near Marvie. Toward nightfall, Ewell concluded he had gone as far with his offensive action as he could in the face of stiff enemy resistance. He ordered his three battalions to break contact with the enemy and to fall back to defend a general line along the high ground to the west of Bizory and Neffe. That night, Ewell returned to McAuliffe's division headquarters where McAuliffe and his G-3 Kinnard looked over and approved his plans for holding the high ground outside Neff.[36]

When walking back through Bastogne, Ewell encountered a sergeant from Company I in an apparently dazed condition who asked him, "Colonel, have you heard about Company I? We have been wiped out." In disbelief, Ewell got back to his radio and discovered the report was nearer correct than Ewell at first supposed. Company I had lost about eighty-five troopers and five officers in heavy combat around Wardin, with the survivors so scattered about that it was no longer possible to form even a platoon. Ewell had just assumed Company I had followed without problem his orders to disengage from the enemy and withdraw to the high ground. Ewell was surprised to learn that seven German tanks and an infantry battalion from Panzer Lehr had pulverized Company I before it could withdraw.[37] This news reinforced Ewell's conclusion that his order had been correct. "Shocked and angered by the loss, the 501st commander had only one consolation: this was conclusive evidence that he had been right in not rushing headlong toward Longvilly, to get sliced up from the rear by the Germans' crack panzer division," journalist Fred MacKenzie commented.[38]

Colonel O'Hara had reached the identical conclusion. At 1530 on the afternoon of December 19, Team O'Hara forces encountered high-velocity fire from the vicinity of Wardin, aimed at knocking out the unit's tanks. But when Team O'Hara's tanks withdrew one hundred yards onto a defilade, the firing ceased. The Nazis advanced close enough to fire a bazooka round at a Team O'Hara tank, but the rocket fell five yards short. Then, when four walking wounded from Company I of the 501st's 3rd Battalion came through the Team O'Hara lines, O'Hara learned of the tragedy that had befallen Company I. Alarmed at the losses taken by Company I, O'Hara radioed Colonel Roberts at 10th Armored CCB's headquarters in Bastogne and requested permission to withdraw. He received a reply, "Contact the friends on your left, hold what you have." When O'Hara realized headquarters did not fully appreciate the combat situation, he sent his assistant, Capt. George A. Renoux, back to Bastogne to explain in person what O'Hara did not want to explain over the radio. At 1715 on, O'Hara received permission to withdraw to the high ground north of Marvie. This suited O'Hara just fine, as this was exactly the area he had selected as the best to defend.[39]

In Ewell's estimate, the success of the 501st on December 19 was measured not by the number of the enemy killed but by the tactical surprise that he had managed to work on the Nazis, so as to bring the German advance to a halt. "I felt it was contact along a wide front where troops were advancing against them which put the Germans off stride," Ewell said in his oral history after the battle. "They stopped to consider and then they could not get started again. Until that time they had been meeting little groups of troops, encircling them and then gobbling them up. We gave them what they least expected to find."

Ewell also credited the success of the 501st to the fact the soldiers were paratroopers. "I think too that discovering that they were up against parachute troops made a difference," Ewell continued. "They captured some of our men at Wardin, and they knew from there on that they were fighting the 101st."[40] When the news of the disaster that befell Company I reached General McAuliffe, he knew immediately that the intelligence estimates of VIII Corps were completely inaccurate. While Ewell had been sent out with a mission to secure the road to the east of Bastogne as far as Longvilly, there was no way this objective could be achieved without taking losses that may have ended right there any chance of successfully defending Bastogne.[41]

MIDDLETON LEAVES BASTOGNE

Early on the morning of December 19, General Middleton departed Bastogne for Neufchâteau in a two-vehicle convoy that arrived shortly after dawn.[42] By midmorning December 19, General McAuliffe had moved his headquarters from the schoolhouse in Mande-Saint-Étienne to the headquarters vacated by General Middleton in the Heintz Barracks. But instead of occupying the two-story brick administration building VIII Corps had vacated, McAuliffe directed his staff to set up their operations room in one of the half-dozen or so relatively modest barracks arranged along the north side of the central courtyard.[43] Kinnard had advised that if the Germans should attack the command post, this position would be easier to defend. The space McAuliffe occupied was partly underground, but there was an exit through a stairway leading to a double-door exit to ground level. As if to stress the determination to defend this command post, the paratroopers even rolled up an anti-tank vehicle, with the gun pointing outward, to cover the exit just in case of a panzer tank attack.[44]

As McAuliffe settled into his new quarters, Danahy, the 101st's G-2 intelligence officer, surveyed the battle situation on the operations map in the new command post. At 1430 hours on December 19, when infantry from Ewell's 501st finally reached Cherry's château command post, they found it had been set on fire by enemy hand grenades. At 1600 hours, Cherry pulled out of the château and moved to Mont, nearly two miles to the west of Neffe. On moving out, Cherry's message to Roberts at the CCB command post in Bastogne was, "We're not driven out. We were burned out. We are not withdrawing. We are moving."[45] Still, Danahy declared success. While the situation remained desperate, Bastogne was still in US hands. "We are throwing everything we've got at them to save Bastogne," Danahy reflected, "but at least the Germans aren't west of Bastogne yet."[46]

THE LOSS OF THE HOSPITAL

A major setback was suffered by the 101st on December 19 when the Germans captured the airborne division's field hospital. The 101st had decided to set up the field hospital at a crossroads northwest of Flamierge and southwest of Bastogne, in an open field at an intersection the GIs had nicknamed "Crossroads X." Middleton and McAuliffe considered it likely the initial fighting would be to the east of Bastogne, as the Nazis advanced out of the Ardennes. Thus, the crossroads area was considered to be in a safe area in the rear. Lt. Col. David Gold, the surgeon of the 101st Division, and Lt. Col. Carl W. Kohls, the division supply officer, put the field hospital here, convinced the crossroads area was a safe location with available water, good access, and several buildings that could provide protection—an ideal location for the division hospital and evacuation center. Working diligently, the medical staff got ready to start receiving casualties.[47]

The attack occurred around 2230 hours, when a half-dozen German armored vehicles including tanks and half-tracks, accompanied by some one hundred infantrymen, ran into an American truck convoy. PFC Don M. Dobbins, who had been transporting injured troops to the field hospital, was captured. Finding the field hospital as a consequence, the Germans hit with machine-gun fire the hospital tents, ignoring the red crosses prominently showing in the light of the burning trucks the Germans had destroyed in the convoy with which Dobbins was traveling. After the truck convoy was destroyed, a German officer approached the medical station and gave Dr. Gold thirty minutes to pack up and load his personnel and his patients for transfer to German POW facilities.[48]

As midnight approached on December 19, the 327th Glider Infantry dispatched a motorized patrol to Crossroads X to investigate reports of machine-gun fire in that vicinity. When the patrol arrived, they found to their astonishment that the hospital was gone. The 327th patrol concluded there must have been a fight. Dead Germans in civilian clothes were found strewn around the ground, evidencing a fight had taken place. But there were no bodies of American soldiers. The 327th patrol concluded Colonel Gold and his entire medical staff had been captured. The Germans took 11 medical officers and 119 enlisted men of the 326th Medical Company, plus seven officers and five enlisted men from surgical units. The bulk of the medical supplies were captured or destroyed, leaving the 101st Airborne Division with a 501st aid station set up in a building in Bastogne that was suddenly the division's only hospital facility.

PFC Elmer Lucas, a member of the 101st's Airborne Division's 326th Medical Company, gave a statement in France in April 1945, in which he explained how the field hospital had been captured. He described that at about 2200 hours on December 19, as the field hospital was yet being established and only a few casualties had been received from the battle around Bastogne, the facility at Crossroads X began receiving fire from automatic weapons. "When the fire began, some of the member of the company were in the main company area near fox holes and stayed there," he said. "Others who were farther west ran into the forest and put a good deal of distance between them and the firing. After fifteen minutes of this sporadic fire, the Germans edged their way forward and, although I am not sure how it occurred, captured some of our officers." Lucas described that the hospital staff were taken by surprise. "I was approximately 100 yards away and in the night I could not see who was captured and could not see if Colonel Gold was among them. Several persons speaking in English—I think that they were our officers—told the men not to resist but to give up." Lucas reported the majority of the Treatment Section, the Surgical Teams, and part of the Headquarters Section were captured. "In the fire I know that some of our people were killed and wounded and I, myself, was taken prisoner by Germans in civilian clothes." Lucas claimed he escaped being taken away by the Germans as a POW by jumping into a ditch when a US truck driver came on the scene, stopped, and began firing on the Germans with his 50-caliber machine gun.[49]

Technical 4 Emil Natalle, who had been assigned to work with the surgical group acting in concert with the 326th Medical Company, described the violence of the German attack on the field hospital and evacuation center:

I was not scheduled for surgical duty so I settled into my foxhole early, as we had been on the move for the previous twenty-four hours. Sleep came quickly but the repose was brief.

About eleven o'clock, out of the dark, broke the light like day. Artillery, mortars, small arms fire, aerial flares combined in a veritable fireworks. German troops and armor were quickly in our hospital area. Firing ceased. The German OIC [Officer in Charge] asked for the US OIC. Finding the US officer in charge, the German asked for our surrender.

The Germans were all over the area. They hollered, laughed, and made noise, just as Germans always do. It was bedlam. And to think that only a few minutes earlier, the place was a peaceful meadow somewhere in the Ardennes.[50]

Natalle was forced to suffer the indignity of driving one of the trucks from the field hospital into captivity. He described the experience as follows:

Meanwhile, back on the hill at the hospital site, the US trucks, trailers, and other vehicles had been loaded with all the hospital's equipment and were set to vacate the area. I was told to drive one of the trucks. It was loaded with the wounded on stretchers (litters). A German soldier rode "shotgun" beside me. The convoy of 326th Medical Company POWs headed east from the crossroads site. It was the beginning of the end for the US Army's first-ever airborne surgical team and some 150 or more personnel of the 101st's unique surgical hospital.[51]

Those captured from the medical facility were on the trucks for several days, moving during daylight, while hiding at night in farm buildings and barnyards. As POWs, the Bastogne medical facility captives joined a larger group of prisoners from the 106th Infantry Division on their march into Germany.

The loss of the field hospital left the 101st at the beginning of the siege in dire straits for adequate medical staff or supplies. Scrounging around, paratroopers of the 101st found a medical supply depot abandoned when VIII Corps moved headquarters from Bastogne to Neufchâteau. That was supplemented by another army medical supply dump located in Bastogne by

Capt. Robert Smith, a civil affairs officer assigned to 101st Division command. These caches contained blankets, litters, splint baskets, and a miscellaneous assortment of medical supplies that helped compensate for the loss.[52] Despite this discovery, the troops still faced a shortage of blankets, litters, penicillin, surgical instruments, other medical equipment, and surgeons. Casualties throughout the siege were brought to the makeshift medical facilities set up in the town of Bastogne. As casualties mounted, medical staff began placing new arrivals on concrete floors without covers. Supply officers went through the town requesting blankets and quilts from the civilians. From the December 19 attack on the Crossroads medical facility, only eight officers and forty-four men of the medical detachment escaped.[53]

To McAuliffe and Middleton, the loss of the hospital facility signified that the Germans had advanced around Bastogne in sufficient numbers that attacks from the west now had to be considered possible, if not likely. The loss of the field hospital also suggested Germans would encircle Bastogne much more quickly than Allied command had initially anticipated.

TEAM DESOBRY AND THE BATTLE FOR NOVILLE

The battle for Noville began at approximately 0530 hours on the morning of December 19, when a group of half-tracks first heard in the distance began approaching Desobry's defenses in the darkness just before dawn. Unable to tell if the approaching troops were friend or enemy, the sentry shouted, "Halt!" four times. When the first vehicle came to a grinding halt a few yards ahead of him, someone in the half-track yelled something in German. Hearing this, US troops from a bank on the right of the road showered down hand grenades on the half-track as German soldiers jumped from the vehicle and lay dead or wounded in the road. At this the rest of the enemy column unloaded and deployed in the ditches along the road. What ensued was a twenty-minute fight punctuated by exploding grenades and the staccato fire of automatic weapons. Seeing German infantry advancing behind the half-tracks, S. Sgt. Leon D. Gantt ordered his men to withdraw from the advance roadblock one hundred yards back toward Noville.[54]

At approximately 1030 hours, the German attack on Noville began in earnest. "The defenders had heard the rumblings of tanks and the puttering of small vehicles out in the fog as if a tremendous build-up were going on," S. L. A. Marshall recorded. "Quite suddenly the fog lifted like a curtain going up and revealing the stage. The countryside was filled with tanks."[55] Desobry's defenders quickly realized Noville stood square in the path of an entire panzer division. Seeing that the leading enemy formations were about one thousand yards away, Desobry's troops opened up fire with whatever weapons they had available. Marshall commented that distance made no difference, even to the men with .50 caliber machine guns, as everybody began firing with whatever weapons they had. When the enemy closed to eight hundred yards, fourteen German tanks on the ridge stopped and began shelling the village. On the left flank of the enemy advance, when the fog curtain fully lifted, enemy tanks were as close as two hundred yards away from Desobry's defenders.[56]

"The events of the next hour were shaped by the flashes of the heavy guns and the vagaries of the ever-shifting fog," Marshall continued. "The guns rolled in measure according to a visibility that came and went in the passage of only a few seconds."[57] Team Desobry soldiers fired at the German infantry, following on foot the tanks moving forward into the battle. At just the right moment, a platoon from the 609th Tank Destroyer Battalion rolled into Noville, adding the firepower of four badly needed tank destroyers to the battle. Nine German Mark IV and Mark V tanks were hit and exploded into flames as the clearing fog along a ridge line made the German tanks stand out "like ducks in a shooting gallery."[58] At a range of six hundred yards, an American cavalryman engaged a panzer tank with his armored car and knocked it out with one shot from his 37mm gun, a shot Marshall called "the most miraculous hit of the morning."[59]

By 1130 hours the initial German assault on Noville had quieted to intermittent shelling. The lifting of the fog had made Desobry acutely aware that the surrounding terrain put his defensive efforts at a tremendous disadvantage. With the Germans occupying the ridges on the three sides of Noville, the enemy could pull their tanks into a protected defilade against the back side of the hills on the ridge to establish a safe position from which they could keep the town under close artillery fire. Much as Roberts had predicted before sending Desobry into the field of battle, Desobry began having second thoughts about falling back to the high ground at Foy. This strategic withdrawal would give him the advantage he believed he needed to make a successful defense of the key road into Bastogne from the north. In the lull of the battle, Desobry called Roberts and requested permission to withdraw down the road to Foy. Roberts was sympathetic to the request, but he urged Desobry to hold out, believing he could get some relief from the 101st Airborne Division that had been pouring into the assembly area west of Bastogne all night.[60]

After talking with Desobry, Roberts left his 10th Armored CCB command post in the Hotel LeBrun in the center of Bastogne to go looking for McAuliffe. Before he found McAuliffe, Roberts encountered Brig. Gen. Gerald J. Higgins, the assistant commander of the 101st Airborne. While they were conferring, the advance elements of the 1st Battalion of the 506th Parachute Infantry Regiment came up behind them, marching into Bastogne from the assembly area under the command of Col. Robert F. Sink. Higgins ordered Sink to send a battalion forward to assist Desobry. Sink in turn gave the assignment to the 1st Battalion under Lt. Col. James LaPrade, ordering LaPrade to proceed immediately up the road north to Noville. Higgins further directed that Sink should hold his 2nd and 3rd battalions in division reserve just north of Bastogne. Roberts then went back to the telephone and urged Desobry to use his judgment about abandoning Noville, advising him that if he could hold Noville, a battalion of paratroopers was on the way to help.[61] Desobry decided to stay in Noville, and LaPrade arrived with the 1st Battalion of the 506th PIR at around 1330 hours that afternoon.[62]

Before being ordered to Bastogne, the 10th Armored Division had been preparing for what they had anticipated would be a big offensive with Patton's Third Army in the south. Accompanying Combat Command B to Bastogne were several two-and-a-half-ton trucks the supply officers of the 10th Armored had loaded with everything they could find—including uniforms and winter clothes, as well as weapons and ammunitions. In the vicinity of Foy, Roberts placed his supply vehicles on either side of the road to accommodate the paratroopers of the 1st Battalion of the 506th as the paratroopers advanced in a typical paratrooper marching formation of two single columns on either side of the road. As the paratroopers marched by, the supply officers of the 10th Armored CCB gave them what they needed, whether it was M-1 rifles, ammunition, or clothes and winter boots.[63]

Members of the 101st Airborne head north out of Bastogne to assist in the defense of Noville. December 19, 1944.

An attempt to attack the Germans as the 506th arrived at Noville stalled. LaPrade had a force of thirteen medium tanks, six tank destroyers, and a thousand men, no match for the Second Panzer's seven thousand men still armed with eighty of their starting eighty-eight tanks, along with a full array of eighty-eights and supplementary artillery. When the American attack failed, the Germans tried an assault of their own, about an hour later, with two columns of sixteen tanks backed by a battalion of Panzer Grenadiers. The German assault failed when the German tanks held back, out of respect for the American bazookas. As the Germans pulled back, smoke from Noville's now burning buildings thickened the fog that covered the battlefield.[64]

By 1700 hours that afternoon, Desobry pulled his troops back into Noville in defensive positions, with everyone near exhaustion given that they had been fighting since 0530 hours that morning. Desobry got word that LaPrade wanted to talk with him, so Desobry proceeded to the command

post that had been set up in the first floor of a small house in the center of
the town. When Desobry arrived, he had his troops push a huge desk up
against the wall to the north for added protection, but the precaution soon
proved insufficient. Desobry described what happened as follows:

> Unfortunately my guys had put the CP up in a house alongside the road
> in the middle of the town, a very small house, on the first floor. When I
> got there and took a look at it, I was a little bit worried and so we took
> a great big huge Belgium schrang, and put it up against the wall, off to
> the north. We did this for added protection. I guess that would not pro-
> tect us too much, but we always think things like that might help. So we
> did that. Then LaPrade and I got over a map on a little table and he was
> showing me where he intended to put his paratroopers in the defense for
> a night. I agreed that well, if you put a company in there, I'll put some
> tanks in there and so on. While we were working on this defense, the
> maintenance officer, who had been evacuating crippled vehicles back to
> Bastogne, drove up in a VTR, a recovery vehicle that looks like a tank, and
> he parked it outside this CP. He came in to tell me that the job had been
> completed and that he was going on back to his company in Bastogne. He
> made the fundamental error, which we are all taught not to do, of driving
> any vehicle right up to a CP because that just shows whoever might be
> watching where the CP is.[65]

As Desobry continued the narrative, the Nazi reaction was predictable:

> The Germans that I had been fighting to the north of town and a little bit
> before apparently saw the VTR in the dark and they started shooting at
> it and as it normally is they missed the VTR and hit the building. When
> they hit the building they really took it down. And they killed LaPrade,
> I guess probably 10 to 12 guys, and I was badly wounded, hit in the face,
> head and eyes. The guys took me down into the cellar and when I came
> to they told me I was badly wounded and the doctor said that I had to go
> back to the hospital.[66]

But Desobry, despite being badly wounded, resisted:

So I said, "Well, I want to go back and talk to Colonel Roberts, the Combat Commander, because I was convinced that we couldn't stay in Noville, and that we had to get back on that ridgeline at Foy where we could do a much better job. But I wanted to go back and tell him. He hadn't come up to see us. The only ones that would come up to see us during the day were General Higgins from the 101st and Colonel [Robert F.] Sink, the [506th PIR] regimental commander, nobody from the 10th Armored. They knew what the situation was and they had agreed with us that we ought to go back to Foy. They didn't have the authority to say that though. So I wanted to go back and see Roberts and so I asked that they get my jeep and take me back there and so the driver went out to get the jeep and he never came back.[67]

Desobry, obviously too seriously wounded to continue in command, was evacuated from Noville. Though he protested he wanted to return to Bastogne to see Roberts, Desobry quickly fell unconscious. An ambulance of the 101st Airborne carried Desobry and other wounded from Noville back to Bastogne, and then on to the field hospital set up by the 326th Medical Group to the west of Bastogne. At the field hospital, Desobry was taken immediately into the operating tent, just in time for the German attack. When the Germans captured the field hospital, Desobry was captured. The first thing after being injured at Noville that Desobry remembered was waking up in the back of an ambulance as it moved down the road, headed for Germany. Desobry quickly realized he was a POW, along with the rest of the wounded and most members of the field hospital unit, including the surgeons. Ironically, being taken POW after the Germans overran the 326th Medical Group's field hospital probably saved Desobry's life.[68] The hospital established in Bastogne, after the capture of the field hospital, was completely destroyed by a direct hit in the fierce German shelling of Bastogne on Christmas Day, a disaster that killed all the wounded and the entire medical staff.

When Desobry was wounded, Maj. Robert F. Harwick, the executive officer of the 1st Battalion, 506th PIR, assumed the command of what then became "Team Harwick." As Harwick explained the situation, he had just arrived at the command post and started to set up a message center in a room adjoining the room where Desobry was meeting with LaPrade, when "a shell came through the window of the command post and I found myself in command of the forces around the town."[69] "About ten o'clock, we briefly contacted the regiment by radio," recalled Harwick, describing how desperate the situation at Noville had become. "I was afraid to tell our true situation over the air, and the message we received was, 'Hold at all costs.' That cost began to mount then, with a tank attack right down the road. Part of our infantry positions were lost, but the tank destroyers got their twentieth tank, which burned at the edge of town, setting fire to one of the few whole buildings."

As the German attack intensified, the 506th fighting at Noville began to realize it was a lost cause. "The situation was so acute that I called in the company and tank commanders. Another attack—surely, two—would end the affair for us. We drew up plans to fight a withdrawal. A jeep with two wounded men and a messenger who volunteered was sent down the road. The message was to General McAuliffe. It just said, 'We can hold out but not indefinitely.' There was no answer."[70] The jeep incident was described in detail in an article written by Collie Small for the *Saturday Evening Post*. "Finally, Captain Rennie Tye, of Memphis, Tennessee, volunteered to make a suicidal dash through the German-held town. Lying flat on the hood of a speeding jeep, with an automatic in his hand, Tye raced through Foy, firing until his ammunition was exhausted. One of two wounded men in the jeep was killed by a German machine gunner, but Tye was untouched."[71]

Late in the afternoon on December 19, McAuliffe telephoned Middleton to explain to the corps that commanders Higgins and Sink were both recommending that the troops pull back from Noville to Foy. Higgins had come to the conclusion that defending Noville might not be worth the price, given the terrain that placed the town effectively in the bottom of a bowl, with the Germans in control of the ridges that swept above the bowl. "I think we're way out on a limb," Higgins told McAuliffe, recommending that McAuliffe authorize a fallback from Noville to Foy. "There is much too much distance between LaPrade [1st Battalion of 506th PIR] at Noville and Strayer [3rd Battalion of 506th PIR] at Foy. It is my judgment that the Noville force had better get out."[72] Colonel Sink, commander of the 506th, had gone into the field and come to the same conclusion. At around 1820 hours, Sink called

McAuliffe and recommended his 1st Battalion be withdrawn to a point north of Foy. In speaking with Middleton, McAuliffe added his own recommendation that US forces should be withdrawn from Noville. Middleton disagreed. "No, if we are to hold on to Bastogne, you cannot keep falling back," he insisted.

McAuliffe called Sink and relayed the orders to hold Noville. By this time, Desobry, who had been removed from Noville unconscious and taken to the field hospital, was on his way to Germany, a prisoner of the attacking Germans who overran the field hospital.[73]

THE 705TH TANK DESTROYER
BATTALION ARRIVES AT BASTOGNE

"Another lucky ace up McAuliffe's sleeve was a fast-moving tank destroyer unit that managed to slip into Bastogne at the last minute," military historians Leo Barron and Don Cygan noted in *No Silent Night*.[74]

The 705th, an experienced unit that fought in the European theater since just after D-Day, was equipped with the lethal M18 "Hellcat" tank destroyer. The M18 was designed primarily to destroy enemy tanks in defensive fighting and was a weapon perfectly suited for what McAuliffe faced trying to hold Bastogne. Barron and Cygan described the M18 as follows: "The tracked vehicle had a powerful 76mm gun designed for penetrating thick German armor. But most incredibly, the Hellcat was one of the fastest military vehicles ever designed. It could travel on good roads at speeds over fifty-five miles per hour powered by its 460-horsepower radial aircraft engine."[75] As noted earlier, the M18 was designed to "shoot and scoot," so that instead of pressing into head-to-head combat with German armor, the M18 could race ahead to ambush German armor and then run away before German tanks could return fire. The only downside, Barron and Cygan noted, was that designers of the vehicle had traded speed for safety, arming the M18 with only one-half to one inch of steel, compared to an M4 Sherman tank's two-and-a-half-inch thick frontal armor. Neither stood up to the three or more inches of armor typically protecting the front of a German Panzerkampfwagen Mark IV tank.[76] Barron and Cygan cite Anthony C. Breder, a member of the 705th, who bluntly summed up the chances of surviving an armor-piercing hit to an M18 as follows: "They were pretty good tanks—the best the Americans ever made. Fast, you know—fifty-five miles per hour. No armor, though. If a German gun shot at you it went right through that armor like paper."[77]

The 705th, commanded by Lt. Col. Clifford D. Templeton, was holding the line at Kohlscheid, Germany, with the US Ninth Army when it received orders on December 18 to head south for Bastogne. A trip that should have been short was delayed and complicated by the "human flotsam and jet-sam" filling the roads, remnants of American units that had fallen victim to the German advance.[78] Having reached the heights outside La Rouche-en-Ardenne at 0915 hours on December 19, Templeton was alarmed at what he saw. "American units were in confusion along the road," S. L. A. Marshall wrote. "They were making little or no effort to adjust themselves to the situation or to set up a local defense. So in midmorning Templeton sent two platoons with four tank destroyers to set up a roadblock to the north of the town."[79] Templeton then left the battalion at La Rouche-en-Ardenne and went on to Neufchâteau to meet with General Middleton in his recently established VIII Corps headquarters. When he arrived at Neufchâteau, Middleton ordered Templeton to go to Bastogne and attach his unit to the 101st Airborne Division.

Templeton's 705th Tank Destroyer Battalion reached Bastogne at 2030 hours on December 19, to the delight of General McAuliffe. With the arrival of the 705th, all the major fighting elements that would be present through the Siege of Bastogne had arrived. "The 101st Division and Combat Command B had begun the fight that morning and the tank destroyers were now ready to link their power with that of the armor and the infantry," S. L. A. Marshall noted. "Men of every unit had morale of the highest quality and with their weapons each was capable of stiffening the other. It was a matter of finding the way through courage, resource, and good will."[80] Military historians Leo Barron and Don Cygan agreed: "To say that Templeton's tank destroyers with their long, 76mm armor-piercing guns would come in handy defending Bastogne from Manteuffel's panzers would be a huge understatement. By the second day of their arrival, they were already proving their worth, successfully defending the northeastern approaches to town."[81]

AFRICAN AMERICANS FIGHTING AT BASTOGNE

Rarely chronicled is the involvement of the African Americans who fought at Bastogne. The 969th Field Artillery Battalion was an African American artillery unit equipped with five 155mm howitzers that was originally assigned to support the 28th Infantry Division. Stranded when the 28th Infantry Division began to collapse, General McAuliffe was happy to reassign the 969th to provide additional much-needed field artillery support. The other African American unit was the 333rd Field Artillery Battalion that moved to Bastogne on December 16 at less than full strength. The 333rd suffered heavier losses in the Siege of Bastogne than any other military unit assigned to VIII Corps, with six officers and 222 enlisted men killed.[82] The 969th received the Distinguished Unit Citation from General Patton for its "unflinching performance" holding Bastogne.[83]

Field artillery unit fires a 155-mm howitzer in action against advancing Germans, Bastogne, Belgium. December 1944.

BASTOGNE ENCIRCLED BUT SECURE

The first round of the battle at Noville had convinced General McAuliffe that the Germans were "full of fight."[84] The general sent the 1st Battalion of the 506th to assist Major Desobry at Noville because he felt Desobry's 10th Armored task force was a "little armed force in trouble."[85] Still, McAuliffe held the remaining two battalions of the 506th in reserve. "All along I figured that it was best to keep the maximum of my forces in hand so that I could quickly meet threats as they developed," McAuliffe recalled in his after-action oral history given to S. L. A. Marshall's field staff. "It was in line with the same policy that some of the battalions which were engaged were maneuvered directly from division—the battalion that fought at Noville, for example."[86] In the afternoon of December 19, McAuliffe ordered Company C of the 705th Tank Destroyer Battalion to the 506th and he moved the 502nd Regiment into place so it could be deployed on the northern flank as needed the following day. Clearly he anticipated holding Noville meant continued heavy fighting.

Wounded paratrooper of 502nd Parachute Infantry Regiment being brought by jeep to the 101st Division aid station at Bastogne. December 21, 1944.

"Yet on the whole, that first night in Bastogne, the situation was good, and it was largely the intuition and hunch and driving energy of the leaders that had made it so," Marshall concluded. "The day of the 19th had proved that in the few minutes allowed him the night before, General McAuliffe had sized up the position properly."[87] Marshall noted that McAuliffe had been tossed into a battle in which nearly all the major facts had been either unknown or obscure. "The first day's results proved the angels had been with him as he made his first decisions," Marshall reflected.[88]

That evening, Colonel Kinnard recommended that to defend Bastogne, McAuliffe should assign each regiment of the 101st Airborne Division to protect a sector of the defense perimeter that was beginning to form like a wheel, with the various roads leading into and out of town serving as the spokes. "The perimeter would be based on the ordinal directions spreading out from Bastogne, with the town center as its hub and headquarters," explained Barron and Cygan in *No Silent Night*. "Each unit would be responsible for that sector's outlying villages or one or more of the seven roads leading into the city. McAuliffe and his staff knew the Germans would try to seize these roads and towns for lines of attack into Bastogne."[89] McAuliffe thought Kinnard's idea made sense. "The German tanks would be forced to use these inroads, as the open fields around Bastogne were soft and muddy," Barron and Cygan explained. "Any remaining land was either too hilly or thick with woodlets—impossible for armored vehicles to penetrate."[90] In addition, by holding the 3rd Battalion of the 506th and the 502nd out of the immediate battle in Noville, McAuliffe realized he could design a centralized reserve of forces that could reach any part of the perimeter quickly, as needed to plug holes or to counterattack as the opportunity presented itself. "Most of all," Barron and Cygan concluded, "McAuliffe wanted to use his artillery and the available armor to separate the German infantry from their tanks. McAuliffe's plan was for the paratroopers to kill the Panzergrenadiers while the tanks, tank destroyers, and antitank guns took care of the panzers."[91] By bringing his artillery to a central location near the hub in Bastogne, McAuliffe figured he could hit almost anything within a seven-mile radius.[92]

McAuliffe explained his thinking to Marshall's historians in his after-action oral account of the battle:

I had eleven battalions of artillery by the time Ewell attacked, and they were all tied in by the morning of 19th December. I estimate that half the enemy attacks were broken up by our artillery: that is what the POWs said. The Germans were full of beans on that first day but each day thereafter they seemed less formidable to me, and I felt that their assaults were not being pressed as hard and as wisely. The attacks which weren't wholly disarranged by artillery fire were at least partly slowed when we put our [artillery fire] down. The marks are there today: in any of the woods around Mont, Marvie, Neffe, Noville, and Champs there are hundreds of bodies blown to pieces. We used massive fire over 360 degrees. All of the 105s had circular gun pits and were ready to fire in any direction. At times we moved some of the guns up to where they could fire direct against the tanks at six hundred yards: this was the only exception.[93]

Barron and Cygan came up with an interesting image to describe McAuliffe's defense strategy: "The Americans must have felt as if they were reliving ancient European history and 'gazing from the ramparts,' like some throwback to a medieval siege. Bastogne was their fortress, with the roaring armor and approaching men of Hitler's vaunted Wehrmacht gathering like barbarians from all four directions to surmount them."[94]

McAuliffe was in the catbird seat as an artillery commander of a paratrooper division. After all, paratroopers were trained to successfully conduct missions being dropped behind enemy lines where by definition the paratroopers expected to be surrounded by the enemy from the get-go. So, for the paratroopers of the 101st Airborne to realize Bastogne was quickly being encircled by advancing German troops was not the same matter of concern a regular infantry division might have felt being surrounded in the field of battle. Still, McAuliffe sorely appreciated the support provided by the 10th Armored.

In "Tigers on the Loose," an episode of *The Big Picture*, a television documentary originally broadcast on ABC in 1965, some twenty-one years after the end of the battle, Col. William Roberts and Gen. Anthony McAuliffe each gave statements in their own words reflecting upon the importance of having both the 10th Armored Division Combat Command B and the 101st Airborne Division in the Siege of Bastogne fighting together. "In thinking it over, I've decided that if we had been in Bastogne without any infantry, we couldn't have held ten minutes," Roberts said, wearing a sport coat and a tie, seated comfortably in what appeared to be the living room or study of his home. "The 101st Airborne without the steel that my outfit afforded could not have held. But the steel of my outfit and the blood and flesh of their outfit made a pretty tough combination." McAuliffe was equally generous. "It seems regrettable to me that Combat Command B of the 10th Armored Division didn't get the credit it deserved at the Siege of Bastogne," McAuliffe said, wearing a suit and a tie, standing outside in sunny, warm weather. "Actually the 10th Armored Division was in there a day before we were and had some very hard fighting before we ever got into it, and I sincerely believe that we would never have been able to get into Bastogne if it had not been for the defense fighting of the three elements of the 10th Armored Division [Team Cherry, Team O'Hara, and Team Desobry] who were the first into Bastogne and protected the town from invasion by the Germans."[95]

GERMANS FAIL TO TAKE BASTOGNE

Michael Collins and Michael King in *The Tigers of Bastogne* noted that after the Battle of the Bulge, German Fifth Army Commander Hasso van Manteuffel claimed the Germans lost the initiative as early as December 18.[96] This was certainly the case at Noville. Collins and King pointed out that a military axiom of war typically predicts attackers with a three-to-one advantage or more have a realistic chance of obtaining their objectives. Yet the Germans of the 2nd Panzer failed to do so, in large part because the vagaries of the ever-shifting fog meant neither side was ever entirely sure how strong the other side was. "As the fog occasionally lifted it became apparent that the Germans had a whole panzer division in the area, but initially there was a lot of muscle flexing and posturing from both sides as they established who had what and who was where," Collins and King observed.[97] In the other sector of heavy fighting on December 19, the paratroopers of the 501st under Ewell in support of Team Cherry consolidated their defensive position to the east of Bastogne, on the road leading to Longvilly and Wardin. "The period of greatest confusion, on the American side at least, was over," concluded historian John S. D. Eisenhower in *The Bitter Woods*.[98]

NEWS ON HOMEFRONT ALARMING

The news reports from the European Theater were becoming increasingly alarming. "Germans Sweep West Through Luxembourg," Drew Middleton reported in the *New York Times* in a front-page article datelined from the Supreme Headquarters of the Allied Expeditionary Force and published on December 23, 1944. "The great German winter offensive smashed westward through Belgium unchecked today for the seventh consecutive day," Middleton wrote. "Although American infantry and tanks have managed to hold positions along the sides of the flood tide of enemy soldiery, the advance in the center shows no signs of slowing down. By late Wednesday panzer units had swept through the duchy of Luxembourg, isolated the great railroad communications center of Bastogne in Belgium and then pushed on thirteen and a half miles northwest to the vicinity of La Roche."[99] While the detail about the developing Bastogne siege was sketchy, Americans reading Middleton's dispatches began consulting their maps and atlases.

SECTION III

PATTON HEADS NORTH

It was impossible, Patton believed, to bear the burden of command and the incomparable stresses of war without divine guidance.

—Michael Keane, *Patton: Blood, Guts, and Prayer*, 2012[1]

A lifelong student of war, Gen. George S. Patton Jr.'s constant standing order was to attack. While Patton's aggressiveness in battle is commonly understood, less well appreciated is his belief in God and his devotion to prayer. Yet for students of Patton who have read his published letters and diaries, there can be no doubt Patton believed in God, to the point where he felt God had destined him to achieve military greatness. Through the many ups and downs of his military career, Patton was also a devout Episcopalian who read the Bible daily.

In 1948, four years after the Siege of Bastogne, the chaplain who wrote Patton's famous prayer for good weather, Chaplain James Hugh O'Neill, relayed a conversation he had with Patton on December 8, 1944, in which Patton explained the importance he gave to prayer. "Chaplain, I am a strong believer in prayer," Patton confessed to Chaplain O'Neill. "There are three ways that men get what they want: by planning, by working, and by praying. Any great military operation takes careful planning, or thinking. Then you must have well-trained troops to carry it out: that's working. But between the plan and the operation there is always an unknown. That unknown spells defeat or victory, success or failure. It is the reaction of the actors to the ordeal when it actually comes. Some people call that getting the breaks; I call it God. God has His part, or margin, in everything. That's where prayer comes in."[2]

Patton explained he was thinking of publishing for all the chaplains assigned to the Third Army a special training letter dedicated to expounding upon the importance of prayer, with the goal of stressing that soldiers in his Third Army should learn to pray no matter where they were, including praying on the field of combat as equal to praying in church. Patton feared that if his troops did not learn to pray in combat they would "crack up" from the stress of battle. He explained:

> Up to now, in the Third Army, God has been very good to us. We have never retreated; we have suffered no defeats, no famine, no epidemics. This is because a lot of people back home are praying for us. We were lucky in Africa, in Sicily, and in Italy. Simply because people prayed. But we have to pray for ourselves, too. A good soldier is not made merely by making him think and work. There is something in every soldier that goes deeper than thinking or working—it's his "guts." It is something that he has built in there: it is a world of truth and power that is higher than himself. Great living is not all output of thought and work. A man has to have intake as well. I don't know what you call it, but I call it Religion, Prayer, or God.[3]

O'Neill left from this conversation to write what he titled Training Letter No. 5, inspired by Patton's reverie on prayer. The next day, Patton read it and without change ordered that it be circulated not only to the 486 chaplains then serving the Third Army by ministering to thirty-two different denominations, but also to every Third Army commander down to and including the regimental level. Three thousand two hundred copies were distributed to every unit in the Third Army over O'Neill's signature as Third Army chaplain.

Issued with a dateline, December 14, 1944, two days before the Battle of the Bulge began, Training Letter No. 5 read as follows:

Our glorious march from the Normandy Beach across France to where we stand, before and beyond the Siegfried Line, with the wreckage of the German Army behind us should convince the most skeptical soldier that God has ridden with our banner. Pestilence and famine have not touched us. We have continued in unity of purpose. We have had no quitters; and our leadership has been masterful. The Third Army has no roster of Retreats. None of Defeats. We have no memory of a lost battle to hand on to our children from this great campaign.

But we are not stopping at the Siegfried Line. Tough days may be ahead of us before we eat our rations in the Chancellery of the Deutsches Reich.

As chaplains it is our business to pray. We preach its importance. We urge its practice. But the time is now to intensify our faith in prayer, not alone with ourselves, but with every believing man, Protestant, Catholic, Jew, or Christian in the ranks of the Third United States Army.

Those who pray do more for the world than those who fight; and if the world goes from bad to worse, it is because there are more battles than prayers. "Hands lifted up," said [French bishop and theologian Jacques-Bénigne] Bossuet, "smash more battalions than hands that strike." Gideon of Bible fame was least in his father's house. He came from Israel's smallest tribe. But he was a mighty man of valor. His strength lay not in his military might, but in his recognition of God's proper claims upon his life. He reduced his Army from thirty-two thousand to three hundred men lest the people of Israel would think that their valor had saved them. We have no intention to reduce our vast striking force. But we must urge, instruct, and indoctrinate every fighting man to pray as well as fight. In Gideon's day, and in our own, spiritually alert minorities carry the burdens and bring the victories.

Urge all of your men to pray, not alone in church, but everywhere. Pray when driving. Pray when fighting. Pray alone. Pray with others. Pray by night and pray by day. Pray for the cessation of immoderate rains, for good weather for Battle. Pray for the defeat of our wicked enemy whose banner is injustice and whose good is oppression. Pray for victory. Pray for our Army, and Pray for Peace.

We must march together, all out for God. The soldier who "cracks up" does not need sympathy or comfort as much as he needs strength. We are not trying to make the best of these days. It is our job to make the most of them. Now is not the time to follow God from "afar off." This Army needs the assurance and the faith that God is with us. With prayer, we cannot fail.

Be assured that this message on prayer has the approval, the encouragement, and the enthusiastic support of the Third United States Army Commander.

With every good wish to each of you for a very Happy Christmas, and my personal congratulations for your splendid and courageous work since landing on the beach, I am G. S. Patton, Jr, Lieutenant General, Commanding Third United States Army.[4]

Chaplain O'Neill ended the recollection by adding, "It was late in January of 1945 when I saw the army commander again. This was in the city of Luxembourg. He stood directly in front of me, smiled: 'Well, Padre, our prayers worked. I knew they would.' Then he cracked me on the side of my steel helmet with his riding crop. That was his way of saying, 'Well done.'"[5]

CHAPTER 7

A DARING PLAN

More than any other single point in his career, this was Patton's
defining moment. He proposed to turn almost an entire army
ninety degrees to the north, force-march it through ice and snow
forty miles or more, then, without rest, commit it to a counterattack
against an enemy tasting victory for the first time in many months.

—Alan Axelrod, *Patton: A Biography*, 2006[1]

When the Germans launched their Wacht am Rhein offensive on December 16, 1944, Patton was only days away from launching his own planned offensive into the Saar on the southern flank of the US line facing Germany. His first impulse on hearing the Germans had attacked Middleton's VIII Corps was to launch his attack immediately, calculating the Germans pushing into the Ardennes would be unable to repulse an attack by Patton in the south. Patton felt certain that if he launched his planned attack now, the Germans would be forced to break off the Ardennes offensive to counter him from plunging a Third Army tank charge deep into the heart of the Nazi Third Reich.

THE REAL DEAL

Believing an army not on the move invites counterattack, Patton quickly blamed Eisenhower and Bradley for having tempted Hitler to take his bold move. On December 17, 1944, the second day of the German offensive, Patton confided the following to his diary:

> The German attack is on a wide front and moving fast. . . . This may be a feint . . . although at the moment it looks like the real thing. If the Germans . . . are intending to attack me, we will stop them as we are very well placed.
>
> Had the V and VIII Corps of the First Army been more aggressive, the Germans could not have prepared this attack; one must never sit still.[2]

As noted earlier, at the start of the Battle of the Bulge, Patton was irate when General Bradley ordered the 10th Armored Division moved from Patton's command and reassigned to Middleton's VIII Corps to help repulse what Bradley characterized as "a rather strong German attack."[3] At that point unaware of the scale of the German attack, Patton protested, arguing to Bradley that the Third Army needed the 10th Armored in case the Germans extended the offensive south into his area. Patton knew Bradley well enough to be concerned that Bradley reassigning the 10th Armored could be the first step in Bradley postponing or canceling his offensive into the Saar. "Bradley admitted my logic but took counsel of his fears," Patton concluded, trying to rationalize why he lost this valued fighting division. "I wish he [Bradley] were less timid."[4]

When Patton had time to recover from his initial anger, he concluded that Hitler had served up an unexpected opportunity to crush the Nazi forces as Hitler advanced beyond his supply lines. Patton, like Bradley, suspected Hitler repeated the identical mistake he had made with his ill-advised counterattack at Mortain during the Battle of Normandy four months earlier. There Hitler ordered a German counterattack led by four panzer divisions with the goal of cutting to the sea at Avranches on the English Channel, cutting through the advancing US forces with the goal of cutting off and isolating Patton's Third Army.[5] Rather than achieve his objective, Hitler ended up exposing the "first really big concentration of enemy tanks seen since D-Day."[6] Pounding Hitler's counteroffensive at Mortain with air attacks and effective artillery fire, "the U.S. Army had asserted a dominance on the battlefield—with firepower, tenacity, and a credible display of combined arms competence—that would only intensify over the next eight months, as the European campaign grew even more feverish."[7] Hitler's blunder led to what is known as the "Falaise Pocket," in which Montgomery from the north and Patton from the south attempted to trap and annihilate the German 5th and 7th Panzer Armies. A decision by Bradley to stop Patton's northward advance at Argentan, regarded as "the most controversial order"[8] Bradley issued in his career, allowed many of the Germans to escape, but only with their lives, as the Germans abandoned battle equipment as they ran. "By any measure, the defeat at Falaise was profound," Atkinson wrote in the third volume of his Liberation Trilogy, *The Guns at Last Light*. "Perhaps ten thousand Germans lay dead and fifty thousand more had been captured. Thunderbolts [P-47 fighter airplanes] buzzed the roads, herding men waving white flags into prisoner columns."[9] After the Hitler-engineered German disaster at Mortain and the Falaise Pocket, the Allies took Paris less than two weeks later, as the Germans retreated across the Seine River.

As a military historian, the German breakout in the Ardennes also reminded Patton of General Ludendorff's ill-advised "all out or nothing" Great Spring Offensive in March 1918, launched as Germany transferred more than five hundred thousand troops to the Western Front from the east after the Bolshevik Revolution forced Russia to pull out of World War I.[10] On December 17, 1944, Patton wrote a letter to Maj. Gen. Fox Connor in Hendersonville, North Carolina, in which he drew this very comparison:

> Yesterday morning the Germans attacked to my north in front of the VIII Corps of the First Army. It reminds me very much of March 25, 1918 [Ludendorff's final offensive], and I think will have the same results.
>
> I have always felt the war will be terminated east of the Rhine and I am convinced that this attack by the Germans will be very thoroughly smashed, and they will have nothing left.[11]

Ludendorff's initial breakout and push into Belgium was viewed with great enthusiasm in Germany, especially when it looked at first like Germany had thrown off the chains of trench warfare and might drive on directly to Paris before the United States could fully deliver a fresh and well-supplied American Expeditionary Force to Europe. Germany's hopes were dashed, however, once Allied resistance stiffened, giving Allied commanders, including French marshal Foch and US general "Black Jack" Pershing, time to consolidate military leadership and counterattack. The Germans, having overextended their supply lines, were forced into a disastrous retreat that ultimately led to the collapse of the Hindenburg Line and the end of the German Empire by November that year.

Studying the combat map, Patton realized Hitler may have blundered again by launching an over-optimistic and ill-conceived offensive that Hitler thought could deliver a decisive blow to the advancing Allies. Even in the early hours of the battle, Patton had begun to consider that the "bulge" created by the rapid advance of the German center into Belgium created an excellent opportunity to counterattack and destroy the Wehrmacht in Belgium. Patton greatly preferred this alternative to slugging out the end of the war against Germany's top notch professional generals. Patton believed top professionals in the German high command would have preferred to delay the Allied advance into Germany with a series of costly defensive battles reminiscent of the Hürtgen Forest. This time, instead of letting the Germans get away by crossing the Seine after Mortain and the Falaise Pocket, Patton envisioned encircling the fleeing Germans to destroy them east of the Rhine, before they could get back to reorganize in the heartland of Germany.

CONFERENCE WITH BRADLEY

At 1030 hours on December 18, Bradley telephoned and asked Patton to meet with him in Luxembourg, and to bring along Oscar Koch, Patton's G-2 intelligence officer; Col. Halley G. Maddox, his G-3 operations officer; and Col. Walter J. Muller, the G-4 logistics officer.[12] Ten minutes after he received the call, Patton departed for Luxembourg as instructed, with his senior staff. When Patton arrived, Bradley began the conference cautiously, worried that Patton would resist abandoning his plans for an offensive in the south. The problem was Eisenhower and Bradley had already decided that Patton had no choice but to cancel his planned offensive because his Third Army was needed to reinforce General Middleton's VIII Corp in defense of Bastogne. By the time of this meeting, Patton had already adjusted his thinking to realize the German attack in the Ardennes was the main thrust of the German counteroffensive, not a feint, and he wanted in on the action. What Bradley did not know was that Patton had completely changed his thinking. By the time the meeting started in Luxembourg, Patton was enthusiastic about canceling his offensive in the Saar, provided he got the opportunity to wheel his massive Third Army north to save Middleton.

Bradley began the conference by showing Patton on the map the extent of the German penetration into Allied lines of defense. Patton readily admitted the German advance was much greater than he had initially appreciated. When Bradley asked Patton what Patton thought he could do, Patton did not hesitate. He told Bradley he could halt the Third Army's 4th Armored Division immediately and concentrate it near Longwy. He also explained he would order the 80th Infantry Division to start heading north in the morning toward Luxembourg. He added that he could alert the 26th Infantry Division to move in twenty-four hours, if necessary.[13] Bradley, satisfied with Patton's response, described the meeting as follows:

> When Patton arrived, I said, "You won't like what I'm going to do, but I fear it is necessary." I briefed him on the extent of the German penetration. I outlined my strategy. We had to break off our attacks eastward, turn Hodges's army [First Army] south and Patton's [Third Army] north. My fears turned out to be groundless. Patton grasped the necessity for the change in the strategy at once and immediately became the most unrestrained champion. I asked what he could do immediately to help Middleton. His answer astounded me. He could have three divisions—the 4th Armored, 80th and 26th Infantry—moving northward within about twenty-four hours. He left, already mentally making plans for swinging his entire Third Army northward.[14]

Bradley noted that when he walked Patton to his jeep, Patton was in good spirits, even though plans for the Saar offensive were now shelved, probably permanently. Patton shrugged to Bradley. "We'll still be killing Krauts."[15]

Leaving Bradley, Patton immediately telephoned his Third Army chief of staff, Brig. Gen. Hobart Gay, and instructed him to inform Maj. Gen. Hugh Gaffey, commander of the 4th Armored, and Maj. Gen. Horace L. McBride, commander of the 80th Infantry, to stop whatever they were doing so they could begin preparing their troops for movement. Patton further instructed Gay that he was placing the 4th Armored and the 80th Infantry under Maj. Gen. John Milliken's III Corps.[16] While Patton was returning from Luxembourg, Bradley phoned Gay and notified him the situation was deteriorating. Bradley told Gay it was a sure thing now that the Third Army would order the 4th and the 80th to move that night, if at all possible. Gay responded that he believed initial elements of the 4th Armored could be moved out immediately, since the unit could move on its own power. The problem was that Gay needed trucks to move the 80th Infantry forward. Despite this, Gay believed the remaining elements of the 4th Armored and the 80th Infantry could be moved out early the next morning.[17] Bradley asked Gay to have Patton call him as soon as Patton arrived.

Patten drove home in the dark, "a very dangerous operation, which I hate," he commented to his diary. Arriving at 2000 hours, he telephoned Bradley, as requested.[18] Bradley told Patton the situation with Middleton's VIII Corps was even worse than he anticipated and that it was imperative that the 4th Armored and 80th Infantry move out as soon as possible. Bradley further told Patton that General Eisenhower had called a conference at Verdun for 1100 hours the next day, December 19. Patton was to attend along with a staff officer. Bradley ended the conversation by informing Patton that he and Eisenhower had decided Middleton's VIII Corps would be reassigned from First Army command to Patton's Third Army command.[19]

US Army military historian Martin Blumenson, in compiling Patton papers for publication after the war, observed that the more Patton thought about the German bulge into the American lines, the more he realized the best thing might be to let the Germans penetrate forty to fifty miles. With the Germans extended that far beyond their supply lines, Patton felt he could make a bold move to cut the German offensive off in the rear, destroying the entire thrust and possibly entrapping thousands of Germany's last remaining troops in a forward position they would find indefensible. "This might end the war altogether," Blumenson observed, "but it would take great nerve and aplomb to permit the Germans to roll forward, for they had a massive force in the Ardennes."[20]

MEETING WITH IKE AT VERDUN

December 19, 1944, began for Patton at 0700 hours with a series of staff meetings reviewing the detailed plans required if the Third Army were to have any chance of pivoting north as rapidly as Generals Eisenhower and Bradley wanted. At 0915 hours, Patton, accompanied by Col. Paul D. Harkins—Patton's deputy chief of staff under Gay, nicknamed "Ramrod Harkins" by the troops—and by his aide Lt. Col. Charles R. Codman, departed for Verdun in two jeeps armed with .30-caliber machine guns.[21] Verdun, the scene of the December 19 conference, had a historic past as the location of several important battles. In 1792, the French Revolutionary forces fought the Prussian Army there during the opening months of what came to be known as the War of the First Coalition; victorious in that battle, the Prussians advanced toward Paris. In the Franco-Prussian war of 1870–1871, Verdun was the last fortress to fall to the Prussians. Then, in 1916, the Germans and the French fought to a virtual stalemate at Verdun, making the battle the most prolonged of World War I and one of the most deadly battles in history, resulting in nearly one million casualties.

Patton, "his stern war face firmly in place," arrived at Verdun with Harkins and Codman at approximately 1045 hours.[22] Also called to meet with Eisenhower at Verdun was Gen. Jacob "Jake" Devers, commander of the Sixth Army, positioned to the south of Patton's Third Army. Rather than attend the meeting in person, Field Marshal Bernard Montgomery, still pouting at not being given the command responsibility he considered his due after Operation Market Garden, sent to attend in his place his chief of staff, Maj. Gen. Francis de Guingand, in a move most interpreted as a calculated insult to Eisenhower and the American commanders present.[23]

In defense of Montgomery, military historian John Rickard, in his 2001 book, *Advance and Destroy: Patton as Commander in the Bulge*, argued that

Eisenhower never invited Montgomery to the meeting.[24] Although several of
the participants subsequently cited Montgomery's chief of staff as being present, Rickard pointed out that Guingand was actually not there, but instead
was making his way back to Europe from England when the conference
was held.[25] Rickard explained that Eisenhower didn't invite Montgomery
because the American general believed the German counteroffensive in the
Ardennes was specifically a problem for US military commanders to solve.[26]

Yet many of those at the conference specifically reference British
officers being present. The reality seems to be that Eisenhower did not want
Montgomery there, or Montgomery would have been directed to attend.
Eisenhower realized that Montgomery's slow and plodding ways were not
what he needed to stop Rundstedt's advance. The only general Eisenhower
had that he could rely upon to get this particular job done was Patton, and
Eisenhower knew it. No other Allied general could reinforce Middleton as
fast as Patton could. Whether they liked Patton or not, even his enemies
had to admit that Patton, much like Ulysses Grant (whom Patton greatly
admired), knew how to press a fight to the enemy, regardless of the cost in
men killed and wounded or fighting equipment lost in the field of battle.

Eisenhower arrived promptly at 1100 hours, driving up to Eagle Main in
Verdun in a heavily armored, bulletproof Cadillac sedan, escorted by military police jeeps armed with machine guns, "looking grave, almost ashen."[27]
Bradley initially planned to drive from his Luxembourg command post to
Verdun but changed his mind when an aid of General Hodges called on the
evening of December 18, warning Bradley that English-speaking Germans
in captured American "ODs," short for Olive-Drab GI-issue uniforms, had
infiltrated US lines in an attempt to panic the rear areas. Volunteers for this
covert effort were recruited by the notorious German Waffen-SS lieutenant
colonel Otto Skorzeny, a favorite of Hitler, whose World War II adventures
included snatching Mussolini out of an Italian hotel in which he had been
imprisoned by the new Italian government following his fall from power
in July 1943. Skorzeny's primary objective appeared to have been to seize
bridges across the Meuse, anticipating the rapid advance of the German
counteroffensive.[28]

Bradley quipped, "Most of these GI-uniformed enemy troops were cut
down before they reached the Meuse but not until a half-million GIs played

cat and mouse with each other each time they met on the road. Neither rank nor credentials nor protests spared the traveler an inquisition at each intersection he passed."[29] Bradley further commented with a note of amused dismay that even he, the second in command to Eisenhower in the European theater, had been stopped three times by nervous US sentries and submitted to an inquisition, forced to prove he was who he said he was. The first time, the GIs stopping Bradley asked him to identify the capital of Illinois. When Bradley answered, "Springfield," the inquisitor was unsure what to do, mistakenly believing the correct answer was Chicago. The second time, Bradley had to identify that on a football team, the position of guard was located between the center and the tackle on a line of scrimmage. And the third time, Bradley had to name the current spouse of movie star Betty Grable. When Bradley was stumped coming up with Betty Grable's current husband, the guard, pleased at having stumped General Bradley, let him pass anyway.[30] Eisenhower most likely took the precautions of traveling to Verdun in the armor-reinforced heavy sedan with beefed up security because a rumor that Skorzeny's real mission was to assassinate Eisenhower had caused consternation at SHAEF headquarters in Versailles. The Battle of the Bulge is characterized in part by the activity of Skorzeny's men roaming the Ardennes by "ambushing convoys, spreading alarm and confusion, altering or removing road signs, and generally raising [expletive] as a guerrilla force."[31]

In his 1948 book, *Crusade in Europe*, Eisenhower shared his thought process preparing for the Verdun conference on December 19:

> In a situation of this kind there are normally two feasible lines of reaction for the defending forces, assuming that the high command does not become so frightened as to order a general retreat along the whole front. One is merely to build up a safe defensive line around the general area under attack, choosing some strong feature, such as a river, on which to make the stand. The other is for the defender to begin attacking as soon as he can assemble the necessary troops. I chose the second, not only because in the strategic sense we were on the offensive, but because I firmly believed that by coming out of the Siegfried the enemy had given us a great opportunity which we should seize as soon as possible.[32]

Eisenhower confided that his purpose in calling the Verdun meeting was to make arrangements for the beginning of the southern assault. Eisenhower and Bradley had decided they would extend Devers' Sixth Army defense north to allow Patton's Third Army to leave the Saar front and head north. By acknowledging the Wacht am Rhein offensive had served up an opportunity, Eisenhower signaled his thinking was not too far dissimilar from Patton's own perception of a chance to end the war more quickly by defeating the bulk of Hitler's remaining forces either by encircling them or by attacking them as they retreated in the field of open battle east of the Rhine. In his 2007 book, *Ike: An American Hero*, Eisenhower historian Michael Korda made a relevant comparison:

> Rundstedt was like Rommel at El Alamein: the farther and the farther he advanced, the more his already tenuous supply line would be stretched, and the more complete his eventual defeat would be. In addition, so long as Bastogne held out, Rundstedt's line of communications was fatally compromised. Ike instinctively rejected the idea of building a defensive line to contain Rundstedt—he wanted to attack him and destroy his forces, now that the German army was at last out in the open from behind the defenses of the Siegfried Line.[33]

In Verdun, they met at Eagle Main, on the second floor of a chilly old French stone-built barracks, in a room warmed only by a pot-bellied stove. Most of the attendees kept their coats on to fight back the cold. Except for a long table and a few chairs prepared for the attendees and the easels on which Eisenhower planned to display battle situation maps, the room was open and bare. Historian D'Este commented that Eisenhower upon arriving at Verdun looked uncharacteristically tense: "As always during periods of crisis, Eisenhower's chief weapon of motivation to defuse tense situations was optimism. However, the cheerfulness he exuded at Verdun seemed forced, and the usual Eisenhower smile could not hide the grimness and the aura of crisis that was present in the room."[34] Still, Eisenhower was resolved to begin the meeting with a note of optimism. "The present situation is to be regarded as one of opportunity for us and not for disaster," Eisenhower said. "There will be only cheerful faces at this conference table."[35]

Hearing Eisenhower begin the meeting on a positive note, Patton simply could not resist the opportunity to chime in with his usual bravado, championing a bold, if not outright audacious, tactic: "[L]et's have the guts to let [them] go all the way to Paris. Then we'll really cut'em up and chew'em up."[36] Typically, Patton blurted out the comment with a snide smile and characteristic abandon that showed a complete disregard for decorum. D'Este noted the room erupted in laughter, but that much of the laughter was nervous and forced.[37] Many at the conference simply interpreted Patton's remark as nothing more than the disrespectful showboating they considered one of Patton's principal faults. What they failed to understand was that Patton meant what he said.

Still, Eisenhower was not going to allow those present to suspect the extent to which he might have agreed, at least at some basic level, with Patton's bold proposal. "George, that's fine," Eisenhower retorted. "But the enemy must never be allowed to cross the Meuse."[38] Typically more reserved than Patton, Eisenhower appreciated that in the fortunes of war, tempting Rundstedt to advance beyond his supply lines was a risky strategy. Depending upon how successful the Germans were in their advance, stopping the Nazi advance might be more difficult than anticipated. What Eisenhower had in mind was a version of Patton's proposal tempered by the reasoned caution for which Eisenhower had become famous in his role as a political general.

Eisenhower's proposal was that they draw a line at the Meuse, beyond which there was to be no further Allied retreat. Anticipating that the Germans would be contained, Eisenhower wanted to counterattack. "George, I want you to command this move—under Brad's supervision of course—making a strong counterattack with at least six divisions," Eisenhower said pointedly to Patton. "When can you start?" This was precisely the opening Patton had longed to hear. "As soon as you are through with me," Patton said with an air of determination. He knew that many in the room would consider it unreasonable to presume he could pivot his huge Third Army and turn it north on a moment's notice, without taking the normal planning time to prepare so bold a redirection. "When can you attack?" Eisenhower asked, following up to make sure he had heard Patton correctly. "The morning of December 21, with three divisions," Patton answered without hesitation.[39]

"Forty-eight hours!" D'Este wrote, noting the astonishment all in the room felt hearing Patton's words. "Eisenhower was not amused, wrongly assuming Patton had once again pieced a very inopportune moment to act boastful," D'Este stressed.[40] Eisenhower responded to Patton in obvious disbelief: "George, if you try to go that early, you won't have all three divisions ready, and you'll go piecemeal. You will start on the twenty-second, and I want your initial blow to be a strong one! I'd even settle for the twenty-third if it takes you that long."[41] Patton was not being flippant. He and his staff had already worked out three different plans of action beforehand, so as to be able to respond immediately and specifically regardless what contingency Eisenhower and Bradley might direct.

D'Este noted that when Patton suggested he could launch his attack within forty-eight hours, there was some laughter. Codman, Patton's aide, witnessed "a stir, a shuffling of feet, as those present straightened up in their chairs." Codman saw skepticism in some faces, but a "current of excitement leaped like a flame" through the room.[42] John S. D. Eisenhower made a similar observation: "The prospect of relieving three divisions from the line, turning them north, and traveling over icy roads to Arlon to prepare for a major counterattack in less than seventy-two hours was astonishing, even to a group accustomed to flexibility in their military operations."[43]

This was the sublime moment of Patton's career, military historian Martin Blumenson noted.[44] All his life, Patton had prepared for just such an opportunity. "When I said I could attack on the twenty-second, it created quite a commotion—some people seemed surprised and others pleased," Patton later commented.[45] Patton, however, had believed it could be done. In the ensuing discussion, Patton repeated that he could bring north three divisions right away, the 4th Armored, followed by the 80th and 24th Infantries. Eisenhower was afraid three divisions might not be strong enough to make the counterattack effective. Patton countered, arguing that he could beat the Germans with three divisions; moreover, if he waited to get more divisions into the effort, he would lose the element of surprise.

Eisenhower approved Patton's plan.

Blumenson noted that much as Hitler's Mortain offensive in August of that year had foreshadowed Hitler's December 1944 offensive in the Ardennes, Patton's move to cut off Hitler's breakthrough in the Falaise Pocket foreshadowed Patton's decision to turn his Third Army north in a wheeling movement to Bastogne. The Verdun conference set US strategy in the Ardennes: an effort would be made to hold Bastogne long enough for Patton to break off his planned offensive and turn his Third Army north, while Devers would extend his left to cover the front Patton was vacating in the Saar.

The boldness of Hitler's Wacht am Rhein was matched by the boldness of Patton's proposal. Blumenson commented:

> Patton's proposal was astonishing, technically difficult, and daring. It meant reorienting his entire army from an eastward direction to the north, a ninety-degree turn that would pose logistical nightmares— getting divisions on new roads and making sure that supplies reached them from dumps established in quite a different context, for quite a different situation. Altogether, it was an operation that only a master could think of executing.[46]

D'Este recorded that Patton with his cigar in hand illustrated his intentions on the map. Pointing to the obvious German "bulge" in the St. Vith–Bastogne region and speaking directly to Bradley, Patton said: "Brad, the Kraut's stuck his head in the meat grinder." Then, turning his fist in a grinding motion, Patton added, "And this time, I've got hold of the handle."[47]

Bradley noted that no one present at the Verdun conference offered an alternative line of action, for the only "alternative" would have involved withdrawal to a winter defensive line on the Meuse.[48] Bradley agreed with Patton's plan, reasoning that Patton's move north was the best chance the US commanders had to save Bastogne. In A Soldier's Life, Bradley explained his reasoning:

> Meanwhile our situation at the crossroads of Bastogne was rapidly shaping into a major crisis. Manteuffel's 5th Panzer Army, in the center of Rundstedt's line, had spilled past that isle of resistance to cut its north and south exit roads. With the encirclement of Bastogne foredoomed, I nevertheless ordered Middleton's VIII Corps to hold on to that vital objective. Even though it might cost us heavy casualties in the airborne division and the two armored combat commands that had reached that

outpost, I could not afford to relinquish Bastogne and let the enemy widen his Bulge. But though I did not minimize the ordeal we inflicted upon its defenders, I was confident that the 101st could hold with the aid of those tankers from the 9th and 10th Armored Divisions. They could hold out I thought at least until Patton's Third Army broke through to relieve them. The relief of Bastogne was to be the priority objective in Patton's flanking attack.[49]

As the Verdun conference was breaking up, Eisenhower commented to Patton that, "Every time I get a new star, I get attacked." Just before the Battle of the Bulge, Eisenhower received his fifth star to become the commanding general of the army, the second-highest possible rank in the US Army. Eisenhower could not help seeing the parallel, remembering that he had been promoted to four-star general just before the American defeat at the Kasserine Pass in February 1943 during the Tunisia Campaign. Patton quipped in return, "And every time you get attacked, I pull you out."[50] After Eisenhower was appointed a four-star general, Patton got command of II Corps, just in time to save Eisenhower from a disastrous defeat in North Africa. The exchange was ironic with Patton taking credit for saving Eisenhower's career, given the number of times during the war Eisenhower had been called upon to come to Patton's defense.

In one incident that proved to be particularly detrimental to Patton's career, he slapped a soldier suffering from battle fatigue. The incident involved Private Charles H. Kuhl of L Company, 26th Infantry Regiment, who had reported to 1st Medical Battalion aid station on August 2, 1943, and was transferred the same day to the 15th Evacuation Hospital near Nicosia for evaluation. Touring the 15th Evacuation Hospital on August 3, 1943, Patton made the rounds, taking time to speak personally with various wounded soldiers. As Patton's biographer Ladislas Farago describes the incident in his 1964 book, *Patton: Ordeal and Triumph*, Patton was about to leave the tent when he saw a soldier in his mid-twenties "who was squatting on a box near the dressing station with no bandage on him to indicate he had been wounded."[51] Kuhl made the mistake of explaining to Patton that, "I just get sick inside myself." Patton became so enraged he started slapping and kicking Kuhl. Pulling his pistol, Patton ordered the hospital commander to send Kuhl back to the front lines. Clearly, the incident occurred in an era before post-traumatic stress disorder, or PTSD, had been diagnosed. Patton, in his bravado for courage under combat, unfortunately concluded Kuhl's mental distress was a cover for cowardice. As it turned out, a blood test determined that Kuhl had been suffering from malaria.[52]

The soldier-slapping incident with Kuhl and a similar incident a few days later in which Patton slapped Private Paul G. Bennett of C Battery, 17th Field Artillery Regiment, 1st Infantry Division, another hospitalized soldier suffering from battle fatigue, nearly ended Patton's military career. Extensive high-visibility media coverage in the United States led to demands from various members of Congress that Patton be relieved of command and sent back to the United States immediately. Eisenhower relieved Patton of command of the Seventh Army that Patton had commanded brilliantly in the invasion of Sicily and he delivered in writing a sharply worded rebuke to Patton. Still, behind the scenes, Eisenhower fought with US military high command in the United States, arguing Patton needed to be retained because his aggressive leadership style in battle was important to winning the war in Europe.

What Eisenhower realized was that Patton was "a master of pursuit." As historian John S. D. Eisenhower explained in *The Bitter Woods*, "This quality, Eisenhower theorized, is one of the rarest to be found in a commander. It has been possessed by others—by Napoleon (who, incidentally, probably lost Waterloo because of his uncharacteristic failure to pursue vigorously after the action at Quatre Bras) and by Grant. Lincoln came within a hair's breadth of firing Meade for his failure to pursue Lee after the Union victory at Gettysburg."[53] Ultimately, Patton had to apologize, not only to Kuhl and Bennett, but to every division of the Seventh Army, forced to go from division to division to explain his behavior.

But, as D'Este commented, if ever Eisenhower was justified for saving Patton's career, it was now, during the Battle of the Bulge, when Patton was the only commander Eisenhower had who was capable of making such a daring maneuver to save Bastogne and turn the tide of the German counter-offensive.[54] Even before he left Verdun, Patton had begun turning the Third Army north by working the phones with his staff officers. Two days after the Verdun conference, as of December 21, 1944, Patton's Third Army was advancing toward Bastogne with an armored and an infantry division. "Within less than a week Patton had switched the bulk of his Third Army, with its guns, supply, and equipment, from fifty to seventy-five miles into the new offensive," Bradley wrote. "More than 133,000 tanks and trucks joined that round-the-clock trek over the icy roads."[55] Before the Battle of the Bulge, Bradley did not share Patton's enthusiasm for his Third Army staff. But after seeing Patton move the Third Army toward Bastogne, Bradley changed his mind, impressed that a greatly matured Patton succeeded in coaxing from his staff a brilliant effort.[56]

Bradley thought Patton was being ambitious in claiming he could begin his northward movement on December 22, only forty-eight hours from the conclusion of the Verdun conference; Bradley noted that any other commander would have "held his breath and believed himself taking a chance on ninety-eight."[57] But after the war, Bradley acknowledged that Patton made good on the start of his attack within two days' time. One week after Patton turned the Third Army north, Rundstedt "charged to a halt on the high water mark of his offensive."[58] Vindicating Eisenhower's decision to retain Patton after the slapping incidents, Bradley wrote in his 1951 memoir, *A Soldier's Story*, that Patton's brilliant shift of his Third Army from its bridgehead in the Saar to the snow-covered Ardennes front became "one of the most astonishing feats of generalship of our campaign in the West."[59]

IKE REBUKES BRADLEY

The morning after the Verdun conference, Patton drove to Luxembourg, arriving at 0900 hours. He was with Bradley when Eisenhower called to give Bradley some bad news.[60] Eisenhower had decided to reassign operational control of the First and Ninth Armies, north of the bulge, to Montgomery, arguing that telephone connections between Bradley in Luxembourg and the First and Ninth Armies were now difficult. This, Eisenhower reasoned, would free Bradley to focus on directing Patton's Third Army and the defense of Bastogne with Middleton's VIII Corps now reassigned from the First Army to the Third Army.[61] Patton immediately knew this was a ruse in that Eisenhower was trying to let Bradley down easy. Patton confided to his diary: "As a matter of fact, telephonic communications were all right, and it is either a case of having lost confidence in Bradley or having been forced to put Montgomery in through the machinations of the prime minister or with the hope that if he gives Monty operational control, he will get some of the British divisions in [to the fight]." Patton summed up the situation with the next sentence: "Eisenhower is either unwilling or unable to command Montgomery."[62]

The backstory of this decision was that Montgomery, after being excluded from the Verdun conference, complained bitterly to Maj. Gen. J. F. M. "Jock" Whiteley, one of Eisenhower's most trusted staff officers, generally regarded as the most able British officer at SHAEF.[63] Montgomery's specific complaint was that First Army under General Hodges was in disarray and that Hodges had performed poorly in countering the German advance in the first hours of the Battle of the Bulge. In defense of Hodges, the suspicion was that Hodges may have been suffering from viral pneumonia and confined to his bed, virtually unconscious, as the attack started. There were reports of Hodges sitting at his desk, his head in his arms, unable to function at a time when First Army command decisions were required. Montgomery also complained that Bradley had failed in his command by not leaving the comfort of his Luxembourg hotel headquarters to visit Hodges in the field.

Whiteley found a ready ally in the person of Maj. Gen. Kenneth Strong, a British intelligence officer also assigned to SHAEF, whom Eisenhower also trusted.[64] Together, Whiteley and Strong approached Gen. Bedell Smith, Eisenhower's chief of staff. Smith, though initially put off by Whiteley and Strong's assessment that First Army needed to be reassigned to Montgomery's command, eventually came around.[65] Smith's assessment was that the First Army "had a very bad staff" and Hodges "was the weakest commander we had."[66] Smith also felt that Bradley "had nothing under control in the opening hours of the German offensive and was in no position to influence the outcome of the battle from his headquarters in Luxembourg."[67]

Finally Eisenhower accepted Smith's recommendation and, on the morning of December 20, he telephoned Bradley to communicate his decision. Bradley received the news with anger. "By God, Ike, I cannot be responsible to the American people if you do this. I resign," Bradley told Eisenhower. Calmly but firmly Eisenhower explained to Bradley that Bradley was not responsible to the American people, but that he—Eisenhower—was.

Eisenhower then added sharply, "Your resignation, therefore, means absolutely nothing." When Bradley continued protesting, Eisenhower ended the conversation with, "Well, Brad, those are my orders."[68] Bradley later rationalized that the fault was that Hodges "was not a man like Patton, who naturally radiated unbounded confidence and dogged determination." He added, "Hodges was sounding more and more depressed at a time when we needed Pattonesque bravado."[69]

Bedell Smith comforted Bradley, explaining the assignment of the First and Ninth Armies to Montgomery was temporary, such that Ike planned to return the First and Ninth Armies to Bradley's command once the crisis of the German advance was over. "Ike wanted me to give my full attention to Patton's offensive, now the key to turning disaster into triumph," Bradley rationalized in *A General's Life*. "We wanted to make sure Patton did not go off half-cocked. Montgomery would merely be *temporarily* (he [Smith] repeated) relieving me of a lot of headaches in the north. So far, Monty had contributed nothing to the battle; as northern land commander he might be more willing to commit British forces to help Hodges [with the First Army] and [General William Hood] Simpson [with the Ninth Army]."[70] Bradley further noted that up until this date in the Battle of the Bulge, Monty had not so much as offered one British platoon to help Hodges.

Bradley never fully recovered from Eisenhower's decision. "Bradley resented Eisenhower's decision precisely because it might be misinterpreted as a loss of confidence in Bradley's efficiency at a time of great emergency," Blumenson, the compiler of Patton's papers, observed. "Moreover, it would enable Montgomery to press for his reappointment to the Allied ground force command."[71] In the final analysis, Eisenhower needed someone to blame for the Allied failure to anticipate and repulse immediately Hitler's surprise Wacht am Rhein offensive, and Bradley was the logical fall-guy. As second-in-command to Eisenhower, Bradley had been responsible for the defensive deployment of the forces in the Ardennes that Hitler so successfully exploited when the Battle of the Bulge began.

Eisenhower and the Allied command at SHAEF found it particularly difficult to accept the collapse of the 106th Infantry Division fighting under the command of General Middleton in VIII Corps, reporting ultimately to General Hodges and First Army command. On December 19, the 422nd and 423rd Regiments of the 106th became cut off from the rest of the division and surrounded by advancing Germans. "Green troops of the 106th Golden Lion Division were rudely awakened from their winter sojourn by the menacing rumble of Tiger and Panther tanks on the move," wrote Michael Collins and Martin King in their 2011 book, *Voices of the Bulge*, describing 0530 hours on the morning of December 16, 1944, when the Battle of the Bulge began.[72] "As I remember it, I was trying to sleep in the ruins of a German farmhouse," recalled John Hillard Dunn, a soldier in the 106th. "It was December, cold and snowing. Squirming about in my sleeping bag, I felt reassured by the three-foot thickness of the wall against which I rested my shivering spine. Sometime in the night, buzz bombs began their cement-mixer noise overhead."[73] Dunn soon realized the area near St. Vith where his unit had been assigned was not the "rest area" he had been led to believe. "The vortex of a tornado is a vacuum," he continued. "And that is where we were—in the center of a storm of armor and artillery roaring into the Ardennes. Already we were being bypassed by the onrushing German tanks, and I for one certainly didn't know it, nor would I have believed it had anyone told us."[74]

Nelson Charron, Company D, 422nd Regiment, 106th Infantry Division, had similar memories of the Battle of the Bulge: "We were awake during the opening morning, and there were buzz bombs going over our heads. We fired quite a lot, but we were just in big trouble because we had no big guns. Our artillery was knocked out, and machine guns against tanks were not going to cut it. There was no way we could have escaped, maybe right off the bat we could have, but we were too weak."[75] The next day, December 17, Charron continued to fight. "We all wanted to fight; it was either be captured or be killed. The officers told us to surrender, and we had to destroy our weapons. On their tanks [Tiger II "King Tiger" Tanks equipped with 88mm guns] they had 88s, and anybody who tried to escape was shot. There was a group who tried to get out, but they did not make it because of those 88s."[76] Finally, on December 18, exhausted from fierce combat resisting the German advance, surrounded, and virtually out of ammunition, the commanders of the two regiments abandoned what looked like fruitless efforts to fight their way out and gave up the battle, calculating that further fighting would simply result in more casualties. To save what lives were left, the

422nd and 423rd Regiments of the 106th surrendered more than seven thousand men of the 106th Infantry Division into German captivity and were ultimately sent to various POW camps in Germany, resulting in the largest mass surrender of US troops in World War II.[77]

At Bradley's request, Patton moved his Third Army headquarters into Bradley's hotel in Luxembourg. "Throughout the entire Battle of the Bulge crisis, we worked in closest contact and saw each other daily, either at his headquarters or mine," Bradley wrote. "We dined together and planned together. We had never been closer or worked in greater harmony."[78]

CHAPTER 8

A PRAYER FOR VICTORY

This is General Patton. Do you have a prayer for weather?

—Gen. George S. Patton Jr., question posed to Chaplain James Hugh
O'Neill, US Third Army, in a telephone call December 8, 1944[1]

In a letter written to his wife, Beatrice, on December 21, 1944, Patton used a fishing analogy to explain his strategy in moving the Third Army north: "Remember how a tarpon always makes one big flop just before he dies. We should get well into the guts of the enemy and cut his supply lines. Destiny sent for me in a hurry when things got tight. Perhaps God saved me for this effort."[2]

All his life, Patton had interpreted events in his life as reflecting the hand of God intervening to move his life in accord with what he sensed was a divine plan for his life.

On September 26, 1918, when Patton was fighting in World War I near the village of Cheppy in Lorraine, France, a German machine-gun bullet "tore through his body, entering his groin and exiting his buttocks, leaving a gaping wound the size of a teacup."[3] As blood poured from Patton's body, he contemplated his death.

Patton imagined he saw the faces of his ancestors: Gen. Hugh Mercer, wounded at the battle of Princeton in the Revolutionary War; grandfather north, his chief of staff, Brig. Gen. Hobart Gay, objected, reminding Patton that the prayer had been written earlier, for the Lorraine Campaign. "Oh, the Lord won't mind," Patton answered. "He knows we're too busy killing Germans to print another prayer."[29] Moreover, when the prayer was distributed, the Third Army was too besieged with a winter blizzard for anyone to believe it would really work.

International News Service correspondent Larry Newman, who covered the Third Army, wrote the following:

> Patton was never disheartened. In the midst of the battle—perhaps the most desperate a U.S. Army has ever had to fight—Patton called a conference of all correspondents. As we filed into the room, the tenseness was depressing. But when Patton strode into the room, smiling, confident, the atmosphere changed within seconds. He asked, "What the [expletive] is all the mourning about? This is the end of the beginning. We've been batting our brains out trying to get the Hun out in the open. Now he is out. And with the help of God we'll finish him off this time—and for good.[30]

Patton then said, "I have a little Christmas card and prayer for all of you." He handed out to the reporters the card he had printed with his Christmas greeting on one side and Chaplain O'Neill's prayer for fair weather on the other side. Patton appeared not to have any doubt the prayer would work. When the weather did break, Newman wrote, Patton explained to the reporters, "The war is almost over. The God of battles always stands on the side of right when the judgment comes out."[31]

Col. Paul A, Danahy, 101st G-2 Intelligence Officer; Gen. Anthony McAuliffe, 101st Airborne Division Commanding Officer; Col. Harry Kinnard, 101st G-3 Operations Officer, hold Bastogne sign for the camera. December 1944.

Unit of 101st Airborne Division marches out of Bastogne during siege to attack German units in neighboring villages. December 1944.

US tank destroyer moving up at crossroads leading into Bastogne, Belgium.
December 1944.

Infantry of 10th Armored Division fight snow and bitter cold conditions, near
Bastogne, Belgium. December 1944.

Members of 501st Parachute Infantry Regime moves out to attack somewhere near Bastogne, Belgium. December 1944.

Tank camouflaged with sheets from village homes. Bastogne, Belgium. December 1944.

A damaged ambulance of the 326th Airborne Medical Company rests in front of the destroyed buildings of Bastogne, Belgium. December 23, 1944.

Members of the 502nd Parachute Infantry Regiment outpost a strategic roadblock just south of Bastogne, Belgium. December 1944.

Sherman tanks in snow outside Bastogne, Belgium. December 1944.

502nd Parachute Infantry Regiment bazooka attack on German tank over terrain that German tanks moved on Christmas Day in the attack on Rolle Château. The German tank in the foreground was destroyed in that attack.

Machine gun unit, 101st Airborne Division, at Bastogne, Belgium. December 1944.

Soldiers of 101st Airborne dug in foxhole, defending Bastogne, Belgium, in the snow and bitter cold. December 1944.

Low-flying C-47s drop desperately needed supplies to the 101st Airborne Division at Bastogne, Belgium. Destroyed German military vehicle seen in foreground, sending a black column of smoke skyward. December 1944.

C-47s circle over field in Bastogne, Belgium, in effort to air-ressupply beseiged US forces. December 1944.

Members of the 326th Airborne Medical Company rush bundles of medical supplies off the "drop zone" after the first aerial resupply mission at Bastogne, Belgium. December 22, 1944.

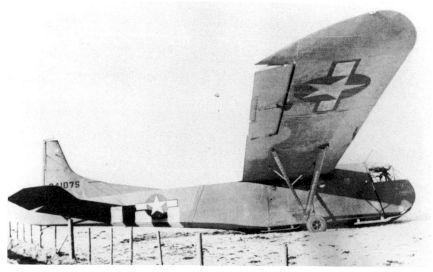

One of the gliders used to fly doctors and medical supplies to the troops fighting at Bastogne, Belgium. December 23, 1944.

Two members of the 3rd Battalion, 327th Glider Infantry Regiment, retrieving medical supplies air-dropped to the surrounded 101st Airborne Division, in Bastogne, Belgium. December 27, 1944.

C-47 shot down over Bastogne, Belgium, in air-resupply effort to surrounded US troops defending the village. December 1944.

US soldiers of 101st Airborne examine a bombed, destroyed building in Bastogne, Belgium. December 1944.

Gen. George S. Patton, Jr., with Brig. Gen. Anthony McAuliffe (left) and Col. Steve Chappuis (center) after awarding both officers the Distinguished Service Cross for their actions in the defense of Bastogne. December 1944.

Gen. George Patton in jeep with Gen. Anthony McAuliffe, Bastogne, Belgium. December 1944.

CHAPTER 9

MCAULIFFE DIGS IN

In the command post, McAuliffe and the division staff had
assembled for a pre-dinner drink. In the course of a hilarious
reunion, I described to them the reaction of the outside world
to the defense of Bastogne. They were incredulous when I told
them they were heroes and indignant when they learned they
had been "rescued." The attitude of the division had been
expressed that first day the German lines closed around the
town—"They've got us surrounded, the poor bastards!"

—Gen. Maxwell D. Taylor, *Swords and Plowshares*, 1972[1]

As December 20 dawned, McAuliffe was wondering "whether
Noville was worth what he may have to pay to hold it, and
was about to make a decision," as battlefield historian S. L. A.
Marshall observed. At approximately 1200 hours on December 20,
General McAuliffe made up his mind: Noville was not sufficiently important to warrant a last-ditch stand, especially given the inferior terrain in
which the Germans held the ridges surrounding the town.[2] McAuliffe
ordered the 3rd Battalion of the 506th to attack at Foy, providing some
diversion for Task Force Harwick and the 1st Battalion of the 506th to
withdraw from Noville along the road heading through Foy, south to

Bastogne. The fighting at Noville had taken a toll, not only in battle casualties, but also in the loss of fighting vehicles. A good deal of ammunition had to be destroyed and some fifty wounded soldiers had not yet been evacuated. Still, when the order to evacuate came, there were enough tanks, half-tracks, and trucks remaining to transport what remained of the fighting force in the withdrawal.[3]

Marshall noted that at 1300 hours, as the withdrawal from Noville was getting underway, another fortunate circumstance occurred. "Then, as if Providence again chose to intervene in their favor, the fog closed around them and screened their departure from the enemy," Marshall wrote. "They knew that they could be heard and they wondered whether the Germans would try to take them in flank while they were on the move. But the fire which might have been turned against the road was spared them and they moved along quite easily, except for an occasional flurry of bullets."[4] By dusk on December 20, the column of vehicles withdrawing from Noville drew into Foy, going past the lines of the 3rd Battalion of the 506th PIR.

Maj. Robert F. Harwick, the executive officer of the 506th's 1st Battalion who took over Team Desobry after Desobry was severely wounded and evacuated from the battlefield, recalled the withdrawal from Noville: "Of the five tanks remaining, I could find crews for only two. Our troopers took over and drove two more. The disabled one was set afire and a five-minute fuse put on what ammunition was left. Four tanks and C Company left first, with orders to push and engage any enemy without further orders. Stopping, we knew, would mean the loss of the entire column. The tank destroyers with A Company formed the rear guard to prevent the Germans from following. All of the wounded were placed on vehicles."[5] Harwick described how the action of the fog helped facilitate the withdrawal. "Under cover of the now wonderful fog, we took off on time. The men did a brilliant job of changing positions, loading wounded, gathering or destroying ammunition and equipment. The wounded had just been put on a vehicle when sounds of fire told of trouble at the head of the column. I hurried up. The first tank was on fire. But we had to push on—if we did not take losses then everybody would be a loss."[6]

But while the evacuation was successful, it was not always orderly.

Capt. John T. Prior, the medical officer for the 20th Armored Infantry Battalion of what had been Team Desobry before Harwick took command, recalled the difficulty of evacuating the wounded from Noville:

> Upon receipt of the withdrawal order, we were given ten minutes to move out. Since I had no functioning vehicular transportation and no litters, I decided to stay and surrender my patients to the Germans. I asked for volunteers to stay with me but the silence was deafening. It looked as if only myself and the tavern owners (an old lady and her husband who said their rosaries aloud for two days in their cellar) would stay behind. At this point, my first sergeant seized the initiative and ran into the street shouting at the departing tanks to swing by the aid station. The tankers ran into our building and, after ripping off all the doors from the walls, strapped our patients to the doors and tied them to their vehicles. The column then moved down the road toward Bastogne where I assumed there was a hospital and fresh defenders.[7]

Unfortunately, Captain Prior would learn the 101st's field hospital had been overrun and captured by the Germans and there were no fresh troops at Bastogne, just the dogged men of the 101st Airborne and the 10th Armored who remained to continue the fight to hold Bastogne against the German advance.

Marshall provided a summary of the action at Noville. Team Desobry had gone to Noville with fifteen tanks and returned with four. The 1st Battalion of the 506th, at full strength when it went forward to assist Team Desobry, paid heavily in blood to hold the town. When the 506th finally withdrew, casualties amounted to twelve officers plus its commander, Colonel LaPrade, killed or wounded, in addition to 169 enlisted men.[8] Together, the armored soldiers and the paratroopers had destroyed or badly crippled somewhere between twenty and thirty enemy tanks, including at least three Mark VI tanks. Headquarters of the 506th estimated the defense of Noville had cost the German infantry the equivalent of half a regiment. "Yet all of these material measurements of what had been achieved were mean and meager weighed against the fact that the men of Noville had held their ground for a decisive forty-eight hours during which time the defense of Bastogne had opportunity to organize and grow confident of its own strength," Marshall concluded.[9]

STOPPING GERMAN TANKS

On December 20, Team O'Hara came under attack to the southeast of Bastogne. At 0645 hours, the Germans shelled a roadblock Team O'Hara had constructed on the road from Bastogne to Wiltz, about thirteen hundred yards east of Marvie.[10] At around 0900 hours, the fog lifted just enough for the US soldiers to spot a dozen German soldiers trying to break up the roadblock. Artillery shells from the 420th Field Artillery Battalion caught the Germans while they were carrying away the felled logs. The enemy next tried to put a smoke cover over the road block to conceal the block and the terrain around it. Fearing an infantry attack was about to start, Team O'Hara blasted the roadblock area with fire from mortars and assault guns. This, US commanders believed, was enough to deter the Germans from attacking O'Hara's front, shifting their assault instead to the area around Marvie where O'Hara had positioned five M5 medium tanks the night before.[11] At Marvie, O'Hara's tank command was assisted by the 327th Glider Infantry under the command of Col. Joseph H. Harper.

PFC Donald J. Rich of the 327th Glider Infantry Regiment's G Company described the fierceness of the tank combat at Marvie. "The bazooka section had not yet been set up when someone yelled, 'There comes a German tank!'" Rich recalled. "I grabbed my bazooka and told one man to come with me. We ran up the street and into a house. I told the man with me to take the bazooka and stay at a window. I went into the next room to watch and told him to wait till the tank went by and then fire at it. He must have stuck his head up before the tank went by because the tanker fired into the house and blew a hole about three or four feet in diameter." This was the difficulty of fighting from within buildings: damage done by German artillery or tanks to the building could end up being life threatening simply from the structural damage and the flying debris, whether or not the defenders were hit directly. "I went rolling across the floor," Rich continued. "I jumped up to see how my buddy made out. He came staggering out of the room. I rushed him to the medics. I never knew if he had serious wounds or if he made it.

I ran back to the house to retrieve the bazooka. It was bent, with the barrel opening sealed. Someone else got the tank further on."[12]

At around 1100 hours on December 20, the 2nd Battalion of the 327th Glider Infantry Regiment, in the process of relieving elements of the 326th Engineers at Marvie, came under artillery fire. Some twenty minutes after the shelling began, four Mark IV tanks, a self-propelled 75mm gun, and six half-tracks carrying German infantry moved out of the woods east of the town. The five M5 medium tanks O'Hara had positioned to assist in the defense of Marvie were out-gunned by the heavier German Mark IV tanks. Yet, what the M5 tanks lost in terms of fire-power, they gained in mobility. "The M5s attempted evasive maneuvers by darting from one place of cover to the next on the northern edge of the village, hoping to avoid drawing fire from the Germans," noted Michael Collins and Martin King in their 2013 book, *The Tigers of Bastogne*. "This tactic did not prove wholly successful because one of the M5s was set ablaze and the other was immobilized by a damaged drivetrain." The extent of the damage became apparent when one of the M5 tanks had to travel in reverse gear all the way back to Team O'Hara's position.[13]

When the Germans saw the M5 tanks retreating from the hillside where they were positioned throughout the engagement, the Germans moved in for what looked like an easy kill. "This gave the medium tanks an opportunity to hit them with a broadside at around seven hundred yards range," Collins and King continued. "One Sherman immobilized a Mark IV while the second Sherman effectively damaged another Mark IV and a half-track. A third Mark IV attempted to extricate itself from the situation and make it back to the corner of the woods, but it was promptly destroyed by a bazooka man from the 327th GIR."[14] While O'Hara's tanks were taking out the Mark IV tanks, the German half-tracks made a dash for the edge of the village. "Once they had reached their destination, the infantrymen they were carrying immediately disembarked and sought refuge in the houses," Collins and King continued. "A house-to-house battle ensued with the men of the 2nd Battalion, 327th GIR, that culminated in thirty Germans being killed with the rest taken POW."[15] December 20 ended with the Americans still in control of Marvie, but with the weather changing for the worse. While no snow had yet fallen, the Ardennes were definitely cold and the ground was frozen hard enough for tracked vehicles to get over the hillsides in any direction.[16]

In many ways, December 20th marked a turning point in the battle to hold Bastogne. The fighting had been desperate, but the three combat teams of the 10th Armored had just enough assistance from the 101st entering the battle to stave off the German attack from opening at least one of the three roads into Bastogne the Germans were trying to take: Noville-Bastogne road in the north, the Longvilly-Bastogne road in the east, and the Marvie-Bastogne in the southeast. "As a result of the preliminary actions, the Bastogne garrison was now consolidated and, except for the loss of a considerable part of Colonel Roberts' armor at Noville and along the Longvilly road and one company of Ewell's men at Wardin, the combat elements were intact and confronting the enemy wherever he appeared," summarized journalist Fred MacKenzie. "General McAuliffe began to dare to believe that the German juggernaut was not so overwhelming an adversary, after all." This assessment was especially poignant because McAuliffe could have decided to withdraw altogether from Bastogne, if he decided the cost of holding Bastogne were as great as the cost of holding Noville had become. "The Airborne commander's reappraisal of his position was important because at this stage of the battle, the General Staff and subordinate commanders knew, he [McAuliffe] could have followed the example of others and sent the Screaming Eagles scampering down the road to Neufchâteau, fighting no more than a rear-guard action."[17] [17]

FATHER SAMPSON CAPTURED BY THE ENEMY

On December 20, Father Sampson was captured by Nazi troops.

After dinner that evening, Father Sampson was sitting around with a group of regimental headquarters men, Dr. Waldman, one of the surgeons, and several of his aid men. "As wounded had really been coming in fast, we were all quite tired from caring for them," Father Sampson recalled in his autobiography. "We were just having a smoke and a short break when Mr. Sheen, the communications warrant officer, came in. 'You should see what I have just seen,' he said. 'A group of troopers machine-gunned on the road about two miles north of here.'"[18] Father Sampson asked him where exactly that place was, thinking perhaps some of the wounded were left there. Sheen could not explain it well on the map, for there were four roads going north out of Bastogne, and he was not sure which road was involved.

Father Sampson recounted what he did next:

> My driver, Cpl. Adams, and I piled into the jeep and went to try to find the place. Since we couldn't find the bodies Sheen had spoken about, I decided to keep going a mile or so farther on to where our division medical company had been captured by the Germans the night before. A few German vehicles, armored cars, etc., had come up from a side road, shot up several American trucks bringing in supplies, and captured our whole medical company at the same time. Our own regimental supply trucks had been captured there too, along with several aid men. Since Doc Waldman told me that we were getting very short of supplies, I decided to salvage some of the stuff that the Germans had left behind. We loaded the jeep with two chests of much-needed equipment and were ready to head back to the regimental aid station.[19]

That is when tragedy struck. Father Sampson was not yet quite ready to give up the search, especially after a soldier on outpost guard told him that there had been quite a skirmish the previous night on the other side of the hill. "Perhaps that was the place Sheen had referred to, I reasoned," Father Sampson continued. "We drove over the hill to see, and just over the crest of the hill we ran into Germans . . . hundreds of them. An armored car leveled its gun at us, and the Germans jumped out from behind trees yelling something. A light reconnaissance vehicle came up quickly." Immediately, Father Sampson knew there was no escape. "Stop the jeep, Adams," he said. "I'm sorry I got you into this mess." Adams was calm. "That's okay, Father," Adams mumbled.

Father Sampson concluded the story simply, but forcefully. "We were captured," he wrote.[20]

MCAULIFFE: "I'M STAYING"

At a staff conference at McAuliffe's 101st headquarters in Bastogne on Wednesday, December 20, the question was what McAuliffe planned to do:

escape from Bastogne by fighting a rear-guard action as the troops withdrew southwest along the still-open road to Neufchâteau, or stand and fight, with the expectation that soon they would be encircled by the advancing Germans. "The 101st Airborne Division was accustomed to the psychological hazards in battles of encirclement, but the paratroopers and glider-borne soldiers knew that this one had not been put down in advance on anybody's planning board," noted MacKenzie. "Shortages of material alone proved that."[21] Colonel Nelson's 907th Glider Field Artillery Battalion had virtually used up its supply of ammunition for its 105mm guns the day before in supporting Ewell's 501st east of Bastogne. This was typical of all artillery units in the field. "The shortage of ammunition worried McAuliffe more than any other difficulty he faced," MacKenzie noted. "They were in a bad way for medical supplies because of the hospital's capture, and food and warm clothing were scarce."[22] The problem was that everything was running short at Bastogne. What was available to be scavenged had already been raided: flour and sugar had been requisitioned from civilian warehouses, and supply stores left behind by VIII Corps had been stripped of what small amounts of food and clothing had been left behind. With severe winter weather moving in, McAuliffe knew air resupply would be out of the question for an indefinite number of days to come.

In a general staff discussion of the battle situation, McAuliffe pored over reports that Germans were wearing US uniforms and operating US tanks, half-tracks, and trucks with the "stars and stripes" emblems painted over with Swastikas. Paul Danahy, the 101st's G-2 intelligence officer learned that eleven Germans who were found dead on the ground when the hospital was captured were wearing a combination of civilian clothes mixed with American uniforms. To make sure this was true, Danahy went out to the site of the captured field hospital to see for himself. What he found was that invariably the Germans killed while wearing American dress had also mixed with some of their own clothing, so the Germans could argue they were in uniform and not operating as spies.[23] "They are using our equipment because they need it," Danahy concluded.[24] These observations inspired Danahy to a prophecy. "Their equipment is augmented by captured US equipment that they do not hesitate to use," Danahy wrote to McAuliffe. "Their morale is excellent but will disintegrate as they come into contact with American airborne troops. It is well known that the Germans dislike fighting. The false courage acquired during their recent successes has so far proved insufficient to prevent their becoming road bound."[25]

Field interrogations with captured German troops also provided intelligence that German field commanders had told their men that supply depots in Bastogne were bursting with American food. Promised that there would be good eating once they captured Bastogne, some of the German forces had gone hungry for three days while trying to reach the American rations. US intelligence had also noticed indications the advancing Germans were short on ammunition. While mortars and artillery fire had hit storefronts in Bastogne and wounded a few soldiers and civilians, German heavy artillery was largely being limited to providing covering fire for tanks and infantry charging forward.[26]

Danahy's intelligence estimates encouraged McAuliffe to conclude Bastogne had already weathered the worst attacks the Germans were capable of launching. US intelligence was beginning to realize the advancing Nazis were behind the rigid schedule Hitler had set for reaching the Meuse. The 2nd Panzer attacked Noville because Noville was in the path of the division's northward sweep attempting to bypass Bastogne. German colonel Meinrad von Lauchert, the commander of the 2nd Panzer Division, a unit Patton considered "the best armored division in the German army," was furious the 2nd Panzer had not captured Bastogne. Late in the day on December 20, as his troops were taking up positions in Noville, Lauchert contacted Gen. Heinrich von Lüttwitz by radio and asked for permission to delay his march west so he could move down the Noville road and take Bastogne. To his surprise, Lüttwitz answered sharply, "Forget Bastogne. Head for the Meuse."[27] US intelligence was also beginning to suspect that the Panzer Lehr Division might break from the battle at Bastogne to bypass the town to the south, making their own rush to reach the Meuse. The honor of capturing Bastogne would be left then to the 26th Volksgrenadier, not a battle-seasoned unit, but a last-ditch army composed of old men, young boys, and soldiers sufficiently recovered from battle injuries to fight again.

At the staff meeting on December 20, McAuliffe made a critical decision. MacKenzie dramatically recorded what happened as follows:

He [General McAuliffe] walked away from the group clustered around the desks, drawing General Higgins with him, and spoke briefly with the assistant commander. Then he moved to near the center of the room and stood alone.

The easy familiarity that characterized most of Tony McAuliffe's relationship with the staff fell away for a moment. A theatrical note that others accepted as appropriate was in his speech as he announced, "I am staying."

The tenor of the general's voice marked what he said as the considered, unalterable decision of the commander, and the staff members experienced the thrill that command decisions always sent coursing through them in situations where their courage was challenged and where their lives could be forfeited.[28]

Military historians Leo Barron and Don Cygan commented, "None of the men in the room knew it at the time, but their commander had just committed them to one of the epic stands in American history." They continued, "The Americans were staying in Bastogne. The staff responded, nodding. The officers and MacKenzie knew what the stakes were. They were taking a stand. Success meant victory and, more important, survival. Defeat meant probable death. McAuliffe's single-minded decision could turn out to be the most famous decision for the 101st Airborne, or it could turn to spell their doom."[29]

Late in the afternoon of December 20, McAuliffe left Bastogne to meet with Middleton in person at VIII headquarters at Neufchâteau. McAuliffe explained he was certain he could hold on at Bastogne for at least forty-eight hours, maybe longer. Middleton warned McAuliffe that the time could come soon when communications between Bastogne and VIII headquarters could not be maintained. Middleton warned that the 116th Panzer Division was advancing on McAuliffe's flank, in addition to the three divisions already attacking the town. McAuliffe said, "I think we can take care of them." But Middleton was not so confident. Middleton agreed that he wanted to hold Bastogne, but he was not sure it could be held indefinitely, in view of recent developments. Middleton advised it was important that the road to the southwest toward Neufchâteau be kept open as long as possible. As McAuliffe walked out the door, Middleton's last comment was, "Now, don't get yourself surrounded." McAuliffe observed that Middleton said this lightly, and he judged it was just Middleton's way of adding a bit of ironic levity into a difficult and tense situation.[30]

McAuliffe left the conference and told his driver to get back to Bastogne as fast as he could. It was a good thing McAuliffe did so, because about a half hour later, the German armor cut the road, effectively completing the encirclement of the town. S. L. A. Marshall commented the timing of the German encirclement was a mixed blessing, for it "brought an important change in the relationship of the forces in the defense."[31] Marshall noted that during the first two days of the Bastogne siege, the infantry and the armor had collaborated but they had not been a team. That was about to change. When Middleton learned the Neufchâteau road had been cut, he telephoned General Roberts directly to inform him that Roberts and the 10th Armored Combat Command B would now serve under McAuliffe's command. "Your work has been quite satisfactory, but I have so many divisions that I can't take time to study two sets of reports from the same area," Middleton explained, letting Roberts down easily.[32] Roberts understood. To show he was willing to comply completely with the order, Roberts agreed to move 10th Armored CCB headquarters from the Hotel LeBrun in the center of Bastogne to McAuliffe's 101st headquarters in the Heintz Barracks. "The result was that coordination was complete," S. L. A. Marshall wrote. "Roberts, a veteran tank commander, was particularly concerned that the armor be used properly, used to the maximum effect and not wasted."[33]

Marshall noted that Roberts strongly resisted the attempts to use his tanks as roadblocks. Up until this point, Roberts had worked specifically to get his armored units released after each engagement so that there would always be a maximum strength to the mobile reserve for the next emergency. Though he accepted Middleton's decision, Roberts still published during the siege a mimeographed memorandum instructing infantry officers on the right way to use tanks.

On December 21, VIII Corps ordered Combat Command B to "hold the Bastogne line at all costs." Middleton had been skeptical Bastogne could be held, but after meeting with McAuliffe, Middleton began to believe the gamble of an encircled force at Bastogne was going to succeed. "There was no longer any doubt or question anywhere in the camp," Marshall wrote.

"From this hour the action of all concerned, the VIII Corps commander, the 101st Division commander, and the armored force commander of Combat Command B—Middleton, McAuliffe, and Roberts—became wholly consistent with the resolve that Bastogne could and would be held."[34]

If McAuliffe had wanted to withdraw from Bastogne, he had many opportunities to do so. But, after conferring with his staff on December 20 and realizing the Germans were suffering as he was, both from shortage of supplies and adverse weather conditions, McAuliffe decided to stay. He was a paratrooper trained to be encircled and was also an artillery commander adept at using artillery to stop an enemy tank-led infantry advance. In the final analysis, McAuliffe concluded he could save more men by standing at Bastogne and fighting than he could if he were forced to fight a rear-guard action in a complex withdrawal.

Suddenly, McAuliffe's situation simplified. He now realized that the only American troops he needed to worry about were "right within the two-and-one-half-mile circle of German forces around Bastogne." That was just fine with him. "The only support he could expect for the time being was just what he had—all within ranging distance of his own 105mm batteries,"

US artillery unit firing 75-mm M1A1 field howitzer, Bastogne, Belgium. December 1944.

S. L. A. Marshall observed. "It was a nice, clear-cut position, and it had materialized in just about the way he had expected upon first reaching Bastogne."[35] As noted earlier, McAuliffe, in his after-action oral history given to S. L. A. Marshall and his staff of field historians, said from the first moments he got to Bastogne, he expected the Germans would surround his defense of the town.

At this point in the narrative, Marshall again made reference to McAuliffe's good fortune: "But what he [McAuliffe] had not foreseen, something that came like a gift from the gods, was that after the first hard collision, the enemy would give him a comparative respite in which to reflect on his situation and knit his armor and infantry close together, now that both were his to work with as he saw fit."[36] Marshall noted the Germans had

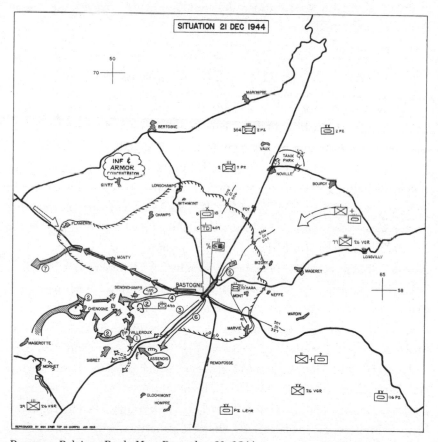

Bastogne, Belgium: Battle Map, December 21, 1944

spent two days trying desperately to break through at Bastogne. When that failed, the Germans spent the next two days trying to ride hard around it. "They had failed to crush it; they would try to choke it," Marshall wrote.[37] But while the Germans were building up around the west and the south of the town, the pressure against Bastogne relaxed, giving McAuliffe much-needed time to fortify his defenses, placing the various units of the 101st strategically around the defensive circle McAuliffe had devised to protect Bastogne at the circle's center. McAuliffe was outnumbered, with eighteen thousand US troops defending Bastogne against German divisions totaling probably forty-five thousand men, attacking from all sides.[38] The worsening winter weather was forecast not to break until after Christmas. But if Bastogne could manage to hold on until a break in the weather permitted air resupply, McAuliffe was confident he could hold this defensive position at Bastogne indefinitely.

COLD, SNOW, HUNGER, AND FROSTBITE

On Thursday, December 21, 1944, another of the enduring images of the battle emerged: snow began falling, covering the mud and frozen terrain in a blanket of white. The troops digging in were already freezing cold, not properly clothed for winter combat, and short on every imaginable type of supply, including food and ammunition. The snow cruelly managed to add another level of misery. "On December 21, it snowed, a soft, dry snow," wrote Stephen Ambrose in *Band of Brothers*, describing how Easy Company, of the 2nd Battalion of the 506th, dug in a reserve position after the pullback from Noville. "It kept coming, six inches, twelve inches. The temperature fell to well below freezing, the wind came up, even in the woods." Ambrose noted that with only their jump boots and battle dress with trench coats, the men of Easy Company were colder than they had ever been in their lives. "No wool socks, no long underwear," Ambrose added. "Runners went into Bastogne and returned with flour sacks and bed sheets, which provided some warmth and camouflage. In the foxholes and on the outposts, men wrapped their bodies in blankets and their boots in burlap. The burlap soaked up the snow, boots became soggy, socks got wet, the cold penetrated right to the bones. Shivering was as normal as breathing." Ambrose commented the men looked like George Washington's army at Valley Forge, except they were getting fired upon, had no huts for shelter, and could not light warming fires for fear of providing target opportunities to the enemy.[39]

Trench foot was a serious medical condition named in reference to World War I trench warfare, where the foot ailment became epidemic in the harsh, insanitary conditions of fighting outdoors in winter in dugout walkways that tended to pool with near-frozen water. Resembling frostbite, trench foot, if untreated, is extremely painful. In severe cases, toes or even the whole foot can turn black, become gangrenous, and require amputation. "For the men of Easy, without decent socks and no galoshes, feet always cold and always wet, trench foot became a problem," Ambrose noted. "Corporal Carson remembered being taught that the way to prevent trench foot was to massage the feet. So he took off his boots and massaged his feet. A German shell came in and hit a tree over his foxhole. Splinters tore up his foot and penetrated his thigh. He was evacuated back to Bastogne."[40] Dick Winters, the commander of Easy Company, in his 2006 book, *Beyond Band of Brothers*, noted that one-third of the casualties his unit suffered at Bastogne came from trench foot and frostbite. "Trench foot results from extreme moisture and cold, which adversely affects the body's circulation," Winters wrote. "The use of burlap only increased the moisture surrounding the foot, causing the skin to become so tender that it was impossible for soldiers to lace their boots."[41] Winters commented that the situation of trench foot became so painful that every soldier carried and transferred morphine ampoule vials from dead soldiers to those who still manned the foxholes.

"Life on the front lines defied description," Winters continued. "The weather was bitterly cold and the ground was frozen solid. Digging foxholes was a job every trooper despised, but it was a necessary chore. Unfortunately, our motor movement to Bastogne had been so hurried that many soldiers lacked entrenching tools to dig textbook fighting positions. And the temperature was horribly cold. Cold is cold. You live in a foxhole. Your feet are wet, and you're wiggling your toes to keep from freezing."[42] To make matters worse, Winters noted, there was no hot food, little sleep, no rest, and ever-present danger of instant death. "The worst time was night, when temperatures plummeted and fog covered the battlefield until mid to late morning," Winters recalled. "The uncertainty of what lay just yards ahead in the next tree line was sufficient to break ordinary men. Not surprisingly, the men became physically exhausted."[43]

Suffering right along with the soldiers on the line were the army chaplains. "Father Maloney came up in his jeep to do Mass for the men," remembered William "Wild Bill" Guarnere and Edward "Babe" Heffron, two of the Easy Company "Band of Brothers" at Bastogne. "The driver of the jeep, a Catholic kid, acted as the altar boy, and if he needed help, one of us would pitch in. When we saw the jeep coming up, we had to separate to walk toward it, you couldn't bunch up. One shell comes in, it could kill up to eight men. So we had to stagger, we all knew to do that, any soldier in any infantry organization knows to do that."

Guarnere and Heffron remembered that it was snowing and Father Maloney gave a pep talk, saying: "You guys are doing a good job for your country, you're heroes, it's a pleasure to be your spiritual guide, and I'm proud to be part of the 506th." Father Maloney used the hood of the jeep as an altar, and the soldiers knelt in the snow to get communion.[44] "Skip Muck was kneeling by me. He was a likeable, funny guy, and Irish and short like me," Heffron commented. "I got my wafer and he got his and Father Maloney ended the Mass saying, 'God bless you, good luck.' In the Catholic faith, when you receive communion and you die, you automatically ascend into heaven. So we walked away. I said to Muck, 'At least if we die, we're going to die in a state of grace.' Muck said, 'You're right, Heffron.'"[45]

At Bastogne, Father John Maloney suffered injuries two days in a row, first in his arm and the second in his shoulder. "The first came while he was visiting troops crouching in their foxholes near the edge of the American defensive lines surrounding Bastogne," wrote Jesuit priest Father Donald F. Crosby in his 1994 book, *Battlefield Chaplains: Catholic Priests in World War II*. "Suddenly he heard the clatter of a German artillery shell flying toward him, and as he ran for cover, a piece of shrapnel put what he called 'a neat hole' in his right forearm." The next day, while tending the wounded at a field hospital, another round of explosives landed nearby, this time giving him a mere "flesh wound," as he called it, in his shoulder. After the war, Father Maloney insisted none of his injuries had been at all "serious" and that he needed almost no care, rest, or hospitalization. His only real wounds, Father Maloney said, were "a decided tendency to duck at squeaking doors and low-flying jeeps," and some "967 gray hairs." The army, taking Maloney's wounds more seriously, awarded him a Purple Heart, later adding an Oak Leaf Cluster to the medal.[46]

Father Crosby believed bravery in combat distinguished chaplains in World War II. "Despite all the dangers they faced, the religious fervor of the men continued to make the chaplains' work worthwhile," Crosby observed. Yet, characteristically, the chaplains were focused not on themselves, but the spiritual well-being of the soldiers. Crosby noted that a priest from Vermont marveled at the goodness and generosity of his infantrymen. "He saw them repeatedly make great sacrifices for each other, especially their wounded comrades," Crosby wrote. "The supervising chaplain of one division reported his 'pride and consolation' were the troops and officers of his unit." Crosby quoted the Vermont priest as saying the following: "The religious life of these men will go down in history as something as outstanding as the great deeds they are accomplishing in battle." Crosby commented the men of the division would continue to be an inspiration to the Vermont priest, "as they had been to most of the chaplains in the Ardennes struggle, both Catholic and non-Catholic."[47]

PATTON PREPARES TO ATTACK

Eisenhower came out of the Verdun conference on December 19 convinced that holding Bastogne was essential to future offensive operations simply because Bastogne controlled the entire road network on the south side of the German bulge. After Eisenhower demoted Bradley, Patton moved to gain operational command over the southern battlefield of the Bulge. Bradley agreed, reassigning Middleton's VIII Corp to Bradley's Third Army group, effectively putting Patton in command of the Bastogne defense. Before he launched his 4th Armored into the spearhead of the Third Army advance north, Patton wanted to make sure he and Middleton were on the same page. Patton ordered Middleton to meet him in Arlon, the headquarters of Maj. Gen. John Milliken's III Corps. Milliken's III Corps commanded the 4th Armored, as Middleton's VIII Corps commanded the 101st at Bastogne. While Patton ultimately came to accept that the decision to hold Bastogne was correct, Patton never completely dismissed the idea that it would have been equally correct if his Third Army had counterattacked Hitler from the south, even if it meant ultimately abandoning Bastogne to the German advance.

On December 20, Patton began the meeting with Middleton in a confrontational manner. "Troy," Patton began, "of all the crazy things I ever heard of, leaving the 101st Airborne to be surrounded in Bastogne is the worst!" John S. D. Eisenhower, in *The Bitter Woods*, explained that Patton and Middleton were in the habit of exchanging frank opinions. "They had been students at Leavenworth together, and Middleton, an expert horseman, was one of the few officers excused from that august institution's equitation course and permitted to help exercise George Patton's fourteen polo ponies," Eisenhower noted. "But aside from their past relationship, Middleton could rely on the axiom: if General Patton is swearing at you, the chances are that you are currently rating pretty high on his list."[48]

Middleton took Patton's verbal assault in stride. "George," Middleton said in his best Mississippi drawl, "just look at that map with all the roads converging on Bastogne. Bastogne is the hub of a wheel. If we let the Boche take it, they will be at the Meuse in a day." Writing in his diary on December 20, Patton summarized the meeting with Middleton: "I told Middleton to give ground and blow up bridges so that we can get the enemy further extended before we hit him in the flank. However, on Bradley's suggestion, in which Middleton strongly concurred, we decided to hang on to Bastogne, because it is a very important road net, and I do not believe the enemy would dare pass it without reducing it."[49]

Then Patton switched gears, asking Middleton that if Middleton were in Patton's position, where would he launch his Third Army attack on Bastogne, from Neufchâteau to the southwest of Bastogne, or from Arlon to the south? "I'd attack with the 4th Armored from the place where our lines are closest to Bastogne," Middleton answered. The highway from Neufchâteau was seven miles closer to Bastogne than the road from Arlon. Middleton continued: "You've got to use both roads, but I'd put the weight on the Neufchâteau road. But as for the main effort of III Corps, I'd put it farther east. You don't cut troops off by pushing them in their front."

Eisenhower commented that as often happens, two graduates of the Command and General Staff School at Leavenworth could take the same set of facts and come up with different solutions. Patton had already decided the III Corps main attack would be made by the 4th Armored up the Arlon road. Milliken's other two III Corps divisions, the 26th Infantry Division and the 80th Infantry Division, would advance to the east, protecting the 4th Armored's right flank. Patton ordered Milliken to move III Corps headquarters to Arlon.

Patton's main preoccupation at this time was Millikin's III Corps attack, scheduled to jump off on December 22, two days after Patton's meeting with Middleton. As historian John S. D. Eisenhower noted, all three of Millikin's III Corps divisions had been either out of the line or in quiet sectors when the Third Army was ordered north. The 80th Infantry was in the best condition. The 26th Infantry was packed with replacements, after losing twenty-five hundred men to casualties during the Lorraine Campaign. The 4th Armored suffered from lack of replacements, but even more from worn-out equipment, much of which had been spent in the unit's constant combat since Normandy. Patton spent considerable time on the telephone arranging for self-propelled tank destroyer battalions, non-divisional tank battalions, hospitals, ammunition, and bridging materials. He directed all three divisions of the III Corps to cannibalize their anti-tank gun units and turn them into riflemen since all three were short of critical infantry replacements.[50]

German panzer tank knocked out by two anti-tank rounds, Bastogne, Belgium. December 1944.

Back in Luxembourg, Patton, with no staff officers present to help him, repeatedly telephoned his Third Army chief of staff, Brig. Gen. Hobart Gay, organizing in incredible detail the complicated logistics required to move the entire Third Army north, taking care to position the units Patton wanted leading the charge. Patton's supply officers had to set up scores of depots and dumps, shifting 62,000 tons of supplies in just 120 hours, working around the clock. His signal crew had to get ready to construct and maintain some twenty thousand miles of field wire under extreme winter conditions in what Patton assumed would be vicious enemy interference. Hundreds of thousands of new maps had to be distributed so field commanders could develop terrain analyses of the suddenly changed battle area.[51] [51]

"It was all wrought quietly and efficiently by a teamwork without parallel in the ETO [European Theater of Operations], a teamwork rooted deeply in great know-how, in great confidence in itself and its commander, and in great fighting spirit." wrote Col. Robert S. Allen, a syndicated columnist before the war who served as an intelligence officer on Patton's staff.[52] [52] Patton credited his team: "Actually the remarkable movement of the Third Army from the Saar to the Bulge was due to the superior efficiency of the Third Army staff."[53] But it took the honesty of Patton's driver to credit the general. At the end of a hectic day organizing the pivot north, Sergeant Mims, Patton's driver, said to him, "General, the government is wasting a lot of money hiring a whole general staff. You and me have run the Third Army all day and done a better job than they do."[54] On December 21, Patton wrote to his wife, "Yesterday I again earned my pay. I visited seven divisions and regrouped an army alone. It was quite a day and I enjoyed it."[55] [55] Military historian Trevor N. Dupuy in his 1994 book, *Hitler's Last Gamble*, agreed:

> While typically immodest, Patton hardly overstated the case—other than the implication that he had done all of this without any help from his efficient staff. He had, in fact, accomplished one of the great feats in military history: halting in its tracks an attacking army of 350,000 men and pivoting this massive force ninety degrees to be able to resume the attack in an entirely different direction in less than seventy hours. He *had* earned his pay![56]

Patton's first order to his troops on heading north toward Bastogne was: "Everyone in this army must understand that we are not fighting this battle in any half-cocked manner. It's either root hog—or die! Shoot the works. If those Hun[s] . . . want war in the raw then that's the way we'll give it to them!"[57] On December 21, the night before the Third Army launched its attack, Patton met with the staffs of three of his four corps. He recorded the event in his diary as follows: "I had all staffs, except the VIII Corps, in for a conference. As usual on the verge of an attack, they were full of doubt. I seemed always to be the ray of sunshine, and by God, I always am. We can and will win, God helping . . . I wish it were this time tomorrow night. When one attacks, it is the enemy who has to worry. Give us the victory, Lord."[58] Typically, even when alone in the quiet of his room overseas at night, after a demanding and stressful day preparing for battle, Patton's thoughts turned to the approaching fight and he felt confident, provided he had the help of God. Always ready to attack, Patton exhorted his corps staff in this final meeting before the offensive to be aggressive. "Drive like [expletive]!" he commanded them.[59]

Bradley knew this was Patton's finest hour:

> True to his boast at Verdun, Patton, having turned his Third Army ninety degrees, attacked on December 22. His generalship during this difficult maneuver was magnificent, one of the most brilliant performances by any commander on either side in World War II. It was absolutely his cup of tea—rapid, open warfare combined with noble purpose and difficult goals. He relished every minute of it, knowing full well that this mission, if nothing else, would guarantee him a place of high honor in the annals of the US Army.[60]

On the eve of the Third Army going into battle, Patton confided to his diary: "This has been a most wonderful move on the part of the whole Army. We will attack at 4 a.m., December 22nd."[61]

PATTON ATTACKS

As Patton had planned, at approximately 0600 hours on December 22, Patton's Third Army began its advance to the north, signaling the beginning of the US counterattack in the Battle of the Bulge. In the advance, Patton gave the battle lead to the 4th Armored Division and its commander, Maj. Gen. Hugh Gaffey. Commissioned in the field artillery in 1917, Gaffey had served as a regimental artillery officer in the Allied Expeditionary Force during World War I. A graduate of the Command and General Staff College at Ft. Leavenworth in 1936, Gaffey had served with Patton in North Africa. In April 1944, after Eisenhower pressured Patton to remove Maj. Gen. Hobart R. "Hap" Gay as his chief of staff during the Normandy preparations because of Eisenhower's concerns over Gay's administrative competence,[62] Patton chose Gaffey as Gay's replacement. In December 1944, Gaffey assumed command of the 4th Armored (in a move that allowed Patton to restore Gay to his position as Third Army chief of staff). "Patton kept watch over the 4th Armored Division with proprietary interest," noted military historian Harold R. Winton in his 2007 book, *Corps Commanders of the Bulge*.[63] Winton further noted that Gaffey clearly understood the objective of the 4th Armored was not to make "a thin, pencil-like thrust into Bastogne," but to establish a corridor sufficiently wide to withstand German counterattack and to permit the use of Bastogne as a base for future operations.[64] Once Bastogne was secure, Eisenhower and Bradley planned to utilize the town as the staging location for the continuance of Patton's counterattack to the northeast.

As the Third Army counterattack began, Patton, characteristically, was out among the troops as much as possible. "More than ever, Patton made it a point to be seen during the Bulge, always riding in an open armored car," noted historian Carlo D'Este in *Patton: A Genius for War*. "The cold was so intense that most soldiers dressed in as many layers of clothing as they could manage, but Patton's only concession to the glacial temperatures was a heavy winter parka or an overcoat."[65] D'Este noted Patton, in direct contrast to Bradley, spent little time in his headquarters, and most of his time each day on the road, so he could be seen by his troops enduring the same wretched weather conditions as they were. "Daily he prowled the roads of the Ardennes, sitting ramrod stiff, often with his arms folded, his face unsmiling," D'Este wrote. "More than once his face froze. Word of Patton's presence managed to filter through the amazing GI grapevine with astonishing rapidity, as did his words of praise for the troops, which were invariably repeated down through the chain of command: 'The Old Man says . . .' or, 'George says . . .'"[66]

D'Este related that one cold, dark, miserable afternoon, Patton encountered a column of 4th Armored moving toward Bastogne. Tanks and vehicles were sliding off the road in thick ice. But someone recognized Patton and let out a shout that began to roll down the column as soldiers in trucks and tanks began cheering. D'Este further related that after the war, a GI told Patton's wife, Beatrice: "Oh, yes, I knew him, though I only saw him once. We were stuck in the snow and he came by in a jeep. His face was awful red, and he must have been about froze riding in that open jeep. He yelled to us to get out and push, and first I knew, there was General Patton pushing right alongside of me. Sure, I knew him; he never asked a man to do what he wouldn't do himself."[67]

In this, Patton and McAuliffe shared an important characteristic: both commanders knew the importance of seeing the battle situation firsthand, observing with their own eyes, and being seen by their troops as willing to do so—willing to be in the front, in direct contrast to those generals that preferred to be safe in a command headquarters to the rear, where they were reduced to making command decisions relying on information gathered secondhand. Patton, like McAuliffe, always seemed to know the right place to be and the right time to be there. Both commanders shared the characteristic of wanting to know every detail of the battle for themselves, even at the risk of placing themselves with the troops, or even ahead of the troops, sensing somehow where precisely at the right time to handle a problem. McAuliffe decided to stay in Bastogne, while Middleton would most likely have staged a strategic retreat. Patton saw no problem turning the Third Army ninety degrees and conducting a forced march through the bitter cold of a raging snowstorm to relieve Bastogne, while other more cautious commanders may not have taken the risk. While McAuliffe might boast he did not need to be relieved, one of the reasons he could hold out fighting was he knew that as long as Patton's Third Army was on the way, there was no need to surrender—if only he could manage to hold on long enough.

Even though the advancing troops were fatigued and reconnaissance had not been sufficient to know for certain what enemy troops the Third Army might face ahead, Patton insisted the Third Army had to keep pushing through the night in order to maintain the initiative. "Patton kept up the verbal pressure all day," military historian Harold Winton noted. "Shortly before noon, he called Col. James H. Phillips, Milliken's diligent chief of staff, and 'directed that we drive like [expletive]. That we keep on attacking tonight,' adding, 'This is the last struggle and we have a chance of winning the war.'"[68]

SECTION IV

"NUTS!"

What may have been the biggest morale booster came with a
reverse twist—the enemy "ultimatum." About noon four Germans
under a white flag entered the lines of the 2nd Battalion,
327th. . . . The rest of the story has become legend . . .

—Hugh M. Cole, *The Ardennes: The Battle of the Bulge*, 1988[1]

Despite being surrounded, Gen. Anthony McAuliffe's composure in the defense of Bastogne was remarkable. "We were never really worried," McAuliffe told army field historians in his oral history given shortly after the Siege of Bastogne. "I never committed my division reserve. I didn't feel at any time that the situation called for it. Kinnard [Lt. Col. Harry Kinnard, G-3 operations officer] and Danahy [Lt. Col. Paul Danahy, G-2 intelligence officer] were never worried. It didn't look like big stuff to us or like an extraordinary situation. We felt it was just one more incident in the general battle. I can say positively that all of the worrying about our situation was done outside of Bastogne."[2]

McAuliffe's confidence was based on his certainty that his artillery strategy could beat back any advances the Germans might make. The troops he now had in the field were paratroopers seasoned by battle, trained to fight even when the enemy encircled them. Yet in a private conference with the regimental commanders of the 101st Airborne Division, McAuliffe acknowledged that withdrawal from Bastogne would have been suicide. As Lt. Col. Steve Chappuis, the commander of the 502nd Parachute Infantry Regiment—nicknamed "Silent Steve" because of his introspective nature— commented, "War is bad enough when you are tied in and the enemy is coming directly into you. When you are moving and he is coming around you, it is hopeless."[3]

On the night of December 20, McAuliffe had his last in-person conversation with Gen. Troy Middleton, commander of VIII Corps, at Neufchâteau. Devising a way McAuliffe could be relayed via radio messages in code to track Patton's progress, Middleton and McAuliffe made up a list of each town along Patton's way, assigning a letter to designate each town. Bastogne, for instance, was designated "K." This permitted McAuliffe to ask Middleton, "Where is Hugh?" meaning Maj. Gen. Hugh J. Gaffey, the commander of the 4th Armored in Patton's advancing Third Army. In response, VIII Corps headquarters could tell McAuliffe, "He's at 'C,'" so McAuliffe could track the progress of the advancing 4th Armored without giving away the position to any enemy that might be monitoring the conversation. "The night of 20 December, when I was in Neufchâteau, Middleton told me that Patton was attacking to the east of Bastogne."[4] Clearly, McAuliffe was tracking Patton closely, obviously concerned about when the 4th Armored relief would arrive.

With Patton approaching from the south, McAuliffe's major challenge was reduced to surviving the bad weather long enough for Patton to arrive. Either that or a miracle had to occur given that the forecast was snow and fog for the foreseeable future, at least until after Christmas. Would the bad weather break before McAuliffe ran out of ammunition? On leaving Neufchâteau after his conference with Middleton on December 20, McAuliffe contemplated that he might have to hold out without air resupply for another five days, until Christmas, and maybe longer. If the artillery guns were silenced and the troops on the line ran out of ammunition, McAuliffe would face the dire consequences of either allowing Bastogne to be overrun by the enemy or withdrawing his troops in a disastrous defeat.

The defense of Bastogne came down to a question of timing, and McAuliffe, as good a commander as he was, could not control the weather.

CHAPTER 10

AN OFFER TO SURRENDER

The men of the 101st chipped deeper into the frozen
earth, smiled grimly at McAuliffe's reply, and waited. The
Yankee spirit of Mac's answer swept through the ranks.

—Publication of the 101st Airborne Division, *Epic of the 101st Airborne: Bastogne*, 1945[1]

By noon on December 22, the 463rd Field Artillery Battalion, supporting the 327th Glider Infantry to the southwest and west in the circle defense perimeter of the town, was down to two hundred rounds of ammunition. Other artillery units were facing the same predicament. Without artillery ammunition, the key principle of McAuliffe's defensive strategy would be rendered non-operative. Throughout the day, infantry commanders observed an enemy build-up opposite their sectors, with tanks and half-tracks loaded with Germans moving "freely and contemptuously" along the lateral roads, making no attempt at concealment even though they were within easy range of the howitzers.[2] McAuliffe was at the point where he might have to ration his guns to ten rounds per day. S. L. A. Marshall observed it made the defenders frantic that a shortage of ammunition prevented them from firing on the Germans as they moved in open view across obvious killing fields.[3]

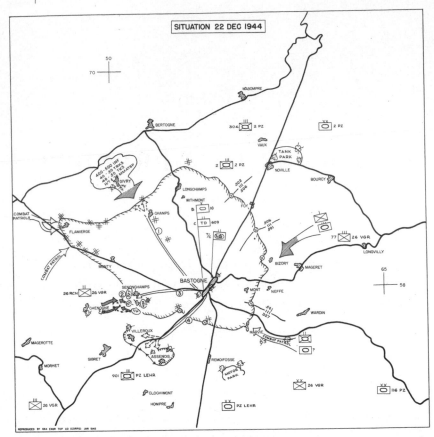

Bastogne, Belgium: Battle Map, December 22, 1944

THE EBB IN SUPPLIES

Meanwhile, the US Army Air Corps was doing everything possible to fight the bad weather in a desperate effort to put C-47s loaded with supplies in the air.

At 1530 hours on December 22, the 101st Division headquarters in Bastogne was notified that air resupply would be attempted later that day. Shortly thereafter, the 101st Division headquarters was notified that the air resupply would be postponed because of bad weather.[4] The defenders at Bastogne would have to hold out yet another day without resupply. As desperately as food was needed, ammunition was the shortage most immediately critical to survival. "They [the Germans] didn't have the coordinated artillery attack on the offense that I had in the defense," McAuliffe explained in the oral history he gave to S. L. A. Marshall's military historians after the battle. "They lacked both the guns and the ammunition. Most of the heavy fire we got from them was from tanks and SP [self-propelled] guns. It was our artillery situation which gave me my chief reason for confidence."[5]

Until supplies ran low, the Bastogne defenders had used freely the ammunition they had. On December 20 alone, seven battalions fired twenty-six hundred artillery rounds, with the majority of the rounds being directed against armor. The problem was unsupported infantry rarely stopped German armor, but infantry supported by artillery fire proved quite effective.[6] "The incomprehensible German failure to attempt to destroy or neutralize American artillery only served to bolster the cannoneers' confidence and determination," Col. Ralph M. Mitchell wrote in his 1986 monograph on the defense of Bastogne. "In his after-action report, one direct-support battalion commander wrote, 'After arriving at Bastogne and going into position, we found ourselves in exactly the situation we had been trained to handle.' Perhaps that was ultimately why they acquitted themselves so well."[7]

"On 23 December, our ammunition supply became critical," McAuliffe admitted in his after-action oral history. "Prior to that, the pinch wasn't too great. We then got down to ten rounds per gun. I began to get a little worried, and I told the batteries not to fire until they saw the whites of their eyes. The infantry and the few remaining [forward artillery] observers screamed their heads off."[8] Without air resupply, the guns defending Bastogne were at the risk of going silent and becoming easy prey for attacking German forces.[9] "We are about to be attacked by two regiments," said one phone message received at the 101st Division command post. "We can see them out there. Please let us fire at least two rounds per gun." Colonel Kinnard listened to the appeal, but had no alternative but to relay McAuliffe's reply: "If you see four hundred Germans in a hundred-yard area, and they have their heads up, you can fire artillery at them—but not more than two rounds."[10]

But everything was running low on supply, not just ammunition. The defenders of Bastogne were continuing to suffer from a lack of food, medical supplies, and winter clothing. The German troops were beginning to appear in the field in white suits and were camouflaging vehicles and guns in a similar fashion, while McAuliffe's defenders in their dark uniforms stood out as easy targets in the snow. General McAuliffe, since he spoke French, went out to the Bastogne townspeople himself to ask for help. "The commander's personal appearance among the villagers seemed to rally them to full active support of the besieged Americans holed up in their midst and around the town," journalist MacKenzie reported. Bed-clothing, tablecloths, and other white goods came from the homes and shops to drape Bastogne's Battered Bastards in forward positions."[11]

The desperation for something to eat was made clear by the extent to which Private E. B. Wallace went after a piece of cheese: "On the first day I threw away a can of K-ration cheese. When I became very hungry three days later, I crawled in that snow that covered the ground and found the cheese. The first cooked food we had was sprouted bean soup from dried beans someone found in a shack by the railroad."[12] The scrounging for food was often dangerous, as was made clear by an incident on the morning of December 22, when two soldiers on the line decided to search a small village for something to eat. PFC John E. Fitzgerald told the story as follows: "They went through one of our outposts and were gone for several hours. On their way back, they became lost in the fog and wandered too far to their left. As they approached our lines, they were cut down by one of the machine guns. Later that morning when the fog cleared, someone spotted their bodies. A detail was sent out to bring them back in. As we watched them being placed onto a jeep, we could see some potatoes rolling from their pockets onto the ground."[13]

Convoying supplies to Bastogne also proved impossible. On December 19, the 426th Quartermaster Company was ambushed trying to convey supplies to the besieged village, only to be met by German resistance, with the supplies diverted to VIII Corps until in Neufchâteau.[14] But even if supplies got to Bastogne, Colonel Kohls at Bastogne had no division-level supply forces or vehicles available either to pick up the resupply packages or manage their distribution. In preparation for the possibility of air resupply, Kohls issued instructions to the various regiments to send at least five quarter-ton trucks to the field to handle the supplies directly and haul them to the dumps. Kohls also instructed the units to report what supplies they had recovered and then distribute them according to orders issued by Kohls's G-4 section. Kohls had assigned the task of recovering aerial resupply to Maj. William H. Butler, S-4 supply officer of the 501st Parachute Infantry Regiment, and to Captain Matheson, S-4 of the 506th.[15]

Despite canceling the air resupply that had been initially scheduled for midday December 22, VIII Corps refused to give up. Col. Carl W. Kohls, the G-4 supply officer of the 101st Airborne, received a radio message at 2115 hours from VIII Corps saying that an attempt would be made to drop that night a portion of the supplies scheduled for air resupply earlier in the day.[16] At the appointed hour Butler went to the air drop area in the large, clear fields on a gentle hillside to the west of the houses of Bastogne, close to the Heintz Barracks, and put out florescent panels. But nothing happened. "Out of great expectation came only great disappointment," military historian S. L. A. Marshall noted.[17]

A WHITE FLAG APPEARS

At around noon on Friday, December 22, 1944, one of the most dramatic moments of World War II began to unfold along the defense perimeter around Bastogne, near a farm belonging to Jean Kessler, not far from the Arlon highway to the south of Bastogne.

Here troops of a platoon of Company F, 2nd Battalion, 327th Glider Infantry Regiment, watched in amazement as four Germans, one of them carrying a large white flag, appeared in front of the foxhole lines.[18]

As PFC Charles Kocourek witnessed the approach of the enemy soldiers, he felt it strange that the enemy would surrender when they were still being fired upon from a distance of many hundred yards.

He described his reaction as follows:

While we were standing around, we heard some firing and I walked over to these positions and asked, "What for?" The men said, "Germans—way out there!" Off in the distance were four Germans with a white flag coming down the road. One guy says, "Three shots and we've got four Germans— not bad!" I said, "Why would four Germans at four hundred yards' distance from our positions want to give up? It doesn't make any sense."[19]

From his outpost in the cellar of an isolated farmhouse, Sgt. Oswald Y. Butler of Company F, 327th Glider Infantry Regiment, also saw the four Germans with the large white flag walking up the road from Arlon toward his outpost. He telephoned Capt. James F. Adams, commanding officer of Company F, at the company command post over a hill to the rear. "There are four Krauts coming up the road," Butler reported. "They're carrying a white flag. It looks like they want to surrender."[20] Butler went out with S. Sgt. Carl E. Dickinson and PFC Ernest D. Premetz, a medical corpsman who spoke German, and the three headed out through the snow-covered fields to meet the Germans. Dickinson described the encounter as follows:

> I went down and met them below our line and one of them who could speak English said, "According to the Geneva and Hague Conventions, we have the right to deliver an ultimatum" and asked to be taken to our commanding officer.
>
> They each carried handkerchiefs for blindfolds and the German major blindfolded the other officer and I, in turn, blindfolded the German major. As soon as this was accomplished, our company medic, Ernest Premetz, not knowing if any of the Germans could speak English, came down as he could speak German. We left the other Germans with PFC Leo Palma in a BAR [Browning Automatic Rifle] position at the side of the road, and Ernest Premetz and I started back to the CP [Command Post] where Sergeant Butler and Lieutenant Smith came to the door to learn what was going on. When we asked them what to do with the two German officers, they told us to take them to the company CP where they stayed until their ultimatum was delivered to General McAuliffe in Bastogne.[21]

"Only the barest essentials of this great hour were remembered thereafter, and they were not always in agreement on minor details for factual reporting," MacKenzie noted regarding the German approach to the US lines.[22] Most accounts identify the four Germans as a major, a captain, and two enlisted men. The officers were dressed in long leather coats and shined boots; the enlisted men were ordinary soldiers in standard army coats. All were observed to be very polite. In most accounts, the German captain, wearing medical insignia, is reported to have stepped forward, saying in English, "We are *parlementaires*, and we want to speak with your officers." Then, after the major spoke in German to the captain, the captain amended his remarks to say, "We want to talk to your commanding general."[23]

As instructed, Dickinson and Premetz took the four Germans to the Company F command post, which was about a quarter of a mile in the woods to the east of the Kessler Farm and the Arlon-Bastogne road. As the Americans led the Germans over a hill, the Americans turned them around several times so they would not be familiar with the location of the command post.[24] In other accounts, Dickinson and Premetz left the two German enlisted men at the platoon command post and blindfolded the two officers before leading them over the hill to the command post of Captain Adams.

From there, word went up the chain of command as Adams called the 2nd Battalion headquarters in Marvie, and Battalion called Regiment in Bastogne, with the 327th headquarters in turn calling the 101st Division headquarters at the Heintz Barracks, relaying the message that some Germans had come in with surrender terms.[25] Maj. Alvin Jones, the 327th duty officer, received the following message: "Four Krauts have arrived at Company B. They came along the Arlon Road. They are carrying a white flag and declare themselves to be emissaries. You'd say they want to surrender!"

Even though the defenders of Bastogne were surrounded, the soldiers on the front line had never for a minute imagined the Germans were advancing toward their lines under a white flag because they wanted the Americans to surrender. Clearly, the first impression as word went up to 101st Division command was that the Germans had given up. "The rumor spread quickly around the front that the enemy had had enough and that a party had arrived to arrange a surrender," military historian S. L. A. Marshall wrote. "Quiet held the front. Many of the American defenders crawled out of their cover and spent the noon hour shaving, washing, and going to the straddle trenches."[26] Journalist MacKenzie agreed: "A rumor spread along the 327th Regiment's front: the Germans were ready to surrender and had sent a party to arrange terms. Men climbed out of their holes, built fires, shaved, visited neighbors."[27]

Major Jones, together with Col. Joseph H. Harper, commander of the 327th Glider Infantry Regiment, set out from the 327th headquarters in Bastogne to the 101st Division headquarters, where they handed to Col. Ned

D. Moore, the acting chief of staff of the 101st, the written message the Germans brought with them. The message, obviously typed on a captured American typewriter, contained the German version of the text on the left side and the English translation on the right side of the one-page message. The message was addressed, "To the USA Commander of the encircled town of Bastogne," and read:

> The fortune of war is changing. This time the USA forces in and near Bastogne have been encircled by strong German armored units. More German armored units have crossed the river Ourthe near Ortheuville, have taken Marche and reached St. Hubert by passing through Hompré-Sibret-Tillet. Libramont is in German hands.
>
> There is only one possibility to save the encircled USA troops from total annihilation: that is the honorable surrender of the encircled town. In order to think it over a term of two hours will be granted beginning with the presentation of this note.
>
> If this proposal should be rejected one German Artillery Corps and six heavy AA [Anti-Aircraft] battalions are ready to annihilate the USA troops near Bastogne. The order for firing will be given immediately after this two hours' term.
>
> All the serious civilian losses caused by this artillery fire would not correspond with the well-known American humanity.

The message was ambiguously signed simply, "The German Commander," not specifying the precise German commander responsible for deciding to issue the surrender demand.

Thankful for the lull in the battle that began Thursday, December 21, and was continuing into Friday, December 22, the Allied commanders in Bastogne were exhausted and getting some much-needed rest. "After five nights and four days of disorder, agitation, and fatiguing tension, the general staff had just instituted a plan in which the members would spell each other in the Operations Room [of 101st headquarters at the Heintz Barracks] so each could get four hours of sleep at regular intervals," noted journalist MacKenzie. "Paul Danahy, scheduled to relieve Colonel Kohls early that morning, had scolded Kohls for permitting him to oversleep his allotted time. 'Aw, I didn't have the heart to wake you,' said Kohls, 'You looked just like my little boy sleeping there.'"[28]

McAuliffe's activity had been so incessant from the moment he left Camp Mourmelon that others in the 101st command post began to worry they must induce him to rest. After assuring McAuliffe that other commanders could take care of minor emergencies and reassuring him that the defense of Bastogne was going well, his staff convinced him he should conserve his energies to meet real crises when they arose. As the pivotal moment developed, McAuliffe, who had been awake all the previous night, was asleep in a basement cubbyhole of the Heintz Barracks, next to the 101st Division command post in the cellar.[29]

So when Jones and Harper arrived at the command post, McAuliffe had to be awakened. MacKenzie described the scene as follows: "Most of the general staff were gathered in the Operations Room at division headquarters without any sign of tension or excitement evident among them when Major Jones arrived, saluted, and told General McAuliffe he had a message from the Germans." MacKenzie's narrative continued as follows:

> "What is it?" the general asked.
>
> "It's an ultimatum, sir," Jones said.
>
> Colonel Moore took the papers and scanned the English translation.
>
> "What does it say, Ned?" McAuliffe asked.
>
> "They want you to surrender," Moore answered.
>
> "Aw, nuts!" the commander blurted, exploding out of the calmness that was characteristic of his behavior under almost any circumstances.[30]

Marshall's account of the moment varied somewhat:

> Colonel Harper, commanding the 327th, went with Jones to division headquarters. The two German officers were left with Captain Adams. Members of the staff were grouped around General McAuliffe when Harper and Jones arrived. McAuliffe asked someone what the paper contained and was told that it was a request for surrender.
>
> He laughed and said, "Aw, nuts!" It really seemed funny to him at the time. He figured he was giving the Germans "one [expletive] of a beating"

and all of his men knew it. The demand seemed out of line with the exist-
ing situation.[31]

Harper, in his after-action debriefing with S. L. A. Marshall's historians had a slightly different account. "Harper had gone on up to present the
terms to McAuliffe as the German officers had been left back at the company command post," the report of Harper's debriefing read. "McAuliffe
laughed when he read the proposal. Then he said to Harper and the others
around him, 'Aw, nuts!'"[32]

The dismissive "Aw, nuts!" reaction shows McAuliffe reacting almost
as if he was disappointed that the Germans had not come forward to surrender to him. Secure that his defensive strategy was winning, McAuliffe
had never imagined the Germans would expect the Americans at Bastogne
would want to surrender. Viewed objectively, it would have to be absurd
to consider that an encircling army, the Germans, would surrender to
the encircled enemy, the Americans at Bastogne. Yet, McAuliffe psychologically never allowed himself to feel he was the underdog in this siege.
"Summing up their collective feeling, General McAuliffe said they all felt
they were giving the Germans 'a beating' and the ultimatum was 'way out of
line,'" MacKenzie wrote.[33]

MacKenzie also reported that the sentence in the ultimatum about
civilians irritated McAuliffe because Germans had shown no concern for
civilians in the battle up to then.[34] McAuliffe thought the Germans were
hypocritical for suggesting they were concerned about the civilians who
would be wounded or killed if McAuliffe refused to surrender and the
Germans started shelling Bastogne. Here it was the height of a severe winter, and the Germans in their advance had destroyed countless homes and
villages all throughout the Belgium countryside.

Besides, as the Siege of Bastogne wore on, the US forces were all too
aware of the various atrocities the SS was committing, including very dis-
turbing rumors involving the SS and American POWS at Malmedy.[35] The
crux of the rumors was that the Nazi SS under Lt. Col. Joachim Peiper's
Kampfgruppe had ordered his troops to brutally machine-gun and massacre
somewhere between eighty and one hundred US soldiers who had surrendered, while the US soldiers were standing unarmed and defenseless in a

snowy field. "Early one afternoon, SS troops discovered an American field battalion, which quickly surrendered," wrote Jesuit priest Father Donald F. Crosby. "At a signal from an officer, the Germans opened fire on the prisoners with machine guns and pistols. At least eighty-six unarmed, defenseless American soldiers perished. When SS troops saw that some of the men still showed signs of life, they smashed them in the head with rifle butts or shot them again. A few Americans managed to escape, and they immediately reported what had happened." Father Crosby noted word of the massacre spread like wildfire through American ranks, stiffening the resolve of the troops to deflect the enemy attack.[36] Crosby commented that at the time of the Malmedy massacre, word had begun to spread among the US troops involved in the Battle of the Bulge that the dreaded SS troops were committing atrocities against both American troops and Belgian civilians. "It was well known that the SS respected no one and considered themselves bound by none of the basic laws of decency," Father Crosby wrote. "When the chaplains heard about the atrocities, they, too, seethed with anger."[37] Chaplain Leo Weigel came to the conclusion, Father Crosby noted, that the SS was "a menace that should be exterminated now because it will not be checked in any other way."[38]

Harper reported that McAuliffe decided to stall for a couple of hours before he made a response. When finally McAuliffe sat down with paper and pencil to compose his answer, he was not sure what he should say. "I don't know what to tell them," McAuliffe said to his staff.

Journalist MacKenzie recorded what happened next.

> Hearing this, Kinnard, the division G-3, piped up, "That first crack you made would be hard to beat, General."
>
> Puzzled, McAuliffe asked, "What was that?"
>
> Kinnard reminded him, "You said, 'Nuts!'"
>
> The general snapped his fingers, "That's it!"
>
> As those present seconded the suggestion, McAuliffe wrote: "To the German Commander. Nuts! From the American Commander."[39]

MacKenzie described how those in the room reacted. "Colonel Harper was summoned. McAuliffe asked him how he would reply to the message.

Harper stood mute in thought until the general handed over his paper. They all burst into an uproar of laughter, delighted with this zany culmination of the affair." McAuliffe asked Harper to make sure the message was delivered. "I will deliver it myself," Harper answered. "It will be a lot of fun."[40] McAuliffe cautioned Harper not to go into German lines.

Harper returned to the Company F command post where the two Germans were standing in the woods, blindfolded and under guard. "I have the American commander's reply," Harper informed them.[41]

The German captain asked, "Is it written or verbal?"

Harper answered, "It is written."

Harper then stuck the message in the German captain's hand. The German captain read and translated the message, informing his associate, the German major, that the message said, "Nuts!"

Confused, the German major asked for clarification: "Is the reply negative or affirmative? If it is affirmative, I will negotiate further."

Colonel Harper was beginning to lose his good temper. "The reply is decidedly not affirmative," he said firmly.

"If you continue this foolish attack your losses will be tremendous," the German threatened.[42]

To make sure the Germans understood the idiom, Harper decided not to compromise on the translation, just to make sure the Germans got the message. "It means, 'Go to [expletive]!'" Harper explained in terms easy to understand.

As US military historian Hugh M. Cole noted, the 101st Division's G-2, Lt. Col. Paul Danahy, saw to it that the story was circulated—and properly embellished—in the daily periodic report: "The Commanding General's answer was, with a sarcastic air of humorous tolerance, emphatically negative."[43]

Harper put the two officers in a jeep and took them back to the main road where the two German privates were waiting with the white flag. He then removed the blindfold and said in English, speaking to the German captain, "If you continue to attack, we will kill every German that tries to break into this city."

The German major and captain saluted very stiffly. The captain said, "We will kill many Americans. This is war."

Military historian S. L. A. Marshall noted it was then 1350 hours, just under two hours since US troops first spotted the four German soldiers advancing toward American lines under a white flag.

"On your way, Bud," Colonel Harper said, "and good luck to you."

As the four Germans walked down the road back to German lines, Harper returned to the command post, regretting that he had sent them off wishing them good luck. MacKenzie commented that Harper regretted his bellicose behavior. "He said later that he could have kicked himself for popping off, because he feared after some second thought that the affronted Germans would throw everything they had at his front, and the men of his command would be the sufferers."[44]

McAuliffe and his second in command, General Higgins, took delight the rest of the day in sitting at the crude, bare table, straight-faced and solemn as they invited visitors to read the exchange.

"The thing caused the reader's wits to reel," MacKenzie reported. "Then the next few moments were crazy with laughter. The generals roared with glee, and the butt of their fun sometimes was close to hysteria because of that amazing word jumping at him off the page."[45] MacKenzie was equally thrilled, writing: "It was marvelous, this answer to the pompous German: 'Nuts!' and nothing else. It was glorious."[46]

McAuliffe's response was easily the most famous single word uttered by any American commander during World War II.

With the delay in reporting on Bastogne to Americans back home, the first story on McAuliffe's reply appeared on New Year's Eve, December 31, 1944. An Associated Press story printed in the *Washington Post* carried the title, "'Nuts' Reply Typical of Gen. McAuliffe." Using the general's nickname, "Old Crock," reporter Edward D. Ball described McAuliffe in heroic terms:

> Offhand, you wouldn't think of this slight man, who weighs 135 pounds, as second in command of one of the world's toughest fighting outfits. He parts his slightly graying hair in the middle, and takes on something of a professorial appearance when he hitches on a pair of shell-rimmed glasses while poring over maps. He parachuted into Normandy on D-Day and landed by glider in Holland. Here he just jumped out of the back of a truck.

The AP report noted that all through the encirclement, McAuliffe was "out in the front line sizing up the situation or back at the command post outguessing the Germans." The article told the story of one of McAuliffe's frequent visits to a crowded hospital, when a GI rose up from his litter and said, "Don't give up on account of us, General Mac." McAuliffe assured the soldier "there would be no giving up."[47]

Despite the celebrity status his "Nuts!" response instantly conferred on McAuliffe with US troops throughout the European theater and worldwide, the commander characteristically took the incident in stride.

"Now as to the request for our surrender, it must be realized the thing really seemed funny to us at the time," McAuliffe explained in simple, unpretentious terms to S. L. A. Marshall's military historians shortly after the Siege of Bastogne had been lifted. McAuliffe told Marshall:

> It was a little out of line for them to tell us that we were beat up and the position was hopeless. When the message was read to me, I said, 'Aw, nuts,' just to dismiss it. But I realized that I had to make some kind of reply and I was thinking it over. I asked the staff what they thought. Kinnard said, 'That first remark of yours would be hard to beat,' and then he recalled what I had said. That made everybody very enthusiastic, and because they thought it was all right, I sent it along. But Kinnard had the inspiration.[48]

Despite his innate humility, McAuliffe's response inspired Patton, a soldier's soldier, who greatly admired what he saw as McAuliffe's courage under fire.

"Anybody that eloquent deserves to be saved," Patton said, drawing inspiration from McAuliffe's laconic reply.

Military historian Harold Winton called the surrender ultimatum "the largest German psychological blunder of the campaign." Realizing German general Lüttwitz was responsible for issuing the ultimatum, Winton argued that Lüttwitz "was obviously motivated by the thought that a victory on the cheap would resolve the tension between continuing the attack toward the west and capturing the transport nexus necessary to support that offensive." Winton believed Lüttwitz may have been encouraged by the surrender of two regiments of the 106th earlier in the battle to hope he might pull off a similar coup. Winton charged that Lüttwitz "utterly misread the mood of McAuliffe, who had absolutely no intention of surrendering and probably realized as much as the 47th Panzer Corps commander [Lüttwitz] did that, all things considered, the defenders of Bastogne had the upper hand."[49]

The 101st Airborne Division's G-2 periodic report for the Bastogne siege took delight in noting that the vengeful artillery assault the Germans promised never materialized: "The catastrophic carnage of human lives resulting from the artillery barrage of astronomic proportions which was to be the fate of the defending troops failed to materialize."[50]

Historian Ladislas Farago noted that on the evening of December 22, McAuliffe launched a series of forays so surprising to the Germans that the Nazis hastily had to scrape forces together to repel the attacks. These forays "now convinced the Germans that they could not gain Bastogne without a struggle." Farago commented that although the siege continued and the future of the town's eighteen thousand defenders remained in the balance, McAuliffe's resolute determination to hold on to Bastogne turned the tide. Farago quoted German general Manteuffel as writing: "From the evening of December 22, the situation at Bastogne was reversed: henceforth the investing forces were to be on the defensive."[51] Manteuffel was angered over the entire episode, not only because he had not been consulted or given permission to Lüttwitz to attempt this scheme, but even more so because the Germans lacked the artillery needed to make good on Lüttwitz's threat to annihilate the Bastogne defenders. "This is crazy," Manteuffel muttered, realizing he would have to request support from the Luftwaffe to carry out Lüttwitz's threat as best he could.[52]

Leo Barron and Don Cygan pointed out that Bastogne had become Lüttwitz's "biggest problem." Barron and Cygan observed:

As he [Lüttwitz] sat in a fine chair in the luxurious château [Lüttwitz's headquarters at Roumont near the town of Libin, Belgium, to the west of Bastogne], Lüttwitz mentally ticked off the disadvantages that the Americans must now be confronting: they were surrounded, could not get resupplied, and were cut off from the rest of the Allied army. The artillery fire seemed to have slackened. That could mean the *Amis* were running out of shells. There had been no major reports of clashes with

American armor, so it was logical to suspect that they had only a scant number of tanks. Lüttwitz knew the 101st Airborne Division, the unit the Allies called the "Eagle Division," was the primary unit ensconced behind Bastogne's walls. A Fallschirmjäger [Paratrooper] unit was not designed to fight very long without supplies, armor, or additional infantry support. Also, the recent turn in the weather could only be making the situation miserable for the Americans.[53]

Lüttwitz also knew the American attempt to defend St. Vith, to the north of Bastogne, was failing.

Baron and Cygan argued that before he committed the 26th Volksgrenadier Division to an all-out attempt to take Bastogne, Lüttwitz had decided he would "throw the dice" and see whether the American commander might accept an offer to surrender.[54] Lüttwitz chose as the emissaries crossing American lines under a white flag Major Wagner from his staff, along with Lt. Hellmuth Henke, the personal adjutant of Gen. Fritz Bayerlein, the commander of the Panzer Lehr Division. Henke spoke perfect English, with a British accent. Lüttwitz decided on his own to issue the ultimatum without first consulting with General Manteuffel to get his approval. "He [Lüttwitz] hoped his gamble would work, for if it did, he would probably be hailed as a hero," Barron and Cygan wrote. "If it didn't, Manteuffel, and probably all of Germany, would unleash their wrath on him instead of the Americans."[55]

When McAuliffe rejected Lüttwitz's ultimatum, Lüttwitz knew he had lost his gamble. At Manteuffel's insistence, the Panzer Lehr Division was ordered to bypass Bastogne to the south as the 2nd Panzer Division had been ordered to bypass Bastogne to the north, with both divisions headed west toward the Meuse River. This left the job of taking Bastogne to Col. Heinz Kokott and the 26th Volksgrenadier Division.

Reflecting on McAuliffe's one-word response to the Germans, S. L. A. Marshall noted, "It was a victory for eloquence at some expense to grammar but in keeping with the other grim humors of the day." That night, Marshall noted, the Luftwaffe began its bombing attack on Bastogne, an assault the Luftwaffe repeated on the next four nights.[56]

CHAPTER 11

THE BAD WEATHER BREAKS

On the twenty-third, skies cleared, snows stopped, and the
weather remained perfect for six days. "Hot dog!" yelped Patton
in glee, "I guess I'll have another 100,000 of those prayers
printed." Chaplain O'Neill, overnight one of the most popular
men in Third Army Headquarters—if only because he made
the "Old Man" happy—had won himself a Bronze Star.

—Gen. Paul D. Harkins, *When the Third Cracked Europe*, 1969[1]

T he Bastogne battlefield was strangely quiet as snow began to fall
after midnight on Friday, December 22. It was that evening, just
before the weather broke, that the Bastogne battlefield was visited
by a seemingly paranormal "ghost patrol" of phantom warriors that added a
note of the supernatural to the battlefield.

A BASTOGNE MYSTERY

In the quiet of the Friday night snowfall, one of the mysterious incidents
that came to characterize the Siege of Bastogne occurred. "The night in all
respects was one for ghostly apparitions," wrote journalist Fred MacKenzie
in *The Men of Bastogne*. "The battlefield was utterly silent, a lively habitat for

specters, queerly illuminated in a kind of twilight." A mysterious procession of eleven figures was observed coming boldly through the snow-whitened fields of no-man's-land a mile and a half southeast of Bastogne. Unchallenged, this eerie procession entered American lines and disappeared. "From reports of the passage and subsequent unexplained disappearance of the strangers, a legend was born: a ghost patrol haunted the centuries-old Ardennes invasion corridor," MacKenzie recorded.[2]

The strange patrol of phantom warriors was first spied by four men of Colonel O'Hara's 54th Armored Infantry Battalion as they were on patrol between positions held between Harper's 327th Regiment on the right and Ewell's 501st Regiment on the left. "A crust was forming on the snow as the temperature dropped and frost settled in the lowlands," MacKenzie noted. "The sound of the crust's breaking underfoot was O'Hara's men first warning of the incursion from the direction of the German positions."[3] The eleven figures advanced without showing any caution as they climbed over fences and moved confidently into the US lines. None of the intruders appeared armed. "The outnumbered Tiger patrol kept quiet and out of sight," MacKenzie continued. "Their initial alarm subsided almost immediately, because they saw no menace in a group lacking the furtive movements of belligerents. The party passed unmolested from sight."[4] The eleven men appeared at various points along the US lines, filing past sentries and walking to within a few yards of various unit command posts without any alarm being raised.

In his after-action interview with S. L. A. Marshall's historians, O'Hara gave a detailed description of the ghost patrol, trying to explain why his men did not fire when they saw the strange intruders. "These men walked upright, went over fences, and entered our position midway between the sector of the 327th and the 54th," O'Hara reported. "They passed sentries, walked within 100 yards of the command post of the 327th and 200 yards of the command post of the 54th. Yet these men seemed so familiar with the area that no challenge was made." O'Hara noted that four different groups reported the patrol and gave an accurate count of the number. "When the command posts heard of the incident, they checked to learn if any adjacent unit had put out such a patrol and found that they had not. Perhaps these men were stragglers. They were never heard from again."[5]

S. L. A. Marshall took O'Hara's story seriously enough that he included it in his classic book on the battle, *Bastogne: The First Eight Days.* "This visitation and its mystery became one of the legends of Bastogne," S. L. A. Marshall wrote.[6]

THE WEATHER BREAKS

On December 22, troops of the Third Army began advancing north in a raging snowstorm with a copy of Patton's prayer for fair weather in their pockets. As they advanced, a sudden, unexpected shift in the weather began taking place in Russia, on the Eastern Front. "German meteorologists on the Eastern Front noted a forming high-pressure system and dutifully reported the information to Generalfeldmarschall Model of Heeresgruppe B [Army Group B] in charge of the battle," noted military historian Danny S. Parker.[7] On the Allied side, the 21st Weather Squadron attached to the 9th Air Force also began paying attention to the lower moisture, accompanied by a rising barometer, in the temperature readings from Russia. "Very early on the morning of December 23, [Maj. Stuart J.] Fuller rushed into the 12th Army Group Tactical Air Command war room with astonishing news," Parker continued. "His forecast identified an eastern high-pressure cell known as a 'Russian High' that would result in good weather all along the front. Hitler's luck had finally run out."[8]

FLYING WEATHER

"December 23 will be remembered all over the Ardennes campaign as the day when the weather broke," noted historian John S. D. Eisenhower.[9] George Patton attributed the unexpected break in the weather to Chaplain O'Neill's prayer. As far as Patton was concerned, unpredicted clearing of the weather was proof Chaplain O'Neill was in the good graces of God. As noted earlier, Patton summoned Chaplain O'Neill to pin a medal. The prayer had to have been a good prayer, Patton was convinced. But even more important Chaplain O'Neill evidently had the ear of God. As far as Patton was concerned, anyone who was in the good graces of God needed to be in the good graces of the Third Army as well. The unexpected clearing of the skies on Saturday, December 23, 1944, elevated the drama of Chaplain O'Neill's prayer for good weather into yet another legend of the Siege of Bastogne.

US Army meteorologists had no explanation why the weather changed so suddenly and unpredictably, but the sun rose on December 23 to a frozen landscape under a clear blue sky. Air resupply of Bastogne was now possible for the first time since the siege began. Equally important, US fighter airplanes could finally assist in pushing back the German forces surrounding the beleaguered village. "Morning. December 23rd. The mists and ground fog slowly faded to show a clear, steely blue winter sky," Parker wrote. "A pale December sun hesitantly rose above the horizon to at last reveal itself. Within hours the sun was like a blazing arc illuminating the snow dusted forests over the embattled hills of the Ardennes. It was, according to one beleaguered GI on the ground, 'the war's most beautiful sunrise.'"[10] George Patton's reaction was predictable: "What a glorious day! Perfect for killing Germans!"[11]

THE C-47S TAKE TO THE AIR

Early on the morning of December 23, the pathfinders who planned to lead the air resupply effort were reloaded into their Douglas C-47 airplanes, this time confident the mission would finally go forward.

Built by Douglas Aircraft, the C-47s, known as "Skytrains" or "Dakotas" (based on the letters "DACoTA" for Douglas Aircraft Company Transport Aircraft), were military transport/cargo aircraft that served as the workhorse aircraft for air resupply missions. Paratroopers used a specially redesigned C-53 "Skytrooper" version throughout World War II. After World War II, the C-47 became the DC-3, a two-engine propeller aircraft that became the workhorse commercial passenger airliner of the 1950s.

The lead aircraft was piloted by Col. Joel L. Crouch of the 9th Troop Carrier Common Pathfinder Group, or 9th TCC Pathfinder Group, of the XVIII Airborne Corps. A member of the pathfinder team on Crouch's C-47 was Richard M. Wright, Company E, 506th Parachute Infantry Regiment, 101st Airborne Division. "It was probably the quickest way to get into the fight against the evil tyranny of Nazi domination that had overwhelmed and brutalized most of Europe," Wright said, explaining why he chose to volunteer as a paratrooper to be a pathfinder. "They explained to us that it was a suicide mission, and I just felt that I had to volunteer for it."[12]

Pathfinders were the first to jump into a drop zone, or "DZ." Their mission was to set up the signaling equipment needed to direct the C-47s of the airborne troop carrier command to drop its supplies on the right location. Specifically, the job of the pathfinders was to set up radar transmitters, AN/PPN-1A Eureka beacon units, that would send out a signal to be received by the APN-2 (SRC-729) Rebecca receivers carried on C-47 troop-carrying and cargo airplanes. The Eureka signal was designed to guide the Rebecca-equipped C-47s to the DZ, regardless how large or small the DZ was.[13] Each pathfinder "stick," consisting of one officer and nine enlisted men, was responsible for marking the DZ and guiding the C-47s to their destination. The executive officer of the 9th TCC Pathfinder Group made the decision to drop two pathfinder sticks into Bastogne, in case one group was dropped into enemy territory or otherwise incapacitated. After the first mission to resupply Bastogne, four pathfinder sticks from the 9th TCC were sent to a French airfield camp in Chateaudon where they stayed for several days on thirty-minute alert for future missions.[14]

PFC John Agnew, a member of "jumpmaster" 1st Lt. Shrable Williams's stick, described the air resupply mission to Bastogne as follows:

> Take-off time was 0645, 23 December 1944, I was in the lead aircraft (#993) piloted by LTC Crouch. We were followed by a second aircraft (#681) piloted by 1st Lt. Lionel Wood. The flight from Chalgrove [England] to Bastogne was uneventful but as we approached the DZ and the red light came on for "hook-up!" tension mounted and you got a lot of funny feelings. Suddenly there was a burst of ground fire and you could see the tracers go by. It came from a German gun emplacement directly in front of our flight path. Quickly, Colonel Crouch dove the aircraft directly at the Germans (we were looking down the barrels of their guns), who, thinking they had shot us down and we were going to crash on top of them, jumped out of their gun emplacement and ran for safety. The colonel then pulled the aircraft back up to jump altitude. However, since we were all standing (loaded with heavy pathfinder equipment), the suddenness of the maneuver caught us by surprise and most of us sank to our

knees due to the "G" force exerted. Luckily, we all recovered our balance just as the green light came on and out the door we went. Upon landing, George Blain signaled the second aircraft to commence their drop.[15]

At 0935 hours, the pathfinders from the first C-47 piloted by Colonel Crouch jumped, followed quickly by the second group in Lieutenant Wood's airplane. The jumpmasters of the two teams were Lieutenants Shrable Williams and Gordon Rothwell.

Lieutenant Williams later recalled:

The drop was successful. Both teams landed okay. Upon landing, Lieutenant Rothwell and I went straight to 101st Division Headquarters to see where they wanted the resupplies dropped. We went to the designated DZ and LZ [Landing Zone] in a low place almost in town. We set up our electronic equipment and in less than an hour later the planes were contacted and were homing in on our signal and the resupply mission was history. We were located on the highest ground in and around Bastogne so we had a front row seat.[16]

After identifying the DZ, the pathfinders quickly laid out their fluorescent orange panels on the white snow to mark a DZ just west of the 101st headquarters in Heintz Barracks. As the other pathfinders worked to mark out the DZ, Agnew, a demolitions specialist, quickly found exactly the right place to set up his Eureka transmitter, on top of a large, ten-foot-tall stack of bricks. This was the highest point in the area, perfect for setting up the radio and Eureka signal transmitting equipment required to help guide the C-47s to the DZ. With Agnew operating the Eureka from a position on top of the pile of bricks, the others in the first pathfinder stick stood behind the pile of bricks, pleased to have found the cover in case the enemy spotted them and opened fire.[17]

The pathfinders on the ground waited until the last minute to turn on their Eureka set, so as to avoid giving their position away to German radio direction finders that were ready to call in artillery fire on the landing zone. Once the pathfinders had radioed back that they had safely landed within the Bastogne defense perimeter, forty C-47s of the 441 TCC Group took off, operating solely on instruments because the still rough weather over England meant visual flying was impossible with the low clouds that continued to hug the ground. About forty miles out from Bastogne, the skies cleared, making instrument flying no longer necessary. About thirty minutes after taking off in England, the C-47s were over the drop zone.

THE C-47S ARRIVE

Flying into Bastogne, the C-47 pilots easily spotted ahead the selected DZ. Technical Sergeant Martin Wolfe, a C-47 radio operator, described what it looked like flying into Bastogne: "The first thing you saw, coming toward Bastogne, was a large, flat plain completely covered with snow, the whiteness broken only by a few trees and some roads and, off in the distance, the town itself. Next, your eye caught the pattern of tank tracks across the snow. We came down lower and lower, finally to about 500 feet off the ground, our drop height."[18]

At approximately 1150 hours, hundreds of brightly colored parachute

Bastogne air-resupply. C-47s drop supplies by parachute. December 1944.

canopies filled the skies above Bastogne, as this first wave of C-47s began to drop their supplies. The parapacks dropped in many different colors, each color-coded to allow easy identification of the loads, with red parachutes signaling ammunition, for instance, green for rations, and blue designating water.[19] "Upturned faces in the headquarters were transfigured with rapture as the planes came on and on like great immortal carriers of goods from heaven," MacKenzie noted, "and when one and another burst into flames from the flak, the watchers were aghast: it was incredible that these bearers of good tidings were vulnerable to earthly assault."[20] MacKenzie observed that parachutes of yellow, red, and blue floated down with huge bundles of supplies upon the plain west of the town and beyond the cemetery. "Some of the sluggish, fat-bodied craft passed less than 1,000 feet overhead, and all around was a vast invigorating throbbing," he wrote. "Men cheered and flung themselves into violent motion, wanting to convey to the pilots a measure of the exultation that stormed in them below."[21]

Radio-operator Don Bolce described the experience of flying within one of the C-47s heading toward Bastogne that day from Ramsbury, England: "We had four squadrons, each with eighteen planes for a total of seventy-two C-47s. Under the planes in racks, we had parapacks, which could be released from the pilots' compartment, and parabundles inside the plane. These we pushed out the open door with static lines in place to open the chutes." Bolce noted he was on the radio during the mission and his Rebecca receiver picked up the Eureka signal about twenty-five miles outside Bastogne. The signal led Bolce's C-47 directly to the DZ. "As we neared Bastogne we could see snow everywhere," Bolce remembered. "We removed the door as we prepared to push the parabundles out over the DZ. I could see German half-tracks with 88mm guns come out of the dark woods to my left. They began shooting their deadly flack directly at our plane, but thankfully their range was short. There were many puffs of black smoke but we never did get hit." When the C-47 reached the DZ, the pilot gave the green light and Bolce helped the other crew members push the parabundles out the open door. "I could see the colored smoke and bright panels on the white snow below us," Bolce continued. "The supplies had been delivered to the defenders of Bastogne!"[22]

By 1606 hours on December 23, 1944, some 241 C-47s had dropped

1,446 bundles weighing 144 tons into the mile-square DZ.[23] The drop pattern was excellent, with the accuracy of the C-47s permitting about a 95 percent recovery of the material dropped. "Working against the approaching darkness, the supply crews threw whole bundles, parachute and all, into the jeeps and shuttled between the drop zone and their dumps as fast as they could tear over the ground," noted military historian S. L. A. Marshall. "All supplies were in the unit dumps by 1700, and even before that time ammunition had been rushed directly to the front lines and battery positions. The artillery was firing part of the resupply ammunition at the enemy before the drop zone had been cleared."[24] General McAuliffe and his staff watched the air resupply from the front entrance to the Heintz Barracks as the sound from the C-47s grew in volume from the southwest. "As the men hollered in joy, the C-47s from Troop Carrier Command spread over Bastogne like angels with olive drab wings," observed military historians Barron and Cygan. "To many watching the drop, the gently falling parachutes reminded them of the gently falling snow the day before."[25]

MacKenzie, observing the air resupply from 101st Division Headquarters, watched carefully as a group of men gathered, looking upward. MacKenzie overheard members of the division staff saying, "Wait and see,"[26] it felt as they scanned the sky "as if Santa and his sleigh would suddenly appear."[27] MacKenzie did not have to wait long to find out what the excitement was about. "Low over field and town then swarmed objects so dear to their straining eyes they might not look upon angel band with greater wonderment and joy," he wrote. "The objects were the foremost planes of a mass flight of 240 C-47 cargo carriers bringing them supplies. Here were the messengers with tidings that the world of friends and decency had not forgotten the defenders of Bastogne. Here was evidence that back somewhere order and planning were restored after a week of uncertainty and snafu."[28] MacKenzie wrote the men of Bastogne looked upon the air resupply as a harbinger of victory. "We'll beat the Krauts now, sir," exulted a soldier MacKenzie observed dancing by.[29]

The air resupply happening on December 23, just two days before Christmas, had a mystical quality to it. MacKenzie recorded an incident in which a soldier was found exhibiting ecstatically a tiny prayer book cradled in both his hands. "Look what I found," the soldier exclaimed. "It was right there on a window sill in plain sight, and all of a sudden I saw it there."[30] MacKenzie commented that the soldier took finding the prayer book just when the C-47 air resupply reached Bastogne as a sign from God, confirming, finally that all would be well.

But that was not the only sign from God that MacKenzie noted that day. "High, high in remote and cloudless heavens a flight of four-motored bombing planes, flecks of gold far up in the rays of the descending sun, cruised eastward," he noted. "Behind the [B-17] Flying Fortresses or [B-24] Liberators, far too high to be identified as either one or the other, propellers churning the thin, cold atmosphere fashioned long trails of cloud. Threads of purest white were spun in formations at which the unoccupied squinted long after the ships passed out of sight."[31] More than one thousand medium bombers of the 9th Air Force and the Royal Air Force Bomber Commands pounded rail centers, roads, bridges, and other check points to the east of the Ardennes with nine hundred tons of bombs through December 23, in a carefully planned campaign of road and rail interdiction east of the German breakout lines, effectively hampering any last-ditch resupply and reinforcement efforts the Germans might have been able to make to support the Wacht am Rhein offensive west of the Rhine.[32]

"When the sun dropped below the bleak Ardennes horizon, its unflung beams painted the distant trailing banners pink and luminously yellow," MacKenzie wrote. The picturesque nature of his prose provided testament to the emotion of the moment. "And as it sank farther, the pencils of vapor dispersed gradually into a lofty roseate overcast, deepened in hue to magenta and to violet and paled to gray, fading beyond the range of vision in the eastern firmament—the East where soon those reared in the Christian tradition might in an extremity look for a significant star to herald a tomorrow of peace and good will."[33] McAuliffe's G-3, Harry Kinnard, was also enthusiastic in his reaction to resupply. "It was a once-in-a-lifetime occasion which all who were there would never forget," he wrote in a letter many years after the war.[34] "The weather cleared very mysteriously on December 23," recalled Phil Burge, Company C, 55th Armored Engineer Battalion, 10th Armored Division, for whom viewing the air resupply was virtually a religious experience. Years after the war, he said, "I can still see those C-47s flying over, dropping supplies. If that had not happened, I would not be here today. That was a miraculous sight. It was an act of God."[35] "Resupply came in that day, and to put it mildly, it helped us," General McAuliffe reported in his characteristic matter-of-fact manner.[36]

The defenders at Bastogne owed their ability to sustain the next round of German attacks not only to the miracle of the weather breaking unexpectedly but also to the skill and courage under fire of the pathfinders who jumped to mark the DZ, as well as the C-47 pilots and crews who steadfastly flew the missions.[37] The GIs watched heavy German anti-aircraft fire bring down several C-47s as the cargo aircraft entered and exited the DZ. Remarkably, the C-47s going down, some even behind enemy lines, did not cause other C-47s to take evasive action.[38] Colonel Harper, commander of the 327th Glider Infantry Regiment spoke highly of the airmen in his after-action history. "Their courage was tremendous," he said, "and I believe that their example did a great deal to encourage my infantry."[39]

After-action records indicate that of the first 40 airplanes from Troop Carrier Command that participated in the December 23 air resupply operation to Bastogne, 4 were shot down, while 35 of the remaining 36 of the surviving aircraft received battle damage. Six of the C-47s were so badly damaged that they had to make emergency landings, unable to return to their home base in Chalgrove, England.[40] Separate after-action records indicate a total of 241 C-47s were involved, with the majority of supplies consisting of 75mm and 105mm howitzer ammunition, plus ammunition for mortars, various types of grenades, as well as .30-caliber and .50-caliber carbine ammunition. The additional supplies dropped included K rations plus various medical supplies including twelve boxes of morphine surettes and three hundred units of plasma.[41] "Informed that the troops had recovered 95 percent of the supplies dropped, McAuliffe's G-3, Colonel Kinnard, allowed as how that was 'close enough for government work.'"[42]

Yet the air resupply on December 23, welcome as it was, still was not sufficient to sustain the continuing siege. "The contents of the bundles were not in balance with the real needs of the troops," observed military historian S. L. A. Marshall.[43] He pointed out too much .50-caliber ammunition had been sent when what was needed was .30-caliber for the M1 Garand rifles the troops of the 101st Airborne relied upon as their basic weapon of choice. The morphine and plasma were needed, but the 101st still lacked penicillin, given the number of wounded soldiers who could not be evacuated to hospitals until the siege was broken. Bastogne also badly needed blankets, not just for the soldiers in the field and wounded, but equally badly for the civilians who had remained in Bastogne. The military had collected so much of the available bedding from the small Belgian community that many citizens were miserably cold at night and asking for blankets.[44] Still, the resupply effort on December 23 kept the defenders going. By nightfall on December 23, Colonel Kohls, the G-4 logistics and supply officer for the 101st Airborne Division, had reports from all the unit supply officers of what supplies they had received, including an inventory of matériel that had reached unit dumps. Kohls talked with VIII Corps again at 0830 hours on December 24, Christmas Eve, asking for specific items to be included in future airdrops.[45]

As Kohls was talking with VIII Corps on Christmas Eve, the first wave of C-47s from the second resupply mission appeared over the DZ, starting a second-day air resupply mission that lasted from approximately 0855 until 1530 hours. In the December 24 air resupply, approximately one hundred tons of matériel were parachuted out of 160 airplanes. This airdrop included various badly needed batteries and gasoline in addition to ammunition and K rations. Still, Kohls was short key items: only 445 gallons of gasoline were on hand, medical supplies continued to be in demand, and the 26,406 K rations that had been received were only enough to resupply the defenders of Bastogne for a little more than a day. The troops were instructed, for a second time during the siege, to forage any food supplies in their areas and to report discoveries to supply officers so the found food could be distributed where it was most needed. Christmas was shaping up to be a K-ration day for those defenders of Bastogne lucky enough to have a K ration, not a holiday the troops in the field would celebrate with a hot meal served complete with turkey, mashed potatoes, and gravy.[46] During the next three days, with the exception of Christmas because of unfavorable weather over the C-47 bases in England, some 962 C-47s dropped an additional 850 tons of supplies.

On December 26, there were eleven gliders that brought in desperately needed surgeons. Knowing that the glider descent into Bastogne encircled by the enemy would be a particularly hazardous undertaking, Dr. Lamar Soutter, the Third Army surgeon who led the team, wrote, "This was something we felt we absolutely had to do." On December 26, the medical

One of the many gliders used to fly doctors and medical supplies to U.S. forces at Bastogne, Belgium. Note African American troops assisting in unloading effort. December 1944.

volunteers took off and caught up with ten other gliders containing 2,975 gallons of 80-octane gasoline. At 1720 hours, the C-47s towing the gliders leveled off at six hundred feet and cut the gliders loose. All landed safely.[47] On December 27, thirty-two gliders made safe landings delivering 736 rounds of ammunition for the larger 155mm howitzers.[48]

P-47 THUNDERBOLTS RULE THE SKY

During the five days of the resupply effort, from December 23 through December 28, 962 C-47s managed to drop 850 tubs of supplies. The Germans attacking Bastogne shot down nineteen C-47s and badly damaged fifty more.[49] The losses would have been greater except for the P-47 Thunderbolt fighters dispatched from airbases in France to accompany the air resupply. When the escort mission was concluded, the P-47s, also known as "Jugs," short for "Juggernaut," were free to attack the Germans encircling Bastogne with bombs, machine-gun fire, and napalm.[50] Hunting German troops and tanks, the P-47 fighter pilots found the enemy left clear tracks in the snow, making it easy to identify enemy positions even when tanks or infantry headed for cover into the thick Ardennes Forest surrounding Bastogne.

The defense of Bastogne was also blessed by the presence of Capt. James E. Parker of the 9th Air Force. On December 17, a call came from Headquarters, 70th Wing, 9th Air Force to the 393rd Fighter Squadron to send a controller to the VIII US Army Corps, then headquartered in Bastogne. The call said the controller should be a pilot with considerable combat service in the European Theater of Operations. Captain Parker was selected for the mission and he arrived at Bastogne at 1400 hours on December 18. Parker, a fighter pilot with combat experience in both the Pacific and European Theaters, was uniquely qualified for this mission. As a combat pilot, Parker had come to the conclusion that he was operating in the dark on combat missions because he did not have sufficient advance information on his targets. As a consequence, he volunteered to go on liaison missions with ground forces. At the time he was ordered to Bastogne, Parker had never participated in any mission that involved ground controllers coordinating with air combat pilots. The truth is that until Parker got involved, that military job description had not yet been created.[51]

When Parker reported to Corps Headquarters at Bastogne, his only equipment consisted of a pocket full of radio crystals, which would only be useful if he could find a very high frequency radio, or VHF, so he could use the radio crystals to communicate with American aircraft in flight. After searching the entire 101st Division without any success, Parker found the attached 10th Armored Division units had two radios of the type he needed—one in a tank and the other in a jeep. On being told that the tank could not be spared, Parker sought out Colonel Roberts, the commander of the 10th Armored Division. Roberts kept the tank but assigned the jeep to Parker. Assisted by Sgt. Frank B. Hotard, a 9th Air Force technician, Parker managed to adapt the jeep's radio with his air-contact radio crystals so that he was ready to work supporting attacking fighter planes. Parker believed he had the radio equipment operational on December 21, but he could not test it because on that day there were no airplanes in the air. Then, at 1000 hours on December 23, Parker heard supporting P-47 fighters accompanying the C-47 cargo planes and he was able to determine his modified radio equipment worked.[52]

Parker's procedure in directing the aircraft was simple. When airborne command assigned a P-47 to a mission supporting the 101st, the fighter pilot checked in with Parker by radio. While the P-47s were on their way to Bastogne, Parker gave them a clear landmark, such as a railroad or highway. Several checkpoints were visualized from the map to give the P-47 pilots a specific approach direction to bring them directly over their target. This procedure enabled the P-47s to drop fast and low so they could gain an element of complete surprise that could never have been achieved if the P-47s had needed to circle in search of targets. Even after the P-47s had expended their bombs and gun ammunition, the fighter airplanes still had enough gasoline to allow them to climb to safe altitudes to patrol either the perimeter of the defenses or a specific area of the battlefield for reconnaissance. Their reconnaissance reports permitted Parker to make improved target selections for subsequent flights, as well as to give ground forces advance information on the buildup of enemy strength.[53]

Using various types of radio-to-phone systems, Parker and a small team were able to coordinate the P-47 Thunderbolts on murderous missions against Nazi tanks and infantry in and around Bastogne. At one point in the battle, Capt. Charles Cherle, assisting Parker with the switchboard air-ground communications, was contacted by a Thunderbolt pilot who came on the air with, "Kingfish leader here, Kingfish leader here. See armor in the woods. Is it ours or is it the Krauts?" Captain Cherle replied, "I don't think we have anything there but hold on until I check." Picking up another telephone, Cherle made sure with Parker the armor was part of an enemy force. He shouted back to the pilot, "Buzzard calling Kingfish. Go ahead and shoot them." A moment later, four P-47s dove out of the sky with machine guns firing and knocked out the German tanks. Parker's air liaison team ended up coordinating with communications officers from various land-based combat units to smash great quantities of German armored equipment that could otherwise have been used to dislodge the Americans from Bastogne.[54]

Captain Parker in his oral history after-action report given to Marshall's military field historians described how useful the snow was to the P-47 pilots trying to locate the enemy. "Tracks led to concealed forest positions which were then bombed," Parker noted. "The forests in this area are fir which blaze quickly from fire bombs. The smoke from the burning forests, towns, and columns made a 360-degree circle around Bastogne until it appeared that the weather was closing in. Every nearby town was hit at least once with explosive and firebombs. Noville was hit ten times."[55] In the first four days of air support, from December 23 to December 26, the fighter planes averaged more than 250 sorties daily, according to Parker's oral history. "On December 23 the enemy was caught completely by surprise and several columns which were moving up to make an attack were so badly cut up that they could not make an organized effort," Parker reported. "This continued to be the case for several days."[56]

Colonel Roberts, watching the fighter planes at work, credited Parker's efforts as being worth the equivalent of two or three infantry divisions.[57] General McAuliffe bracketed the work of Parker and the fighter planes as a key factor why Bastogne was saved, along with the superiority of his artillery and the courage of the men on the ground. "It wasn't unusual during the siege to have an infantryman call in that five tanks were coming down on him and then see six P-47s diving at the tanks within twenty minutes," General McAuliffe commented after the battle.[58] During the critical days of good flying weather, as many as nineteen squadrons of fighter planes circled Bastogne, with Parker's switchboard giving directions to as many as five squadrons at a time.[59] In the first six days of good flying weather over Bastogne, Parker estimated some two thousand P-47 sorties were made. Only two P-47s were lost in combat, and in one of these, Parker reported, the pilot was rescued.[60]

CHAPTER 12

THE GERMAN ATTACK
RESUMES

That evening [December 23] only a few minutes after the
German attack began in the Marvie sector, Lt. Col. Harry W.
O. Kinnard (the 101st Airborne Division G-3) telephoned his
opposite number at the VIII Corps command post. The gist of
his report, as recorded in the G-3 journal, was this: "In regard to
our situation it is getting pretty sticky around here. They [the 4th
Armored Division] must keep coming. The enemy has attacked
all along the south and some tanks are through and running
around in our area. Request you inform 4th Armored Division
of our situation and ask them to put on possible pressure."

—Hugh M. Cole, US Military Historian, *The Ardennes: Battle of the Bulge*, 1988[1]

D espite the turn in the battle that accompanied the change in
weather, the Germans besieging Bastogne were not ready to give
up. "The Germans were becoming desperate," military historian
Col. Ralph M. Mitchell wrote.[2]

THE BATTLE FOR MARVIE

To the southwest of Bastogne, at approximately 1730 hours on December 23, German Panzer Lehr tanks and infantry moved out of the woods a thousand yards off and began advancing along a narrow country road to the south of Marvie.

About five hundred yards southwest of Marvie, Hill 500 was defended by Company G of the 2nd Battalion of the 327th Glider Infantry, under the command of Lt. Stanley Morrison, who had briefly been held captive by the Germans when they first broke into Marvie on Wednesday morning. At approximately 1840 hours, a panzer force surrounded Hill 500. German infantry clad in white snowsuits crawled into the farm buildings around the base. The situation became critical as four German tanks began advancing up the hill. From his regimental command post at Bastogne's southern limits, Col. Robert Harper, the commander of the 327th, telephoned Morrison about the situation. "I see tanks just outside my window," Morrison replied, speaking calmly. "We are continuing to fight back, but it looks like they have us."[3] A few minutes later, Harper telephoned Morrison again. "We're still holding on," Morrison said. Just then the line went dead.[4] Harper learned what he feared most had happened: Morrison and the other defenders of Hill 500, nearly one hundred men in total, were overrun. The end came for Lieutenant Morrison's detachment sometime after 1900 hours on the evening of December 23. With the Germans overrunning Hill 500, the first breach in Bastogne's outer defenses was in the process of developing, and the Germans were finally positioned for a direct, frontal assault on Bastogne.[5]

"Frenzied, flare-lit pandemonium followed," journalist Fred MacKenzie wrote. "The enemy infantry came on the run across the weirdly illuminated snow, firing wildly and yelling in a crazy chorus that soon was punctuated by piercing screams of pain as many fell under the American fire."[6] The outnumbered Screaming Eagles in Marvie fought desperately to prevent the German attackers from breaking through. Before the German advance could be contained, two German tanks prowled into Bastogne and shot up houses in the vicinity of Harper's 327th command post. Anti-tank weapons in Bastogne quickly incapacitated these two tanks, but the breach into the town was nerve-wracking for the defenders.

South of Bastogne, the situation was equally desperate for Task Force O'Hara, as Col. James O'Hara's remaining men were the only US forces preventing the Germans from advancing into Bastogne from the south along the road to Wiltz. Before Hill 500 fell, when Harper called O'Hara's command post to see if Harper could assist Morrison, Harper learned that Team O'Hara was under enemy attack as well. "They are attacking me and are trying to come around my north flank," O'Hara explained.[7]

In his after-action report to Marshall's historians, O'Hara gave a vivid account of the fighting. "The enemy were yelling, firing flares, and acting like a pack of mad men," he explained. "Tracer fire was everywhere, much of it wild." A German tank blasted a house nearby, setting it afire. "The loft was filled with hay and the effect was to make the entire area as light as day," O'Hara continued. "In their snow suits, the enemy looked like a group of ghosts dancing about a fire. They made no attempt to be quiet." From only a hundred yards away, the men from Team O'Hara watched, firing on the enemy as the Germans tried to infiltrate to the north.[8]

O'Hara recalled in particular what happened to one of his unit who had failed to withdraw, only to find himself surrounded. "He played dead when they came to his fox hole, even when they said, 'Hello, Hello,' kicked him, sat on him, took his BAR [Browning Automatic Rifle], and rifled his pockets." The man kept absolutely still. In the ensuing fight, he heard the Germans bring up two artillery pieces on the left, one large and the other smaller. "The Germans fired the small one indiscriminately in hopes of getting return fire that they could then shoot at with the big one," O'Hara related. "Yet during the night, the large gun did not fire." The man in the foxhole also heard German ambulances make many trips to the area to carry out the dead and wounded.[9]

"Most [German] tanks were destroyed after they had penetrated the defenses and had been separated from their infantry," noted military analyst Col. James P. Mitchell, in his monograph on the 101st Airborne's defense of Bastogne. "The task was most frequently accomplished by direct-fire artillery, anti-tank weapons, and bazooka fire at close range." As an example, he cited an incident on December 23 in Marvie. "There PFC Norman Osterberg, a member of the 327th Glider Infantry Regiment, exposed himself to enemy fire and, using his bazooka, repeatedly drove attacking tanks away even though they came within ten yards of his position. Wounded in the process, he continued his stand for three hours, thus stopping the attack in his sector." Mitchell noted such bravery was common in the Siege of Bastogne. "Fighting against tanks, soldiers quietly discovered that digging in around a town was far preferable and more effective than occupying its buildings and being crushed in the rubble. Teamwork, cooperation, effective combined arms attacks on targets, and stubborn and brave resistance gave the paratroopers the fighting edge they never relinquished."[10]

When a German half-track and a group of tanks tried to move down Hill 500 to attack Marvie, a lucky shot disabled the half-track. "The wreckage proved an invaluable block," MacKenzie noted. "German tanks trying to smash into Marvie that night found they could not pass over or around the ruin in the narrow roadway."[11] Team O'Hara's tanks and assault guns stopped a major German penetration by gunning down the panzers silhouetted in the glare of burning buildings, allowing the Americans to hold on to the northern half of Marvie.[12] "An hour before dawn on the twenty-fourth, the battle ended and quiet came to Marvie," noted US military historian Hugh Cole. "O'Hara's troops had accounted for eight panzers in this fight, but the village was still clutched by both antagonists."[13]

Shortly after dawn on Sunday, December 24, Christmas Eve, Harper went down to Marvie to examine his lines. He was still there at 1340 hours when six P-47s bombed the location, dropping five-hundred-pound bombs and strafing the streets with .50-caliber machine-gun fire. Harper survived the P-47 attack by jumping in a foxhole. He then continued to examine the tanks of Team O'Hara along the road to Wiltz. Harper instructed the Sherman tanks to start pounding on the houses in the lower part of Marvie that concealed the German infantry.[14]

MCAULIFFE ADJUSTS THE DEFENSE

The battle on the night of December 23 demonstrated that McAuliffe's command was overextended at a number of points. The artillery concentrated in a center to the west of Bastogne was exposed, and segments of the defense perimeter were not as well coordinated as they might be. The tankers of Colonel Roberts' 10th Armored were not as sure of airborne positions, and most likely the regiments of the 101st were equally hazy as to the location of 10th Armored tanks and tank destroyer detachments on their flanks.[15]

To correct the situation, Colonel Kinnard, whose tactical sense was highly regarded by McAuliffe and the other commanders, drew up a plan on December 24 to regroup the Bastogne forces. His idea, which General McAuliffe implemented immediately, was to place all four regiments of the 101st Airborne on the line as combined rifle teams supported by armor and backed up by artillery. The idea was to ring Bastogne with defenders from the four 101st regiments such that each of the regiments had some tank or anti-tank support attached to give the paratroopers armored punch against advancing German tanks.

Around the circle perimeter defense, Kinnard positioned Col. Julian Ewell's 501st to the east, defending the road leading to Longvilly; Col. Robert Sink's 506th to the northeast, protecting the road to Noville; to the northwest Col. Steve Chappuis's 502nd, defending the road to Longchamps; and Col. Joseph Harper's 327th to the west and southwest, protecting the roads to Mande-St.-Étienne and the road to Neufchâteau. To provide the units with tank and tank destroyer support, Kinnard proposed breaking the 705th Tank Destroyer Battalion into units that could be assigned to the various 101st regiments arranged along the outer defense perimeter. The various teams of the 10th Armored were assigned to the various 101st regiments, such that Team O'Hara was assigned to Ewell's 501st, with Team Cherry and Team SNAFU held in reserve to be assigned where needed.[16]

Military historian Cole noted the readjustment of the 101st positions suggested by Kinnard's plan resulted in a "taut and tenuous line" of defense consisting of approximately sixteen miles in the defense perimeter circled around Bastogne. "That it could not be defended in equal strength at all points was not only a military aphorism but a simple fact dictated by the troops available and the accidents of the ground," Cole commented.[17]

Gen. Gerald Higgins, second in command to McAuliffe in the 101st Airborne, was concerned about the northwest sector, a gently rolling hill country with no natural obstacles and little tree growth. Higgins felt confident the northwest—particularly the area around the village of Flamierge, defended by Harper's 327th, and the area around the towns of Champs and Longchamps, defended by Chappuis's 502nd—were the places where the Germans would most likely launch their next tank attack. Higgins warned McAuliffe that he expected the brunt of the German attack would next come from the northwest. "The Germans are a sentimental people," Higgins explained to McAuliffe. He suggested the German military would like nothing better than making a Christmas present of Bastogne to Hitler.[18]

PATTON'S 4TH ARMORED BATTLES NORTH

On Saturday, December 23, Patton was frustrated because the news was both good and bad. The good news was that the weather had cleared and Bastogne had been resupplied by air. It also cheered Patton that the United States Army Air Force was once again bombing Germany, in coordination with the British Royal Air Force. The bad news was that the Third Army advance north was not moving as fast as he wanted.

That day he wrote the following entry in his diary:

> We have not done so well today as I hoped but have advanced from two to five miles and have beaten the enemy wherever we have met him . . . not yet reached Bastogne, but they are resupplying it by air.
>
> The weather is fine today. We had seven groups of fighter bombers, eleven groups of medium bombers, one division of the VIII Air Force, and some RAF planes assisting us. I hope it got results.[19]

In moving the 4th Armored Division forward on December 22, Maj. Gen. Hugh Gaffey, the commander, had ordered Brig. Gen. Herbert L. Earnest to take his Combat Command A up on the right, advancing along the Arlon-to-Bastogne highway, while Brig. Gen. Holmes E. Dager took Combat Command B forward on the left; advancing on secondary roads west of the Arlon-to-Bastogne highway, Brig. Gen. Wendell Blanchard's Combat Command Reserve, CCR, was in reserve, along with the 704th Tank Destroyer Battalion. Gaffey's plan was to spearhead the drive with CCB. Accordingly, Gaffey had instructed Dager: "You will drive in, relieve the force [at Bastogne], and proceed from Bastogne to the northeast."[20] Albin "Al" Irzyk, the tank commander of the 8th Tank Battalion in Brig. Gen. Dager's

Combat Command B, understood the order: "Our objective was clear and simple—Bastogne. Our mission—get there as fast as we could."[21]

The advance proved difficult. A single machine gun and six enemy soldiers held up CCA's advance through Martelange, a town some fourteen miles south of Bastogne. Meanwhile, CCB advanced twelve miles to Burnon in two and a half hours, but waited there for CCA to catch up, violating a Patton tactical tenant that admonished against halting simply because some other unit is stuck. Patton insisted upon pressing forward, reasoning that pressing ahead might release the situation to allow the stuck unit to begin moving once again.[22] At any rate, fighting through the countryside traversing Belgium's snow-covered and icy roads was slow going. The Germans had multiple opportunities to challenge Patton's advance by establishing roadblocks and taking up defensive positions within the many small towns and villages along the way.

As the 4th Armored began settling in for the night at the end of the first day of their advance, an order came down that the unit was to continue moving forward through the night of December 22–23. By ordering the 4th Armored to advance through the night, Patton risked stretching the endurance of tired and frozen troops who were already beginning to suffer frostbite. Irzyk observed Patton's order to attack at night jolted the troops. In his 1996 autobiography, *He Rode Up Front for Patton*, Irzyk described the troops' reaction as follows: "This one was a lulu. It staggered all hands. They were just in the process of settling in for the night, when they were slapped hard in the head. That brought them awake in a hurry. The new orders were, 'Move all night!'"[23] Irzyk found out that the order had come from Patton directly. Evidently, the progress of CCB in the first hours of battle got Patton "fired up and his juices flowing."

Irzyk continued:

So, figuratively, he [Patton] was using his spurs and riding crop to get there 'firstest and quickest.' At this point, he had already made believers of General Eisenhower and his senior officers. He had already met and even exceeded the promises he made to them many hours earlier, and already had, no doubt astonished them. It was also later learned that Patton had ordered the night move with the very optimistic, but completely unrealistic, belief that the forces could reach Bastogne by daylight. He probably almost smelled the touchdown.[24]

So, at midnight on the night of December 22–23, Irzyk noted, they were on the move again. It was a bitter cold night, and the visibility was extremely poor, but the Third Army followed orders and the advance resumed. Ironically, the 4th Armored Division, after being withdrawn on December 8 from fighting around the Maginot Line some nine miles from the German border, had been in Bastogne before the Battle of the Bulge began. In that earlier movement, elements of the 4th Armored had actually come within one kilometer of the same spot they would return to six days later.[25] This fact fit into Irzyk's description of how miserable the night move on December 22–23 turned out to be:

> So at midnight, it was hit the road again, Jack. These were the guys who had made that difficult, trying one hundred sixty-one mile forced march. They had been on the move patrolling, outposting and had gone in and out of Bastogne. They had moved back to the rear and had been up since 3:00 a.m. and on the move ever since.
>
> As they were moving out again, it was almost the exact hour merely three days ago that they were departing from Domnon and they had hardly stopped—it was unbelievable. How much living can you squeeze into seventy-two hours? How much can a man endure? How long and how far can you drive him? That all remained to be seen. So, as ordered, they moved all night. The task was slow, difficult, and turned out to be particularly painful and costly.[26]

Irzyk conceded the Third Army made progress that day but "the ratio of effort expended to results gained was hardly favorable."[27] At first light on December 23, their good fortune ran out. About a mile outside Chaumont, Germans were waiting in force, with paratroopers from the 14th Regiment, 5th Fallschrimjäger [Paratrooper] Division and assault guns from the German 11th Assault Gun Brigade ready to stop their advance.

The 8th Tank Battalion was ordered to lead the move into the heavily defended village. Irzyk decided to execute a deliberate attack on Chaumont to occupy it, not skirt it as Patton had directed.[28] Irzyk reasoned that if he was going to Bastogne, the best way was to follow the road through Chaumont, and then on to the next town. There really was no alternative since Iryzk's tanks could not leave the road to the right or the left. But Chaumont presented problems in addition to having just the one road. Like many of these small villages on the way to Bastogne, Chaumont had only one road passing through the town. Chaumont sat low on the ground, "much like being in the bottom of a saucer." To advance into the town, Iryzk's forces would be going downhill sharply, but once committed, the only way to go forward was through the town. "There was no right, left, or back up," Irzyk wrote in his autobiography.[29]

Irzyk was confident he had developed a sound plan for attacking Chaumont, even though it meant dividing his forces. He ordered Company B to attack the town by driving down from the high ground, while Company C operated on the ridge to the left and Company A rode the ridge to the right. As Company C began to move forward, Irzyk received a totally unexpected jolt. The ground was not frozen solid and his bogged-down tanks "were mired so deep in the soft earth that they could not budge forward or backward."[30] He had counted on the ground being frozen solid, knowing that this was one of the coldest winters in forty to sixty years. But what he had not realized was that a fast-moving stream still flowed through Chaumont softening the earth around despite the cold winter. Irzyk quickly realized his five lead tanks in Company C were useless and vulnerable to German attack. So, despite having executed an attack maneuver that was worthy of being taught in military school, Iryzk's entire left flank was left unprotected. The good news was that Company B had moved successfully into Chaumont and, having seized the town, was now moving to the outskirts on the other side.

That's when the Germans unleashed the fury of their counterattack. Irzyk described the action as follows:

> It was the frightening, demoralizing, intimidating, unreal sounds, screeches, and screams of high velocity tank gun rounds hitting, crashing, exploding, and ricocheting all around them. It shook, staggered, numbed, alarmed and unnerved the men. It had happened so suddenly, so unexpectedly, that for a brief instant, there was panic. What had happened?

Then there was instant realization that this was a heavy enemy tank counterattack. The fire was so powerful and they were so vulnerable that as they reacted their thoughts flashed—was this doomsday, wipeout?[31]

Before he was finished with Chaumont, Irzyk had a life-threatening experience. As he drove his tank through the town, what happened was the one thing Irzyk and his tank crew feared might one day happen. Irzyk described the experience in vivid terms:

There was a low, loud, deafening, earsplitting sound, followed by a terrible, horrible powerful, frightening blow. The tank was shoved violently forward. It was as though the tank had been hit in the back by a huge sledge hammer, and picked up and thrown forward by a superhuman hand.

The three in the turret were tossed and bounced like rag dolls. Stunned and dazed, they quickly untangled themselves and got back on their feet. This was not easy. While on the turret floor, they had been part of the clutter and utter chaos in the tank. The large heavy tank gun rounds, which had been clamped upright, were now strewn like huge matchsticks on the turret floor. Every single item in the tank had been tossed about and pitched hither, thither, and yon. It was as if a giant hand had grabbed everything in the turret, and tossed it violently about. Not a single item was anywhere near its original resting place. The inside of the tank looked as though a bunch of tables at a rummage sale had been picked up and upended.[32]

Realizing their tank had been hit and could be hit again if they did not move quickly, Irzyk recovered enough to give the order, "Keep moving!" When he had a minute to survey the damage, Irzyk realized to his utter astonishment that the turret had been hit and cracked by a high-velocity round from an enemy tank. But somehow the round had not penetrated the turret's armor. The tank was damaged, but basically intact and operational. Irzyk could not believe it; he "was convinced that it was a minor miracle—that they had been spared and uniquely blessed by the Supreme Being." As he described the experience, Irzyk commented that it "was as though he had received a tap on his shoulder from the back, reassuring him that someone was behind him, protecting him." He described it as "an unreal, mystical feeling."[33]

What he realized next was that the mitten on his right hand was soggy with blood. Examining the hand more closely, he saw that the thumb and the area around it seemed to have been sliced and mangled, with blood oozing though. But at that moment Irzyk had more important things to think about. As quickly as he could, Irzyk drove his tank along the twisting, uphill road out of Chaumont and out of danger. Irzyk's tank had been hit by a Tiger tank with a 78mm high-velocity cannon capable of hitting a Sherman tank at two-miles' distance. Irzyk later figured he was lucky. The round from the Tiger tank had evidently hit the turret of Irzyk's Sherman tank at an angle and ricocheted off, sparing Irzyk the full impact of the shot.

The battle for Chaumont lasted two days before CCB finally seized the town around midday on December 24.[34] What Irzyk realized after Chaumont was that "Bastogne was a lot farther away than one day" and from here on, the 4th Armored "could feasibly have a tough fight for almost every yard."[35] Patton was coming to the same conclusion. He called General Milliken at III Corps barking orders. "There's too much piddling around!" Patton insisted. "Bypass these towns and clear them up later. Tanks can operate on this ground now."[36] But bypassing the small towns might not be as simple as it sounded. The 4th Armored in moving north toward Bastogne had no choice but to encounter a sequence of small towns. Even if the 4th Armored could bypass a particular town or village, the Germans would calculate another place north to face the 4th Armored in counterattack regardless what route Patton chose through the hill-bound valleys of the Ardennes to reach Bastogne.

Early on December 24, Gaffey, frustrated that the advances of the 4th Armored's CCA and CCB were stalled by stiff German resistance, made a command decision ordering CCR to move up on the left of the 4th Armored Division's advance, to begin attacking along the Neufchâteau-Bastogne axis.[37] Through the day of December 24, CCB regrouped after the bloody battle at Chaumont, while CCA continued making modest progress fighting north from Martelange. "If there was any hope for relief of Bastogne in the near future, it probably lay with CCR," military historian Harold Winton wrote.[38] This was a reality Patton soon came to see he had no choice but to accept. Ironically, the new line of attack taken by CCR after the redeployment from being held in reserve to assuming the left flank along the Neufchâteau road to Bastogne was the axis that Middleton had recommended in the first place. CCR, commanded by General Blanchard, consisted of two maneuver battalions, the 37th Tank Battalion, commanded by Lt. Col. Creighton W. Abrams, and the 53rd Armored Infantry Battalion, commanded by Lt. Col. George Jacques. It was supported by two 105mm howitzer battalions and a battery of 155mm howitzers.[39] During the night of December 24–25, CCR closed in on Bastogne, having road-marched to Neufchâteau.[40]

GERMANS REGROUP FOR A FINAL ATTACK

The battle was fairly quiet at Bastogne, as Lüttwitz regrouped for a major attack on Christmas Day. German general Heinz Kokott, the commander of the 26th Volksgrenadier Division, was primarily responsible for directing the attack on Bastogne after Manteuffel's 5th Panzer Army had pushed on to the west. In interrogations after the war, Kokott said that seeing the C-47s resupply Bastogne on December 23 made him think the Americans were getting new paratrooper reinforcements. This sight, Kokott remarked, "increased the disorder" in the German ranks.[41] Up until noon on December 23, Kokott thought the battle for Bastogne was going pretty well. He knew the 26th Reconnaissance Battalion, together with some panzers from the 2nd Panzer Division, were ready to attack from the east of Bastogne, while the 77th Volksgrenadier Regiment was moving to attack from the southwest. Intelligence reports indicated that German forces had taken Flamierge, to the northwest of Bastogne, although at noon that was not yet confirmed.

What disturbed Kokott, in addition to seeing the air resupply of the besieged town, was what appeared to be a surprising number of German troops retreating into a leaderless mob. Kokott identified the soldiers streaming past his division headquarters as German paratroopers, Fallschirmjägers, recognizable by their squared-off helmet rims and Luftwaffe smocks. Kokott concluded the retreating soldiers belonged to the 5th Fallschirmjäger Division, part of the 7th Army to the south—the German army tasked with blocking the northward advance of General Patton's Third Army. Looking at the faces of the retreating paratroopers, Kokott recognized the signs of a beaten and demoralized fighting force. One of Kokott's staff soldiers asked one of the paratroopers what had happened. "The enemy has broken through! He moved to the north with tanks and has captured Chaumont!"

Kokott soon learned that Patton's 4th Armored had wiped out the Fallschirmjäger battalion defending Chaumont.[42] "For a moment, Kokott felt sorry for the men who were retreating," military historians Barron and Cygan noted. "Like many *landsers*, these men were not hardened infantry soldiers. Though many were young and fit, a majority of them had served most of the war in the rear echelons as clerks, cooks, and technicians."[43] Barron and Cygan observed that most of these men were Fallschirmjäger only in name, having never received parachute training or participated even in a single parachute jump. Despite the brave fight these men had put up, it was ridiculous to think inexperienced and poorly trained soldiers like these could stop George Patton's Third Army, probably the best of the armored fighting forces the Allies possessed. Seeing this retreat, Kokott had to doubt the ragtag allotment of young and old gathered to form his 26th Volksgrenadier Division would fare much better against the battle-hardened 101st Airborne Division, especially after the Screaming Eagles were reinforced by Patton.

To make matters worse, Kokott realized with the clearing weather, the American fighter planes would be in the air once again. "The traffic jam of disorganized men, plodding horses, wagons, and idling vehicles moving along at a snail's pace in the bright sun was just too easy a target for the Allied pilots," Barron and Cygan added. "Once again, Kokott braced for destruction."[44] Kokott knew his men were unprepared for the "Jabos," German slang for "Jagdbombers," translated "Fighter-Bombers," the German name for Allied fighter-bombers like the P-47 now prowling the skies. That Saturday afternoon, at 1206 hours on December 23, P-47s from the 514th Fighter Squadron took off from Mourmelon—the exact base in France from which the 101st Airborne Division had departed on their night-run to Bastogne. Less than a half hour later, at 1230 hours, the P-47s arrived at Bastogne to provide cover for a C-47 resupply mission headed to the town. Within moments of linking up with the C-47s, the P-47 pilots spotted a convoy of twenty German vehicles, some of which were pulling artillery, in the vicinity of Silbret and Hompre to the west of Bastogne. The P-47s attacked. "The flight commander gave a 'Tallyhoo!'" noted Barron and Cygan. "With a roar from the huge turbo-charged Pratt & Whitney engines, the fighters peeled off and started to line up to strafe the convoy. For the pilots of the 514th, it was a turkey shoot. Howling down from the skies over Bastogne, scores of silver jug-shaped fighters dived on anything German around the perimeter."[45]

On the night of December 23, while Kokott's forces were attacking Marvie to the southeast of Bastogne, General Manteuffel, the commander of the 5th Panzer Army, visited Kokott at his command post. In his debriefing with US military intelligence after the war, Kokott claimed he never knew that the attack on Marvie led by the 901st Panzergrenadier Regiment of the Panzer Lehr Division had broken the US line at Hill 500, or that some of its tanks had actually ventured into the outskirts of Bastogne. In the interrogation after the war, Kokott explained German forces in the field reported only that they had occupied the first few houses in Marvie and stopped when they captured the village. "I acted on the assumption that they were telling the truth," Kokott said. "This is a very common error in our operations."[46]

So, when Manteuffel arrived to pay Kokott a visit on the night of December 23, Kokott was dispirited, convinced he was fighting against very difficult odds. Manteuffel brought with him word that an order had come down from German 47th Panzer Corps that Bastogne would be attacked again on Christmas Day. Manteuffel had come to Kokott's headquarters to give him specific and direct orders to take Bastogne immediately. Military historian S. L. A. Marshall summarized the discussion as follows: "In other words, German high command realized Bastogne had to be taken by German forces before Patton's Third Army had time to break the encirclement and relieve the 101st Airborne Division." Manteuffel added, "Bastogne must be taken at all costs."[47]

Manteuffel had been hopeful earlier on December 23, when Hitler released two new divisions from the Führer Reserve—the 9th Panzer Division and the 15th Panzergrenadier Division—that he would get assistance in taking Bastogne. Manteuffel, along with his subordinate, General Lüttwitz, the commander of the 47th Panzer Corps, became convinced Kokott needed considerable reinforcement if he was to take Bastogne. On hearing Hitler had released two divisions from the Führer Reserve, Manteuffel had hoped to get both assigned to him. Instead, Manteuffel's superior officer, Field Marshal Walter Model, head of German Army Group B, sent all but one regiment of the 15th Panzergrenadier Division to support the drive to the Meuse.[48] The one regiment not committed to the drive to the Meuse was the only reinforcement Manteuffel was able to obtain to continue his attack on Bastogne, provided Lüttwitz wanted to continue the attack on Bastogne.

Learning this, Manteuffel sent a message on December 23 to Gen. Alfred Jodl, German chief of the operations staff of the German Armed Forces Command, Oberkommando der Wehrmacht, or OKW, that reached Hitler himself. Manteuffel had asked what he should do: Dedicate all his available resources to taking Bastogne, or continue the drive to the Meuse? "Having insisted in advance of the offensive on the utmost importance of Bastogne, Hitler at that point appeared to have lost interest in it," wrote US military historian Charles B. MacDonald. "The message came back from Jodl: Use all available forces to gain the Meuse."[49]

MacDonald explained that Hitler had become ambivalent about Bastogne. Hitler hated that apparently a small American force could hold on to Bastogne despite a massive German assault. On reading Manteuffel's message to Jodl, Hitler instructed an aide, Maj. Johann Mayer, who was at the front, to go to the headquarters of the 47th Panzer Corps on December 24 to find out what was wrong. There, General Lüttwitz, the corps commander, managed to convince Mayer of the stiffness of the Bastogne resistance. Mayer agreed to pass this on to Hitler, but only after he let Lüttwitz know that Hitler insisted Bastogne had to be taken the next day, Christmas Day. "This conformed in any case with what General Manteuffel was planning," MacDonald wrote. "For any experienced military man, continuing enemy holdout astride the nexus of almost all roads in the area was unacceptable. Since the regiment of the 15th Panzergrenadier Division was arriving that night, he [Manteuffel] ordered an all-out attack for the following morning."[50] MacDonald explained Manteuffel's reasoning that an attack on Christmas Day might take the Americans by surprise. Besides, Manteuffel knew the Luftwaffe was planning a massive bombing of Bastogne for Christmas Eve, a bombing that along with the Christmas Day offensive Manteuffel calculated might provide the Germans with the psychological advantage needed to turn the tide at Bastogne in their favor.[51]

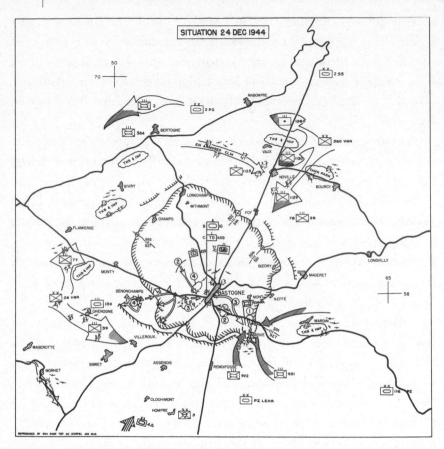

Bastogne, Belgium: Battle Map, December 24, 1944

Manteuffel asked Kokott what his plan of battle would be. Kokott explained the Americans would be looking to the east and the south for the Germans to attack, and that their strength would be in that direction, with the Americans providing the weakest defense to the northwest of Bastogne, exactly where the German troops were the freshest. About this, Kokott was wrong. Actually, McAuliffe had anticipated the Germans would attack from the northwest, and that was where McAuliffe and Higgins had decided to position the freshest of the US forces, the 502nd Parachute Infantry Regiment, under the command of "Silent Steve" Chappuis. Kokott also argued the terrain in the northwest was the most favorable for the deployment of armor, being mostly open rolling hills and relatively firm ground, so that attacking German tanks would not have to be confined to the roads, where American artillery were effective at knocking them out, effectively turning the damaged German tanks into roadblocks. Manteuffel agreed to put the arriving regiment of the 15th Panzergrenadier Division under Kokott's command, reassuring Kokott these were experienced troops who had fought on the Italian front and would arrive in good condition.[52]

The way the decision developed, Manteuffel could conclude he had given Lüttwitz the choice as to how best to use the newly arriving regiment of the 15th Panzergrenadier Division, either to continue the attack on Bastogne, or to secure crossings at the Meuse River. After the war, the chief of staff of the 5th Panzer Army, Carl Wagener, wrote that he had strongly suggested that the 47th Panzer Corps use these divisions for the Meuse crossing. Lüttwitz rejected that option. "He [Lüttwitz] never liked the concept of leaving Bastogne behind as Manteuffel's forces barreled toward Antwerp," Barron and Cygan wrote. "For Lüttwitz, it was finally time to lance the Bastogne boil."[53] Lüttwitz was disappointed with the regiment of the 15th Panzergrenadier Division when they finally arrived. What he received was a combat team at less than full strength with one-and-a-half rifle battalions, a reconnaissance battalion of about thirty armored personnel carriers, a mixture of twenty tanks and assault guns, an engineering company, and two artillery battalions.[54] Though not nearly what Lüttwitz had hoped to receive, he assigned the arriving troops to Kokott to use in the planned Christmas Day attack on the northwest perimeter around Bastogne.

SECTION V

BASTOGNE HOLDS

A Christmas Day Miracle

I remember going to a barn on Christmas Eve with the other men.
A chaplain was there and we had a church service with the familiar
"Silent Night," of course. I was thinking of everyone at home.

—PFC Gordon Bernhardt, 463rd Parachute Field Artillery

Battalion, Bastogne, December 24, 1944[1]

C hristmas Eve at Bastogne was sufficiently quiet that Colonel
Danahy had time to prepare a situation report with a map depict-
ing the enemy positions encircling the town, bordered with the
traditional Christmas color of red, white, and green. He highlighted it with
the words "Merry Christmas" scrawled merrily in green crayon across the
middle of the map where the besieged US defenders continued to hold the
center of the town.[2]

A TALE OF TWO CHRISTMAS MESSAGES

Colonel Kinnard joined Danahy in a creative enterprise of his own, drafting for General McAuliffe a Christmas greeting to the troops.[3] In this inspired communiqué, McAuliffe told his men about the German demand for surrender and how he had given the Nazis advancing under a white flag his famous one-word answer, "Nuts!" The rest of the commander's Christmas message read as follows:

> What's merry about all this, you ask. We're fighting—it's cold—we aren't home. All true, but what has the proud Eagle accomplished with its worthy comrades of the 10th Armored Division, the 705th Tank Destroyer Battalion, and all the rest? Just this: We have stopped cold everything that has been thrown at us from the north, east, south and west. We have identifications from four German panzer divisions, two German infantry divisions, and one German parachute division. These units, spearheading the last desperate German lunge, were heading straight west for key points when the Eagle Division was hurriedly ordered to stem the advance. How effectively this was done will be written in history; not alone in our division's glorious history but in world history. The Germans actually did surround us, their radios blared our doom.
>
> Allied troops are counterattacking in force. We continue to hold Bastogne. By holding Bastogne we assure the success of the Allied armies. We know that our division commander, General Taylor, will say: "Well done!"
>
> We are giving our country and our loved ones at home a worthy Christmas present and, being privileged to take part in this gallant feat of arms, are truly making for ourselves a merry Christmas.[4]

"General McAuliffe's greeting to his troops proved to be in every part a prophetic utterance," US military historian S. L. A. Marshall respectfully noted.[5]

McAuliffe's brave message countered the propaganda leaflets the Germans fired by artillery shells into American lines on Christmas Eve. On one side, the German propaganda leaflet pictured a little girl and a lit

Christmas candle, with a pitiful image of a severely wounded US soldier dimly portrayed in the background. On the reverse side, with a border illustrated with a shooting Christmas star, angels, Christmas cookies, and Christmas candles, the title read: "Hark . . . the Herald Angels sing!"

The copy was designed to play on the heartstrings of the cold GIs in their foxholes on the front line, wishing one and all that they were home that night, warm in their beds, surrounded by a loving family, preparing to celebrate one of the holiest days of the year, Christmas Day, the day Jesus Christ was born. "Well, soldier, here you are in 'No-Man's Land,' just before Christmas far away from home and your loved ones," the leaflet read. "Your sweetheart or wife, your little girl, or perhaps even your little boy, don't you feel them worrying about you, praying for you? Yes, old boy, praying and hoping you'll come home again, soon. Will you come back, are you sure to see those dear young ones?"

As if that emotional message were not enough, the leaflet continued, "This is Christmastime . . . the Yule log, the mistletoe, the Christmas tree, whatever it is, it's home and all that you think fine to celebrate the day of our Savior. Man, have you thought about it, what if you don't come back . . . what of those dear ones?" The end was equally difficult to read: "Well, soldier, 'PEACE ON EARTH GOOD WILL TOWARD MEN' . . . for where there's a will there's a way . . . only 300 yards ahead and MERRY CHRISTMAS!"[6]

While the message was clear, no Americans were surrendering.[7]

According to Bastogne lore, General McAuliffe left division headquarters that Christmas Eve night to take a walk around town for some fresh air. As he walked past the police station that held captive several hundred German prisoners, he heard the German POWs singing in German various Christmas carols we share in English, including "O Tannenbaum," ("O, Christmas Tree") and "Stille Nacht" ("Silent Night"). Moved by the German prisoners sharing what must have been his own homesick feelings, McAuliffe went inside the prison, accompanied by the guards. Inside, the German prisoners could not help taunting McAuliffe in English, saying: "We will be at Antwerp in a few weeks," and "We will soon be free and you will be the prisoner."

McAuliffe waited quietly until their brave insults stopped. "I was just here to wish you a Merry Christmas," he said quietly. From there, McAuliffe left in his jeep, determined to wish his men on the line an equally Merry Christmas.[8]

Anticipating the Germans would make one last fierce effort to take Bastogne on Christmas, McAuliffe wondered for how many of his men this night might be their last.

As Christmas Eve drew to a close, McAuliffe quietly slipped into a Christmas Mass. While no one knows what General McAuliffe prayed that night, it is a reasonable guess he prayed that Bastogne would hold, no matter how much fury the Germans managed to throw their way over the next few hours.

CHAPTER 13

THE CHRISTMAS EVE BOMBING

Allied air activity on the twenty-fourth had heartened the men
on the ground. When night fell they could see the fires left as the
aftermath of the fighter-bomber strikes blazing all the way around
the perimeter. (Twice during the night of 24 December, however,
the Luftwaffe retaliated with very damaging and lethal bombing
sorties on Bastogne and the surrounding area.) Less obtrusive but of
considerable impact was the confidence that the commanders and the
troops had in each other; a lesson for future commanders may be read
in the considerable effort put forth by McAuliffe, Roberts, and the
regimental commanders to apprise all the troops of the "situation."

—Hugh M. Cole, US Military Historian, *The Ardennes: Battle of the Bulge*, 1988[1]

As night descended on Bastogne on December 24, 1944, the quiet
was deceptive. On Christmas Eve, the men in Bastogne said goodbye to one another possibly fearing what they may have anticipated
lay ahead. The experienced combat troops of the 101st Airborne who shoul-
dered so much combat since D-Day may well have anticipated the Germans
would in a surprise and dramatic move utilize Christmas, one of the most
sacred days of the year to all Christians, to make a last fierce try to capture
this pesky Belgian crossroads village they had besieged so far to no avail.

German general Heinz Kokott had quietly assembled the major part of his artillery to the northwest of Bastogne, around Flamierge. Kokott had devised a tight schedule, with the attack planned to start with two Luftwaffe bombing raids on Bastogne during the night of December 24. An infantry assault from the northwest was to begin at 0400 hours, to break through the American rifle line by 0600 hours, at which time an artillery attack was designed to fire on targets of opportunity so as to give the advancing German tanks the ability to move in toward Bastogne at maximum speed. Kokott's goal was to rush an armored group from the 15th Panzer Grenadier into Bastogne between 0800 and 0900 hours on Christmas Day, hoping to capture the town before the American fighter-bombers took to the air.[2]

CHRISTMAS EVE WORSHIP

Catholic soldiers spread the word that a Christmas Mass would be celebrated at headquarters at 1900 hours on Christmas Eve. A photograph of the event that survived the war shows Father McGettigan, a Catholic priest, as a young chaplain in vestments, consecrating the Eucharist before a group of Screaming Eagles kneeling before him, their bare heads absent helmets bowed in prayer. The few soldiers of the 101st that stand are alongside windows heavily draped so as to adhere to blackout conditions. Journalist Fred MacKenzie recorded that a hundred or more men entered the headquarters building where a large room had been converted into a chapel. Candles on the improvised altar furnished the light, as tapers burned in makeshift fixtures along the walls. "The simple service and dimly lighted room were wondrously appropriate to this place where the human spirit sometimes seemed recognizable, a naked and vibrant thing, apart from fleshly woes," MacKenzie wrote. "It was as though one were dying, or being born, in travail."[3] In a brief sermon, MacKenzie wrote, the chaplain noted that sacrifices were required and called for trust in God. "Do not plan," the priest counseled, "for God's plan will prevail."[4] At the end of the service, the soldiers returned to their battle stations in the Christmas Eve moonlight.

After the war, Maj. Stuart Seaton, the executive officer for the 463rd Parachute Field Artillery Battalion, recalled attending Christmas Eve services in Hemroulle, a small town to the northwest of Bastogne:

Father McGettigan celebrating Christmas Eve Mass at 101st Division headquarters. December 24, 1944.

One could hardly forget the night before, Christmas Eve. The division chaplain came to our town for a Christmas Eve service. We had the service in a stable. Somehow that service had a distinct significance. A rather humble setting, somewhat reminiscent of an event some two thousand years previous. I have often thought back to that night and that service.[5]

PFC Leland G. Jones of the headquarters company of the 401st Glider Battalion and his men were making the best of their rations having run out on Christmas Eve:

On Christmas Eve three of us melted a roll of Life Savers to make a cup of "hot soup"—all we had left. But we three then started singing Christmas carols, every one we could remember and we talked of Christmases we recalled at home with our families. Today, still, all good Christmases, before and since, seem to be lumped together. I remember only that horrible Christmas at Bastogne. I cannot listen to "I'll Be Home for Christmas," "White Christmas," or "Silent Night" without choking up.[6]

Private Mike Zorich was on outpost duty on Christmas Eve:

We were dug in on a bald hill overlooking the Germans who were in a patch of woods two hundred yards to our front. I was sent on outpost duty with Herman Sheets and we managed to crawl out to this little patch of trees for cover, overlooking the Germans who had their two men out for duty like we did. The Germans started singing Christmas songs, one of them being "Silent Night." It was strange. It was unbelievable that we were lying on that cold snowy ground, teeth chattering and trying to sing "Silent Night." We were keeping it to ourselves, afraid to let the Germans know we were there. They didn't mind. They were very strong with their voices. That's how strong Christmas is to soldiers out in the field.[7]

All along the line, troops did what they could to decorate small fir trees from the Ardennes. A photograph of some fifteen or twenty men of the mortar platoon of 2nd Battalion Headquarters Company of the 506th Parachute Infantry Regiment shows them with most wearing their helmets

General McAuliffe and 101st Airborne Division staff at Christmas Dinner, Heintz Barracks, Bastogne, Belgium. December 25, 1944. (McAuliffe is seated at the head of the table, farthest from the camera, upper right, with his arms folded and his eyes closed.)

and several sporting burlap bags wrapped into shoe coverings around their boots, standing in the snow on a sunny Christmas Eve around a scrawny fir tree they had roughly decorated.[8]

Another often published photograph shows General McAuliffe and his headquarters staff sitting for Christmas dinner in metal folding chairs, dressed in their field jackets, around a table with a sheet-like tablecloth. The centerpiece consists of a cluster of spruce boughs topped off with a paper star and adorned with a few crudely fashioned ornaments. While the photograph shows plates and silverware, there is not much visible evidence left on the plates. Stephen Ambrose, in *Band of Brothers*, reported the men of Easy Company of the 506th Parachute Infantry Regiment had cold white beans for their Christmas Eve dinner, while General McAuliffe and the 101st Division headquarters staff had "a turkey dinner, served on a table with a tablecloth, a small Christmas tree, knives and forks and plates."[9] What the surviving photo shows is a serious group of commanders sitting around what appears to be not much more than a folding-legs card table adorned with a scrawny fir tree. While the food served is not shown, the turkey dinner had to have been modest. Still, that the commanders at Bastogne had any turkey dinner at all when the troops in the trenches were lucky to have K rations remains a statement about the perquisites of military rank in the World War II era—limited though the perquisites often were in combat situations.

That evening the officers of the 502nd Parachute Infantry Regiment attended Christmas Eve Mass in the tenth-century chapel of the beautiful Rolle Château that they were then using as a command post. By all accounts, it was a happy and peaceful occasion, well attended by the neighboring Belgians who had generously contributed to the fare offered that night by the regimental messes by providing flour and sides of beef from their own meager provisions.[10]

Military historian S. L. A. Marshall noted that while the journal entries of the various units at Bastogne all use the word *quiet* to describe Sunday, December 24, 1944, that description does not do justice to what must have been the tumult in the thoughts and emotions of the men defending Bastogne that night. "Such was their reaction to the Christmas and to the memories surrounding it, that for the first time all around the perimeter men felt fearful," Marshall wrote. "It seemed to them that the end was at hand."[11] As night

Protestant Christmas service in one of a 101st Division operations building, Bastogne, Belgium. Christmas Eve 1944.

fell on Christmas Eve, many of the men shook hands with their comrades and said goodbye. Col. Julian Ewell, in his after-action report, commented that he thought the special fear observed in the troops on Christmas Even had no tactical foundation. Ewell judged it was "purely a nervous reaction because the men all began thinking of home at one time and it seemed to sweep through all ranks that they would not live through Christmas Day."[12]

PATTON DELAYED

On Christmas Eve, General McAuliffe had received a message from General Patton. It read: "Xmas Eve Present Coming. Hold On."[13]

Privately, that night, on the phone with General Middleton, McAuliffe expressed what war historian S. L. A. Marshall took to be his true feelings about Patton and the 4th Armored. "The finest Christmas present the 101st could get would be a relief tomorrow," McAuliffe told the corps commander.[14]

Regarding these messages and communications, military historian Charles B. MacDonald commented that Middleton was aware there was little chance Patton's 4th Armored would be able to break through the determined German defenses to reach Bastogne on Christmas Day. MacDonald wrote:

Indeed, in view of all the problems the 4th Armored Division was encountering, General Patton was ill-advised to send his message, for it raised false hopes. It had taken [the 4th Armored's] CCA [Combat Command A] until midday on December 24 to clear the first village beyond the Sûre River on the Arlon-Bastogne highway, the village of Warnach, still nine miles from Bastogne. Although CCB [Combat Command B] on the secondary roads west of the highway was less than five miles from Bastogne, that combat command was still battling the assault guns and Ferdinands [tank destroyers] that had appeared the day before with such effect at Chaumont. And the threat posed east of the highway by an arriving Führer Grenadier Brigade had prompted General Gaffey to commit CCR

Screaming Eagle soldiers attend a Protestant service in a 101st Division operations building, Bastogne, Belgium. Midnight, Christmas Eve, 1944. Shortly after this photo was taken, German bombers attacking Bastogne broke up the prayer service.

[Combat Command Reserve] there to protect the division's flank. Hopes of a quick, bold thrust on Bastogne had faded.[15]

The combat at Warnach demonstrated that Gen. Herbert L. Earnest's CCA was doing no better than Gen. Holmes E. Dager's CCB in advancing the Third Army toward Bastogne. Historian Don Fox, in his 2003 book, *Patton's Vanguard: The United States Army Fourth Armored Division*, described the ferocity of the fighting at Warnach:

> With the last remnants of daylight clinging to the battlefield, the leading vehicles started up Highway N4 west of Warnach. The tanks moved by without incident, but when the vulnerable half-tracks of C/51 came into view, German anti-tank gunners within Warnach opened fire, and quickly knocked out two of the half-tracks. With darkness descending, bypassing the town was now out of the question. There was no telling at the moment just how strong the enemy force was. If it was large, CCA could not risk leaving an enemy stronghold in its rear area as they continued moving to the north. So D Company was brought to a halt, and the light tanks and Sherman assault guns were turned to face Warnach.[16]

As five light tanks fought their way into Warnach, the commander of one of the M5 tanks instructed his gunner, Private W. King Pound, to fire the tank's .30-caliber machine gun at the thatched roofs of the houses, with the hope of setting them on fire with the tracer bullets. The commander calculated that the light from the burning roofs would reveal the enemy in what was developing as a night fight. "Private Pound poured lead from his machine gun into the buildings until the desired effect was achieved," Fox wrote. "But as the roofs began to burn, the enemy returned fire and sent an anti-tank round slamming into Pound's tank." Pound did not feel the impact, but he reacted when his tank commander began yelling at him to get out.

Fox continued the narrative:

> Pound erupted from the tank, and along with the other crew members, began to race toward a distant tree line that reflected the fires burning at the edge of Warnach. Small arms fire arched overhead as the men

scrambled through the deep snow. Pound had gotten about fifty yards away from the tank when he was struck by the startling realization that he had left the turret of the tank positioned in such a way that the driver couldn't exit out of his hatch. "Squirrel" Hayden was still inside the disabled M5, trapped as a result of Pound's understandable oversight.[17]

When Pound ran back to the tank, he found Hayden was trapped. Even worse, his foot had been shot off. Without hesitation, Pound climbed back into the tank and moved the turret to free the driver's hatch. He then climbed up on the front of the tank and helped pull Hayden out of the hatch. Unable to walk, Hayden held on to Pound's back as Pound scrambled out of the open field and headed toward the tree line where the two other crew members were waiting. "After a close brush with some Germans who came within twenty yards of their hiding place, the tankers later navigated the half mile or so back to the lines of CCA," Fox wrote, concluding the story.[18]

Finally, after two days of brutal and deadly street-to-street infantry fighting and tank combat, Patton prevailed, taking Warnach.

The battle at Warnach was the fiercest the 4th Armored's CCA fought in its drive north. The battle continued over three days, ending with the Americans capturing the town at 0515 hours in the afternoon on December 24, Christmas Eve.[19] After Warnach, General Earnest had come to the surprising conclusion for a regimental tank commander in Patton's Third Army that the advance to Bastogne was not going to be accomplished by his tanks, but by his infantry.[20]

On Christmas Eve, Patton expressed in his diary frustration that the Third Army had not reached Bastogne in the record time upon which he had set his expectations:

This has been a very bad Christmas Eve. All along our line we have received violent counterattacks, of which forced . . . the 4th Armored back some miles with the loss of ten tanks. This was probably my fault, because I had been insisting on day and night attacks. This is all right on the first or second day of the battle and when we had the enemy surprised, but after that the men get too tired. Furthermore, in this bad weather, it is very difficult for armored outfits to operate at night.[21]

In his 1947 book, *War As I Knew It*, Patton repeated what he wrote above in his journal, adding: "Unless you have very bright moonlight and clear going, armored battle at night is of dubious value. I remember being surprised at the time at how long it took me to learn war. I should have known this before."[22] All considered, Patton concluded, "The day of the twenty-fourth was rather discouraging."[23]

On the evening of December 24, Maj. Gen. John Milliken, the commander of III Corps and the general most directly responsible for managing movement of Patton's Third Army divisions north toward Bastogne, issued orders to "stabilize lines with all-around defense and active patrolling . . . Troops will be rested as much as possible . . . Attack will be resumed just before daylight 25 December." Military historian Harold Winton concluded

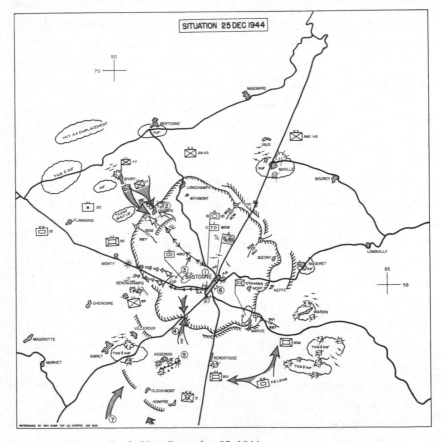

Bastogne, Belgium: Battle Map, December 25, 1944

Milliken's order was a result of Patton finally realizing that his insistence upon continuous day and night attacks in the conditions under which the Third Army was operating simply could not be sustained.[24]

On Christmas Eve, Patton went to candlelight communion at an Episcopal Church in Luxembourg. "It was very nice and we sat in the former Kaiser Wilhelm I's box," Patton noted simply in a diary entry written on December 25, 1944.[25]

THE CHRISTMAS EVE BOMBING

As planned, the Nazis began their Christmas assault on Bastogne with two bombing attacks that commenced on Christmas Eve.

The first reports of German aircraft approaching were received by radio at around 1925 hours, and within thirty minutes bombs were falling in the center of town. "Adolf Hitler had unleashed his fury and frustration on the little Belgian town," wrote Barron and Cygan. "Snarling like fat mosquitos, the bombers and the eruptions of their payloads—high explosive, fragmentation, incendiaries, and bright magnesium flares—blasted the still winter night."[26] The drone of the German bombers was easily recognizable as it

Main Street of Bastogne, as seen by the 101st Airborne Division, after Christmas Eve bombing. Christmas Day 1944.

involved a sound uncharacteristic of American bombers. Some eighty-eight German bombers, most of them Junkers JU-88s, attacked Bastogne in two waves, each lasting about a half hour, dropping a total of two tons of bombs on the village, with the first attack commencing at around 2000 hours and the second at 0300 hours in the early morning hours of Christmas Day.[27] While the German bombing raids were small in comparison to US bombing raids in Europe that were typically in the magnitude of twenty tons of bombs dropped, the German bombing raids were large enough to do massive damage in a village as small as Bastogne. In each attack, the German bombers led with magnesium flares that lit up the center of the town brighter than day, illuminating in a ghostly white glare the village's main square and central buildings. Then the bombs began dropping, with each of the two bombing runs concluded the same way, with the raiding marauders strafing the town with machine-gun fire before they departed into the night.

Historian John Toland noted that when the German bombing raid began on Christmas Eve, the thirty-five hundred civilians trapped in the town during the siege were just beginning to settle down in their cellars for another night.

> Hundreds were huddled on the damp floors of the great seminary cellar. The sisters of the clinic circulated in the flickering candlelight, trying to comfort the old people and the children. Living in the cellar on filthy mattresses, crowded but cold and infested by lice, was hardest on the old. Several had already died; several had gone mad; some were nearing the point of madness or were so petrified by fear they could no longer take care of personal needs. Carbolic acid, mixed with water, had been sprinkled around, but it did little to counteract the nauseating stink of human excrement.[28]

A stick of bombs dropped near the seminary, Toland reported. The lamps and candles blacked out. "Overhead came the thunder of falling timbers and stones," he wrote. "A snowstorm of dust filled the cellar. An old man banged the sides of his bed, screaming wildly. Then he shook the bed next to him. A woman jumped up and grabbed the long hair of one of the sisters, screaming, 'Let me out of here!'"[29]

Nor were the troops in Bastogne's center spared the horror of the German Christmas Eve bombing attack. A bomb hit the command post of Team Cherry, killing Capt. William R. Ryerson and Lt. Edward P. Hyduke, who had figured so prominently in the action around Longvilly in the early hours of the Bastogne siege on December 18. Journalist Fred MacKenzie wrote that his experience of the bombing raid began when he was headed down a corridor that led to the 101st Division command post at Heintz Barracks. "Suddenly, three petrifying explosions, within a short interval of time between the blasts, stilled all voices and movement," he wrote. "There was no mistaking these sounds—bombs were falling." Before he could seek cover, MacKenzie found himself under attack from the air. "Three more dropped, nearer. Then they heard the swelling throb of airplane engines. An all but imperceptible movement swept along the passage. It seemed to begin at one end, pass through each man, and go on down the corridor. It was like the stirring of leaves through which a vagrant wind passes; they were drawing their physical parts into tight knots to resist shock."[30] Then bombs drew nearer.

A thin, shrieking whistle and a thunderous roar beat down their senses. The cellar rocked. They crouched down along the walls.

A second shriek, almost instantaneously after the first, pierced benumbed senses. But the shattering blast of the second bomb blotted out the sensation its falling produced, benumbing them anew. A man seemed buffeted between the heaving walls.

The third bomb of the stick came down mercifully fast to fracture violently against the ties between conscious mind and body pressuring desperately against the unyielding concrete to escape.[31]

As terrified as MacKenzie clearly was, the bombing raid was not centered on the Heintz Barracks. Quickly, the wave of bombers passed over. Off in the town, MacKenzie could see flames roaring into the sky, silhouetting the rooftops.

The 81st Anti-Aircraft Battalion could do little to stop the JU-88s with their .50-caliber machine guns. Because they had been zeroed in on ground targets, the bigger guns were equally useless. For what seemed like an eternity to those on the ground, the German bombers were virtually unimpeded as they roared in at full speed, low in the sky, at an altitude estimated to be between 900 and 1,800 feet.[32] "The citizens of Bastogne hid in their basements, shivering with cold and fear," Barron and Cygan wrote. "As each Luftwaffe plane buzzed over, more flares fell, sputtering and photo-flashing against the stone facades before thudding to the streets. The flares, as much as the bombs, created a freakish effect—strobe lights in the hellish night."[33] The two military historians noted the bomb concussions could be felt easily around the perimeter of Bastogne. From their foxholes on the defensive perimeter, the US troops in the field were equally unequipped to do anything but watch in awe as the center of the village was rocked by explosion after explosion and went up in flames.

THE "ANGEL OF BASTOGNE"

The story of the Siege of Bastogne is not complete without telling the story of Renée Lemaire, a young woman who became known as the "Angel of Bastogne." "Renée Lemaire, thirty years old, was a beautiful young woman with strikingly blue eyes and a thick cascade of brown hair," recorded Charles B. MacDonald. "She had studied and trained for four years at the Brugmann Hospital in Brussels to become a visiting nurse and then worked under the auspices of the Ixelles Hospital in Brussels."[34]

MacDonald tells the story of how Renée met Joseph, the son of an elderly widower for whom she was providing nursing care. Renée and Joseph shared a mutual interest in the piano—Renée loved to sing while Joseph played. Soon the two were fiancés, planning marriage. Near the end of February 1944, Renée returned from night duty at the hospital, only to find that the doors and windows at Joseph's home were locked. She learned that the Gestapo had taken Joseph and his father away because they were Jews. Devastated, Renée continued her work as a nurse. In the late fall of 1944, Renée got permission to spend a month with her family in Bastogne, where her father, Gustave, owned a store on the town's main square. Her mother, an older sister named Gisèle, and a younger sister named Maggy, lived in Bastogne with Gustave. When the Americans came to Bastogne, the Lemaires welcomed American soldiers to their home.

MacDonald continued the narrative:

Renée was swiftly caught up in the glories of the liberation, the laughter of the Americans, the delights of their K-rations, their coffee and chewing gum, their kindness "made in USA." Soon Renée was laughing again, her eyes sparkling. She played the piano in the living room while the soldiers sang, and she learned their songs: "Mexicali Rose," "I'll Walk Alone," "Paper Doll." One of the soldiers, Jimmy, tall and handsome, started coming often to the house and the two went on long walks together.[35]

On December 17, 1944, as the Battle of the Bulge was starting, Jimmy came one final time to tell Renée his unit had been give sudden orders to leave. He promised Renée that he would be back soon.

When the fighting drew close to Bastogne, the Lemaires retreated to their cellar, as did most of the residents of the town that decided to stay through what was certain to be the return of the war to the town. There are various versions of how Renée was recruited by the Americans to serve as a nurse, but one of the most commonly retold involves a US dentist named Lee Naftulin, assigned to the 10th Armored Division. Known by his nickname, "Naf," to his friends, Naftulin was born in Romania in 1907, and his family immigrated to the United States the following year. He had graduated with a degree in dentistry from Ohio State in 1931.[36] The troops at Bastogne had been scrambling ever since the Germans overran the medical station at crossroads "X." After the capture of the 101st's field hospital, those few medical professionals who were left at Bastogne had to struggle to find anyone with medical training who would be willing to help. Looking for locals with medical training in Bastogne, Naftulin knocked on the door of Gustave Lemaire's store in the town's main square. When Renée answered the door and Naftulin learned she was a trained nurse, he recruited her to assist him.[37]

Renée mentioned there was another nurse in town at that time, Augusta Chiwy, an immigrant from the Belgian Congo who had come to visit her uncle in Bastogne just as the Battle of the Bulge was beginning.[38] Finding Chiwy, Naftulin soon recruited her as well. Augusta agreed to work with Renée at the makeshift medical aid station the 10th Armored Division had set up in the Sarma department store near the railroad station, under the

US wounded cared for in makeshift aid station in Bastogne, Belgium, after Germans captured the 101st Division hospital. Wounded lie on floor. December 1944.

direction of the 10th Armored Division's surgeon, Capt. John T. Prior. Born in St. Albans, Vermont, Prior was educated at the University of Vermont and did his graduate work at the medical college at the University of Vermont. He ended up being one of the most highly decorated physicians of World War II, being awarded the Bronze Star, the Silver Star, the Legion of Merit, the Belgian Croix de Guerre, and the medals of the cities of Bastogne and Metz.[39]

Caring for the wounded soldiers in Bastogne was not easy, given the few medical supplies available and the difficulty transporting the wounded from the snow-covered front in jeeps. All the makeshift medical stations, including Prior's, were forced to become hospitals. A surgeon, Prior struggled to keep alive the one hundred or so wounded soldiers under his care, including some thirty who were seriously injured. "The patients who had head, chest, and abdominal wounds could only face certain slow death since there was no chance of surgical procedures," Prior explained in a memoir written after the war. "We had no surgical talent among us, and there was not so much as a can of ether or a scalpel to be had in the city."[40] In none of the Bastogne aid stations were there beds for the wounded. The wounded men had to lie on the floor and contend with the cold with what few blankets could be found.[41]

Prior described how his two volunteer nurses worked together:

> They played different roles among the dying—Renée shrank away from the fresh, gory trauma, while the Congo girl was always in the thick of the splinting, dressing, and hemorrhage control. Renée preferred to circulate among the litter patients, sponging, feeding them, and distributing the few medications we had (sulfa pills and plasma). The presence of these girls was a morale factor of the highest order. This decaying medical situation was worsening—with no hope for the surgical candidates, and even the superficial wounds were beginning to develop gas infection. I never did see any tetanus develop during the entire siege.[42]

Many years after the war, Chiwy remembered, "The snow was very deep that year and you could have cut the fog with a knife. I don't think that I have ever been as cold. The wounded just kept arriving and their number was growing by the hour. The worst problem was supplies. We had almost nothing except a bit of sulfa powder but no anesthetic."[43] The problem was the same for all the various medical aid stations improvised around Bastogne. The medical aid facility established by the 101st Airborne Division at a riding hall in the Heintz Barracks complex had six hundred litter patients on a dirt floor, being sustained much the same, with minimal medical supplies and limited medical staff racing just to keep pace.

Just before the Christmas Eve bombing started, Prior remembered being in the building next to his hospital, preparing to write a letter for a young lieutenant to send to his wife. "The lieutenant was dying of a chest wound," Prior recalled. "As I was about to step out the door for the hospital, one of the men asked if I knew what day it was, pointing out that on Christmas Eve we should open a champagne bottle."[44]

Prior remembers being startled by the bombing attack. "As the two of us filled our cups, the room, which was well blackened out, became as bright as an arc welder's torch," Prior recalled. "Within a second or two, we heard the screeching sound of the first bomb we had ever heard. Every bomb as it descends seems to be pointed right at you. We hit the floor as a terrible explosion next door rocked our building."[45] What Prior feared immediately was that the bombing attack had killed Renée.

Prior ran outside to discover the three-story Sarma department store serving as his hospital was a flaming pile of debris about six feet high. The magnesium flares the German bombers were dropping lit up the night brighter than day. The German bomb had scored a direct hit, collapsing the entire building down on the cellar where Prior and his small medical staff had established the meager medical aid station that served as his "hospital." While Prior and those of his staff not injured in the collapsing building raced to the top of the debris to clear away burning timber in their search to see if any of the wounded had survived, the German bomber, seeing the action below, dropped down to strafe with machine guns those rushing to help. Prior and the others scrambled under some nearby vehicles for safety as the German bomber repeated the strafing run several times over.

When the German bomber finally left the scene, several men volunteered to be lowered into the smoking cellar on a rope, struggling to pull to safety two or three of the injured who could be rescued before the entire building fell into the cellar. "I estimated that about twenty injured were killed in this bombing, along with Renée Lemaire," Prior wrote. "It seems that Renée had been in the kitchen as the bomb came down and she either dashed into, or was pushed into the cellar before the bomb hit. Ironically enough, all those in the kitchen were blown outdoors since one wall was glass." Prior commented that he had often wondered how the German pilot picked this hospital as a target. "There were no external markings but, as some of the men said, the bomb must have come down the chimney," he speculated. "Many tanks and half-tracks were parked bumper to bumper in the street in front of the hospital, so it seems probable he simply picked an area of high troop concentration."[46]

Journalist Fred MacKenzie recorded a bucket brigade of soldiers passing water along in "a woefully puny fire-fighting effort" to save the wounded in the collapse of the building. "The flames leaped up beyond all control," he recorded. "The only sound was the whoosh of the flames leaping skyward from the interior of the tall, stoutly built old structure, like the fires of a blast furnace." MacKenzie thought it was impossible that anyone still lived in the fiercely burning pyre. "Yet in the shadow of the towering walls a few soldiers were pounding and prying at the corner bricks while the flames of the inferno within whipped from windows and doors and soared five stories above them at the top of the fiery cupola." MacKenzie noted that one of the men had observed Nurse Renée Lemaire was caught under a falling timber just as she was nearly out.[47]

Prior wrote in his memoir that before his unit left Bastogne, the rubble was cleared and the majority of the bodies, including that of Renée Lemaire, were identified. He remembered specifically Renée's last day alive. On December 23, when Bastogne had received its first air resupply, Renée had spent much of the day looking to recover for herself one of the silk parachutes, saying she wanted to save it to make a wedding dress for herself one day. Unbeknownst to Renée, Prior had gotten one of the silk parachutes for her, and he was planning to present it to her as a Christmas Day present. Sadly, Prior used that same parachute to wrap Renée Lemaire's remains and bring them to her father.[48] Nurse Augusta Chiwy miraculously survived the blast with only minor cuts and bruises even though she was among those blown through the kitchen wall by the bomb.[49]

Prior wrote the following commendation for Renée:

This girl, a registered nurse in the country of Belgium, volunteered her services at the aid station, 20th Armored Infantry Battalion in Bastogne, Belgium, 21 December 1944. At this time the station was holding about 150 patients since the city was encircled by enemy forces and evacuation was impossible. Many of these patients were seriously injured and in great need of immediate nursing attention. This girl cheerfully accepted the herculean task and worked without adequate rest or food until the night of her untimely death on 24 December 1944. She changed dressings, fed patients unable to feed themselves, gave out medications, bathed and made patients more comfortable, and was of great assistance in the administration of plasma and other professional duties. Her very presence among those wounded men seemed to be an inspiration to those whose morale had declined from prolonged suffering. On the night of December 24 the building in which Renée Lemaire was working was scored with a direct hit by an enemy bomber. She, together with those whom she was caring for so diligently, were instantly killed.[50]

Prior commented that he never heard what action was taken on this commendation.

Most observers put the number of killed in the medical station bombing at around thirty wounded GIs. In the lore that developed over the disaster, Renée Lemaire has become known as the "Angel of Bastogne" for her unselfish devotion to the wounded and the tragic fate that awaited her efforts.

CHAPTER 14

THE CHRISTMAS DAY ATTACK

About 0300 a few German planes droned over the 502nd
lines and dropped bombs indiscriminately around
Rolle, the regimental command post. This seems to
have been the Luftwaffe support promised Kokott.

—Hugh M. Cole, US Military Historian, *The Ardennes: Battle of the Bulge*, 1988[1]

Christmas Day, December 25, 1944, came on a Monday. It had been one week exactly since the 101st Airborne Division was in bivouac, resting at Camp Mourmelon in France.

The main damage in the Christmas Eve bombing was done to the buildings around the Bastogne town square. "A town that had hardly been touched earlier in the war at that point 'wore the ghastly air of desolation' that had come to so many other places in Europe," noted Charles MacDonald.[2] Photographs of Bastogne taken immediately after the Christmas Eve bombings show the massive rubble typical of European villages unfortunate enough to have become the center of a World War I or World War II battle.

Remarkably, the German aerial bombing on Christmas Eve night and in the early hours of Christmas Day did little damage to the US troops defending the perimeter of Bastogne, despite the extensive damage done to the town itself. "The German shelling that reached into General McAuliffe's headquarters in the Christmas morning attack was the curtain-raiser for the most desperate hours of the siege," journalist MacKenzie wrote. "It flayed the snow-blanketed forward area west of Bastogne, but with no recorded damage to the men in scattered foxholes, slit trenches, and buildings along the perimeter."[3]

Only one week since they had been rushed to Bastogne from bivouac, in the early hours before Christmas Day dawned, the US troops on the western perimeter defending Bastogne would have to repulse a desperate German attack designed to take the town once and for all.

THE PRE-DAWN ATTACK BEGINS

At 0245 hours on Christmas Day, the Germans opened up with intense artillery shelling on the northwestern perimeter, in the sector defended by the 502nd Parachute Infantry Regiment, only hours after the unit's Christmas Mass service had ended in the elegant tenth-century chapel at the Rolle Château.[4] Obviously, there was to be no Christmas truce at Bastogne this December 25.[5] At approximately 0300 hours, Kokott's all-out assault to take Bastogne at all costs began with an infantry attack to the northwest, in the area of the perimeter defended by "Silent Steve" Chappuis's 502nd Parachute Infantry Regiment.[6] Within a few minutes of the infantry assault commencing, Chappuis learned by radio that Company A of the 502nd was battling in Champs against a large force of Germans in hand-to-hand and house-to-house combat. When communications went dead between division headquarters at the Heintz Barracks and Chappuis's headquarters at Rolle Château, the headquarters staff at the 101st Divisional Command Post in the Heintz Barracks decided it was time to wake up McAuliffe, even though he had barely had time to hit the sack after returning to Bastogne from midnight Christmas.[7] Kokott's tank assault was certain to follow.

First Lieutenant Al Wise, an assistant platoon leader with Company A of the 502nd, provided a vivid description of the German attack on Champs. When the action began, he was situated in a farmhouse on the outskirts of the village, with the troops dug in about 150 yards in front of the command post about 300 yards in front of the US front lines. He wrote:

We stayed up until midnight Christmas Eve to wish each other a "Merry Christmas" and then turned in. About 0225 our area came under very heavy shelling, lasting approximately 15 minutes. During a lull in the shelling, one of the men from our forward outpost came running into the command post requesting a medic, as one of the men on the outpost had been severely wounded in the back by shrapnel. As the medic and Lt. Harrison started to leave, they noticed some white-clad strange figures surrounding our command post and also the 1st Platoon command post. At approximately the same time a German machine gun, situated about 20 feet from one of the windows of our house, opened the attack by firing directly through the window into the house in which we were standing. At the same time, a machine gun on the opposite side of the house, fired alongside our house, preventing our using the door. The machine gun firing through the window hit our stove, upsetting same and setting fire to the same. About that time another Jerry team, using their bazookas, let go at the walls. We returned fire but as we could see little, the fire was out of control and smoke filled the entire house.[8]

Wise and the others with him survived by running into the barn attached to the house. From there, they ran some 25 yards to a hedgerow, shedding everything in the run—coats, gloves, bedrolls, blankets, and grenades—keeping only their rifles and ammunition.

As the Germans began infiltrating US front lines around Champs, Colonel Chappuis at the regimental command post at Rolle Château found it impossible to shift reinforcements to units under fire because in the darkness it was impossible to distinguish between friends and enemies. In his after-action report, Chappuis recalled that as day broke, Lt. Sam Nichols of the 1st Battalion came running into the command post and said, "There are seven enemy tanks and lots of infantry coming over the hill on your left."

At this time, the Rolle Château command post emptied out. Cooks, clerks, chaplains, and radio men were gathered together under Capt. James C. Stone, the command post manager, and rushed to the next hill. Left in the Rolle Château command post were only Chappuis, his executive officer Lieutenant Colonel Cassidy, a radio operator, and Maj. Douglas Davidson, the battalion surgeon who had been taking care of his own wounded at Rolle

Château. When Davidson saw the German tanks coming over the hill, he routed out all his wounded men who were able to walk, gave them rifles, and led them over toward the point of the attack.[9]

In his after-action report, Chappuis described a similar situation developing at Company A. Capt. James Hatch was in the command post of Company A when he heard the fight going on outside. "Hatch grabbed his pistol and opened the door," Chappuis noted. "He was looking straight into the mouth of the tank's 75-mm gun at a range of 15 yards. He closed the door, saying to the others, 'This is no place for my pistol.'"[10]

General Middleton described Kokott's Christmas Day assault as "a nutcracker squeeze" applied to the American defenders of Champs and Hemroulle, a village located halfway between Champs and Bastogne. As Middleton explained, Kokott's "upper jaw" bit into the 1st Battalion area of the 502nd Parachute Infantry positions at about 0300 hours with a

One of two American tank destroyers knocked out in the German breakthrough on Christmas Day at Champs, Belgium. The haystack behind which the tank destroyer was concealed can be seen smoldering in the background. December 1944.

Volks-grenadier regiment. Delaying the movement of the "lower jaw," at 0530 hours Kokott sent his panzer regiment against the 1st Battalion of the 327th Glider Infantry to the south of Champs. Near Mande-Saint-Étienne, on the left flank of Chappuis's 502nd, a line of eighteen Mark IV giant armored tanks started moving against Company A of the 3rd Battalion of the 327th Glider Infantry Regiment. Advancing in a single column, the Mark IV tanks were followed by hundreds of German infantry on foot.[11]

The German panzer assault roared on toward Hemroulle, where Captain Towns of Company C called Col. Ray C. Allen, commander of the 3rd Battalion of the 327th Glider Infantry who, on December 23, had pulled back to what he considered his final defensive perimeter east of Flamierge. "Tanks are coming toward you!" Towns shouted into the telephone. "Where?" Allen asked. "If you look out your window now, you'll be looking right down the muzzle of an 88," Towns answered. Allen looked out the window and saw Towns was right. Advancing on his position, Allen could make out a tank in the dim light. The tank fired as it headed directly for the house Allen occupied. It was 0715 hours, and Allen decided he needed to call the division commander Col. Joseph Harper immediately. When Allen explained the German tanks were attacking his position, Harper asked, "How close?" Allen explained, "Right here!" The tanks were firing point-blank on Allen from a range of 150 yards. "My units are in position, but I have to run," Allen shouted. Allen, along with two members of his staff, barely escaped into the woods, with the German tanker firing at them as they ran in the early-morning twilight.[12]

THE MYSTERY OF THE "LOST TANKS"

At the height of the battle, the eighteen German tanks and accompanying infantry broke though the defensive perimeter held by the 327th Glider Infantry and got to within one mile of Hemroulle. To the north, German tanks entered the city of Champs.

Having made the breakthrough, German tank commanders radioed back to Kokott's headquarters that they were within striking distance of Bastogne. US military historian Hugh Cole reported:

The tank group on the right of the German line drew ahead of its marching partner, and an hour and a quarter after the advance had begun, reported to Kokott that the only evidence of American reaction was some tank or tank destroyer fire coming in from the south. Thirty minutes later a brief and optimistic radio message flashed to the rear: the tanks and the infantry battalion festooned thereon had reached the western edge of Bastogne. But the elation at the German command post was short-lived; word that the German tanks were in the streets of Bastogne never came. The commander of the 115th Panzer Grenadier Division [a company of tank destroyers] sent a liaison officer forward to find the battalion or its tanks, without success. German forward observers were alerted to listen for the sound of German tank fire—but all they could hear was the crash of artillery fire and the crump of exploding mortar shells.[13]

When the German command could not verify that German tanks had entered Bastogne, the mystery of the "lost tanks" developed. Military historian Charles B. MacDonald cleared up part of the mystery. "The commander of the German tanks had early radioed Colonel Kokott's headquarters that he had reached the western edge of Bastogne," MacDonald noted, as had Hugh Cole. "Although Kokott for long believed the report and thought he was at last about to achieve the success that had so long eluded him, the tank commander had confused Hemroulle with Bastogne."[14]

The remainder of the mystery is explained by the effectiveness of the US troops once the Germans had broken through the defense perimeter. Just west of Hemroulle, about half the German tanks wheeled left and proceeded down a cart path that led to the road between Champs and Bastogne. They soon encountered Companies B and C of the 502nd that Colonel Chappuis had called forward to assist the paratroopers in Champs. As Chappuis turned the companies toward the oncoming attackers, two tank destroyers from Company B of the 705th Tank Destroyer Battalion absorbed the initial shock of the German tank advance. Both tank destroyers were knocked out as they fell back toward the Champs road. As the panzers rolled forward, Company C made an orderly withdrawal to a wooded lot midway between Champs and Hemroulle. "Now it was the paratroopers' turn," Hugh Cole wrote. "They showered the tanks with lead, and the German infantry clinging to the decks and sides fell to the snow. The tank detachment again wheeled into column, this time turning toward Champs. Two of the 705th tank destroyers, which were backing up Company C, caught the column in the process of turning and put away three of the panzers; the paratroopers' bazookas accounted for two more."[15]

In his after-action report, Chappuis described what appears to be the same action. A column of German tanks with infantry riding on the tanks headed toward Champs, only to pass troops from the 502nd's Company C. With the flank of the tank column exposed, two soldiers from Company C each hit and knocked out a tank with their bazookas, while two tank destroyers knocked out three additional German tanks and the German infantry riding on the tanks were cut to pieces by automatic rifle fire. Chappuis reported there were sixty-seven Germans dead and thirty-five taken prisoner as the action drew to a close. One tank broke through Company B and got into Champs. But Company A fired bazookas at it and let loose with 57mm gunfire. "Both scored hits and what type of fire finally stopped the tank is not known," Chappuis reported. "The hull is still in Champs."[16]

The other half of the advancing panzer column encountered stiff resistance from four different sources: a group of four tank destroyers from the 705th; Sherman tanks accompanying Team Cherry of the 10th Armored called up from reserves to join in the fight; the 463rd Parachute Field Artillery Battalion; and bazookas handled by the 327th Glider Infantry. As S. L. A. Marshall observed, "The German tanks were fired at from so many directions and with such a mixture of fire that it was not possible to see or say how each tank met its doom."[17] Marshall confirmed that eighteen German tanks had been seen on the 327th Glider Infantry's front that morning. Marshall also confirmed Chappuis' report that one of the tanks got away into Champs. Marshall also recorded that the 502nd's Company A fired bazookas at the tank and that the tank was shelled by a 57mm gun positioned in the village. "The tank was hit by both types of fire but which weapon made the kill is uncertain," Marshall wrote.[18] Marshall further documented that when the fighting ended, there were "at last eighteen disabled German tanks, many of them with fire-blackened hulls scattered out through the American positions along the ridges running from Hemroulle to Champs."[19] At noon on Christmas Day, General

Lone German Panzer tank to penetrate US lines at Champs, destroyed by US bazooka and 57-mm gunfire, northwest of Bastogne, Belgium. Christmas 1944.

Kokott finally learned the tanks he thought broke through to Bastogne were officially "lost." What happened to the tanks remained a mystery to the German headquarters.[20]

In the end, only one German tank charged into Champs. In fierce hand-to-hand combat, the 502nd held. By the middle of the morning on Christmas Day, the German attackers withdrew from Champs so German artillery could attempt to blast the US paratroopers out of the village and the surrounding woods. In early afternoon, General Kokott called the battle at Champs to a halt, planning to resume the battle under the cover of night.

The wire maintenance men of the 502nd Signal Corp had kept working right through the firefight, so that by 0900 hours, the telephone lines of communication were reestablished between Colonel Chappuis's headquarters at the Rolle Château and 101st division headquarters in Bastogne.[21] In the end, Kokott's attack plan failed. The German tank column that struck out toward Champs was all but wiped out by rifle and bazooka fire from two companies of the 502nd and the 705th tank destroyer battalion. The other tank column, heading into Bastogne, also met devastating fire from the 327th and the reinforcements from the 10th Armored's Team Cherry. "Colonel Kinnard's plan of the day before to position tank destroyers and tanks close to the perimeter was clearly vindicated," military historian Harold Winton concluded.[22]

Still, there were many tense moments in the early morning hours of Christmas Day, especially as reports came in to the 101st division headquarters at Heintz Barracks that German tanks and infantry were advancing on Hemroulle, less than two miles away. Adding to the tension was that the defense of Champs was unknown once communications with "Silent Steve" Chappuis's 502nd's headquarters at Rolle Château broke off. Journalist MacKenzie wrote:

> The appearance of German armor and infantry bearing down on the heart of the defenses seemed more and more a probability, and if it did appear, the defense of Bastogne could deteriorate almost at once into a wild and disorganized struggle at the multiple crossroads. For the first time since the start of the siege, General McAuliffe was alarmed. The danger of being overrun was close at hand. Headquarters personnel privy to the secrets of the operations room looked to the condition of their own arms and thought it probable they would be forming their own force of combative cooks, clerks, drivers, and helpers.[23]

The situation in those early Christmas Day hours looked desperate, as reported by MacKenzie, with the fighting deteriorating into "a form of guerrilla warfare waged at intervals in some sectors by men mad with suffering and anxiety."[24]

In the end, McAuliffe's combination of paratrooper riflemen, bazookas, tanks, tank destroyers, and artillery prevailed. "The German commander had counted on smashing into Bastogne by eight o'clock," MacKenzie wrote. "If he did not, American airpower would catch him on the open plains in broad daylight and end all chance of a Christmas Day victory."[25] Not a single German tank that penetrated the US defensive lines escaped destruction in that fierce early morning Christmas Day battle. "Two American battalions with their attached weapons smashed the Germans' last serious chance of getting into Bastogne," wrote histo-rian Frank James Price in his 1974 biography of Gen. Troy Middleton. "It was close, but as the maneuvers unfolded all the advantages came to the Americans. Having shaken two sizable German armored forces out of their Christmas stocking, the Americans on the west side of Bastogne had finished their job by 9 a.m."[26]

P-47S TO THE CHRISTMAS RESCUE

With daylight on December 25, the P-47 Thunderbolts swarmed overhead to pound back the German attackers, exactly as Kokott had anticipated. In total, the 406th Fighter Group flew 115 sorties on Christmas Day, accom-panied by the 512th and the 513th fighter squadrons that flew six missions each, while the 514th flew five. The P-47s gave the Germans surrounding Bastogne a return beating of their own. The 406th claimed their fighter planes struck forty-seven gun positions, nineteen armored vehicles, one mobile gun, eleven buildings, one hundred twenty eight motor transports, and ten tanks. "Just as Kokott had predicted, the Jabos were everywhere Monday [December 25], enjoying the fair and clear flying weather and pinpointing the men and vehicles of the Reich who were still trying to carry out their orders that Christmas Day," military historians Barron and Cygan observed, pointing out Kokott's worst fears had been realized in that he failed to take Bastogne before the P-47s appeared in the skies. "The Americans once again owned the airspace over Bastogne, and after Christmas, it would never again be contested. Simply put, it spelled disas-ter for any further large-scale German attempts to attack Bastogne during daylight or good weather."[27]

By Christmas Day, Captain Parker of the Ninth Air Force stationed his radio-equipped jeep in the central courtyard of the 101st Airborne's division headquarters in the Heintz Barracks. This positioning permitted him to be an even more effective ground controller, coordinating directly with staff operations in General McAuliffe's command post. Paul Danahy, the G-2 intelligence officer of the 101st, placed red symbols on the Enemy Situation Overlay, such that when the transparent sheet was applied to a map of the surroundings, Parker could tell exactly where German military units were positioned. "Captain Parker stood by his jeep with his map [and Danahy's overlay] spread on the hood and chattered on the radio almost constantly to the pilots," MacKenzie observed. "Danahy fed him information gathered by his intelligence crew. Parker directed the planes to the indicated targets."[28]

As Christmas Day came to a close, General McAuliffe could be satisfied he had held the Germans off from making a much-desired present for Hitler out of Bastogne. "The day seemed less grim than those that had passed," MacKenzie reflected. "Perhaps it was the knowledge that the Air Force was shellacking the foe, or perhaps mere survival on Christmas Day lifted spirits, since many had indicated that they would not see its dawn."[29] Late in the afternoon of Christmas Day, after the combat subsided, a flight of 160 C-47 cargo airplanes resupplied Bastogne once more with the Bastogne defenders cheering them on with renewed enthusiasm. "The relative cheerfulness of the daylight hours gradually was dissipated with the coming of the night," MacKenzie pointed out, aware that the Siege of Bastogne was not yet over. "After all, the Germans were out there, and the men were still cold and hungry."[30]

In his diary on Christmas Day, General Patton recorded that he had left his Luxembourg headquarters early that day, determined to visit in the field all the divisions of the Third Army in direct contact with the enemy. "All were very cheerful," he noted, ready to add a note of caution. "I am not, because we are not going fast enough."[31] He mentioned he made sure that in most cases the men in the Third Army advancing on Bastogne got hot turkey sandwiches for their Christmas dinner. That night, Patton had dinner with General Bradley back in Luxembourg. Both commiserated upon hearing that British general Montgomery, after being given command of the US First Army, was not prepared to attack Germany for three months. It was a delay both Patton and Bradley considered typical for Montgomery, but still unusually slow.

In Bastogne, Christmas Day ended with Colonel Chappuis and Colonel Cassidy sitting down to a table spread with a can of sardines and a box of crackers. That night, General McAuliffe, disappointed that no relief force had yet arrived from Patton's Third Army, telephoned General Middleton and said simply, but to the point, "We have been let down."[32]

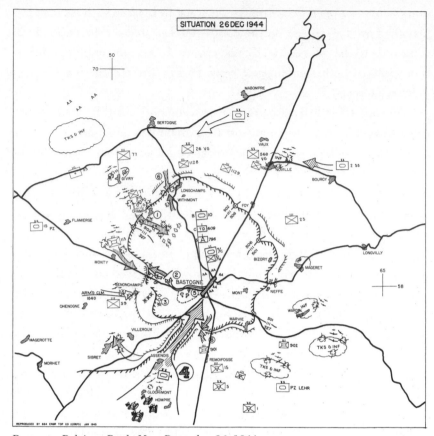

Bastogne, Belgium: Battle Map, December 26, 1944

THE DAY AFTER CHRISTMAS:
PATTON BREAKS THROUGH

What appears to have motivated the decision of the forward units of Patton's 4th Armored to push ahead into Bastogne was the daring efforts of the C-47 pilots and crews.

At approximately 1500 hours on the day after Christmas, the battalion commanders of the 4th Armored Combat Command Reserve came to a decision. Col. Creighton W. Abrams, commander of the 37th Tank Battalion, and Col. George Jacques, commander of the 53rd Armored Infantry Battalion, were ready to implement the battle plan as directed by General Blanchard, the CCR commander. This called for Abrams and

Jacques to pivot toward the west and head for the town of Sibret to the southwest of Bastogne. "As 'Abe' Abrams and 'Jigger' Jacques were discussing their next move, a huge armada of cargo planes began to fill the sky," noted historian Don M. Fox in his 2003 book, *Patton's Vanguard*. Abrams and Jacques realized the cargo planes were headed to Bastogne. In a matter of minutes, the two battalion commanders watched as parachutes gently floated to the ground carrying bundles of much-needed supplies. "Transport planes appeared with gliders in tow, which were then cut loose for their silent descent toward the landing sites within the perimeter. Not all of the aircraft made a safe return, as bursts of flak from the German AA guns peppered the flight path of the paratroopers. The odd cargo plane could be seen falling out of formation, sometimes aflame, dropping toward an unseen fate over the horizon."[33]

The scene was inspiring. "As Abrams and Jacques watched the precious supplies drift downward and out of sight, and witnessed the bravery of the unarmed pilots risking their lives to deliver the lifeblood of supplies to the surrounded paratroopers, a fresh sense of urgency stirred within them," Fox noted.[34] Abrams had an idea. Instead of diverting to the west to take on the Germans defending Sibret in a fight Abrams anticipated would be time consuming and costly, "an uncertain fight that would put them no closer to Bastogne," why not simply continue north along the road from Clochimont to Assenois, and then directly on to Bastogne itself? "Let's take a dash through Assenois straight into Bastogne," Abrams suggested to Jacques. Assenois, a little more than two miles to the southwest of Bastogne, was the last village that separated Abrams and Jacques from Bastogne. As Abrams explained the idea to Jacques, referring to the C-47 pilots they had just observed, "If those fellows can take that, we're going in right now."[35]

Abrams ordered Jacques's 53rd Armored Infantry Battalion and told Capt. William A. Dwight of Grand Rapids, Michigan, the battalion S-3 logistics officer equivalent to a G-3 logistics officer at the division level, to lead the tank-infantry charge into Bastogne.[36] Riding high in the turret of his Sherman tank named "Thunderbolt," Abrams supervised the coordinated attack. The charge caught the German 5th Fallschirmjäger [Paratrooper] and 26th Volksgrenadier Divisions defending Assenois by surprise. "There was no hesitancy among Abrams's and Jacques's men," Fox commented. "They too had been a witness to the drama being played out in the skies above Bastogne, and it proved all the motivation they needed."[37]

Lewis Sorley, a West Point graduate who served in Vietnam, in his 1992 biography of Creighton Abrams, entitled *Thunderbolt: From the Battle of the Bulge to Vietnam and Beyond: General Creighton Abrams and the Army of His Times*, noted that by commanding the first tanks of Patton's Third Army that managed to reach Bastogne, Abrams earned a permanent place in US military history. By deciding to drive directly to Bastogne, Abrams built an enduring reputation as an "aggressive man" who was also a brilliant tactician.[38] After World War II, this reputation would catapult Abrams into a distinguished military career in which he commanded all US forces in Vietnam from 1968 through 1972, at the height of the US military buildup. Subsequently, Abrams served as the chief of staff of the US Army from 1972 until shortly before his death in 1974.

In a letter to his wife dated December 26, General Patton rejoiced in the successful tank charge to relieve Bastogne: "Ever since the twenty-second, we have been trying to relieve Bastogne. Just now at 1845, Gaffey called to say we had made contact. Of course we did not do it with much, but we did it."[39]

A company of five tanks and a half-track carrying infantrymen commanded by Lt. Charles P. Boggess, in his Sherman tank affectionately named "King Cobra," led the charge into Bastogne. Entering Bastogne, Boggess was greeted by engineers of the 326th Airborne Battalion who were startled and delighted to see their sudden arrival. Abrams's biographer Lewis Sorley also described with an appropriate sense of drama how Boggess entered Bastogne:

> Then Boggess spotted some foxholes with what had looked like men in American uniforms. He called out to them, "Come on out, this is the 4th Armored," but nobody moved. "I called again and again," said Boggess, "and finally an officer emerged from the nearest foxhole and approached the tank. He reached up a hand, and with a smile said, 'I'm Lieutenant Webster of the 326th Engineers, 101st Airborne Division. Glad to see you.' It was 4:30 p.m., and getting dark, on the day after Christmas, 1944."[40]

When word reached General McAuliffe at the 101st division head-quarters that the 4th Armored party had reached the perimeter, he set out immediately for the southern front with his aide, Lieutenant Starrett. As recorded by journalist Fred MacKenzie, at approximately 1710 hours on December 26, General McAuliffe shook hands with the tankers of the 4th Armored. "I'm glad to see you," McAuliffe said with characteristic understatement.[41]

"The Siege of Bastogne, for purposes of historic record, may be considered ended at 1645 on 26 December when the 326th Airborne engineers reported contact with 'three light tanks believed friendly,'" recorded US military historian Hugh Cole in the US Army's official history of the Battle of the Bulge. "True, the breach in the German-held ring opened by the 4th Armored Division was narrow and precarious, but it would not be closed despite the most strenuous enemy efforts in coming days."[42] Cole noted the staunch defense of Bastogne had impeded the German 5th Panzer Army drive to the west, demonstrating a military axiom that "no salient thrust into the defender's position can be expanded rapidly and successfully if the shoulders of the salient are firmly held by the defender."[43]

Put in non-military terms, the point was that by holding the cross-roads town of Bastogne, despite being encircled, General McAuliffe and the US troops under his command had slowed down the German advance to the Meuse, making it difficult for Hitler and his field generals to achieve the tactical objectives initially stated for the Wacht am Rhein offensive. "The human cost of the Bastogne battle, therefore, probably was not out of proportion to the military gains achieved," Cole concluded.[44] The 101st Airborne Division suffered battle casualties at Bastogne numbering 105 officers and 1,536 men. The 10th Armored Division's Combat Command B had suffered the loss of 25 officers and 478 men. Cole acknowledged appropriately that there was no way of measuring the human cost of defending Bastogne by simply totaling the dead and the wounded.[45]

Patton's Third Army advance north to Bastogne took five days, and III Corps fired more than 55,000 rounds of artillery—some 4,387,746 pounds, or 2,194 tons—to get there, noted military historian John Nelson Rickard.[46] Maj. Albin F. Irzyk, in his autobiography *He Rode Up Front for Patton*, called Patton's decision to swing Reserve Command behind CCA and CCB, so as to successfully commit it to action on the left flank of the division and corps, "a stroke of absolute genius." Acknowledging there was some doubt where the decision to do so arose, Irzyk wrote, "It had to be the brainchild of a keen armor mind." Irzyk considered the bold idea could have come from Colonel Abrams, as Abrams "had proved over and over that he was bold, aggressive, imaginative, and far-reaching." Irzyk also considered the idea could have been attributed to General Gaffey, the commander of the 4th Armored Division, because Gaffey had been Patton's chief of staff and as such "had been privy to that man's [Patton's] thoughts and methods of operation." But ultimately Irzyk decided the idea had to have been General Patton's. It had to be the "Old Man," Irzyk reasoned, because the move had all the earmarks of Patton's type "of explosive, surprising, audacious, visionary maneuver."[47] In a sense, Irzyk was right: credit for the bold move started with Patton, was implemented by Gaffey, and was brought to fruition by Abrams.

Patton himself took claim for the decision, writing in his diary an entry on December 26 that seemed self-serving, as if he wanted to make sure his version of events was on the record: "At 1400 Gaffey phoned to say that if I authorized the risk, he thought that . . . Col. Wendell Blanchard could break through to Bastogne by rapid advance. I told him to try it. At 1845 they made contact, and Bastogne was liberated. It was a daring thing and well done." Then Patton added a few lines to make sure he emphasized, again for the record, the remarkable nature of the Third Army's unprecedented pivot to race north in record time: "Of course they may be cut off, but I doubt it . . . The speed of our movements is amazing, even to me, and must be a constant source of surprise to the Germans."[48]

For Patton, the relief of Bastogne was the capstone of a stellar military career, and Patton knew it. "The relief of Bastogne is the most brilliant operation we have thus far performed and is in my opinion the outstanding achievement of this war," he stressed in a letter to his wife dated December 29, 1944, three days after the Third Army broke the Bastogne siege. "Now the enemy must dance to our tune, not we to his. In the morning we are starting on a new series of attacks which will be decisive if I can only get Destiny to use reserves to attack and not to defend. This is my biggest battle."[49]

It was 0100 hours on the morning of December 27 before the 53rd Armored Infantry Battalion was finally able to clear all the Germans from Assenois, thereby ensuring a secure corridor into Bastogne, noted military historian Charles B. MacDonald. Yet even before the route was secure, MacDonald observed, twenty-two ambulances and ten trucks carried from Bastogne two hundred and twenty of the most seriously wounded of the soldiers who had so bravely defended the town.[50]

When the toll was counted, only 42 tanks remained of the 240 tanks with which the 4th Armored Division began the move north. "The other 200 were blackened hulks beside the shattered tree stumps on the road to Bastogne," wrote Gen. Paul D. Harkins in his 1969 book, *When the Third Cracked Europe*.[51]

With the Third Army opening a corridor to Bastogne, the besieged town was no longer "the hole in the donut," but "a balloon at the end of a string."[52]

While World War II still had months more to wage, McAuliffe and the defenders of Bastogne had broken the back of Hitler's winter offensive in the Ardennes.

"The relief of Bastogne signaled the defeat of the German army in the Ardennes offensive," US military historian S. L. A. Marshall concluded simply. "But it had cost the 4th Armored Division a price comparable to that exacted from the defenders of Bastogne themselves. In the seven days during which its forces were moving to the relief of Bastogne the Division lost about 1,000 men."[53]

SURGEONS ARRIVE BY AIR

On December 26, a C-47 towing a glider airlifted a much-needed surgical team into Bastogne, the only one-glider mission planned for the entire European theater of operation in World War II.[54] Gen. John B. Coates Jr., the executive officer of the medical section of the Third Army headquarters, recalled after the war that the medical team that included five surgeons had originally volunteered to parachute into Bastogne, though few had ever flown and none had ever had any jump training. Lt. Charlton W. "Corky" Corwin Jr. recalled piloting the glider that carried the volunteer medical team to Bastogne:

I believe that the glider flight into Bastogne, carrying the medics, was not only the only single glider mission in World War II, but also may have been the only glider to have landed twice on the same combat mission. We took off at Orleans, France. Benjamin F. Constantino was my copilot; the trusty towship, a C-47, was piloted by Capt. Raymond H. Ottoman . . .

We landed on the fighter base at Etain, France. It was a thrill to bring that glider down on that P-47 strip.

While we were again briefed at the operations office at Etain, the medics loaded the glider. The briefing was an exact repeat of an earlier briefing we had at Orleans in the presence of Colonel Krebs, our group commander. Some fighter pilot captain conducted the briefing. It was a relief to know that we could have an escort, or support of four P-47s.[55]

After the medics loaded the glider, Lieutenant Corwin briefed the passengers, informing the medical team there were no seatbelts on the glider. "I told them to grip the metal tubing upon coming in to land, in the event we crashed. No one had parachutes."[56] Corwin recalled the early afternoon flight from Etain to Bastogne was uneventful because the Germans were caught off guard. The glider cut off properly at three hundred feet and drew small-arms fire. The medical team reported being under fire when they landed. Forced to make a break for cover, the team was pinned down for about an hour before paratroopers of the 101st Airborne recovered them.

At the central medical facility then established in a maintenance garage in Bastogne, Dr. Henry M. Mills, an army captain, encountered in his first impressions what he recalled as the smell of gangrene. "Some of the wounded had been in there for days," he related after the war. "It looked like the Atlanta railroad station scene in *Gone with the Wind*."[57] The five surgeons found some eight hundred wounded soldiers lying on the floor when they arrived, with another seven hundred or so scattered in basements at the various other makeshift hospitals set up around Bastogne. Most of the immediate surgical work involved amputations of arms and legs. Operating conditions were primitive, but the airlift arrival of the surgical team was essential to saving lives that otherwise would have been lost.

On December 26, at approximately 1720 hours, a group of ten C-47s pulling gliders resupplied Bastogne with gasoline. Altogether, C-47s airlifted some three hundred tons of food, clothing, and ammunition to Bastogne the day after Christmas, providing troops not yet willing to depend on Third Army relief with the supplies they needed to keep on fighting.[58]

On December 27, pilot 2nd Lt. Albert S. Barton was flying a CG-4A glider to Bastogne filled with ammunition. Just prior to takeoff, four urgently needed surgeons were brought to his aircraft. Squeezing in with the ammunition, the surgeons sat down on the bench seats. Like the five surgeons the day before, these four were also volunteers. Barton recalled that legroom, because of the ammunition, was limited. In two letters written after the war to Capt. Ernest Turner, the pilot of the C-47 towing Barton and the surgeons in their glider to Bastogne, Barton remembered years later the harrowing nature of that trip. He watched from the glider as the Germans fatally crippled the C-47 towing them to the landing zone:

> It had been a smooth flight until a few minutes before when the puffs of smoke from the anti-aircraft guns below made me feel uneasy. Then the towship's left engine began leaving a trail of smoke, and gradually our speed dropped below 100 mph. I knew that you were in trouble when your left engine began skywriting trails, but now I learn that the Germans weren't satisfied with that. They went after anyone in the cockpit, and finally the right engine too. When the cut-off came, as I knew it must, it was academic. That nylon rope just dropped. Such a contrast; usually a cut-off necessitated a sharp pull-up to avoid that metal hook-up ring snapping back toward the glider. Now it's easy to understand—by that time your ship was almost a well-ventilated glider.[59]

With skill, Barton brought the glider to a safe landing in the Bastogne landing zone. In the letters written to Turner after the war, Barton noted he was relieved when the glider wheels finally trundled down the field. "My four doctor passengers shook hands and said they guessed they better go to work," Barton wrote. "It was a few minutes before the airborne lads appeared, and I had time to think. If you had cut me off just ten seconds earlier I wouldn't have been able to fly out of that black curtain of anti-aircraft fire. It's nearly forty-two years late, Ernie, but I surely do want to thank you for that last ten seconds."[60]

NO GREATER VALOR

"The Belgium people remember their American liberators."

—Inscription on Mardasson Memorial, erected to the memory
of the American soldiers who fought in the Battle of the
Bulge, near Bastogne, Belgium, dated July 4, 1946

Bastogne, symbol of the battle, also became the costly epilogue of the Battle of the Bulge," wrote Guy Franz Arend in concluding his chronology of the Bastogne siege. "The town was to enter history with an importance which was the result of publicity as well as of military actions. For the Americans, it is the symbol of a great battle. It is worth remembering that the battle did not take place in the town of Bastogne. Many of the veterans who return on their pilgrimages did not set foot in the town itself before. Most fought outside the town, in the surrounding villages which bore the horror of the major fighting."[1]

Arend tells the story of Gen. Bruce C. Clarke, the commander of the 7th Armored Division, CCB, that fought with great distinction at St. Vith. After the battle, Clarke sent a staff officer to the press conference General Eisenhower held in his Versailles headquarters. Arend wrote: "This Major Treece was interrupted as he explained the situation, maps in hand, by a journalist who asked: 'Did General Clark say anything in the battle like

"Nuts"?' 'I don't believe he did,' replied Treece. Whereupon the journalists declared that they had heard enough and Treece was dismissed. He returned to his headquarters in disgust."[2]

On Christmas Day 1944, the *New York Times* led with a large-print headline that read, "Nazi Push Halted by Air and Ground Blows." War correspondent Drew Middleton eloquently reported the good news: "The halting of the enemy drive on which the Germans gambled so heavily—a Christmas gift for all those who cherish freedom—may be only temporary, but it is apparent that the German smash has lost its first edge and that whenever his offensive is renewed the enemy will attack with greatly reduced forces against Allied divisions ready to resume their own offensive in the life-and-death struggle over the rugged, snow-covered hills and narrow valleys of the eastern Ardennes."[3]

The victory at Bastogne marked the final turning point of the war in Europe. This Patton appreciated, perhaps more than any other US general, including Eisenhower. "I believe that today ends the Bastogne operation," Patton wrote in his diary on January 11, 1945, as the Third Army was preparing to press the battle into Germany. "From now on it is simply a question of driving a defeated enemy." The next day, Patton added, "I believe that the Bastogne operation is the biggest and best the Third Army has accomplished, not excluding the battle of France, and I hope the troops get the credit for their great work."[4]

When the Bastogne siege was broken on December 26, the war in Europe was not over, but the defenders of Bastogne had withstood the worst the Nazis could throw their way.

For the remainder of his life, General McAuliffe rejected the notion that Bastogne needed to be "relieved" by Patton's Third Army. McAuliffe maintained this despite the urgency he expressed during the siege, anticipating Patton's arrival. Still, McAuliffe typically dismissed any notion that Bastogne had ever been in any real trouble of being overrun. He struck this tone in the oral report he gave S. L. A. Marshall and his military field historians immediately after the Siege of Bastogne:

> I continued to warn my infantry that the tanks would break through and
> that they were to be mentally prepared for such penetrations, since there

was really nothing to worry about. We had our stuff disposed in depth and it would be able to take care of any tanks which got through the infantry line. Well, they did break through—the chief breakthrough coming on Christmas morning—and they got it from all sides: bazookas, 75s, 76s, and rifle fire. One wounded German corporal who had been with the Africa Corps survived that attack. We asked him what had happened. He kept saying over and over, "We didn't know for nothing. We didn't know for nothing." That was all we could get him to say and the only way we could translate it.

Finally, the defense held because our dispositions were right. But about all we commanders could do was decide where the ground should be defended. We put the men there: they held. Many of them were cut to pieces by tank machine gun fire from ten to twenty yards range, but there were others in the foxholes who did not move. Someone on my staff said on Christmas: "The mistake the Germans have made was always to hit us where we happened to be strongest at that moment." That about sums it up.[5]

In 1964, General McAuliffe, accompanied by his wife, Helen, returned to Bastogne. "Men and towns sometimes like to meet again," wrote Jack Anderson, the nationally syndicated columnist and renowned investigative reporter covering the event. "So it happened that the general took his wife to Bastogne. For both, it was a mission of memory—the memory of a Christmas when he and his men battled against overwhelming odds, and Helen McAuliffe, three thousand miles away, endured every hour of the battle with her heart."[6]

The visit for McAuliffe was clearly emotional. "It's the contrast that gets you," General McAuliffe thought back as he stood on the site of his old command post. "To see it, you would have thought that the spirit of Christmas had vanished from the world," McAuliffe said. "You could hear the rumble of the artillery, everywhere, incessantly. The dead were all around, frozen into grotesque shapes. I remember a German tankman, stretched half out of his tank, with horror of death stamped across his face. German infantrymen had been snared on barbed wire, then caught in a crossfire until they were left like terrible stiff scarecrows. There was a GI sprawled in a foxhole, trying to stop an agony he could not feel."

In musing back on the battle, McAuliffe's mind turned immediately to God. "I drove into the town on December 18 with Colonel Kinnard, my assistant chief of staff," McAuliffe recalled. "We took a car and drove around for about an hour, and I showed him where every unit should be. I don't want to sound conceited, but the Lord must have led me by the hand. I had no map or anything and yet the disposition turned out just right. It permitted us to commit all our regiments to the best advantage."

Twenty years later, McAuliffe assessed once more how the US troops managed to survive encirclement, outnumbered by the enemy. "We had about sixty guns," McAuliffe explained. "We figured the angle of the shell and time on target and we placed them in such a way that each could swing 360 degrees and zero in on any section of the battlefield. Within two minutes, we could hit any point where the Germans were breaking through. That was why artillery played a big part in the victory."

Returning twenty years later, the battle in McAuliffe's mind was like it happened yesterday. "Then the Germans began to attack," he continued his narrative. "They attacked first from the east, then northeast, then southeast. But they attacked piecemeal. We had time to shift our forces and bring our strongest to bear on each threat."

The general paused for a moment. "Long afterwards, I talked to the German general, Manteuffel, who commanded the 5th Panzer Division here. I told him if I had been General Lüttwitz, in charge of the attack, I would have hit the American position from all directions simultaneously. He agreed. He said that Lüttwitz was too worried about his flanks. Manteuffel said he didn't realize what Lüttwitz was up to until casualties were too high to change the plan."

In writing the account of McAuliffe's 1964 visit to Bastogne, Jack Anderson commented, "The general thinks history has given too much emphasis to his classic, no-surrender reply. But words—even a four-letter one—can change history when they express the resolution of death before defeat. And the words have certainly immortalized McAuliffe."

Anderson observed that as he and McAuliffe strolled around Bastogne, word quickly spread of their coming. "McAuliffe *est ici!*" or, in English, "McAuliffe is here!" was shouted from door to door. "Our stroll and talk was a triumphal procession of a returned hero," Anderson wrote. On Bastogne's main street, Gerard-Marie Collard, a fruit seller, presented McAuliffe with a bunch of grapes. A butcher thrust a sausage into his hand. The town pharmacist asked for his autograph. A youth dashed away for his camera. Anderson marveled at the enthusiasm with which McAuliffe was welcomed back to Bastogne.

In strolling around the fields in which the battle had been fought, McAuliffe recalled his worst setback—when the field hospital, complete with surgeons, patients, and medical supplies, was captured. Anderson noted the wounded endured terrible suffering, only partly eased by cognac that the VIII Corps had left behind. "I visited the wounded only once, early in the battle," McAuliffe said. "I didn't go again. I was afraid it would affect my decisions."

McAuliffe also spoke of one of the men he considered a true hero of the battle—Lt. Col. "Silent Steve" Chappuis, the commander of the 502nd Parachute Infantry Regiment. On Christmas Day, when German tanks broke through the 502nd's lines, McAuliffe called Chappuis on the field telephone. "I asked, 'How are things going, Steve?'" McAuliffe recalled. "'To tell you the truth, General, they're kind of rugged.' I knew that if Chappuis thought a situation was 'kind of rugged,' it must be desperate. I rushed tanks and reinforcements to his help. They stopped the breakthrough."

But most of all, McAuliffe recalled how he had spent Christmas in Bastogne during the siege. "They struck on Christ's birthday," he said with bitterness. "It was a terrible attack from the west, and we thought we won a great victory. There was a great spirit of thankfulness to God. I hadn't planned to go to mass that day, but I happened by this large and imposing home with steeple-like roof on my way to the command post. I knew the priest and I could see him inside and I felt I should go in. Inside you could hear the guns rumbling in the distance. There was a very large attendance, for the religious feeling was widespread."

THE CROSS AND THE SWORD

The US army that fought at Bastogne was a brave and distinguished military force that welcomed God into their midst, trusting defeating the Nazis was necessary regardless of the cost, if only because these soldiers shivering in the cold of their foxholes could not bear the idea that the evil at the core of Nazi Germany might one day triumph to destroy the goodness they saw in their parents, their brothers and sisters, their spouses, their children, and possibly—God willing—even someday their grandchildren.

At Christmas 1944, Father Sampson, the chaplain of the 101st Airborne captured by the Germans at Bastogne, had just completed a forced march with a large group of POWs, walking from Luxembourg to Prum, Germany, on his way to Stalag II-A, in the cold without breakfast or lunch. Herded into a large auditorium of a good-sized school where Hitler and Goering's pictures covered the front wall, the US soldiers were given a supper of one half of a boiled turnip, a half slice of bread, and a cup of warm water, nothing else. Noting that the men were ready to riot, Sampson asked if he might hold a short Christmas service. Father Sampson wrote in his autobiography:

> It was a black night and the city was being bombed constantly. The school we were in was the most dangerous place in the city, right in the middle, and not far from the railroad station. A near miss would collapse the building. We sang "Silent Night, Holy Night" with the roar of planes overhead and bombs dropping near enough to make the building shiver.[7]

When one of the POWs started to read the gospel by the light of a small candle, a German officer came into the auditorium and took the candle away.

> In pitch dark without being able to see my congregation of eight hundred tired, hungry, and desperate soldiers, I said a prayer and then spoke to them for about fifteen or twenty minutes. The idea of the sermon was that Christ is always where He is least expected to be, and that He was just as surely among us that night as He was in the manger in the smallest and least-known village of Judea nineteen hundred years ago. Though we might be thousands of miles from home, in enemy hands, cold and hungry, we had that which makes Christmas, and He was stretching forth his infant hand to each of us to give us courage and help as we knelt to adore Him.[8]

A few months before his retirement, Father Francis Sampson, as chief of chaplains for the US Army, gave a speech on July 31, 1971, in which he addressed a question on the minds of those called to military service in Vietnam:

I have spoken at various universities and have been challenged by this misunderstanding. I have been asked how I can wear the uniform that symbolizes war and also wear the cross upon it symbolizing peace.

One would think that they should find the answer to the very question they proposed—for such questioners are of lofty academic standards, positions, and responsibilities. It is very easy for me to tell them that, by law and statute, the mission of the military of the United States is, first, to preserve peace.

Second, to provide for the security of our country, its borders and internal security. And third, to implement national policy as it pertains to peace treaties with friendly nations which of themselves cannot repel the aggression of avaricious neighbors.

I see nothing in this mission that does not appeal to the highest ideals of any man—regardless of his religion.

Indeed, it was Cardinal O'Neal, the great Churchman, who once said if he had not been a priest he most certainly would have had to be a soldier, because they are both called to the identical things—that is—the preservation of peace, the establishment of justice when it has been lost, and providing the security with protection for the weak and the innocent.[9]

In the Korean War, Father Sampson participated in a parachute drop behind enemy lines north of Pyongyang, on October 20, 1950. Prior to takeoff, he went from airplane to airplane, delivering the eucharist to the paratroopers about to go into battle. He died on January 28, 1996, the feast of the Angelic Doctor. On his tombstone, Father Sampson had inscribed, "Lord, make me an instrument of your peace."[10]

DISTINGUISHED SERVICE CROSS

On January 14, 1945, General Patton presented to General McAuliffe the Distinguished Service Cross for his valor during the Siege of Bastogne. The citation read:

The President of the United States takes pleasure in presenting the Distinguished Service Cross to Anthony Clement McAuliffe (0–12263),

Brigadier General, US Army, for extraordinary heroism in connection with military operations against an armed enemy while serving as Acting Commander, 101st Airborne Division, in action against enemy forces from 17 to 26 December 1944, at Bastogne, Belgium.

During this period General McAuliffe was in command of the 101st Airborne Division during the Siege of Bastogne, Belgium, by overwhelming enemy forces. Though the city was completely surrounded by the enemy, the spirit of the defending troops under this officer's inspiring, gallant leadership never wavered. Their courageous stand is epic.

General McAuliffe continuously exposed himself to enemy bombing, strafing, and armored and infantry attacks to personally direct his troops, utterly disregarding his own safety.

Brigadier General McAuliffe's courage, fearless determination, and inspiring, heroic leadership exemplify the highest traditions of the military forces of the United States and reflect great credit upon himself, the 101st Airborne Division, and the United States Army.[11]

After the war, General McAuliffe continued his career with the army, serving during the Korean War as the commander of the Seventh Army in 1953, and as commander in chief of the US Army in Europe in 1955. In retirement, he lived with his wife, Helen, in their home in Chevy Chase, Maryland. He died on August 11, 1975, at the age of seventy-seven. He is buried along with his wife, son, and daughter in Arlington National Cemetery.

McAuliffe's legacy is that he died as he lived, a gentleman Christian warrior in the tradition of Father Sampson, who managed to experience firsthand the horrors of war, only to emerge with his faith strengthened by the experience. McAuliffe, perhaps the most famous Irish American soldier in World War II,[12] was not so arrogant or preoccupied by the coming battle or confident of success that he failed to attend a packed Christmas Mass with the troops at Bastogne on Christmas Eve.

Military historians will continue to debate the lasting importance of the Bastogne siege. Army colonel Ralph M. Mitchell, in his 1986 assessment, *The 101st Airborne Division's Defense of Bastogne*, was surprisingly dismissive about the reasons the US forces at Bastogne won the siege:

In the final equation, moral strength, luck, and the "fog of war" must also be considered. The Americans had advantages in all three of these categories. The right combination of events and situations—conditions unfavorable to the Germans and favorable to the Americans—produced the American victory at Bastogne. At Bastogne, a light infantry division, properly augmented by good artillery and armor support, was able to defeat a numerically superior and heavier opponent. But the conditions of that victory were particular, not universal in application.[13]

Yet, even in dismissing the legacy of Bastogne as not ultimately important or determinative as a military lesson to be applied for all times and places, Mitchell still listed as his first important characteristic of the outcome "moral strength." Is moral courage a quality that US military forces fighting in the field of battle should always presume will be present, much as is the element of luck? Or, is moral courage of a different quality than luck, in that moral courage will distinguish even those who lose in battle, but luck alone will never be considered to have bestowed valor alone upon those who won? What distinguished McAuliffe and the other brave Americans who fought at Bastogne during the Battle of the Bulge was that no greater valor could ever be expected than for soldiers to suffer extreme hardships and be willing to lay down their own lives in the field of battle not because they were ordered to do so but because they believed in their hearts and souls that serving a higher purpose gave them no other choice.

Even seasoned warriors like Maj. Dick Winters, the commander of Easy Company of the 501st at Bastogne, learned to see with eyes that surpass earthly eyes. "As I went through the war, it was natural to ask myself, *Why am I here? Why am I putting up with the cold, the constant rain, and the loss of so many comrades? Does anyone really care?*" he pondered in his 2006 memoir, *Beyond Band of Brothers*. "A soldier faces death on a daily basis, and his life is one of misery and deprivation. He is cold; he suffers from hunger, frequently bordering at starvation." But when Winters saw for himself the German concentration camps that the 101st Airborne liberated after Bastogne, he had his answer. "The impact of seeing those people behind that fence left me saying, if only to myself, *Now I know why I am here! For the first time I understand what this war is all about.*"[14]

President Harry S. Truman's address on April 3, 1953, on the occasion of laying the cornerstone of the New York Avenue Presbyterian Church, perhaps expressed best what the Bastogne siege has confirmed for me about what the Founding Fathers understood concerning the nation they resolved to bring forth. "In the world at large, as well as in our domestic affairs, we must apply moral standards to our national conduct," Truman said. "At the present time our nation is engaged in a great effort to maintain justice and peace in the world. An essential feature of this effort is our program to build up the defenses of our country. There has never been a greater cause. There has never been a cause which had a stronger moral claim on all of us."

Truman continued: "I do not think that anyone can study the history of this nation of ours—study it deeply and earnestly—without becoming convinced that divine providence has played a great part in it. I have the feeling that God has created us and brought us to our present position of power and strength for some great purpose. And up to now we have been shirking it. Now we are assuming it, and now we must carry it through."

Truman admitted this conviction derived solely from his faith: "It is not given to us to know fully what that purpose is. But I think we may be sure of one thing. That is, that our country is intended to do all it can, in cooperation with other nations, to help create peace and preserve peace in this world. It is given to us to defend the spiritual values—the moral code—against the vast forces of evil that seek to destroy them."[15]

Given the often mindless cruelty and often senseless violence of war, perhaps the greatest concern of a moral nation should always be that a God-fearing people have no choice but to embrace the heart of darkness to defeat a truly evil foe. While no one may ever be able to prove Patton's prayer was the reason the winter weather unexpectedly improved on December 23, 1944, the true miracle that insured Allied victory at Bastogne, we know one thing for certain: at Bastogne in December 1944, America did not give up on God, and God did not give up on America. As these final pages testify, Gen. Anthony McAuliffe lived his senior years not as a conquering hero, but as a husband and father, thankful to God that he had survived and humbled by the opportunity God had served him to honor himself and our nation by commanding so brilliantly in a battle that sealed the fate of the Third Reich.

To return to a theme in the introduction, in a world certain once again to be "nasty, cruel, brutish, and short," as political philosopher Thomas Hobbes famously warned, how much of our moral fiber will we lose as a nation if we turn our backs on God? I end up with the same concern with which I started. If we go forward as a nation in which the citizens cannot say publicly, "In God we trust," or if our disrespect of Judeo-Christian values becomes the norm, how much of what made victory at Bastogne possible will we have thrown away, mindless we are disregarding the most important quality we possess as the land of the free and the home of the brave?

The true heroes at Bastogne in December 1944 were the GIs—not only of the 101st Airborne, the 10th Armored, and the Third Army, as well as the many others who fought along side them—who were inspired to give their all because an encircled US field commander who had truly never advanced beyond the rank of artillery commander yet had the courage to say "Nuts!" to Hitler. In adopting this one-word rebuke as their own, the heroes of Bastogne fighting through the siege to victory said "Nuts!" not only to Hitler, but "Nuts!" as well to all evil tyrants and empires who would dare bring ever again a Malmedy massacre or the horror of a Holocaust against a moral people steeled by their belief in a just God.

Writing a historical book, picking up the pieces of history, and confronting the puzzles of the past is an exhilarating experience. As I end this book, I like to think that my father and his friends who fought with him would say that despite its flaws, in the final analysis, "This is the book we would have been proud to write." It honors those who fought and prayed and died at Bastogne and all the others on bloodstained battlefields across the world where Americans distinguished themselves, our nation, and God. Truly "No Greater Valor" applies to them all.

BIBLIOGRAPHY

Author's Note: There are many different editions and printings of the books cited in this bibliography that have been published. The edition cited here first in each listing is not the first edition published, but the edition and printing used in establishing the footnote page references used in the text.

Addor, Don. *Noville Outpost to Bastogne: And Other Experiences with the 20th Armored Infantry Battalion, 10th Armored Division, Patton's Third Army.* Victoria, BC, Canada: Trafford, 2004.

Alexander, Larry. *Biggest Brother: The Life of Major Dick Winters, the Man Who Led the Band of Brothers.* New York, NY: NAL Caliber, 2005.

Ambrose, Stephen E. *The Band of Brothers: E Company, 506th Regiment, 101 Airborne from Normandy to Hitler's Eagle's Nest.* New York, NY: Simon & Schuster, S&S Classic Edition, 2001.

Arend, Guy Franz. *"Bastogne" and The Ardennes Offensive.* Bastogne, Belgium: Bastogne Historical Center, 1974.

———. *The Battle for Bastogne: "If You Don't Know What Nuts Means."* Bastogne, Belgium: Bastogne Historical Center, 50th Anniversary Edition, 1984.

———. *The Battle for Bastogne: "The Hole in the Doughnut."* Bastogne, Belgium: Bastogne Historical Center, 40th Anniversary Edition, 1974.

Astor, Gerald. *A Blood-Dimmed Tide: The Battle of the Bulge by the Men Who Fought It.* New York, NY: Donald I. Fine, Inc., 1992.

Atkinson, Rick. *The Guns at Last Light: The War in Western Europe, 1944–1945.* New York, NY: Henry Holt and Company, 2013.

Axelrod, Alan. *Patton: A Biography.* New York, NY: Palgrave MacMillan, 2006.

———. *Patton's Drive: The Making of America's Greatest General.* Guilford, Connecticut: The Lyons Press, 2009.

Barron, Leo and Don Cygan. *No Silent Night: The Christmas Battle at Bastogne.* New York, NY: NAL Caliber, 2012.

Baumbach, Werner. *Broken Swastika: The Defeat of the Luftwaffe.* New York, NY: Dorset Press, English Translation, 1960.

Blumenson, Martin. *Patton: The Man Behind the Legend, 1885–1945.* New York, NY: William Morrow and Company, Inc., 1985.

———. *The Patton Papers 1940–1945.* Boston, Mass.: Houghton Mifflin Company, 1975.

Boland, B. E. *Patton Uncovered: The Untold Story of How the Greatest American General Was Disgraced by Scheming Politicians and Jealous Generals.* Voorhees, New Jersey: Melody Publishing Co., 2002.

Boykin, William G. with Lynn Vincent. *Never Surrender: A Soldier's Journey to the Crossroads of Faith and Reason.* New York, NY: FaithWords, Hachette Book Group USA, 2008.

Bowen, Robert M., edited by Christopher J. Anderson. *Fighting with the Screaming Eagles: With the 101st Airborne from Normandy to Bastogne.* Mechanicsburg, Pennsylvania: Stackpole Books, 2001.

Bradley, Omar N. *A General's Life: An Autobiography.* New York, NY: Simon and Schuster, 1983.

———. *A Soldier's Story.* New York, NY: Henry Holt and Company, 1951.

Brighton, Terry. *Patton, Montgomery, Rommel: Masters of War.* New York, NY: Crown Publishers, 2008.

Burgett, Donald R. *Seven Roads to Hell: A Screaming Eagle at Bastogne.* Novato, California: Presidio Press, 1999.

Carpenter, Alton E. and A. Anne Eiland. *Chappie: World War II Diary of a Combat Chaplain.* Mesa, Arizona: Mead Publishing, 2007.

Cole, Hugh M. *The U.S. Army in World War II: The European Theater of Operations, The Ardennes: Battle of the Bulge.* Washington, DC: Office of the Chief of Military History, US Army, 1988.

Collins, Michael and Martin King. *The Tigers of Bastogne: Voices of the 10th Armored Division in the Battle of the Bulge.* Havertown, Pennsylvania: Casemate Publishers, 2013.

———. *Voices of the Bulge: Untold Stories from Veterans of the Bulge.* Minneapolis, Minnesota: Zenith Press, 2011.

Cosby, Donald F. *Battlefield Chaplains: Catholic Priests in World War II.* Lawrence, Kansas: The University Press of Kansas, 1994.

D'Este. Carlo. *Eisenhower: A Soldier's Life.* New York, NY: Henry Holt and Company, 2002.

———, *Patton: A Genius for War.* New York, NY: HarperCollins Publisher, Inc., 1995.

DeFelice, Jim. *Omar Bradley: General at War.* Washington, DC: Regnery History, 2011.

Door, Robert F. and Thomas D. Jones. *Hell Hawks! The Untold Story of the American Fliers Who Savaged Hitler's Wehrmacht.* Minneapolis, Minnesota: Zenith Press, 2008.

Dorsett, Lyle W. *Serving God and Country: U.S. Military Chaplains in World War II.* New York, NY: Berkley Books, 2012.

Dupuy, Trevor N., with David L. Bongard and Richard C. Anderson, Jr. *Hitler's Last Gamble: The Battle of the Bulge, December 1944—January 1945.* New York, NY: HarperCollins Publishers, Inc., 1994.

Eisenhower, Dwight D. *Crusade in Europe.* Garden City, NY: Doubleday & Company, Inc., 1948.

Eisenhower, John S. D. *The Bitter Woods: The Dramatic Story, Told at All Echelons—From Supreme Command to Squad Leader—of the Crisis that Shook the Western Coalition: Hitler's Surprise Ardennes Offensive.* New York, NY: G. P. Putnam's Sons, 1969.

Elstob, Peter. *Ballantine's Illustrated History of World War II, Battle Book No. 4: Bastogne: The Road Back.* New York, NY: Ballantine Books, 1968.

Essame, E. *Patton: A Study in Command*. New York, NY: Charles Scribner's Sons, 1974.

Evans, Richard J. *The Third Reich at War*. New York, NY: The Penguin Press, 2009.

Farago, Ladislas. *Patton: Ordeal and Triumph*. New York, NY: Ivan Obolensky, Inc., 1964.

Forty, George. *4th Armored Division in World War II*. Minneapolis, Minnesota: Zenith Press, 2008.

Fox, Don M. *Patton's Vanguard: The United States Army Fourth Armored Division*. Jefferson, North Carolina: McFarland & Company, Inc., Publishers, 2003.

Frankel, Nat and Larry Smith. *Patton's Best: An Informal History of the 4th Armored Division*. New York, NY: Hawthorn Books, Inc., 1978.

Green, Michael and James D. Brown. *Patton's Third Army in World War II*. Minneapolis, MN: Zenith Press, 2010.

Grinker, Roy R. and John P. Spiegel. *Men Under Stress*. Philadelphia, Pennsylvania: The Blakiston Company, 1945.

———. *War Neuroses*. Philadelphia, Pennsylvania: The Blakiston Company, 1945.

Guarnere, William "Wild Bill," and Edward "Babe" Heffron, with Robyn Post. *Brothers in Battle, Best of Friends: Two WWII Paratroopers from the Original Band of Brothers Tell Their Story*. New York, NY: The Berkley Publishing Group, 2007.

Hastings, Max. *Armageddon: The Battle for Germany, 1944–1945*. New York, NY: Alfred A. Knopf, 2004.

Hawkins, Paul D. with the editors, Army Times Publishing Company. *When the Third Cracked Europe: The Story of Patton's Incredible Army*. Harrisburg, Pennsylvania: Stackpole Books, 1990.

Heinz, Joss. *In the Perimeter of Bastogne: December 1044—January 1945*. Ostend, Belgium: Omnia, 1982. Translated by Nenette Lorimer.

Hirshson, Stanley P. *General Patton: A Soldier's Life*. New York, NY: HarperCollins Publishers, Inc., 2002.

Irzyk, Albin F. "Al." *He Rode Up Front for Patton*. Raleigh, North Carolina: Pentland Press, Inc., 1996.

Jordan, Jonathan W. *Brothers, Rivals, Victors: Eisenhower, Patton, Bradley, and the Partnership That Drove the Allied Conquest in Europe*. New York, NY: NAL Caliber, 2011.

Keane, Michael. *Patton: Blood, Guts, and Prayer*. Washington, DC: Regnery History, 2012.

Keegan, John. *An Illustrated History of the First World War*. New York, NY: Alfred A. Knopf, 2001.

Kennedy, Nancy B. *Miracles & Moments of Grace: Inspiring Stories from Military Chaplains*. Abilene, Texas: Leafwood Publishers, 2011.

Korda, Michael. *Ike: An American Hero*. New York, NY: HarperCollins Publishers, 2007.

Koskimaki, George. *The Battered Bastards of Bastogne: A Chronicle of the Defense of Bastogne, December 19, 1944—January 17, 1944*. Havertown, Pennsylvania: Casemate, 1994.

MacDonald, Charles B. *A Time for Trumpets: The Untold Story of the Battle of the Bulge*. New York, NY: William Morrow and Company, Inc., 1985.

MacKenzie, Fred. *The Men of Bastogne*. New York: David McKay Company, Inc., 1968.

Malarkey, Don, with Bob Welch. *Easy Company Soldier: The Legendary Battles of a Sergeant from World War II's "Band of Brothers."* New York, NY: St. Martin's Press, 2008.

Marshall, S. L. A. *Bastogne: The First Eight Days*. Washington, DC: United States Army Center of Military History, Facsimile Reprint, 2004). Originally published as: Colonel S. L. A. Marshall, assisted by Captain John G. Westover and Lieutenant A. Joseph Webber, *Bastogne: The Story of the First Eight Days in Which the 101st Airborne Division Was Closed Within the Ring of German Forces*. Washington, DC: Infantry Journal Press, 1946.

McManus, John C. *Alamo in the Ardennes: The Untold Story of the American Soldiers Who Made the Defense of Bastogne Possible*. Hoboken, New Jersey: John Wiley & Sons, Inc., 2007.

Merriam, Robert Edward. *Dark December: The Full Account of the Battle of the Bulge*. Chicago, Illinois: Ziff-Davis Publishing Company, 1947.

Metcalf, George Reuben. *With Cross and Shovel: A Chaplain's Letters from England, France, and Germany 1942–1945*. Cambridge, Massachusetts: The Riverside Press, 1960.

Mitcham, Samuel W., Jr. *Panzers in Winter: Hitler's Army and the Battle of the Bulge*. Westport, Connecticut: Praeger Security International, 2006.

Mitchell, Ralph M. *The 101st Airborne Division's Defense of Bastogne*. Bennington, Vermont: Merriam Press, 2013. Colonel Ralph M. Mitchell, *The 101st Airborne Division's Defense of Bastogne*. Fort Leavenworth, Kansas: U. S. Army Command and General Staff College, Combat Studies Institute, September 1986.

Parker, Danny S. *Battle of the Bulge: Hitler's Ardennes Offensive, 1944–1945*. Conshohocken, Pennsylvania: Combined Books, Inc., 1991.

———., editor. *Hitler's Ardennes Offensive: The German View of the Battle of the Bulge*. Mechanicsburg, Pennsylvania: Stackpole Books, 1997.

———. *To Win the Winter Sky: Air War over the Ardennes, 1944–1945*. Conshohocken, Pennsylvania: Combined Books, Inc., 1994.

Patterson, Eugene. *Patton's Unsung Armor of the Ardennes: The Tenth Armored Division's Secret Dash to Bastogne*. Xlibris Corporation, Xlibris.com, 2008.

Patton, George S., Jr. annotated by Colonel Paul D. Harkins. *War As I Knew It*. Boston, Mass.: Houghton Mifflin Company, 1975 Reprint.

Price, Frank James. *Troy H. Middleton: A Biography*. Baton Rouge, Louisiana: Louisiana State University Press, 1974.

Province, Charles M. *Patton's Third Army: A Chronology of the Third Army Advance, August, 1944 to May, 1945*. New York: Hippocrene Books, 1992.

Rappaport, Leonard and Arthur Northwood, Jr. *Rendezvous with Destiny: A History of the 101st Airborne Division*. Sweetwater, TN: 101st Airborne Division Association, 1948.

Rickard, John Nelson. *Advance and Destroy: Patton as Commander in the Bulge*. Lexington, Kentucky: The University of Kentucky Press, 2011.

Rottman, Gordon L. *World War II Infantry Anti-Tank Tactics*. Oxford, U.K.: Osprey Publishing Ltd., 2005.

Sampson, Francis L. *Look Out Below!* Washington, DC: The Catholic University of America Press, Inc., 1958.

———. *Paratrooper Padre*. Washington, DC: The Catholic University of America Press, 1948.

Sasser, Charles W. *God in the Foxhole: Inspiring True Stories of Miracles on the Battlefield*. New York, NY: Threshold Editions, Simon and Schuster, Inc., 2008.

Shapiro, Milton J. *Tank Command: General George S. Patton's 4th Armored Division*. New York, NY: David McKay Company, Inc., 1979.

Showalter, Dennis. *Patton and Rommel: Men of War in the Twentieth Century.* New York, NY: The Berkley Publishing Group, 2005.

Smith, Jean Edward. *Eisenhower in War and Peace.* New York, NY: Random House, 2012.

Sorley, Lewis. *Thunderbolt: From the Battle of the Bulge To Vietnam and Beyond: General Creighton Abrams and the Army of His Times.* New York, NY: Simon & Schuster, 1992.

Stanton, Shelby L. *Order of Battle: U. S. Army, World War II.* Novato, California: Presidio Press, 1984.

Taaffe, Stephen R. *Marshall and His Generals: U.S. Army Commanders in World War II.* Lawrence, Kansas: University of Kansas Press, 2011.

Taylor, John M. *General Maxwell Taylor: The Sword and the Pen.* New York, NY: Doubleday, 1989.

Taylor, Maxwell D. *Swords and Plowshares.* New York, NY: W. W. Norton & Company, Inc., 1972.

Toland, John. *Battle: The Story of the Bulge.* New York, NY: Random House, 1959.

Tolhurst, Michael. *Battle of the Bulge: Bastogne.* Barnsley, South Yorkshire, U.K.: Pen & Sword Books, 2001.

Von Hassel, Agostino and Ed Breslin. *Patton: The Pursuit of Destiny.* Nashville, TN: Thomas Nelson, Inc., 2010.

Weintraub, Stanley. *11 Days in December: Christmas at the Bulge, 1944.* New York, NY: Free Press, [date].

Whiting, Charles. *Ballantine's Illustrated History of World War II, War Leader book, No. 1: Patton.* New York, NY: Ballantine Books Inc., 1970.

Winters, Dick, with Colonel Cole C. Kingseed. *Beyond Band of Brothers.* New York, NY: Berkley Publishing Group, 2006.

Winton, Harold R. *Corps Commanders of the Bulge: Six American Generals and Victory in the Ardennes.* Lawrence, Kansas: University of Kansas Press, 2007.

Young, Charles H., editor. *Into the Valley: The Untold Story of USAAF Troop Carrier in World War II: From North Africa through Europe.* Dallas, Texas: PrintComm Inc., 1995.

Zaloga, Steven J. *Battle of the Bulge (2): Bastogne.* Oxford, U.K.: Osprey Publishing Ltd., 2004.

ARCHIVAL REFERENCES

During World War II, Army Chief of Staff George C. Marshall decided to establish a program to preserve, as the war was ongoing, primary historical documentary sources, with the goal of using these sources to prepare the Army's official history of the war. Lt. Col. (later Brig. Gen.) S. L. A. Marshall pioneered the Army's oral history project by drawing on his experience as a journalist to develop what he called the "interview after capture." He began to develop his technique of taking oral histories immediately after combat actions from key participants in November 1943, when he interviewed members of the 3rd Battalion, 165th Infantry after a fierce engagement on Malkin Island in the Pacific.

In 1944, Marshall went to Europe with a team of historians trained on his interview techniques to take after-action oral histories from combatants in the 82nd and 101st Airborne Divisions. During the Battle of the Bulge, Marshall and his assistants, including Capt. John G. Westover and Lt. A. Joseph Webber, interviewed members of the 101st Airborne and its attached units soon after the Bastogne siege was lifted. These field histories formed the backbone of S. L. A. Marshall's definitive history of the siege, *Bastogne: The First Eight Days*, first published in 1947.

After nearly two years of searching through records in the National Archives and Records Administration at College Park, Maryland, several of these original oral histories were located, including the following interviews listed here:

CHAPPUIS and CASSIDY—Lt. Col. Steve A. Chappuis, commanding officer, and Lt. Col. Patrick J. Cassidy, executive officer, 502 Parachute Infantry Regiment, 101st Airborne Division, interview conducted by Col. S. L. A. Marshall over the period Jan. 4–10, 1944, at Château Rolle, Belgium.

CHERRY—Lt. Col. Henry T. Cherry, commanding officer, Team Cherry, 10th Armored Division, "Team Cherry, 18–21 December 1944," interview conducted by Capt. John G. Westover at Bastogne, Belgium, Jan. 18, 1945.

CLARK—Capt. L. B. Clark, 4th Armored Division, "Narrative Summary of Operations of the 4th Armored Division in the Relief of Bastogne, 22–29 Dec. 1944," no location, no date.

EWELL—Lt. Col. Julian J. Ewell, commanding officer, 501st Parachute Infantry Regiment, 101st Airborne Division, "Action of 501st Regiment at Bastogne," interview conducted by Col. S. L. A. Marshall, Jan. 6, 1944, at Bastogne, Belgium. "Notes made after conversations with Colonel Ewell on 12 March 1945," interview conducted by Col. S. L. A. Marshall, no location, no date, one page.

HARPER—Col. Joseph H. Harper, commanding officer, 327th Glider Infantry Regiment, 101st Airborne Division, interview conducted by Col. S. L. A. Marshall, Jan 8, 9, and 10, 1944.

KINNARD—Lt. Col. H. W. O. Kinnard, G-3, 101st Airborne Division, "G-3 Account of Bastogne Operation," interview conducted by Col. S. L. A. Marshall over the period Jan. 3–11, 1944.

LUCAS—Pfc. Elmer E. Lucas, Medical Detachment, 506th Parachute Infantry Regiment, 101st Airborne Division, statement in Historical Section office, Paris, France, April 6, 1946.

McAULIFFE—Brig. Gen. Anthony C. McAuliffe, commanding officer, 101st Airborne Division, "Commander's View of Situation," interview conducted by Col. S. L. A. Marshall at Bastogne, Jan. 5, 1944.

MIDDLETON—Maj. Gen. Troy H. Middleton, commanding officer, 8th Corps, interviewed by Capt. L. B. Clark, at Zeulenroda, Germany, on April 20, 1945.

NELSON—Lt. Col. Clarence F. Nelson, commanding officer, 907th Glider Field Artillery Battalion, "Artillery in the Neffe Action," interview conducted by Col. S. L. A. Marshall at Bastogne, no date.

O'HARA—Lt. Col. James O'Hara, commanding officer, Team O'Hara, 10th Armored Division, "Team O'Hara," interview conducted by Capt. John G. Westover, no location, no date.

PARKER—Capt. James E. Parker, 9th Air Force, member of liaison group attached to 101st Airborne during Bastogne operation, "Air Support Party at Bastogne," interview conducted by Capt. John G. Westover at Bastogne, Belgium, January 1, 1945.

ROBERTS—Col. William L. Roberts, commanding officer, 10th Armored Division, "CCB, 10 Armored Division, 17–18 Dec. 1944," interview conducted by Capt. John G. Westover at Vaux-Lez-Rosieres, January 12, 1945.

Letter to Col. S. L. A. Marshall, dated Feb. 18, 1945, containing a 4-page summary titled, "Reflections and Impressions of Bastogne."

SINK—Col. Robert F. Sink, commanding officer, 506th Parachute Infantry Regiment, "501–506 Contact Story," from an interview conducted by Capt. John G. Westover, at Camp Mourmelon, France, March 20, 1945.

Among the records at the National Archives and Records Administration at College Park, Maryland, the following unit reports on the Bastogne operation were particularly useful:

3rd ARMY—Lt. Gen. George S. Patton, Jr., commanding officer, Third Army, "Notes on Bastogne Operation," Headquarters, Third U.S. Army, Jan. 16, 1943.

"Third U.S. Army Operations, December 1944–March 1945," June 15, 1945.

10th ARMORED DIVISION—"After Action Report of CCB—2 Dec. 1944 thru 1 Jan. 1945," CCB, 10th Armored Division, APO 260, U.S. Army, no date.

"Recommendation for Unit Citation, Third Tank Battalion, CCB, 10th Armored Division," Headquarters, Third Tank Battalion, APO 260, U.S. Army, Jan. 14, 1945.

101st AIRBORNE DIVISION—"After Action Report for December 1944," Headquarters, 101st Airborne Division, March 16, 1945.

"After Action Report, 17 Dec 1944 to 27 Dec 1944," Office of the Chief of Staff, Headquarters, 101st Airborne Division, March 16, 1945.

"Report on Air Resupply to 101st Airborne Division at Bastogne," Jan. 11, 1945.

"Transportation Corps at Bastogne," no location, no date.

327th GLIDER INFANTRY REGIMENT, 101ST AIRBORNE DIVISION—"After Action Report, Belgium and France, December 1944," March 12, 1945.

501st PARACHUTE INFANTRY REGIMENT, 101st AIRBORNE DIVISION— "After Action Report, Dec. 21, 1944 to Dec. 31, 1944," no date.

502nd PARACHUTE INFANTRY REGIMENT, 101st AIRBORNE DIVISION— "After Action Report, Belgium and France, December 1944," March 12, 1945.

506th PARACHUTE INFANTRY REGIMENT, 101st AIRBORNE DIVISION— "After Action Report, Belgium and France, December 1944," March 9, 1945.

NOTES

Introduction

1. Lyle W. Dorsett, *Serving God and Country: US Military Chaplains in World War II* (New York: Berkley Caliber, 2012), 49.
2. Ibid., 4–5.
3. Ibid., 6.
4. Thucydides, *History of the Peloponnesian War,* with an English Translation by Charles Foster Smith, in Four Volumes (Cambridge, Mass.: Harvard University Press, 1965), Loeb Classical Library, No. 108–No. 110, and No. 169.
5. H. D. Westlake, *Individuals in Thucydides* (Cambridge, UK: Cambridge University Press).
6. Lieutenant General (Ret.) William G. Boykin with Lynn Vincent, *Never Surrender: A Soldier's Journey to the Crossroads of Faith and Reason* (New York: FaithWords, an imprint of Hachette Book Group USA, Inc., 2008), 314–18.
7. David I. Kertzer, *The Pope and Mussolini: The Secret History of Pius XI and the Rise of Fascism in Europe* (New York: Random House, 2014), 120–22.
8. Ibid., 224.
9. Stephen E. Everett, *Oral History: Techniques and Procedures* (Washington, DC, Center of Military History, US Army, 1992), 4. Available online at http://www.au.af.mil/au/awc/awcgate/oralhist.htm.
10. Ibid., 5.
11. S. L. A. Marshall, assisted by Captain John G. Westover and Lieutenant A. Joseph Webber, *Bastogne: The First Eight Days* (Washington, DC: Center of Military History, US Army, Reprint 2004). Originally published in 1946 by the Infantry Journal Press, Washington, DC.
12. George Koskimaki, *The Battered Bastards of Bastogne: A Chronicle of the Defense of Bastogne (December 19, 1944–January 17, 1945)* (Havertown, Pennsylvania: Casemate, 1994).

Section I: "Hold Bastogne!"

1. Hugh M. Cole, *The Ardennes: The Battle of the Bulge* (Center of Military History, United States Army, 1988), 445. Published in the series of volumes entitled *United States Army in World War II, The European Theater of Operations.*

2. Marshall, *Bastogne*, 1.

3. Ibid.

4. Price, *Troy H. Middleton* (Baton Rouge: Louisiana State University Press, 1974), 68.

5. Ibid.

6. Ibid., 68–69.

7. Ibid., 136–137.

8. Guy Franz Arend, *Bastogne: "If You Don't Know What Nuts Means"–A Chronology of the Battle of Bastogne with Comments* (Sagato, S.A.: Bastogne Historical Center, 1987), 27.

9. Price, *Troy H. Middleton*, 215.

10. Drew Middleton, "Nazi Offensive Pierces First Army Lines," *New York Times*, December 18, 1944, page 1.

11. Harold Denny, "German Assault is a Major Effort," *New York Times*, December 18, 1944, page 1.

Chapter 1

1. Cole, *The Ardennes*, 305.

2. Omar N. Bradley, *A Soldier's Story* (New York: Henry Holt and Company, 1951), 467.

3. Omar N. Bradley and Clay Blair, *A General's Life: An Autobiography by General of the Army Omar N. Bradley and Clay Blair* (New York: Simon and Schuster, 1983), 354.

4. Ibid.

5. The account of the SHAEF meeting of December 17, 1944, is drawn from Marshall, *Bastogne*, 8.

6. Bradley and Blair, *A General's Life*, 357.

7. Danny S. Parker, *Battle of the Bulge: Hitler's Ardennes Offensive, 1944–1945* (Conshohocken, PA: Combined Books, Inc., 1991), 37.

8. Leo Barron and Don Cygan, *No Silent Night: The Christmas Battle for Bastogne* (New York: NAL Caliber, 2012), 20–21.

9. Ibid., 43.

10. Marshall, *Bastogne*, 6.

11. Ibid.

12. John C. McManus, *Alamo in the Ardennes: The Untold Story of the American Soldiers Who Made the Defense of Bastogne Possible* (New York: John Wiley & Sons, 2007), 52–54.

13. Ibid.

14. Ibid., 75.

15. Ibid., 76–77.

16. Ibid., 77.

17. Ibid., 78.

18. Marshall, *Bastogne*, 10.

19. Fred MacKenzie, *The Men of Bastogne* (New York: David McKay Company, Inc., 1968), 12–13.

20. Ibid., 13.

21. Ibid., 13–14.

22. Ibid., 9.

23. Ibid., 10.

24. Ibid.

25. Ibid.

26. Taken from a comment made by war correspondent Fred MacKenzie. Ibid., 5.

27. Barron and Cygan, *No Silent Night*, 46.

28. MacKenzie, *The Men of Bastogne*, 10–11.

29. Ibid., 11.

30. Ibid., 20.

31. Stephen F. Ambrose, *Band of Brothers: E Company, 506th Regiment, 101st Airborne from Normandy to Hitler's Eagle's Nest* (New York: Simon & Schuster, 1999), 174.

32. "G-3 Fred Kinnard Account of Bastogne Interview," noted in pencil on the original as "Kinnard Interview." Found among the Bastogne papers at the National Archives and Records Administration, College Park, Maryland. Note at the beginning of the transcript: "This narrative developed from a series of interviews with Lt. Colonel Kinnard in the period 3 Jan to 11 Jan. During these interviews Colonel Danahy was present most of the time and General Higgins part of the time." The original interview bears the handwritten signature in pen of Col. S. L. A. Marshall.

33. Ibid.

34. There is confusion in the military records of the Siege of Bastogne in that S. L. A. Marshall in his *Bastogne: The First Eight Days* records that McAuliffe and his command party left Camp Mourmelon before the advance party left (p. 13). An After-Action Report covering the period Dec. 17, 1944, to Dec. 27, 1944, documents the advance party left Camp Mourmelon at 1215 on Dec. 18, 1944, followed by General McAuliffe, who departed at 1225. "Subject: Action Report, 17 Dec 1944 to 27 Dec 1944," Office of the Chief of Staff, Headquarters of the Chief of Staff, APO 472, US Army, 28 December 1944," directed to "Commanding Officer, 101st Airborne Division." Document found in Bastogne records at the National Archives and Records Administration, College Park, Maryland.

35. McAuliffe, "Forward," dated Feb. 4, 1968, in MacKenzie, *The Men of Bastogne*, vii.

36. Ibid., vii–viii.

37. Ibid., viii.

38. Arend, *Bastogne*, 47.

39. Marshall, *Bastogne*, 11.

40. John S. D. Eisenhower, *The Bitter Woods: The Battle of the Bulge* (New York: De Capo Press, Paperback Edition, 1995), 243–44.

Chapter 2

1. Cole, *The Ardennes*, 305–306.

2. Ambrose, *Band of Brothers*, 165.

3. Ibid., 166.

4. Koskimaki, *The Battered Bastards of Bastogne*, 9–10.

5. Ibid., 26.

6. "Bastogne: The Hole in the Doughnut," *The Story of the 101st Airborne Division* (Stars and Stripes Publication, one of a series of GI Stories of the Ground, Air, and Services Forces in the European Theater of Operations, a publication of the Information and Education Division ETOUSA, date stamped Sept. 23, 1947), 19. Found in the Bastogne records at the National Archives and Records Administration, College Park, Maryland.

7. Arend, *Bastogne*, 47.

8. Robert M. Bowen, *Fighting with the Screaming Eagles: With the 101st Airborne from Normandy to Bastogne*, ed. Christopher J. Anderson (Stackpole Books: Pennsylvania, 2001), 161.

9. Ibid., 161–62.

10. Cole, *The Ardennes*, 309.

11. Marshall, *Bastogne*, 19.

12. William "Wild Bill" Guarnere and Edward "Babe" Heffron, with Robyn Post, *Brothers in Battle, Best of Friends: Two WWII Paratroopers from the Original Band of Brothers Tell Their Story* (New York: Berkley Caliber, 2007), 157–58.

13. Ibid., 158.

14. Ibid.

15. After-Action Report for December 1944, Headquarters 101st Airborne Division, APO 472, L-450, March 16, 1945. National Archives and Records Administration, College Park, Maryland.

16. "Transportation Corps at Bastogne." Found in the Bastogne records at the National Archives and Records Administration, College Park, Maryland. The discrepancy between the After-Action Report of the 101st Airborne Division putting troop strength at 11,035, and the Transportation Corps After-Action Report putting troop strength at 14,000 on leaving Camp Mourmelon is noted, but not resolved. The more correct figure appears to be 11,035.

17. Ibid.

18. Koskimaki, *The Battered Bastards of Bastogne*, 34.

19. Ibid.

20. Ibid., 37.

21. Ibid.

22. Arend, *Bastogne*, 61.

23. Marshall, *Bastogne*, 19.

24. MacKenzie, *The Men of Bastogne*, 42.

25. Ibid.

26. Chaplain (Lt. Col.) Francis L. Sampson, *Look Out Below! A Story of the Airborne by a Parachute Padre* (Washington, DC: The Catholic University of America Press, Inc., 1958), 3.

27. Ibid., 59.

28. Ibid.

29. Ibid.

30. Tom Longden, "Sampson, Francis L.," *The Des Moines Register*, Feb. 4, 2008, http://www.desmoinesregister.com/article/99999999/FAMOUSIOWANS/712160326/Sampson-Francis-L-. Also, see: Donald R. McClarey, "Father Major General," The American Catholic, November 18, 2008, http://the-american-catholic.com/2008/11/18/father-major-general/.

31. Sampson, *Look Out Below!*, 78.

32. Ibid., 79.

33. Ibid.

34. Ibid.

35. Ibid., 86.

36. Ibid., 85–86.

37. Ibid., 94.

38. Ibid., 101–102.

39. Ibid., 102.

40. Ibid., 102–103.

41. Ibid., 103.

42. Ibid., 104.

43. Ibid.

44. Ibid., "Author's Introduction," xviii.

45. Major Dick Winters, with Colonel Cole C. Kingseed, *Beyond Band of Brothers: The War Memoirs of Major Dick Winters* (New York: The Berkeley Publishing Group, 2006), 16–17.

46. Ambrose, *Band of Brothers*, 15–16.

47. Ibid., 21.

48. Cole, *The Ardennes*, 307–308.

49. Ibid., 308–309.

50. Ralph M. Mitchell, Colonel, US Army, *The 101st Airborne Division's Defense of Bastogne* (Combat Studies Institute, US Army Command and General Staff College, September 1986); subsequently republished (Bennington, VT: Merriam Press, 2000, Fifth Edition 2013), 21.

51. Ibid., 21–22.

52. Ibid., 23–24.

53. MacKenzie, *The Men of Bastogne*, 23.

54. Ibid.

55. Ibid., 24.

56. Marshall, *Bastogne*, 12.

57. MacKenzie, *The Men of Bastogne*, 24.

58. Ibid., 25.

59. Ibid., 26.

60. "Caserne Heintz," or "Heintz Barracks," Reg Jans Battlefield Experience, http://www.regjans.com/?page_id=2186.

61. Marshall, *Bastogne*, 12.

62. MacKenzie, *The Men of Bastogne*, 29.

63. Ibid., 29–30.

64. Ibid., 30.

65. Michael Collins and Martin King, *The Tigers of Bastogne: Voices of the 10th Armored Division in the Battle of the Bulge* (Havertown, Pennsylvania: Casemate Publishers, 2013), 22. Biographical information on Colonel Roberts was sourced here.

66. Ibid., 11.

67. J. Eisenhower, *The Bitter Woods*, 308.

68. Marshall, *Bastogne*, 13.

69. Ibid.

70. Gordon L. Rottman, *World War II Infantry Anti-Tank Tactics* (Long Island City, NY: Osprey Publishing Ltd., 2005), [page].

71. Parker, *The Battle of the Bulge*, 60–61. This and the preceding paragraph describing German tanks was sourced here.

72. J. Eisenhower, *The Bitter Woods*, 310.

73. Ibid., 310–11.

74. Colonel S. L. A. Marshall, Interview with General McAuliffe, Conducted at Bastogne on January 5, 1944. Marshall noted: "The words are put down as he said them." Document found at the National Archives Records Administration, College Park, Maryland.

75. Collins and King, *The Tigers of Bastogne*, 123.

76. Marshall, *Bastogne*, 18.

77. Harold R. Winton, *Corps Commanders of the Bulge: Six American Generals and Victory in the Ardennes* (Lawrence, Kansas: University of Kansas Press, 2007), 173.

78. Matthew B. Ridgway, *Soldier: The Memoirs of Matthew B. Ridgway*, as told to Harold H. Martin (New York: Harper and Brothers, 1956), 115.

79. Marshall, *Bastogne: The First Eight Days*, 16.

80. J. Eisenhower, *The Bitter Woods*, 310.

81. "G-3 Fred Kinnard Account of Bastogne Interview," National Archives and Records Administration, College Park, Maryland.

82. MacKenzie, *The Men of Bastogne*, 39.

83. Ibid., 2.

84. Ibid., 3.

85. Ibid., 7.

86. Ibid., 6.

87. Ibid.

88. Koskimaki, *The Battered Bastards of Bastogne*, 33.

89. Barron and Cygan, *No Silent Night*, 73–74.

90. Ambrose, *Band of Brothers*, 176.

91. Sampson, *Look Out Below!*, 104.

92. Ibid., 104–105.

93. Charles B. MacDonald, *A Time for Trumpets* (New York: William Morrow and Company, 1985), 505–506.

94. Ibid, 506.

95. General Paul Harkins, *When the Third Cracked Europe*, 45.

Chapter 3

1. Cole, *The Ardennes*, 5–6.

2. John Keegan, *An Illustrated History of the First World War* (New York: Alfred A. Knopf, 2001), 19–21; Barbara Tuchman, *The Guns of August* (New York: Scribner, 1962); Hans Ehlert, Michael Epkenhans, Gerhard P. Gross, David T. Zabecki, editors, *The Schlieffen Plan: International Perspectives on the German Strategy for World War I* (Lawrence, Kansas: The University of Kansas Press, 2014); see also, "The Schlieffen Plan," Alpha History, http://alphahistory.com/worldwar1/schlieffen-plan/. The discussion of the Schlieffen Plan was sourced here.

3. Cole, *The Ardennes*, 40. See also "The Schlieffen Plan," *Alpha History*, alphahistory. com/worldwar1/Schlieffen-plan.

4. Bradley and Blair, *A General's Life*, 356.

5. Ibid., 354–55.

6. Ibid., 356.

7. Ibid.

8. Ibid., 352.

9. Dwight D. Eisenhower, *Crusade in Europe* (Garden City, New York: Doubleday & Co., 1948), 342.

10. Ibid.

11. MacDonald, *A Time for Trumpets*, 21.

12. Parker, *Battle of the Bulge*, 34. Information in this paragraph regarding General Rundstedt's career was sourced here.

13. Ibid.

14. Ibid.

15. D. Eisenhower, *Crusade in Europe*, 344.

16. Bradley and Blair, *A General's Life*, 356–57.

17. Ibid., 345.

18. Parker, *Battle of the Bulge*, 31.

19. Bradley and Blair, *A General's Life*, 349.

20. Ibid., 337–38.

21. Parker, *The Battle of the Bulge*, 31

22. Ibid.

23. Carlo D'Este, *Eisenhower: A Soldier's Life* (New York: Henry Holt and Company, LLC: 2002), 627.

24. Ibid.

25. Ibid.

26. Ibid.

27. Barron and Cygan, *No Silent Night*, 13.

28. Parker, *Battle of the Bulge*, 35. Information of Field Marshal Walther Model's career was sourced here.

29. Samuel W. Mitcham, Jr., *Panzers in Winter: Hitler's Army and the Battle of the Bulge* (Westport, Connecticut: Praeger Security International, 2006), 59.

30. US National Archives, "Records of the United States Strategic Bombing Study [USSBS], established pursuant to a presidential directive, Sept. 9, 1944, Record Group 243, http://www.archives.gov/research/guide-fed-records/groups/243.html.

31. Parker, *Battle of the Bulge*, 32.

32. Collins and King, *The Tigers of Bastogne*, 30.

33. Parker, *Battle of the Bulge*, 39.

34. Ibid., 42.

35. Bradley and Blair, *A General's Life*, 351.

36. Ibid., 350.

37. Ibid.

38. Ibid.

39. Ibid., 351.

40. Ibid.

41. Bradley, *A Soldier's Story*, 461.

42. Ibid., 464.

43. Max Hastings, *Armageddon: The Battle for Germany, 1944–1945* (New York: Alfred A. Knopf, 2004), 198.

44. Ibid.
45. Bradley, *A Soldier's Story*, 461–62.
46. Bradley and Blair, *A General's Life*, 353.
47. Ibid., 354, italics in original.
48. D. Eisenhower, *Crusade in Europe*, 341.
49. Ibid.
50. Bradley's conversation with Patton recalled in: Bradley, *A Soldier's Story*, 465.
51. Ibid.
52. Ladislas Farago, *Patton: Ordeal and Triumph* (New York: Ivan Obolensky, Inc., 1964), 698.

Section II: The Defense of Bastogne Takes Shape

1. Mitcham Jr., *Panzers in Winter*, 125.

Chapter 4

1. Cole, *The Ardennes*, 449.
2. Website of the 2VIII Infantry Division, Pennsylvania National Guard, http://pa.ng.mil/ARNG/28ID/Pages/default.aspx.
3. J. Eisenhower, *The Bitter Woods*, 204.
4. Ibid.
5. Mitcham Jr., *Panzers in Winter*, 125.
6. J. Eisenhower, *The Bitter Woods*, 205.
7. Ibid.
8. Mitcham Jr., *Panzers in Winter*, 124.
9. Cole, *The Ardennes*, 192.
10. Ibid., 191–192.
11. Mitcham Jr., *Panzers in Winter*, 125.
12. Ibid.
13. Ibid., 126.
14. Ibid., 127
15. J. Eisenhower, *The Bitter Woods*, 312.
16. Mitcham Jr., *Panzers in Winter*, 127.
17. Ibid.
18. "After-Action Report, 10 December 1944 to 31 December 1944, Headquarters 2VIII Infantry Division, 'In the Field,' 15 January 1945," signed for the Commanding General by J. L. Gibney, Colonel, GSC, Chief of Staff, 2VIII Infantry Division. Found in Bastogne papers at the National Archives and Records Administration, College Park, Maryland.
19. Cole, *The Ardennes*, 211.
20. Ibid.

21. Ibid.

22. Marshall, *Bastogne*, 51.

23. Francis L. Sampson and F. Spellman, *Paratrooper Padre* (Washington, DC: The Catholic University of America Press, 1948), 76.

24. Roy R. Grinker and John P. Spiegel, *Men Under Stress* (Philadelphia, PA: Blakiston, 1945).

25. Joan Cook, "Obituary: John P. Spiegel, 80, Expert on Violence and Combat Stress," *The New York Times*, July 19, 1991, http://www.nytimes.com/1991/07/19/obituaries/john-p-spiegel-80-expert-on-violence-and-combat-stress.html.

26. Jennifer D. Keene, *Doughboys, the Great War, and the Remaking of America* (Baltimore, MD: John Hopkins University Press, 2001), 66–67.

27. Field Interview with Col. William L. Roberts. Original order was written in capital letters throughout.

28. MacDonald, *A Time for Trumpets*, 503.

29. Ibid.

30. Field Interview with Col. William L. Roberts.

31. Ambrose, *Band of Brothers*, 177.

32. Koskimaki, *The Battered Bastards of Bastogne*, 197.

33. MacDonald, *A Time for Trumpets*, 505.

34. Marshall, *Bastogne*, 139.

35. "Tigers on the Loose," YouTube video, an episode of *The Big Picture*, a television documentary originally broadcast on ABC in 1965, posted by "USA Patriotism!", December 5, 2012. http://www.youtube.com/watch?v=R3uCl6PpUsw. World War II combat history of the 10th Armored Division, with a focus on battles fought around Metz and in Bastogne. US Army, Department of Defense. Army public-service films mixed with Signal Corps archival footage, occasional dramatization, and interviews with key combat participants. Lorene Greene, narrator.

36. Parker, *Battle of the Bulge*, 189.

37. Ibid., 189–90.

38. Bradley, *A Soldier's Story*, 479.

Chapter 5

1. Collins and King, *The Tigers of Bastogne*, 11.

2. Ibid., 24.

3. Field interview with Lt. Col. Henry T. Cherry, "Team Cherry, 18–21 December 1944." Written from information gained from an interview with Lt. Col. Henry T. Cherry, Maj. William B. McChesney, Capt. William R. Ryerson, and Lt. Edward P. Hyduke. The interview took place in Bastogne, Belgium, 18 January 1945. Signed by Captain John G. Westover, working as a military historian collecting oral histories in the field under the direction of S. L. A. Marshall. Found among the Bastogne papers in the National Archives and Records Administration, College Park, Maryland. A

typed note at the beginning of the report reads: "While the interview was in progress the Team was ordered to return to the line and the interview was never completed. Ryerson is now KIA [Killed in Action]. Beyond the point covered in the interview the material is from the After-Action Report of the 3rd Tank Battalion, the After-Action Report of the 10th Armored Division CCB, and the Unit Journal of the CCB. All of the unit records of the 3rd Tank Battalion were lost in the Bastogne air raid on Christmas eve."

4. Collins and King, *The Tigers of Bastogne*, 55.
5. Field interview with Lt. Col. Henry T. Cheery, "Team Cherry, 18–21 December 1944."
6. Collins and King, *The Tigers of Bastogne*, 55–56.
7. MacKenzie, *The Men of Bastogne*, 48–49.
8. Ibid., 49.
9. Marshall, *Bastogne*, 25–26. The discussion of Team Cherry is largely drawn from Marshall and from Lt. Col. Cherry's field interview.
10. MacDonald, *A Time for Trumpets*, 488.
11. Arend, *Bastogne*, 91.
12. Collins and King, *The Tigers of Bastogne*, 25.
13. Ibid., 26.
14. Ibid., 56–57.
15. Field Interview with Lt. Col. James O'Hara, no date or details. Typed report carries handwritten signature of Capt. John Westover, a historian from S. L. A. Marshall's staff.
16. Collins and King, *The Tigers of Bastogne*, 23–24.
17. Marshall, *Bastogne*, 14. The discussion of Team Desobry relies heavily on Marshall.
18. Ibid.
19. MacKenzie, *The Men of Bastogne*, 45.
20. Collins and King, *The Tigers of Bastogne*, 57.
21. Ibid.
22. Ibid., 65.
23. Quoted in Collins and King, Ibid., 63.
24. Ibid., 64.
25. Arend, *Bastogne*, 73.
26. MacKenzie, *The Men of Bastogne*, 45–46.
27. Ibid., 46.
28. Collins and King, *The Tigers of Bastogne*, 57–58.
29. Ibid., 57.
30. Marshall, *Bastogne*, 51.
31. MacKenzie, *The Men of Bastogne*, 61.
32. Marshall, *Bastogne*, 53.
33. Collins and King, *The Tigers of Bastogne*, 74.

34. Ibid., 74.

35. Ibid., 76.

Chapter 6

1. "Bastogne: The Hole in the Doughnut," *The Story of the 101st Airborne Division*, 21.

2. Marshall, *Bastogne*, 30.

3. Ibid.

4. MacKenzie, *The Men of Bastogne*, 36.

5. Ibid., 37.

6. Field interview with Lt. Col. Julian Ewell, no date. A note at the beginning of the interview titled "Action of 501st Regiment at Bastogne," that begins with a detailed note: "The following narrative comes from an interview with Lt. Col. Julian Ewell, Regimental Commander. The work was started on 6 Jan. That afternoon Col. Ewell, Col. Kinnard, and the Historical Officer made a reconnaissance over the entire area in which this action had been fought proceeding to Neffe, Mont, Marvie, Bizory and then going along the road to Wardin until finally we had to turn back because of the machine gun fire from the enemy lines. This narrative covers only the first three days of the regimental action. That is so because on the day following the reconnaissance Col. Ewell was hit [wounded in action] and so was the Battalion Commander and his Executive from First Battalion. However it was only in the first three days that the 501st Regt. took a decisive part in it. Thereafter it continued to hold on the defensive line which is indicated in the narrative." The interview is hand-signed in pen by Col. S. L. A. Marshall, Historical Officer.

7. LTC Patrick N. Kaune, US Army, "General Troy H. Middleton: Steadfast in Command," Monograph AY 2011–01, School of Advanced Military Studies, United States Army Command and General Staff College, Fort Leavenworth, Kansas, May 19, 2011, http://www.dtic.mil/cgi-bin/GetTRDoc?AD=ADA546318.

8. Notes made after Col. S. L. A. Marshall interviewed Ewell on March 12, 1945. Found among the Bastogne papers in the National Archives and Records Administration, College Park, Maryland.

9. Kaune, "General Troy H. Middleton: Steadfast in Command."

10. Field interview with Lt. Col. Julian Ewell,

11. Field interview with General McAuliffe.

12. Ibid.

13. Price, *Troy H. Middleton*, 238.

14. Marshall, *Bastogne*, 33. The discussion of Ewell and the 501st draws heavily from Marshall and Ewell's field interview.

15. Ibid., 29.

16. Ibid., 33.

17. MacKenzie, *The Men of Bastogne*, 53.

18. Marshall, *Bastogne*, 34.

19. Koskimaki, *The Battered Bastards of Bastogne*, 45.

20. Price, *Troy H. Middleton*, 238.

21. Field interview with Lt. Col. Julian Ewell.

22. PFC John Trowbridge, in Koskimaki, *The Battered Bastards of Bastogne*, 49.

23. PFC Lawrence C. Lutz, in Koskimaki, *The Battered Bastards of Bastogne*, 50.

24. Koskimaki, *The Battered Bastards of Bastogne*, 52.

25. Marshall, *Bastogne*, 38.

26. Ibid.

27. Mitcham Jr., *Panzers in Winter*, 128.

28. Ibid., 128–29. Note, Mitcham attributes the comment that "If Bayerlein can't read a map, then he should have let one of his staff officers do it!" to Lüttwitz, contradicting Charles MacDonald who attributed the remark to Manteuffel.

29. Price, *Troy H. Middleton*, 238.

30. Ibid., 238–39.

31. Sampson, *Look Out Below!*, 105.

32. Ibid.

33. Koskimaki, *The Battered Bastards of Bastogne*, 50.

34. Ibid., 51.

35. Sampson, *Look Out Below!*, 105–106.

36. Field interview with Lt. Col. Julian Ewell. Also covered in Marshall, *Bastogne*, 45–46.

37. Ibid.

38. Marshall, *Bastogne*, 45-46; also, MacKenzie, *The Men of Bastogne*, 74–75.

39. Field interview with Lt. Col. James O'Hara, 4–5.

40. Field interview with Lt. Col. Julian Ewell, 11–12.

41. MacKenzie, *The Men of Bastogne*, 75.

42. Price, *Troy II. Middleton*, 235.

43. MacKenzie, *The Men of Bastogne*, 69.

44. Barron and Cygan, *No Silent Night*, 74.

45. Field interview with Lt. Col. Henry T. Cherry, "Team Cherry, 18–21 December 1944."

46. Barron and Cygan, *No Silent Night*, 75.

47. Marshall, *Bastogne*, 67–68.

48. "Volunteers Only: Gliderborne Surgical Team," Chapter 13, "The Ardennes: Surprise Attack and Urgent Airsupply," in Col. Charles H. Young, ed., *Into the Valley: The Untold Story of USAAF Troop Carrier in World War II, From North Africa Through Europe* (Dallas, Texas: PrintComm, Inc., 1995), 348–50, at 348.

49. Field interview with PFC Elmer E. Lucas, 36683900, Medical Detachment, 506 Parachute Infantry Regiment, APO 472, 6 April 45, in the Historical Section office, Perice, France. Found among the Bastogne papers in the National Archives and Records Administration, College Park, Maryland.

50. Koskimaki, *The Battered Bastards of Bastogne*, 100.

51. Ibid., 104–105.

52. Marshall, *Bastogne*, 68. Also, "Medical Evacuation and Supply, Bastogne," an Army report found among the Bastogne papers in the National Archives and Records Administration, College Park, Maryland.

53. J. Eisenhower, *The Bitter Woods*, 317.

54. Marshall, *Bastogne*, 53–54. The discussion of Team Desobry relies heavily on Marshall.

55. Ibid., 56.

56. Ibid., 57.

57. Ibid., 57.

58. Ibid.

59. Ibid.

60. Major William R. Desobry, unpublished interview, Carlisle Barracks, quoted in Collins and King, *The Tigers of Bastogne*, 103–110, at 106–107; also Price, *Troy H. Middleton*, 242.

61. Price, *Troy H. Middleton*, 242.

62. Ibid.

63. Desobry, unpublished interview, Carlisle Barracks, quoted in Collins and King, *The Tigers of Bastogne*, 107–108.

64. Price, *Troy H. Middleton*, 242.

65. Desobry, unpublished interview, Carlisle Barracks, quoted in Collins and King, *The Tigers of Bastogne*, 109–110.

66. Ibid.

67. Ibid., 110.

68. Koskimaki, *The Battered Bastards of Bastogne*, 105.

69. Major Robert F. Harwick, quoted in George Koskimaki, *The Battered Bastards of Bastogne*, op.cit., 78–79. From an account authored by Robert F. Harwick published in the November-December 1945 issue of "The Magazine of the Gulf Companies," 2–3.

70. Koskimaki, *The Battered Bastards of Bastogne*, 112.

71. Collie Small, "Bastogne: American Epic," *Saturday Evening Post*, February 17, 1945, 18–19; reported in Koskimaki, *The Battered Bastards of Bastogne*, 112–113.

72. Marshall, *Bastogne*, 65.

73. Ibid., 66.

74. Barron and Cygan, *No Silent Night*, 69.

75. Ibid.

76. Ibid., 69–70.

77. Ibid., 70.

78. Ibid.

79. Marshall, *Bastogne*, 21.

80. Ibid.

81. Barron and Cygan, *No Silent Night*, 73.

82. Collins and King, *The Tigers of Bastogne*, 119.

83. Parker, *Battle of the Bulge*, 216.

84. Field interview with General McAuliffe.

85. Ibid.

86. Ibid.

87. Marshall, *Bastogne*, 67.

88. Ibid.

89. Barron and Cygan, *No Silent Night*, 80.

90. Ibid., 81.

91. Ibid.

92. Ibid., 80.

93. Field interview with General McAuliffe.

94. Barron and Cygan, *No Silent Night*, 81.

95. "Tigers on the Loose," YouTube video.

96. Collins and King, *The Tigers of Bastogne*, 112.

97. Ibid.

98. Eisenhower, *The Bitter Woods*, 318.

99. Drew Middleton, "Germans Sweep West Through Luxembourg," *New York Times*, December 23, 1944, 1.

Section III: Patton Heads North

1. Michael Keane, *Patton: Blood, Guts, and Prayer* (Washington, DC: Regnery Publishing, Inc., 2012), 159.

2. Msgr. James H. O'Neill, "The True Story of the Patton Prayer." Originally published in *The Military Chaplain*, 1948. Republished in *The Review of the News*, October 6, 1971, http://pattonhq.com/prayer.html.

3. Ibid.

4. Keane, *Patton* 214–216

5. O'Neill, "The True Story of the Patton Prayer," loc.cit.

Chapter 7

1. Alan Axelrod, *Patton: A Biography* (New York: Palgrave Macmillan, 2006), 148–49.

2. Martin Blumenson, *The Patton Papers: 1940–1945* (Boston: Houghton Mifflin Company, 1974), 595.

3. D'Este, *Patton: A Genius for War*, 673.
4. Blumenson, *The Patton Papers*, 595.
5. Rick Atkinson, *The Guns at Last Light: The War in Western Europe, 1944–1945* (New York: Henry Holt and Company, 2013), 154.
6. An RAF patrol report, cited in Atkinson, Ibid., 156.
7. Atkinson, *Guns at Last Light*, 158.
8. Ibid., 160–161.
9. Ibid., 169.
10. Keegan, *An Illustrated History of the First World War*, 352.
11. Blumenson, *The Patton Papers*, 596.
12. Ibid.
13. Patton, *The War As I Knew It*, 189–190.
14. Bradley and Blair, *A General's Life*, 358.
15. Bradley, *A Soldier's Story*, 469.
16. Blumenson, *The Patton Papers*, 596–597.
17. Ibid, 597.
18. Ibid.
19. Ibid.
20. Ibid., 598.
21. Patton, *The War As I Knew It*, 190; also John Rickard, *Advance and Destroy: Patton as Commander in the Bulge* (Lexington, Kentucky: The University Press of Kentucky, 2011), 100.
22. D'Este, *Eisenhower*, 644; also, D'Este, *Patton*, 679.
23. Ibid.
24. Rickard, *Advance and Destroy*, 100.
25. Ibid.
26. Ibid., 100–101.
27. D'Este, *Eisenhower*, 644.
28. Bradley, *A Soldier's Story*, 467.
29. Ibid.
30. Ibid., 467, 469.
31. D'Este, *Patton*, 679.
32. D. Eisenhower, *Crusade in Europe*, 350.
33. Michael Korda, *Ike: An American Hero* (New York: Harper, 2007), 537.
34. D'Este, *Eisenhower*, 644.
35. Ibid.
36. Ibid.
37. Ibid.
38. Ibid.
39. Ibid. All quotes in this paragraph come from this source.

40. Ibid., 644–45.

41. Ibid., 645.

42. Ibid.

43. J. Eisenhower, *The Bitter Woods*, 257.

44. Blumenson, *The Patton Papers*, 599.

45. Ibid., 599–600.

46. Ibid., 600.

47. D'Este, *Eisenhower*, 645–46.

48. Bradley, *A Soldier's Story*, 470.

49. Ibid., 472.

50. Blumenson, *The Patton Papers*, 600.

51. Farago, *Patton*, 324–327, at 325. Farago is also a key source on the slapping incident involving Private Paul Bennett. See Farago, 341–367.

52. Ibid., 327.

53. J. Eisenhower, *The Bitter Woods*, 332.

54. D'Este, *Eisenhower*, 646.

55. Bradley, *A Soldier's Story*, 472–473.

56. Ibid., 473.

57. Ibid., 472.

58. Ibid.

59. Ibid.

60. Blumenson, *The Patton Papers*, 601.

61. Bradley and Blair, *A General's Life*, 364.

62. Blumenson, *The Patton Papers*, 601.

63. D'Este, *Eisenhower*, 643.

64. Ibid., 647.

65. Ibid.

66. Ibid., 646.

67. Ibid., 648.

68. Ibid., 648.

69. Bradley and Blair, *A General's Life*, 363.

70. Ibid., 364. Parenthesis in original; brackets added for clarity.

71. Blumenson, *The Patton Papers*, 601–602.

72. Michael Collins and Martin King, *Voices of the Bulge: Untold Stories from Veterans of the Battle of the Bulge* (Minneapolis: Zenith Press, 2011), 1.

73. Ibid., 25.

74. Ibid., 27.

75. Ibid., 39.

76. Ibid., 63.

77. "The Battle of the Bulge," The 106th Infantry Division, http://106thinfantry.webs.com/historyofthe106th.htm.

78. Bradley, *A General's Life*, 357–58.

Chapter 8

1. Msgr. James H. O'Neill, "The True Story of the Patton Prayer." Originally published in *The Military Chaplain*, 1948. Republished in *The Review of the News*, October 6, 1971, http://pattonhq.com/prayer.html.

2. Blumenson, *The Patton Papers*, 603.

3. Keane, *Patton*, 1.

4. Ibid., 85.

5. Ibid., 86.

6. Ibid., 147.

7. Ibid.

8. Ibid., 147–48.

9. Ibid., 205–206.

10. Ibid., 206.

11. George S. Patton Jr., annotated by Col. Paul D. Harkins, *War As I Knew It* (Boston: Houghton Mifflin Company, 1947), footnote on 184–86.

12. Ibid., text, 184.

13. Ibid., footnote, 184.

14. Ibid., footnote, 184–85.

15. Ibid., footnote, 185.

16. Ibid., footnote, 185–186.

17. Ibid., footnote, 186.

18. O'Neill, "The True Story of the Patton Prayer."

19. Ibid.

20. Ibid.

21. Ibid.

22. Ibid.

23. Ibid.

24. George Reuben Metcalf, *With Cross and Shovel*, 184–85.

25. Ibid., 185.

26. Ibid., 184.

27. Keane, *Patton*, 217.

28. Ibid., 216–17.

29. John Toland, *Battle: The Story of the Bulge*, 190.

30. "Larry Newman Sees 'Blood and Guts' at the Battle of the Bulge," in Louis L. Snyder, editor, *A Treasury of Great Reporting* (New York, 1949), 669–670. Also reported in D'Este, *Patton*, 688.

31. Ibid. Marshall, *Bastogne*, 92.

Chapter 9

1. Taylor, *Swords and Plowshares*, 102.
2. Marshall, *Bastogne*, 86.
3. Ibid., 92.
4. Ibid., 93.
5. Koskimaki, *The Battered Bastards of Bastogne*, 113.
6. Ibid., 115.
7. Ibid., 114.
8. Marshall, *Bastogne*, 97.
9. Ibid., 98.
10. Ibid., 99.
11. Ibid.
12. Koskimaki, *Battered Bastards of Bastogne*, 137.
13. Collins and King, *The Tigers of Bastogne*, 145–46.
14. Ibid., 146.
15. Ibid.
16. Marshall, *Bastogne*, 106.
17. MacKenzie, *The Men of Bastogne*, 104.
18. Sampson, *Look Out Below!*, 107–108.
19. Ibid., 108.
20. Ibid.
21. MacKenzie, *The Men of Bastogne*, 105.
22. Ibid., 108.
23. Marshall, *Bastogne*, 110.
24. MacKenzie, *The Men of Bastogne*, 109.
25. Marshall, *Bastogne*, 111.
26. Ibid., 110.
27. Arend, *Bastogne*, 138–39.
28. MacKenzie, *The Men of Bastogne*, 110.
29. Barron and Cygan, *No Silent Night*, 91.
30. Marshall, *Bastogne*, 107.
31. Ibid., 108.
32. Ibid.
33. Ibid., 108–109.
34. Ibid., 109.
35. Ibid., 110.
36. Ibid.
37. Ibid.

38. Robert Edward Merriam, *Dark December: The Full Account of the Battle of the Bulge* (Chicago and New York: Ziff-Davis Publishing Company, 1947), 179.

39. Ambrose, *Band of Brothers*, 181.

40. Ibid., 182.

41. Winters, *Beyond Band of Brothers*, 171.

42. Ibid., 172.

43. Ibid., 173.

44. Guarnere and Heffron, *Brothers in Battle*, 164–65.

45. Ibid., 165.

46. Donald F. Crosby, *Battlefield Chaplains: Catholic Priests in World War II* (Lawrence, Kansas: The University Press of Kansas, 1994), 152–53.

47. Ibid., 156.

48. J. Eisenhower, *The Bitter Woods*, 333–34.

49. Blumenson, *ThePatton Papers*, 602.

50. Eisenhower, *The Bitter Woods*, 334.

51. Patton Jr., *War As I Knew It*, 196. Also noted in: J. Eisenhower, *The Bitter Woods*, 334.

52. Farago, *Patton*, 710.

53. Patton Jr., *War As I Knew It*, 196.

54. Ibid.

55. Blumenson, *The Patton Papers*, 603.

56. Trevor N. Dupuy, with David L. Bongard and Richard C. Anderson Jr., *Hitler's Last Gamble: The Battle of the Bulge, December 1944–January 1945* (New York: HarperCollins Publishers, 1994), 202.

57. Charles Whiting, *Patton* (New York: Ballantine, 1970), 94.

58. Blumenson, *The Patton Papers*, 603–604.

59. Dennis Showalter, *Patton and Rommel: Men of War in the TwentiethCentury* (New York: The Berkley Publishing Co., 2005), 395.

60. Bradley, *A General's Life*, 367.

61. Blumenson, *The Patton Papers*, 603.

62. Jonathan W. Jordan, Brothers, *Rivals, Victors: Eisenhower, Patton, Bradley and the Partnership That Drove the Allied Conquest in Europe.*

63. Winton, *Corps Commanders of the Bulge*, 217.

64. Ibid.

65. D'Este, *Patton*, 688.

66. Ibid.

67. Ibid., 688–89.

68. Winton, *Corps Commanders of the Bulge*, 220.

Section IV: "Nuts!"

1. Cole, *The Ardennes*, 468.
2. Interview with General McAuliffe, after-action oral history, January 5, 1944.
3. Ibid. See also, interview with Lt. Co. Steve Chappuis and Col. Patrick J. Cassidy. A note on the Chappuis-Cassidy file reads, "The narrative was put together through interviews with Col. Chappuis, commanding, and Lieut. Col. Cassidy, Exec, during the period of 4 to 10 Jan, at Chateau Rolle." The note was signed Col. S. L. A. Marshall.
4. Interview with General McAuliffe, after-action oral history, January 5, 1944.

Chapter 10

1. Publication of the 101st Airborne Division, *Epic of the 101st Airborne: Bastogne*, a blue and white spiral-bound publication, 1945. Found in the Bastogne files at the National Archives and Records Administration, College Park, Maryland.
2. Marshall, *Bastogne*, 133.
3. Ibid.
4. "Subject: Report on Air Resupply to 101st Airborne Division at Bastogne," Headquarters 101st Airborne Division, Office of the Division Commander, January 11, 1945. Found among the Bastogne papers at the National Archives and Records Administration, College Park, Maryland.
5. Interview with General McAuliffe, after-action oral history, January 5, 1944.
6. Mitchell, *The 101st Airborne Division's Defense of Bastogne*, 22.
7. Ibid., 23.
8. Interview with General McAuliffe, after-action oral history, January 5, 1944.
9. Mitchell, *The 101st Airborne Division's Defense of Bastogne*, 22.
10. MacKenzie, *The Men of Bastogne*, 162–63; also, Marshall, *Bastogne*, 134.
11. MacKenzie, *The Men of Bastogne*, 164.
12. Koskimaki, *The Battered Bastards of Bastogne*, 198.
13. Ibid.
14. Mitchell, *The 101st Airborne Division's Defense of Bastogne*, 29.
15. Marshall, *Bastogne*, 135.
16. Ibid., 136.
17. Ibid.
18. MacDonald, *A Time for Trumpets*, 511.
19. Koskimaki, *The Battered Bastards of Bastogne*, 204.
20. MacKenzie, *The Men of Bastogne*, 166.
21. Koskimaki, *The Battered Bastards of Bastogne*, 204–205.
22. MacKenzie, *The Men of Bastogne*, 165.
23. Ibid., 166.
24. Marshall, *Bastogne*, 115.

25. Ibid.

26. Ibid.

27. MacKenzie, *The Men of Bastogne*, 167.

28. Ibid., 165.

29. Koskimaki, *The Battered Bastards of Bastogne*, 205.

30. MacKenzie, *The Men of Bastogne*, 167.

31. Marshall, *Bastogne*, 115–16.

32. Interview with Col. Joseph H. Harper. A note at the beginning of the document reads in part, "This narrative was put together in three conferences 8, 9, and 10 January." The introductive note lists Col. J. H. Harper as the first participant in these conferences. The note was signed by S. L. A. Marshall.

33. MacKenzie, *The Men of Bastogne*, 168.

34. Ibid.

35. Barron and Cygan, *No Silent Night*, 144.

36. Crosby, *Battlefield Chaplains*, 150.

37. Ibid.

38. Ibid.

39. MacKenzie, *The Men of Bastogne*, 168–169.

40. Ibid., 169.

41. Interview with Col. Joseph H. Harper; also, Marshall, *Bastogne*, 117.

42. Interview with Col. Joseph H. Harper.

43. Cole, *The Ardennes*, 468; "G-2 Periodic Report, Headquarters 101st Airborne Division, December 22, 1944," found in the Bastogne files at the National Archives Research Administration.

44. MacKenzie, *The Men of Bastogne*, 170.

45. Ibid., 171–72.

46. Ibid., 172.

47. Edward D. Ball, Associated Press, "'Nuts' Reply Typical of McAuliffe: That's 'Old Crock' for you, GIs Say on Note to Nazis," *Washington Post*, December 31, 1944, 3.

48. General McAuliffe, after-action oral history, January 5, 1944.

49. Winton, *Corps Commanders of the Bulge*, 220–21.

50. "G-2 Periodic Report, Headquarters 101st Airborne Division, December 22, 1944."

51. Farago, *Patton*, 717–18.

52. J. Eisenhower, *The Bitter Woods*, 324.

53. Barron and Cygan, *No Silent Night*, 104–105.

54. Ibid., 105.

55. Ibid., 106.

56. Marshall, *Bastogne*, 118.

Chapter 11

1. Harkins, *When the Third Cracked Europe*, 44.
2. MacKenzie, *The Men of Bastogne*, 159.
3. Ibid., 160.
4. Ibid.
5. Interview with Lt. Col. James O'Hara, no date.
6. Marshall, *Bastogne*, 121.
7. Parker, *The Battle of the Bulge*, 191.
8. Ibid.
9. J. Eisenhower, *The Bitter Woods*, 325.
10. Danny S. Parker, *To Win the Winter Sky: Air War over the Ardennes, 1944–1945* (Conshohocken, Pennsylvania: Combined Books, 1994), 221.
11. Ibid.
12. Thomas D. Potter, "Brave Men of World War II," originally published on the website of the 506th Parachute Infantry Regiment, 2003.
13. "World War II: Pathfinders Resupply 101st Airborne Division Troops in Bastogne Via Daring Parachute Drop," HistoryNet.com, June 12, 2006, http://www.historynet.com/world-war-ii-pathfinders-resupply-101st-airborne-division-troops-in-bastogne-via-daring-parachute-drop.htm.
14. Koskimaki, *The Battered Bastards of Bastogne*, 221.
15. Ibid., 223.
16. Ibid., 224.
17. Ibid.
18. Ibid., 227.
19. Maj. Raymond C. Altermatt, Q.M.C., "Aerial Delivery of Supplies," *The Quartermaster Review*, September–October 1945, http://www.qmmuseum.lee.army.mil/WWII/aerial_supplies.htm.
20. MacKenzie, *The Men of Bastogne*, 187.
21. Ibid.
22. Potter, "Brave Men of World War II."
23. Marshall, *Bastogne*, 137.
24. Ibid., 137–38.
25. Barron and Cygan, *No Silent Night*, 131.
26. MacKenzie, *The Men of Bastogne*, 186.
27. Barron and Cygan, *No Silent Night*, 131.
28. MacKenzie, *The Men of Bastogne*, 186.
29. Ibid., 187.
30. Ibid., 187–88.
31. Ibid., 188.
32. Parker, *To Win the Winter Sky: Air War over the Ardennes*, 232.

33. MacKenzie, *The Men of Bastogne*, 188.

34. Letter from Lt. Gen. Harry W. O. Kinnard to Thomas Potter, 2003; quoted in Barron and Cygan, *No Silent Night*, 132.

35. Collins and King, *Voices of the Bulge*, 189.

36. Interview with General McAuliffe, after-action oral history, January 5, 1944.

37. Noted in: "World War II: Pathfinders Resupply 101st Airborne Division Troops in Bastogne Via Daring Parachute Drop."

38. Marshall, *Bastogne*, 138.

39. Interview with Col. Joseph H. Harper.

40. Airborne Pathfinder Operation "Nuts," to commanding general, XVIII Airborne Corps, dated January 7, 1945, found in the Bastogne files at the National Archives Research Administration in College Park, Maryland. Also, see: Koskimaki, *The Battered Bastards of Bastogne*, 221.

41. "Report on Air Resupply to 101st Airborne Division at Bastogne," Headquarters 101st Airborne Division, dated January 11, 1945, found in Bastogne files at National Archives Records Administration, College Park, Maryland.

42. MacDonald, *A Time for Trumpets*, 522.

43. Marshall, *Bastogne*, 138.

44. Ibid.

45. Ibid., 137–39.

46. "Report on Air Resupply to 101st Airborne Division at Bastogne," Headquarters 101st Airborne Division, dated January 11, 1945; see also Marshall, *Bastogne*, 138–39.

47. "World War II: Pathfinders Resupply 101st Airborne Division Troops in Bastogne Via Daring Parachute Drop."

48. "Report on Air Resupply to 101st Airborne Division at Bastogne," Headquarters 101st Airborne Division, dated January 11, 1945.

49. MacDonald, *A Time for Trumpets*, 522.

50. Parker, *To Win the Winter Sky*, 231.

51. Interview with Capt. James Parker, in Bastogne, Belgium, January 1, 1945. Signed by Capt. John G. Westover, from Marshall's headquarters staff. Found in Bastogne files at National Archives Research Administration, College Park, Maryland.

52. Interview with Capt. James Parker (Ibid.); also, see Marshall, *Bastogne*, 140–141 and 145–146.

53. Ibid.

54. Koskimaki, *Battered Bastards of Bastogne*, 230.

55. Interview with Capt. James Parker.

56. Ibid.

57. Marshall, *Bastogne*, 146.

58. Interview with General McAuliffe, after-action report, January 5, 1944. See also, Marshall, *Bastogne*, 146.

59. Koskimaki, *The Battered Bastards of Bastogne*, 231.

60. Interview with Capt. James Parker, in Bastogne, Belgium, January 1, 1945.

Chapter 12

1. Cole, *The Ardennes*, 472.

2. Mitchell, *The 101st Airborne Division's Defense of Bastogne*, 19.

3. MacKenzie, *The Men of Bastogne*, 192–93; see also, Marshall, *Bastogne*, 124–25.

4. MacKenzie, *The Men of Bastogne*, 193; see also, Marshall, *Bastogne*, 124.

5. MacKenzie, *The Men of Bastogne*, 194; see also, Marshall, *Bastogne*, 124.

6. MacKenzie, *The Men of Bastogne*, 194.

7. Marshall, *Bastogne*, 124.

8. Interview with Lt. Col. James O'Hara.

9. Marshall, *Bastogne*, 125–26.

10. Mitchell, *The 101st Airborne Division's Defense of Bastogne*, 24–25.

11. Ibid., 193.

12. Cole, *The Ardennes*, 472.

13. Ibid.

14. Marshall, *Bastogne*, 130–31.

15. Cole, *Ardennes*, 472.

16. Ibid., 472–74.

17. Ibid., 473.

18. Marshall, *Bastogne*, 132.

19. Blumenson, *The Patton Papers*, 604–605.

20. Rickard, *Advance and Destroy*, 150–51.

21. Ibid., 151.

22. Ibid.

23. Brig. Gen. Albin F. Irzyk, *He Rode Up Front for Patton* (Raleigh, North Carolina: Pentland Press, Inc., 1996), 246.

24. Ibid., 247.

25. Brig. Gen. Albin F. Irzyk, U S Army (ret.), "Firsthand Account 4th Armored Division Spearhead at Bastogne," originally published by *World War II* magazine, published online by Historynet.com on August 19, 1999, at http://www.historynet.com/firsthand-account-4th-armored-division-spearhead-at-bastogne-november-99-world-war-ii-feature.htm .

26. Irzyk, *He Rode Up Front for Patton*, 247.

27. Ibid.

28. Rickard, *Advance and Destroy*, 161.

29. Irzyk, *He Rode Up Front for Patton*, 248.

30. Ibid.

31. Ibid., 250.

32. Ibid., 251.

33. Ibid., 252.

34. Devin Cooley, "Cavalry to the Rescue: Patton's Cavalry in the Relief of Bastogne," Osprey Publishing, March 17, 2008, http://www.ospreypublishing.com/articles/world_war_2/cavalry_to_the_rescue/.

35. Irzyk, *He Rode Up Front for Patton*, 247.

36. J. Eisenhower, *The Bitter Woods*, 340.

37. Winton, *Corps Commanders of the Bulge*, 223.

38. Ibid.

39. Ibid.

40. Ibid.

41. Marshall, *Bastogne*, 195–96.

42. Barron and Cygan, *No Silent Night*, 127–28.

43. Ibid., 128.

44. Ibid.

45. Ibid., 128–29.

46. Marshall, *Bastogne*, 196.

47. Ibid., 196–97.

48. MacDonald, *A Time for Trumpets*, 524.

49. Ibid.

50. Ibid.

51. Ibid., 524–25.

52. Marshall, *Bastogne*, 197.

53. Barron and Cygan, *No Silent Night*, 149.

54. Price, *Troy H. Middleton*, 258.

Section V: Bastogne Holds

1. Koskimaki, *The Battered Bastards of Bastogne*, 256.

2. Marshall, *Bastogne*, 155–56.

3. MacKenzie, *The Men of Bastogne*, 217–18.

4. Marshall, *Bastogne*, 155.

5. Ibid., 156.

6. Ibid., 250.

7. Barron and Cygan, *No Silent Night*, 178.

8. Ibid., 175–76.

Chapter 13

1. Cole, *The Ardennes*, 475.

2. Ibid., 476–77.

3. MacKenzie, *The Men of Bastogne*, 211–12. Photograph of Father McGettigan celebrating the Catholic mass on Christmas Eve in Koskimaki, *The Battered Bastards of Bastogne*, 257.

4. Ibid., 212.

5. Koskimaki, *The Battered Bastards of Bastogne*, 256.

6. Ibid., 256–57.

7. Ibid., 257–58.

8. Ibid., 252.

9. Ambrose, *Band of Brothers*, 189.

10. Marshall, *Bastogne*, 157; Collins and King, *The Tigers of Bastogne*, 193–94.

11. Marshall, *Bastogne*, 157.

12. One page of typed notes, with the introductory paragraph reading: "These notes were made after conversations with Colonel Ewell on 12 March 1945, and following his reading of the manuscript. The interview was done by Colonel Marshall." The manuscript discussed appears to be an early draft of what S. L. A. Marshall published in book form in 1947, entitled *Bastogne: The First Eight Days*. Found in the Bastogne files at the National Archives Research Administration, College Park, Maryland.

13. MacDonald, *A Time for Trumpets*, 525.

14. Marshall, *Bastogne*, 155–156.

15. MacDonald, *A Time for Trumpets*, 525–526.

16. Don M. Fox, *Patton's Vanguard: The United States Army Fourth Armored Division* (Jefferson, North Carolina: McFarland and Company, Inc., 2003), 347.

17. Ibid., 347–48.

18. Ibid., 348.

19. Ibid., 349–350.

20. Ibid., 350.

21. Blumenson, *The Patton Papers*, 605.

22. Patton Jr., *War As I Knew It*, 201.

23. Ibid.

24. Winton, *Corps Commanders of the Bulge*, 224.

25. Blumenson, *The Patton Papers*, 606.

26. Barron and Cygan, *No Silent Night*, 178.

27. MacDonald, *A Time for Trumpets*, 527.

28. Toland, *Battle*, 237.

29. Ibid., 238.

30. MacKenzie, *The Men of Bastogne*, 212.

31. Ibid., 212–213.

32. Barron and Cygan, *No Silent Night*, 178.

33. Ibid.

34. MacDonald, *A Time for Trumpets*, 507.

35. Ibid.

36. Michael Collins and Martin King, "The story of Nurse Augusta Chiwy 'The Forgotten Nurse,'" from "The Battle of the Bulge: An American Legacy," http:// users.skynet.be/fa531049/mypage/index.html.

37. Collins and King, *The Tigers of Bastogne*, 150–51.

38. Martin King, "African Nurse Saved GIs at Battle of Bulge," Army News Service, Feb. 22, 2011, http://www.blackfive.net/main/2011/12/band-of-brothers-nurse-augusta-chiwy-someone-you-should-know.html. Also see: Martin King, *L'Infirmière Oubliè: L'histoire inconnue d'Augusta Chiwy, heroine de la bataille des Ardennes* (Paris: Racine, 2012).

39. "Obituary: John T. 'Jack' Prior," *Post Standard*, Syracuse, Nov. 25, 2007, http://obits.syracuse.com/obituaries/syracuse/obituary.aspx?pid=98590675.

40. Jack T. Prior, "The Night Before Christmas, Bastogne 1944," originally published in the Bulletin of the Onondaga County Medical Society, Inc. Posted on the website "Battle of the Bulge Memories," Jan. 2, 2011, last updated June 17, 2013, http://www.battleofthebulgememories.be/fr/stories/us-army/565-the-night-before-christmas-bastogne-1944.

41. Description of aid stations operating as makeshift hospitals in this paragraph drawn from MacDonald, *A Time for Trumpets*, 511.

42. Prior, "The Night Before Christmas, Bastogne 1944."

43. Collins and King, *Voices of the Bulge*, 215.

44. Prior, "The Night Before Christmas, Bastogne 1944."

45. Ibid.

46. Ibid.

47. MacKenzie, *The Men of Bastogne*, 215.

48. Collins and King, *The Tigers of Bastogne*, 191.

49. Ibid.

50. Prior, "The Night Before Christmas, Bastogne 1944."

Chapter 14

1. Cole, *The Ardennes*, 478.

2. MacDonald, *A Time for Trumpets*, 527.

3. MacKenzie, *The Men of Bastogne*, 225.

4. Marshall, *Bastogne*, 157.

5. Collins and King, *The Tigers of Bastogne*, 197.

6. Marshall, *Bastogne*, 157.

7. MacKenzie, *Bastogne*, 227.

8. Koskimaki, *Battered Bastards of Bastogne*, 284–85.

9. Interview with Lt. Col. Steve Chappuis and Col. Patrick J. Cassidy.

10. Ibid.

11. Price, *Troy H. Middleton*, 259.

12. MacKenzie, *The Men of Bastogne*, 230–31.

13. Cole, *The Ardennes*, 478.

14. MacDonald, *A Time for Trumpets*, 528–29.

15. Cole, *The Ardennes*, 478–79.

16. Interview with Lt. Col. Steve Chappuis and Col. Patrick J. Cassidy.

17. Marshall, *Bastogne*, 166.

18. Ibid.

19. Ibid., 167.

20. Cole, *The Ardennes*, 479.

21. Marshall, *Bastogne*, 167.

22. Winton, *Corp Commanders of the Bulge*, 225.

23. MacKenzie, *The Men of Bastogne*, 234.

24. Ibid., 236.

25. Ibid., 238.

26. Price, *Troy H. Middleton*, 260.

27. Barron and Cygan, *No Silent Night*, 309.

28. MacKenzie, *The Men of Bastogne*, 239–40.

29. Ibid., 241.

30. Ibid., 242.

31. Blumenson, *The Patton Papers*, 606.

32. Marshall, *Bastogne*, 169.

33. Fox, *Patton's Vanguard*, 404–405.

34. Ibid., 405.

35. Lewis Sorley, *Thunderbolt: General Creighton Abrams and the Army of His Times* (New York: Simon and Schuster, 1992), 77.

36. Winton, *Corps Commanders of the Bulge*, 226.

37. Fox, *Patton's Vanguard*, 406.

38. Rickard, *Advance and Destroy*, 177.

39. Blumenson, *The Patton Papers*, 607.

40. Sorley, *Thunderbolt*, 80.

41. MacKenzie, *The Men of Bastogne*, 259.

42. Cole, *The Ardennes*, 480.

43. Ibid.

44. Ibid.

45. Ibid., 481.

46. Rickard, *Advance and Destroy*, 178.

47. Irzyk, *He Rode Up Front for Patton*, 271.

48. Blumenson, *The Patton Papers*, 607.

49. Ibid., 608.

50. MacDonald, *A Time for Trumpets*, 532.

51. Harkins, *When the Third Cracked Europe*, 46.

52. MacDonald, *A Time for Trumpets*, 533.

53. Marshall, *Bastogne*, 173.

54. "Volunteers Only: Gliderborne Surgical Team," Chapter 13, "The Ardennes: Surprise Attack and Urgent Airsupply," in Young, ed., *Into the Valley*, 348–50.

55. Koskimaki, *The Battered Bastards of Bastogne*, 313.

56. "Volunteers Only: Gliderborne Surgical Team," Chapter 13, "The Ardennes: Surprise Attack and Urgent Airsupply," in Col. Charles H. Young, ed., *Into the Valley*, 350.

57. Ibid.

58. Koskimaki, *The Battered Bastards of Bastogne*, 314.

59. Albert S. Barton, "Doctors Among the Ammo," in Young, ed., *Into the Valley*, 364–65.

60. Ibid.

Conclusion

1. Arend, *Bastogne*, 317.

2. Ibid., 316.

3. Drew Middleton, "Foes Losses Mount," *New York Times*, December 25, 1944.

4. Blumenson, *Patton*, 622.

5. General McAuliffe, after-action oral history, January 5, 1944, (see [to come])

6. Jack Anderson, "Twenty Years After He Told the Nazis 'Nuts,'" *Parade Magazine*, Sunday newspaper supplement, December 20, 1964, http://news.google.com/newspapers?nid=1955&dat=19641220&id=VYgtAAAAIBAJ&sjid=dpwFAAAAIBAJ&pg=2216,3607115.

7. Sampson, *Look Out Below!* 116–17.

8. Ibid., 117.

9. William J. Hourihan, "The Battle of Normandy: A Paratrooper Chaplain—the Life and Times of Chaplain Francis L. Sampson," http://www.normandy1944.org.uk/new_page_22.htm.

10. Donald R. McClarey, "Father Major General," The American Catholic, November 18, 2008, http://the-american-catholic.com/2008/11/18/father-major-general/.

11. "Anthony Clement McAuliffe, General, United States Army," Arlington National Cemetery Website, http://www.arlingtoncemetery.net/amcauli.htm.

12. Darren McGettigan, "Brigadier General Anthony McAuliffe—the most famous Irish American soldier of World War II," Family History Ireland, 2011 Irish Genealogical E-Handbook, June 3, 2011, http://www.familyhistoryireland.com/genealogy-blog/item/22-irish-americans-in-the-us-army.

13. Mitchell, *The 101st Airborne Division's Defense of Bastogne*, 32–33.

14. Winters, *Beyond Band of Brothers*, 215.
15. President Harry S. Truman, "Address at the Cornerstone Laying of the New York Avenue Presbyterian Church," April 3, 1951, The American Presidency Project, at http://www.presidency.ucsb.edu/ws/?pid=14048.

INDEX

ABOUT THE AUTHOR

J EROME R. CORSI, PH.D., is the author of two #1 *New York Times* best-selling books: *Unfit for Command* (coauthored with John E. O'Neill) and *The Obama Nation*. Since 2004, Dr. Corsi has written six *New York Times* bestsellers on subjects including presidential politics, the economy, and Iran. He has appeared on Fox News, Fox Business, and MSNBC, as well as in hundreds of radio interviews. Dr. Corsi, who received his Ph.D. from the Department of Government at Harvard University in 1972, is a senior staff reporter with WND.com.